FRONT ROW
An Anthology of Plays

TEACHER'S EDITION

James A. MacNeill
R. Garnet Colborne
Jonathan Kaplan

NELSON CANADA

Published in 1984 by
Nelson Canada,
A Division of International Thomson Limited
1120 Birchmount Road
Scarborough, Ontario
M1K 5G4

ISBN 0-17-602055-1

Canadian Cataloguing in Publication Data

Main entry under title:
Front row : an anthology of plays

Teacher's ed.
Supplement to: Front row.
ISBN 0-17-602055-1

1. Canadian drama (English)—20th century.*
2. American drama—20th century. I. MacNeill, James A., 1933-
II. Colborne, R. Garnet. III. Kaplan, Jonathan, 1947-

PS8307.F762 1983   C812'.5   C84-098015-9
PR9196.3.F762 1983

Permission to reprint copyrighted material is gratefully
acknowledged:

"Friends and Relations" by Hugh Hood. Reprinted by
permission of the author.

Printed and bound in Canada

1234567890/JD/0987654

Contents

INTRODUCTION

An Anthology of Plays

Edited by James A. MacNeill, R. Garnet Colborne, Jonathan Kaplan

Friends and Relations

THE UGLY DUCKLING

FEATHERTOP

RIEL

A Storm in Summer

Come away, Come away

SHOWDOWN AT SAND VALLEY

Saint Joan

Still Stands The House

VISIT TO A SMALL PLANET

CYCLONE JACK

RIDE TO THE HILL

Overview

Front Row is an anthology of twelve short plays and excerpts from longer plays by playwrights from Canada and around the world, suitable for use in the early secondary grades. A wide variety of dramatic forms is presented: one-act and full-length stage plays, television plays, and radio dramas, in traditional and contemporary formats. Both adult and adolescent protagonists are featured, with large and small casts.

The anthology features a clear and concise organization—the plays are paired under six thematic headings. This juxtaposition invites direct contrast and comparison between the two plays within a thematic framework that provides a context for study. The units are as follows:

Unit 1: Youth and Age
Unit 2: Decisions
Unit 3: Follies and Foolery
Unit 4: Winners and Losers
Unit 5: Courtroom Justice
Unit 6: The Unexpected

The objectives of the anthology are twofold:

1. To provide the students with pleasurable and stimulating reading experiences:

- The high-interest content is designed to appeal to the young adolescent. Plays were chosen on the basis of literary quality and impact for the students. They all have a strong narrative line, contain characters the students can identify with, and are capable of being enjoyed and "imagined" by themselves, without the props of production. The plays utilize such elements as suspense, twist endings, conflict, and humour.

- All the plays have had successful stage, television, or radio performances and have received critical acclaim. The editors themselves have also used some of the plays effectively in the classroom; several of them have stood the test of time as traditional classroom favourites. "Meaty" plays such as these foster discussion, critical thinking, and writing.

- The plays are written at a variety of reading levels.

- The plays express a variety of points of view. Students are exposed to the sensibilities of young and old, male and female, dynamic and introspective, commonplace and eccentric.

2. To present the students with the opportunity to examine the main elements of drama:

- The anthology exposes students to a variety of types of drama: one-act and full-length stage plays, works for radio and television, plays involving melodrama, satire, tragedy, humour, legend, and science fiction. The anthology also presents various cultural and historical backgrounds and values.

- Each play has been chosen for a specific teaching purpose, whether it be to illustrate plot, mood, setting, characterization, writing style, and so on.

- The plays juxtaposed in each unit will not only suggest comparison and contrast but also encourage both discussion and written response. Thus the teacher can compare and contrast themes and also the playwrights' methods of developing plot, character, setting, and mood within each unit. Wrap-up questions have been included at the end of each unit to facilitate comparison.

This Teacher's Edition contains study material for each of the anthology plays. A description of this material and suggestions for its use can be found beginning on page T14. In addition, the section beginning on page T7 presents a basic four-step approach to teaching the play—a framework into which the study material can be effectively incorporated. Since a play is meant to be seen and heard as much as it is meant to be read, the section starting on page T10 provides some material on the production of drama in the classroom.

The final section in the Teacher's Edition, beginning on page T17, offers a detailed, integrated lesson plan for each of the twelve plays in the anthology. Each makes use of the four-step approach mentioned above and aims at a comprehensive approach to the work under discussion. Suggestions for improving the students' skills in reading, writing, speaking, listening, and viewing are part of each lesson plan. Not all of the suggestions need be followed. Select questions and activities according to the interests and abilities of your students.

Because each classroom situation may be slightly different, you will want to read each play before assigning it to your students. Thus you will be able to anticipate any problems they might have with the selection.

Teaching Drama

A significant trend in the teaching of literature in recent years has been the move away from a purely structuralist view of literature toward a look at the response of the reader. This approach has particular significance for the study of plays as, of all the genres, drama is certainly the most obvious one to study from the viewpoint of student response. Theatre is magic: the darkened room, the shared sense of anticipation, the emotional release that Aristotle speaks of—all of these are possible and, indeed, are expected with drama.

Although reading a play in the classroom is, admittedly, not the same as viewing a performance, it is still absolutely essential that the students become personally involved in the work. The necessity for such an affective, or "feeling," response on the part of the students has governed both the selection and organization of the plays represented in *Front Row*.

Almost any lesson on the drama will benefit from the four-step approach outlined on the following pages; this approach can be applied to other literary genres as well. The four steps are:

1. Pre-reading Activities
2. Reading the Play
3. Comprehension
4. Follow-up Activities

Though not all the steps need be done with each play, this overall approach will assist in developing all the communication skills—listening, speaking, reading, writing, viewing—and will provide variety to the drama lesson.

Sample strategies and activities are suggested for each of the steps.

1. PRE-READING ACTIVITIES

Pre-reading activities will provide the students with a context for what they are about to read, help to develop motivation, and offer an opportunity for them to practise listening and speaking skills. The amount of pre-reading teaching will naturally vary considerably from play to play. The following are some examples of possible activities.

(a) Before Beginning Each Theme Unit

- Discuss the title of the theme with the students. What does the title suggest to you? What kinds of plays do you expect to find in this unit?

- Refer the students to the table of contents. Read the play titles and names of the authors in the unit. What might these plays be about? Which title appeals to you more? Why? Have you read or seen works by either of these authors before? If so, what were the works about? What were they like? Did you enjoy them?

- Read the editors' introduction to the unit. Discuss it with the students to clarify their understanding of the ideas presented and the issues raised. Do you agree with what the editors are saying? Explain.

(b) Setting the Scene for the Play

- Provide suitable introductory material related to the content of the selection. This could take the form of showing pictures or films to the students or having them read articles or reference books. For example, the selection from *Riel* could be introduced by providing the students with background about the North West Rebellion in order to create a context for the events in the play.

- Give students an opportunity to share personal experiences related to the play. For example, *A Storm in Summer* could be preceded by a discussion about prejudice, how students have observed it in their own lives, and how (or if) they have tried to counter it.

- Have the students read or listen to literary selections related to the author or play. The author could be introduced through other works. For example, selections from Winnie the Pooh tales could be read to the students to demonstrate A. A. Milne's sense of whimsy and humour. Materials related to the theme or content of the selection could be presented. For instance, read and discuss a story such as Washington Irving's "The Legend of Sleepy Hollow" as an introduction to *Feathertop*. Both works deal with the supernatural and are set in colonial America. Read the students Hugh Hood's short-story version of "Friends and Relations," reprinted in the Teacher's Edition. Discuss the theme of the story with them; ask them to identify the central character(s).

- Create a mood for the play by having students listen to songs, music, or poetry, or look at photographs and paintings. Some of these activities may lead to the students writing poems, personal anecdotes, stories, or research papers.

(c) Before Beginning to Read the Play

- Have the students discuss the title of the play. This will help to create interest and assist the students to set their own purposes for reading. What questions does the title *Friends and Relations* bring to your mind? What might a story titled *The Ugly Duckling* be about? What atmosphere or mood is set by the title *Showdown at Sand Valley*?

- At this point you could introduce some of the vocabulary or literary-technique activities in this Teacher's Edition. Studying vocabulary for some selections will aid the students in comprehension. Literary devices such as irony and satire could help the students appreciate the play and lead to a more critical reading with sensitivity to form.

- With some of the plays written for television, you might want to introduce some technical words such as *close-up* or *frame*. (The glossary in the anthology contains a list of such terms.) Ask the students to discuss their own memories of the use of certain devices in TV shows or films, such as a *dissolve* or a *pan*.

- Discuss the content and mood of the illustrations. Each unit begins with one or two illustrations; each play also contains an artist's depiction of a scene from that play or photographs from actual stage productions of the work. Ask the students to comment on the mood that an illustration establishes, or how a certain visual image contributes to the theme of the unit.

- Read the quotation from the play (found after the list of characters) to the students. What does this tell you about the play? What questions does it raise in your mind about the play?

2. READING THE PLAY

There are a number of ways to approach the reading of the play. Assess the selection (its level of difficulty, content, style, vocabulary) and your students (their needs and abilities) before deciding which method to use. Also keep in mind the need to provide variety for your students. The methods are not, of course, mutually exclusive; you might begin by reading a selection to the class and later having the students read the entire play on their own.

- Have students listen with their books closed while you read part of the selection. You might choose one or two speeches of the old man in *Come Away, Come Away* or the King's instructions to Dulcibella in *The Ugly Duckling*. If you have a student who reads well and confidently in class, consider reading a dialogue between two characters with that student (after he or she has had time to practise) while the others listen with their books closed; some appropriate selections in this instance might be drawn from *Come Away, Come Away*, *Showdown at Sand Valley* (the scene

between Montana Bill and Mrs. McAllister), or the excerpt from *Riel* (a scene between one of the attorneys and one of the witnesses). Both of these approaches will help the students appreciate the language of the play, aid in understanding and interpretation, and help bring out such elements as humour, suspense, and irony.

- Have students read along in the anthology as you (or you and one pupil) read the play. Less able readers in particular benefit from this approach when it is used with difficult plays such as *Saint Joan*.

- Conduct an oral or silent guided reading of the selection. Find out where the natural breaks in the play occur. Have the students read section by section; follow each section with general discussion and suitable comprehension questions chosen from the Teacher's Edition. Then have the students set questions and goals for themselves before they go on to the next section of reading. Long plays such as *A Storm in Summer* or plays with involved plot lines such as *Cyclone Jack* can be handled effectively in this way. Less able readers tend to benefit from this step-by-step approach.

- Have the students read the entire play silently and independently. This could be done in class or at home. Most of a student's reading is done this way, as an individual activity, with student meeting author on a one-to-one basis.

3. COMPREHENSION

After the play has been read, give the students an opportunity to express their personal reactions to the material. Did you like the play? Why or why not? Did it have a good plot? Were the characters interesting? Did you like the ending? What do you think of the ideas expressed by the author and/or characters?

This is also the time to have the students discuss what problems they had with the play, such as understanding the plot, character motivation, or idiomatic vocabulary.

Then have the students demonstrate their comprehension of the selection by answering comprehension questions. Encourage them to consider thoughtfully what has been read and weigh the worth of the ideas and message presented by the author. The Teacher's Edition gives suggestions for questions that test two aspects of comprehension. Those labelled "A" deal with the literal aspect; those labelled "B" deal with the interpretative/critical aspect. Strive for a combination of oral and written responses to questions. Try to vary the approach you take; that is, don't make the students feel that every lesson consists of an inevitable (and ultimately boring) pattern of first reading the play, then answering a lot of questions, and finally memorizing the meanings of a list of words.

Discuss with the students the literary techniques used by the author. Exposing the students to the technical aspects of literature—that is, how an author develops setting, characterization, climax, figurative language, theme, and conflict—will help them become more mature and perceptive readers and add to their reading enjoyment.

4. FOLLOW-UP ACTIVITIES

As a follow-up to reading the play, you may wish to have the students do activities that extend the context of the play and aid in developing all the various communication skills. Consider the interests and needs of the students when you assign tasks.

(a) Listening and Speaking

- Have the students listen while you read other selections by the same author. Let them discuss these selections and compare or contrast with the reading selection.
- Students might discuss the concepts and values presented in the play or stage a debate around an issue.
- Have the students put on a classroom production of all or part of the play you have just read. Such a production might be no more complicated than a reading by several students from the front of the classroom. They might use a few simple props or costumes. See the section on the production of drama in the classroom, beginning on page T10.
- Have the students improvise a scene using the same characters from the play they have just read. You might choose to have them set the scene at a point before the play begins or after it ends, or you might ask them to create a scene that is only referred to in the play itself. See the section on improvisation, page T11.
- The students could conduct class or school surveys on issues raised by the reading material. The information could then be presented orally, using visual aids such as graphs and photographs.
- Let the students practise and then read a related favourite story or poem to the class.

(b) Reading

- Have the students read other literature on the theme topic or issue presented in the play.
- Have the whole class prepare a poetry or story collection on the theme of the play or unit. Produce the collection as a booklet.
- Have the students make a book display on the unit theme for extra reading in class.
- Have the students prepare book or story reports to the class about the related material they have read. The presentations could be oral or written.

(c) Writing

- The students could rewrite the play and alter it in some way—for example, changing the ending, altering characters, inserting additional dialogue, writing from a different point of view, changing the form to a newspaper article or diary kept by one of the characters. The play could be expanded to include further adventures of the main character, or what happened before or after the play takes place.
- Ask the students to write an essay responding to the concepts or values in the play: "Do you agree or disagree? Why?"
- Have students write personal anecdotes related to the play's events or characters.
- Prepare a time line of the play's events in prose form.
- Have the students write an original story, play, or poem related to the play or theme topic.

(d) Viewing

- From time to time, discuss the illustrations. "How are they appropriate to this play? What light do they shed on the play? Why were these particular illustrations chosen?" Alternatively, a discussion could take place before the play is read. "What questions about the play do these illustrations raise in your mind? What do you think will be the mood of this play?"
- Present related films or film strips to the students.
- The students could prepare a photo essay or picture collection related to the theme unit, developing a particular idea or point of view. This could then be displayed in the classroom.
- The play could be drawn as a comic strip by a student or group of students.

Production of Drama in the Classroom

CAUTION

Each of the plays and excerpts presented in this anthology is protected by copyright. The discussion that follows pertains *only* to staging *within a classroom context*, as one means of teaching the play and its various literary and dramatic techniques. If you are considering producing the play on any other basis—for other classes, for parents, or for the public (either with admission charge or free of charge)—it is your responsibility to contact the appropriate person or organization and get permission to produce the work out of the classroom setting. You will find the contact person or organization listed at the end of each play.

AIMS

The primary concern for any teacher considering class presentations of plays must be to achieve the involvement of all the students in the class in a speaking role. This is not to suggest that all roles be of equal size, because skills and enthusiasm are not equal, but every student must be required to undergo the discipline of preparing a role.

The benefits to the students of such an activity are many, including the development of confidence in speaking before a group; the mental exercise of memorization; and the development of oral interpretation skills.

For some students, particularly those with a keen interest in acting and who have some degree of skill, live productions give them a chance to try on new characters and situations in a relatively non-threatening environment and expand their repertoire of experience.

Student actors become observers of human nature. They notice how different people walk and talk, how they dress, and what mannerisms they have. Drama gives students a chance to "become" someone else for a while, to adopt a new perspective on some aspect of human nature. It allows for empathy, understanding, and shared emotions. Drama leads to increased tolerance of others, because the actor has a chance to explore another person's identity for a while.

ACTIVITIES

If time permits, the teacher should lead into the actual script preparation in stages. Preliminary exercises in voice, movement, and improvisation help to break down inhibitions to some extent and make the actors aware of the bodily components involved in drama. Exercises for voice and body and improvisation often work best in small groups, so the teacher may wish to cast the plays first, then deal with each small group (the cast of a show) separately, leading them through warm-ups and improvisations.

Ideas for exercises are readily available in books about acting found in libraries.

In classroom drama presentations, the teacher should insist on full memorization of lines. This is the basis for any acting, and nothing of any consequence can be achieved in terms of character development until the lines are learned.

Unless the students are extremely competent, the teacher should assume the role of director for each of the plays. This would involve choosing the plays, casting, blocking, and direction of character development. Naturally, the students should be allowed a say in the selection of plays in which they will participate, but final choice in case of a conflict should rest with the teacher.

Casting the plays presents several possibilities. The first priority must be to put some responsible students in each group, because much of the rehearsal time will be unsupervised. The teacher just cannot be in six places at once.

The teacher must also decide if he or she wants the best actors in one group, or students with varied acting skills together, or if friends should work together. All these possibilities carry both advantages and disadvantages; final decisions must be based on what the teacher feels is most appropriate for the particular students in the class.

Blocking, or determining "who stands where, when," can be complicated. Many people spend their lives as directors studying the intricacies of staging. For classroom drama, however, a few brief and simple suggestions will suffice:

- Use varied levels. Do not have all the characters on stage standing or sitting at the same time. If all must be sitting, have some sitting in chairs, some on top of desks, some on the floor, and so on.

- Movement on stage takes place only when there is motivation to move given in the lines. If there is no reason for an actor to change position, the actor should not move.

- Avoid having all the actors onstage standing in a straight line.

Costuming and sets for classroom production should be kept simple and representative. Let the students find or make their own costumes as much as they can. Students in the early secondary grades—and even older students—still enjoy "dressing up," although they likely would not admit it.

HINTS FOR STUDENT ACTORS

Developing a character is something only each individual actor can do for himself or herself. The presentation will be a unique mixture of the nature of the character in the play, the attitude of the playwright, the ideas of the director, and, most importantly, the personality of the actor.

Actors must be observers of humanity. They must cultivate the habit of watching people's faces, actions, expressions, gestures, mannerisms, and idiosyncrasies.

A useful exercise is to make a character sketch or develop a history of a character's life before the time of the play. Where was the character born? What did the character enjoy? What was the character's home like? What events in the character's life made him or her think the way he or she does in the play? These questions and others like them help to bring a character to life and make that character real to the actor preparing to adopt that personality.

When an actor is on stage, there are some "don'ts" that are worthy of note:

- Don't "dance." Keep your feet still unless they have to take you somewhere.
- Don't turn your back to the audience unless there is a valid reason for doing so indicated by the circumstances of the play. If you must turn your back and you are speaking, remember to raise your voice to compensate.
- Don't let other actors hide you. If someone moves in front of you, it is your responsibility to counter the movement and get out from behind.
- Don't upstage another actor. If someone has a line, you should not, through a gesture or movement, cause the audience to focus on you instead of on the speaker. If you do so, you are guilty of upstaging. The character speaking is generally the most important character on the stage at that time.

IMPROVISATION

Derek Bowskill, author of *A Complete Guide to Acting and Stagecraft*, said, "It is one of the functions of improvisation to help the student get away from the dull, the routine, and the cliché." Improvisation or creative drama is a means by which the spontaneous and the imaginative become more important than the prescribed and the predetermined.

When applied to a literary text, dramatic or otherwise, improvisation has the ability to heighten awareness of the text, characterization, mood, and setting. Students improvising from and around a text are also led to explore some of the choices an author had to make.

Improvisation is a process of imagination, exploration, and discovery. It can range from the writing of a background "life" for a chosen character, through changing the climax and ending of a story or play by making different choices from those the author made, to taking the characters from one setting to another and predicting their response and actions. All of the above improvisations can be done on paper or through acting out the situations and characters.

There are, of course, improvisations that can only be done by acting or physically exploring a situation.

Students may explore emotions while improvising, either through exercises whereby the face registers the various emotions or by devising situations where the emotion is brought on by circumstances surrounding the characters. Emotions such as joy, sorrow, fright, anger, surprise, pain, and boredom can all be fitted out with characters in a setting and explored "from the inside" by the students.

Improvisation is an important tool for both the actor and the student of literature to use in the exploration of a text, a character, or a role.

BIBLIOGRAPHY

The following list is brief, but it attempts to provide the teacher with reference materials for warm-up exercises, voice exercises, simple staging techniques, audition and exercise pieces for oral interpretation, and suggested plays for high-school drama club and classroom production.

- Barton, Robert et al. *Nobody in the Cast*. Don Mills, Ont.: Longmans Canada, 1969.
- Bowskill, Derek. *A Complete Guide to Acting and Stagecraft*. Toronto: Coles Publishing Company, 1977.
- Cavanagh, G., and Trip, G. Van V. *The Players (Books One and Two)*. Toronto: McClelland and Stewart, 1970.
- Sternberg, Patricia. *On Stage!* New York: Julian Messner, 1982.
- Tanner, Fran Averett. *Basic Drama Projects*. Caldwell, Idaho: Clark Publishing, 1977.
- Voaden, Herman. *Look Both Ways: Theatre Experiences*. Toronto: Macmillan, 1975.
- Writers' Development Trust. *Spotlight on Drama*. Toronto: Hunter Rose, 1981.

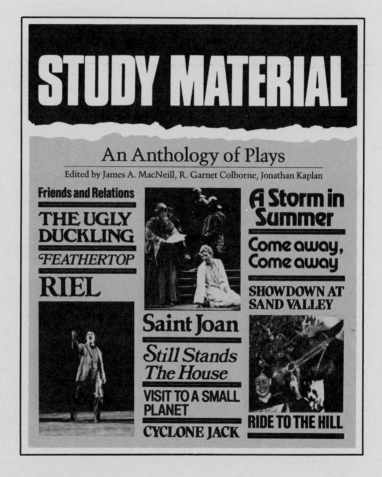

General Suggestions

The study material is designed to provide opportunities for developing all aspects of the language arts—listening, speaking, reading, writing, and viewing.

The material for each play is presented in a consistent format. Each section begins with a summary of the play, a brief note about the author, and a level of difficulty rating for the teacher's reference. Next is a selection of pre-reading activities to set a context for the play itself. The questions and activities that follow are organized under the headings Vocabulary, Comprehension, and Literary Technique. Then comes a series of follow-up activities, intended to extend the context of the play. Following that, and in fact a part of it, are production notes for a classroom presentation of the play. At the end of each unit are wrap-up questions that invite comparison between the two plays.

Naturally there are many other teaching approaches possible, but these lesson plans may be especially helpful to the teacher who is not familiar with handling drama in the classroom.

Not all the activities and questions in these lesson plans need be dealt with. The teacher should select material based on the needs and interests of the class, his or her own teaching style, and the time available.

A number of pre-reading activities are suggested for each play. After the students have read the play, you might proceed in the following manner:

- Let the students react to the play orally before leading them into the study questions. Ask for personal responses by the use of such questions as "Did you like it? Why or why not? Could you 'see' it? What was your favourite section? What was your least favourite section? Are the characters real people? Was there something about the play you did not like?" Also, deal with any confusions about the play that might remain.

- Deal with any questions the students were to consider during their reading of the play.

- Have the students respond to the comprehension questions. Some responses could be oral, others in written form. Not all the questions need be answered. Encourage the students to provide support from the play for their answers.

- Have the students deal with the questions and comments on literary technique, allowing them to analyse some of the technical aspects of the play—characterization, plot, dramatic technique, and so on.

- Refer the students to the sentences in the play which contain the vocabulary words. Have them try to figure out the meanings of the words from the context in which they appear.

- Finally, make a selection from the follow-up activities provided.

The production notes for the plays contain general suggestions for teachers who may be unsure of directing techniques. The notes give warnings of pitfalls to be avoided in attempting productions, suggestions for staging and characterization, and insights gained by the editors, who have participated in productions of some of these plays.

Classroom productions of the plays can be handled in at least two different ways, assuming the teacher wants to involve the entire class. (Also see the section on the production of drama in the classroom, beginning on page T10.) The more traditional approach is to have the class do the production as a final assignment to culminate the study of the play. In that case, the play will have been read and discussed in class beforehand. A more innovative approach is to cast the play before studying it as a class; have the students read aloud or act out scenes from the play (if not the whole work). Thus a play can be presented and discussed as literature *and* theatre at the same time, based on what the students have heard, seen, and read.

A television drama can be handled in the classroom in much the same way as a stage play. One obvious difference is that the director and writer, through the use of the camera, sometimes focus a specific aspect of a scene for the viewer. This might be done by giving the viewer the point of view of a character in the scene or by coming in for a close-up of a certain detail of that scene. When attempting a classroom production of scenes from a television play, the teacher should keep this fact in mind. From the viewpoint of literary study, stage and television plays are not different from one another.

The same is true of a radio script. Without the use of any sort of visual device, the author and director must make their points by other means—sound effects, inflections of the actors' voices, and so on. Have the students suggest ways that a radio play can be produced so as to maximize its dramatic qualities. Again, from a literary point of view, a radio script is much like a stage play.

Half-Hour, Please:
An Introduction

When *Front Row* is first introduced in the classroom, have the students skim the book by themselves for a few minutes. They should notice that in addition to plays, the book contains photographs, illustrations, and pages that divide one unit from another. Point out to them the table of contents at the front. Show that the book is organized in six thematic groups, each with two plays in it. Tell the students that the book contains a variety of forms of drama—plays from television, radio, and the stage.

Next draw students' attention to the photo essay "Half-Hour, Please," beginning on page 7. The essay shows what goes on at a professional production half an hour before the curtain goes up. It identifies the various roles and functions that people perform behind the scenes in such a production. Note that the essay has a progression—it begins by pointing out the technical side of the production (costume shop, sound and lighting technicians, the stage manager and her assistant) and then goes on to look at the performers as they prepare to go on stage.

Allow the students to read the material and then ask them if any have had experience in a school or amateur production. Some students may have been involved behind the scenes; others may have been performers. Ask these individuals to talk about their experiences. What was the play like? Did they enjoy working on the show? How did *they* feel half an hour before curtain? If any of your students have acted before an audience, ask them how they felt about being on a stage. Sometimes students who might be reticent to talk about a play as a piece of literature will feel more comfortable talking about it as a stage presentation.

There will probably be some students in your class who have not been involved in a production but who have seen a live performance. Ask these students to discuss their experiences as audience members. What play did they see? What was it about? Did they enjoy being in the audience? Did they feel that the play was "real"? How did the experience differ from watching television?

An examination of the photo essay and the discussion that grows from it will help the students to realize that the plays in *Front Row* are not simply for reading but are also intended for acting. They can, even at this early stage, start to think about elements that might go into the classroom production of plays in the anthology.

Unit 1: Youth and Age

A Storm in Summer /Rod Serling (television play)
Come Away, Come Away /Mavor Moore (radio play)

This unit demonstrates the similarities between young people and old people—that despite the years that separate them, they have the same hopes and fears, the same need for human consideration. In both *A Storm in Summer* and *Come Away, Come Away*, an older character learns a lesson in human nature from a young child. The children in each play are contrastable figures, for in *A Storm in Summer* the young boy learns as much as his grown-up companion, while in *Come Away, Come Away* the ultimately mysterious young girl is largely an emotionally uninvolved tutor for her older partner.

Most people think of youth and old age as being at opposite ends of the human spectrum, but the young and the old can and do share a great deal.

A playwright can show these similarities and differences in a dramatic way, setting up characters who speak and interact right before our eyes. Through the use of comparison and contrast, the writer can demonstrate that despite the so-called generation gap, the young and the old have the same fears and hopes, the same needs for human warmth and consideration.

A Storm in Summer, an award-winning television play by Rod Serling, is the story of a lonely and bitter old man and an equally bitter young boy from the ghetto. In Mavor Moore's radio play *Come Away, Come Away*, a small girl acts as a catalyst for an old man and helps him to come to grips with the conflicts in his life.

A STORM IN SUMMER

Rod Serling

PLAY SUMMARY

In this full-length play for television, an old, disgruntled man is forced into being a surrogate father to a bitter black ghetto boy. Together the two learn about caring, hurt, and compassion.

ABOUT THE AUTHOR

Rod Serling (1924-1975) was one of the most influential figures in the early days of television. He won many awards for his television series and plays, including "Requiem for a Heavyweight" and the science-fiction/horror series "Twilight Zone" and "Night Gallery." He also wrote the script for the motion picture *Planet of the Apes*.

LEVEL OF DIFFICULTY

Probably more time should be spent on this play than on some of the others in the anthology. There are two reasons for this suggestion. First, this will be, for some students, their first reading of a play; they should be shown *how* to read it and *what* to look for. In addition, *A Storm in Summer* is a television script, so that some time should be spent with the technical aspect of the work as well as the text itself.

Students might need some help with the colloquial language of both Shaddick and Herman. The speeches of the former contain some Yiddish terms and references to historical and literary figures. Herman's speeches contain black American slang of the 1960s.

Still, the play can easily be read silently. Indeed, because of the intensity of the final act, it is recommended that the students begin the study of the play text by reading it to themselves.

PRE-READING ACTIVITIES

1. Ask the students if they have ever encountered prejudice directed at them or someone they know. Have them discuss the emotions involved in such an encounter.

2. Ask the students to provide examples of "compassion" that would help to define the term. The incidents could be either factual or invented by the students.

3. Have the students look at the technical television terminology for camera angles, setting, and so on contained in the play. Have them identify the meaning of the terms, some of which are included in the glossary at the end of the anthology. Assist the students when they are unfamiliar with a term or phrase. Bring other items of vocabulary to their attention at this time also.

4. Introduce the characters of the play. Give the setting both in terms of locale and history (the Vietnam War).

5. Have the students watch for particular events and occurrences as they read, such as the changing relationship between Shaddick and Herman and the changing characterization of Gloria Ross.

6. Ask the students to pay attention to the camera directions and check if they can "see" the play unfold in their minds as they read.

VOCABULARY

1. *Nu* (p. 15) a Yiddish word that roughly translates as "So?" or "What can I do for you?" "...(turns to Gloria) *Nu*."

2. *Scrooge* (p. 16) any stingy, mean-spirited person; from the central character in Charles Dickens's *A Christmas Carol*. "What's he like?...*Scrooge*!"

3. *Booker T. Washington* (p. 16) American black education theorist and writer (1856-1915). "The kid's name is *Washington*....As in *Booker T*."

4. *Mr. Rockefeller* (p. 17) a reference to the rich American philanthropic (charitable) family established by John D. Rockefeller in the nineteenth century. "A moment please, *Mr. Rockefeller*. An item of unfinished business. Namely, your last philanthropy."

5. *brass section* (p. 17) a metaphor for calling attention to an act. "A good deed must be accompanied by a *brass section* and a photographer."

6. *anti-Semite* (p. 20) a person who is prejudiced against Jews. "I don't need a three-foot-tall Ethiopian *anti-Semite*!"

7. *Humphrey Bogart* (p. 20) an American film actor famous for his "tough-guy" roles. "You're the only ten-year-old kid on earth who sounds like *Humphrey Bogart*."

8. *Huckleberry Finn* (p. 21) a character, created by Mark Twain, who ran away from home to spend a lazy life travelling the Mississippi River. "...and this fisherman from a Hundred Thirty-Sixth Street thinks I got nothing better in life to do than play *Huckleberry Finn*."

9. *Achilles heel* (p. 21) a point of weakness and vulnerability. "You know what an *Achilles heel* is?"

10. *bobbin* (p. 22) a float for a fishing line that indicates when a fish is biting. "Keep your eye on that *bobbin*."

11. *Harlem* (p. 24) a district of New York City, now largely a black ghetto. "You don't take a child off a *Harlem* street..."

12. *Mazeltov* (p. 24) a Yiddish phrase that means "good luck." "*Mazeltov* to all the sociological problems in the world."

13. *Mister Charlie* (p. 26) a phrase used by some blacks to refer to a white man. "He say he don't care if *Mister Charlie* hates him..."

14. *tommy-gun* (p. 26) a Thompson submachine gun, able to be carried and operated by one person. "Man, anybody know you gotta guard the back door when you got two bad cats up in a building and you know they got *tommy-guns* too."

15. *Myrna Loy* (p. 28) an American film actress of the 1930s and 1940s. "This is the first movie I've seen since *Myrna Loy*."

16. *boychik* (p. 28) a Yiddish word of endearment, similar to "sonny." "Listen, my little *boychik...*"

17. *Moyshe Dayan* (p. 29) former Israeli minister of defence and soldier. "You remind me of that the next time I go crazy and think I'm *Moyshe Dayan*."

18. *maitre d'* (p. 29) an abbreviation for maître d'hôtel, a head waiter. "(Mrs. Parker, a formidable dowager at another table, calls over *maitre d'*...)"

19. *Lawrence of Arabia* (p. 30) T. E. Lawrence, British soldier and writer who took part in the Arab revolt against the Turks (1916-1918). "*Lawrence of Arabia* and Joe Louis rolled into one."

20. *Joe Louis* (p. 30) black American boxer who held the world heavyweight title from 1937 to 1949. "Lawrence of Arabia and *Joe Louis* rolled into one."

COMPREHENSION

A

1. Why does Shaddick talk to Benjy? How does the fact that he was killed in war foreshadow the ending?

2. What do Abel Shaddick and Herman Washington have in common?

3. How does the author establish Shaddick as a compassionate man just before the end of Act One?

4. Why can Gloria Ross not find a family that belongs to the club willing to take Herman for the two weeks?

5. How does Gloria show Shaddick that perhaps he is as hypocritical and selfish as he accuses her of being?

6. What does Shaddick mean when he says that Gloria Ross's invitation is "reeking of perfume and misplaced contrition"?

7. How do we know the lessons on compassion have been learned by the end of the play? Consider the final actions of Herman, Gloria Ross, and Shaddick.

B

1. The author has said of this play that it indicates "the irrefutable value of compassion." Show how the theme of compassion is central to the ideas and characters of the play.

2. Does Shaddick enjoy the role of martyr, do you think?

3. Herman says that Stanley and Shaddick share the same traits—they both hide themselves behind a false exterior. Explain how this is true. Why does this comparison make Shaddick take Herman fishing?

4. What do the events of the play teach Shaddick about himself?

5. How has Bill assumed mythical proportions for Herman?

6. What is the significance of the title?

LITERARY TECHNIQUE

1. Discuss how the author establishes one aspect of Shaddick's character as early as the teaser. What aspect of character is shown?

2. Do the Jewish and black dialects add to or detract from the impact of the play?

3. How necessary is the scene with the hot rodders? Does it add anything to the development of the characters or the theme? If so, what?

4. How necessary is the scene with Mrs. Parker in the country club? Does it add anything to the development of the characters or the theme? If so, what?

5. Look at the way the author decides how Herman hears the news about Bill. Is it effective? Why or why not?

FOLLOW-UP ACTIVITIES

1. Have the students extend the story by writing a short "biography" of Herman D. Washington after he grows up. Do it twice: once, as he would have been without the compassion shown him by Shaddick; second, as he might become having known Shaddick.

2. Have the students watch another television show and make use of their new knowledge of camera angles and types of shots as they analyse the camera work.

3. Ask the students to imagine a fishing scene several years after the play has ended. Herman has come back

to visit Shaddick, as he promised he would. What might their dialogue be like? The students may present the material in any of a number of forms—they may write the dialogue, two of them might act it out, or it might be presented in the form of a short story.

4. At this point, the teacher may wish to begin work on dramatic presentations of the play itself. Because *A Storm in Summer* is a long work, scenes from the play rather than the entire work are probably the best way to stage the material in the classroom. For more suggestions, see the production notes that follow.

PRODUCTION NOTES

Classroom presentation would probably be best if it were restricted to individual scenes, chosen for their thematic importance or the students' abilities to enact them. Among the most playable scenes would be those between Shaddick and Herman or Shaddick and Gloria Ross. No properties or costumes would be needed.

Note that both Shaddick and Herman are motivated to some extent by both hurt and anger. How can these emotions be shown subtly? How is Shaddick's growing compassion shown in performance? Work on characterizations for an elderly man and a young boy—how do such characters move? Talk? React?

The scene in the country club allows for good character differentiation. Here costuming can make a point about the social backgrounds of those involved.

If your school has video equipment, you might be able to tape some of the scenes and make use of the students' knowledge of camera angles and technique. Try recording the same scene from different points of view—Shaddick's, Herman's, or Gloria's. How is the scene altered by changing the point of view?

COME AWAY, COME AWAY

Mavor Moore

PLAY SUMMARY

An old man who has been abandoned by friends and relatives over the years meets a young girl in a park. He recounts his experiences while the child gathers dead leaves. We discover at the play's conclusion that the child symbolizes death, come to gather in the old man's life.

ABOUT THE AUTHOR

Mavor Moore is a Canadian playwright, actor, director, producer, composer, and critic, born in Toronto in 1919. He has taught theatre at York University. He has written over a hundred dramas for stage, television, and radio; these works have been produced in both North America and Europe. Moore has also headed the Canada Council.

LEVEL OF DIFFICULTY

Since this is a radio play, the entire effect of the work depends on the words and the occasional sound effect. Because there are only two characters, easily differentiated, there is no difficulty figuring out who is talking. The students might encounter some problems when the old man brings up old memories; the line between past and present might blur a bit. This is, however, one of the points of the play. Prepare the students for the man's reminiscences so that they will understand what is happening. The vocabulary is relatively simple, except for some legal terms. The text contains an occasional mild expletive.

PRE-READING ACTIVITIES

1. In this play we discover that a child is symbolic of death. Discuss symbols with the students, showing how a symbol is that which stands for something else. For example, a flag may stand as a symbol for a country; *V* stands as a symbol for victory. The students may be divided into groups and asked to put together a group of symbols; these symbols can then be presented to other groups, which have to guess what the symbols stand for. Alternatively, the students can be asked to write about a symbol and explain what it means. They might enjoy trying to figure out how an object came to stand for what it symbolizes. You might investigate various coats of arms, the symbolism of certain colours (red, white, purple), the national symbolism of certain animals (beaver, eagle, bear), and so on.

   If the students have a basic understanding of symbolism, the meaning of the play should become clear to them. Do not, however, reveal the ending of the play in your discussion before the students have read the work.

2. Discuss the fears and memories that accompany old age. For example, what do the elderly think about as they approach the ends of their lives? Do they fear death? Welcome death? Why or why not? What memories would be particularly outstanding to them? Their failures? Successes? Why?

3. Discuss fantasy and hallucination, particularly as it may affect people who are in the grip of strong emotion or who are suffering illness. Have the students refer to their study of *Saint Joan* if they have covered the excerpt at this point. Initiate a discussion about Joan's "voices" in terms of fantasy and hallucination. This discussion will help prepare the students for the fantasy which the old man has about death. An interesting discussion at the end of the play might centre on reality and fantasy.

4. The students might collect various visual representations of old age—photographs, paintings, and so on. What kinds of comments do these visuals make about the nature of old age? If you have any artists or photographers in the class, they might bring in their own representations of old age.

VOCABULARY

1. *umbrage* (p. 37) feeling offended. "(mock *umbrage*)"
2. *Great War* (p. 40) the First World War. "It was a long time ago. In the *Great War*."
3. *deck tennis* (p. 41) a game similar to tennis, in which a ring of rope or rubber is tossed back and forth over a net. "And *deck tennis*, with a quoit..."
4. *quoit* (p. 41) the ring used in deck tennis. "And deck tennis, with a *quoit*..."
5. *whereas the aforesaid; inasmuch as notwithstanding; do hereby jointly and severally; the party of the first part and the party of the second part* (p. 41) legal terminology.
6. *seal* (p. 41) a design stamped on a piece of wax or other substance to show authenticity, as on official government documents. "...and then bang—the *seal*."

7. *per stirpes* (p. 43) Latin, by descent. "To be divided among my children *per stirpes*."

8. *jovially* (p. 43) in a good-humoured manner. "Dying? (*jovially*) Well, an old fellow in a white nightshirt comes along..."

9. *lay* (p. 44) a song or tune. "(There is a long pause in the guitar music; then the mournful *lay* starts gently up again.)"

COMPREHENSION

A

1. What things does the girl collect? Why are they significant?

2. What do we learn about the old man's family from the play? His granddaughter Millie, his wife, his son, his grandchildren?

3. What sort of routine does the old man follow every day?

4. The old man reveals his strengths and weaknesses in his conversation with the girl. Explain, using examples from the play to support your answer.

5. Apart from strengths and weaknesses, the old man reveals the fears that engulf some elderly people. What fears does he express? Are the fears justified by the circumstances surrounding the old man? Why or why not?

6. What are the most important sound effects in the play?

7. How does the old man die at the end of the play?

B

1. What is the connection between the title and the play itself? Suggest another appropriate title.

2. As the play progresses, we discover that the young girl is symbolic of death. Explain this symbolism. Why does she say that her name is "Mort"?

3. What is the progression of memories that the old man has? Why is it significant?

4. What is the significance of the means of the old man's death? Is there a connection between the leaves the girl collects and the old man?

5. What does the old man mean when he says, "When you get old, you grow four eyes"?

6. What does the old man mean when he says, "It's not the ones you hate who kill you. . . . And it's not the ones you hate who die."?

LITERARY TECHNIQUE

1. Because *Come Away, Come Away* is a radio play, the actors are unseen. The playwright must, therefore, make his characters recognizable by what they say and how they say it. Explain how the playwright has developed his characters through speech and voice. What is the mood of the play?

2. By what means does the playwright establish the mood? Are these means of establishing mood common to most radio plays? Explain.

3. To what extent does the author rely on stereotypes of the old man and the young girl in setting forth his characters? How does he vary from the stereotypes?

FOLLOW-UP ACTIVITIES

1. Have the students search out appropriate sound effects and music for the play. What could they use to make the various sound effects?

2. Hold a discussion of old age. Do the students have a different awareness of old people as a result of reading the play?

3. Have the students develop stories or written scenes based on the threads of the old man's memories—his relationship with his son, for instance, or with his grandchildren.

4. Read the song from Shakespeare's *Twelfth Night* that begins "Come away, come away, death" (Act Two, Scene Four). Ask the students to comment on the song either orally or in writing.

5. Divide the students into groups and have each group make a tape recording of a section of the play. What different interpretations has each group presented? Discuss these differences.

6. Discuss turning the radio play into a television or stage play. What changes would have to be made in the script? What would have to be added or removed? There is a stage version of the play available, which you might present to the students to read after they have come up with their own ideas for a stage presentation.

PRODUCTION NOTES

Although this play is set up as a radio play, it could also be done, in whole or in scenes, as a stage play. If the radio format is kept, the sound effects should be left in— or modified to fit availability of material—to enhance the atmosphere of the play. If you choose to stage the play in the classroom, consider using only selected scenes because of the static nature of the work.

The actress playing the girl must show a sense of confidence and control of situations without crossing the line to being "smart-alecky." It is the function of the girl to prepare the old man for his death. This element of leading and preparing must be brought out in the characterization.

The old man must show a developing openness and friendliness to the girl. Throughout the play, he makes many significant statements about life and death. Although these lines are significant and can be emphasized, they must not sound like declamations.

There is little action in this play, so the dialogue must be delivered with variety in tone and pace to avoid losing audience interest.

UNIT 1: WRAP-UP QUESTIONS

1. In a brief essay show how the theme of death runs through both dramas.

2. Is death the *main* theme for both plays? Explain.

3. One of these plays is a television script; the other is a radio play. What are the differences between the two?

4. The playwrights of both dramas have messages for the audience. What are the messages?

5. Compare the character of Shaddick in *A Storm in Summer* with that of the old man in *Come Away, Come Away*.

6. In what way has life treated both Shaddick and the old man in the same manner? What has been different about their lives?

7. Which of these two plays had a greater effect on your emotions? Why? Examine both plays again and briefly note the thoughts and feelings that are suggested rather than stated.

Unit 2: Decisions

Friends and Relations /Hugh Hood (television play)
Still Stands the House /Gwen Pharis Ringwood
(stage play)

This unit presents the importance of decision-making in each person's life. Decisions often concern not only those who make them, but others as well. In both *Friends and Relations* and *Still Stands the House*, characters have to choose between a radical change in lifestyle and maintaining the pattern that has been followed for years. In the former play, the central figure gains control of her life and establishes a new and positive identity for herself. In the latter play, an attempt to change a family's way of living begins a movement that ends in tragedy.

DECISIONS

Everyone faces decisions countless times a day. The decision might be as small as choosing what to have for breakfast or what clothes to put on in the morning. It is almost as if these were practice for the larger decisions in our lives, such as what career we want to pursue or what sorts of relationships we want to establish with others.

These larger decisions are the stuff of which good drama is made. A "life-and-death" decision puts a great deal of responsibility on the person with the alternatives. The repercussions might affect not only the decision-maker but also other people. It is in these moments of conflict and tension that a good play can give us insight into how we ourselves might solve our own conflicts.

In Hugh Hood's *Friends and Relations*, a widow has to decide whether she will follow the societal role assigned to her or establish a life of her own and explore her "personhood." Gwen Pharis Ringwood's *Still Stands the House* shows a family in conflict, with each of its three members making choices that involve the other two. Should the family unit change or should it go on as it has for decades?

FRIENDS AND RELATIONS page 46

Hugh Hood

PLAY SUMMARY

Ruth Bird's husband has died, leaving her little in terms of finances for her support. The play is the story of her struggle to become independent and a successful business person in the face of opposition displayed by her friends and relations.

ABOUT THE AUTHOR

Hugh Hood is a Canadian playwright, novelist, short-story writer, essayist, and critic, born in Toronto in 1928. He received his Ph.D. from the University of Toronto and taught at St. Joseph's College in Connecticut. Hood has received several prizes for his writing, including the President's Medal, University of Western Ontario, and a Canada Council Fellowship.

LEVEL OF DIFFICULTY

As with most television plays, the visual aspect is important in making the author's point. Call to the students' attention that some scenes flow into the next; others begin even before the previous scene has ended. Have them watch the change in Mrs. Bird—is it sudden or is there an initial resolve on which she can draw? The language of the play is not difficult, apart from some financial and real-estate terms. It is important that the students understand that this play is not simply about Mrs. Bird's financial success, but about her independence as a human being.

PRE-READING ACTIVITIES

1. Discuss the basis of friendships. Have the students list what they believe are the true qualities of a friend. Have them also discuss what kind of support a friend should give in time of need. Finally, discuss how many good friends one can expect to have with all of the qualities they have listed. These discussions will help prepare the students to understand the motives of the friends and relations of Mrs. Bird as they oppose or assist her.

2. Have the students separate into groups and discuss the importance of making careful decisions in terms of the effect these decisions will have upon their futures. Then have the groups share their ideas with the class as a whole and discuss the various considerations. This discussion will help show students that for every decision there is a consequence and that decisions affect other people.

The students should be helped to see that by remaining true to herself, by sticking to her decision, Mrs. Bird acts in her own best interests.

3. Have the students research the rights of a widow. How secure is her financial situation? What does the law entitle her to? The students might also explore some women who have become successful—in business, in the arts, in the sciences—after their husbands have died.

4. Have the students write about the roles that society expects of men and women. What are those roles? Have there been changes in the roles in recent years? Alternatively, set up a panel discussion of the same topic.

VOCABULARY

1. *pokey* (p. 49) small; confined; cramped. "But Christine, your apartment's so *pokey* . . ."

2. *accounts receivable* (p. 50) a list showing the amount of money owing to a firm by customers. "The other big item is the *accounts receivable* at the office."

3. *epitaph* (p. 50) a final judgment on a person or thing. "(This is Lawson's *epitaph*, in a way.)"

4. *closing* (p. 51) in real estate, to complete a deal successfully. "How to manage a *closing*."

5. *mimed* (p. 56) actions performed without words. "(We should be able to watch *mimed* action through this window.)"

6. *intangibles* (p. 56) things incapable of being touched or easily understood by the mind. "She can see the *intangibles*."

7. *equity* (p. 57) the amount that a property or business is worth beyond what is owed on it. "I've always used the house *equity* to finance inventory in the showroom . . ."

8. *zoning* (p. 57) building restrictions in a section of a town, such as only permitting residential or business establishments in a certain area. "The *zoning* forbids it."

9. *Thousand Islands* (p. 59) a group of about 1500 islands on the border between the United States and Canada, in the upper St. Lawrence River. "*Thousand Islands* Tours . . ."

10. *backchat* (p. 60) impudent answers; talking back. "Did you come in just to gossip and pass *backchat*?"

11. *frontage* (p. 61) the width of a lot of land. "At this very moment you're supposed to be in Bert Leventritt's

office, telling him the *frontage* I proposed isn't enough..."

COMPREHENSION

A

1. What do we discover about the attitudes of the other characters toward Mrs. Bird and her dead husband in the first three scenes?

2. How did the doctor die? In what financial state has he left his widow? What immediate suggestions do the friends and relations make with regard to her future? How does she respond?

3. Uncle Lou's character is revealed in Scene Four. Tell what he is like. What information do we get about Mrs. Bird and her husband?

4. Mrs. Bird says that she wants to learn the real-estate business "from scratch." What is Sampson Willey's attitude toward this plan? How does he feel about women purchasing houses?

5. Tell how Uncle Stanley tries to cheat Ruth Bird. How does she stop him?

6. How does Willey cheat Mrs. Bird? What does she do about it?

B

1. What are Mrs. Bird's secrets of success?

2. In Scene Eight Mrs. Bird says to her daughter Christine, "Better than all right. Much, much better than just 'all right.' I'm going to have my life." What does she mean?

3. How does Ruth Bird eventually gain independence from and triumph over her friends and relations?

4. What does Mrs. Bird learn about business ethics during the course of the play?

LITERARY TECHNIQUE

1. In order to hold our attention, the playwright must deliver the important circumstances of a drama immediately. What do we discover about the plot within the first two scenes?

2. The playwright first reveals Mrs. Bird's character in Scene Three through what she says and does. Explain, using examples from this scene to support your answer.

3. In Scene Five, the playwright foreshadows the action to come. Quote a specific line from this scene and explain the foreshadowing.

4. The playwright uses Scene Twelve to show us that Ruth Bird is living an active, independent life of her own. What is said and done in this scene that reveals this fact?

5. Discuss how the montage sequence of Scene Nine furthers the action of the play.

FOLLOW-UP ACTIVITIES

1. Have the students create a series of scenes, some of which show Mrs. Bird and her family while her husband is still alive and others that show a meeting of Mrs. Bird with Christine and Jim after the end of the play. Have the students act out these scenes.

2. Have the students research women who have been successful in some sort of career. Direct them as much as possible to Canadian women who have "made good in a man's world." (One reference text for this question is Grant MacEwan's...*And Mighty Women Too: Stories of Notable Western Canadian Women*.)

3. The sets and costumes for this show can make a strong statement about Mrs. Bird's progression. Have the students discuss or illustrate (by drawing, cutting out pictures from magazines, or other means) Mrs. Bird's wardrobe and the settings around her from the play's first scene to its last.

4. Read to the students the original short story (below) from which Hugh Hood adapted his television script. The short story appeared in 1973 in the literary journal *Seven Persons Repository*. (The television script is a different handling of the same material, written for the CBC television series *The Play's the Thing*, February, 1974.)

Begin a discussion by going over any vocabulary that the students do not understand. Then discuss changes in form that have occurred between the two versions. What is the tone of the story? Who is the central character in the story? In the play? Does the story focus on anyone that the play does not? Are there changes in characterization between story and play? What details have been taken from the story? What details have been left out? Do we have an initially different view of Mrs. Bird in the two forms? What is the time sequence of the play and of the story? Are there any important shifts in time in either form?

You might also ask students to pair individual scenes from story and play. What is left out in one that becomes important in the other? Why?

These questions can be discussed orally in small groups or by the whole class, or they can be answered in written form.

The story offers a more mature version of Mrs. Bird's situation. You may want to read it to yourself first to see if it is appropriate for your students.

Friends and Relations

Hugh Hood

Millicent Holman wept incoherently, self-indulgently, and without real sorrow, sitting in the bathtub splashing water on her pretty face and, as always, refusing to think through a matter which genuinely puzzled her. She left such exercises to her husband. Faced with a puzzle or a mystery, especially if other people were involved, she preferred simply to stare at it with her pretty pout, hoping that it would solve itself or disappear.

"I'm hopeless, I know," she wailed without meaning it. She was by no means hopeless; she was very young-looking, had a little money inherited from a great-aunt, and had stayed married, and in fact meant to go on staying married.

"I can't understand mother at all," she moaned, her voice muffled by bubbles. She fished around for the soap, seized it, and began to scrub her back and shoulders energetically.

"Do me lower down!" she commanded her husband, who was shaving.

James Holman put down his razor with an imperceptible sigh, twisted his face into a grimace at the mirror, and bending, began to soap his wife's back. He felt the soap bump over her vertebrae with a seesaw motion.

"There's no need to cry," he said hopefully, "she'll come another time." He admired his mother-in-law, the redoubtable Mrs. Lawson Bird, genuinely and extravagantly, and never quite knew what she was up to.

"I'm her only daughter," wept Millicent, "and I love her dearly. And she refuses to come and see us."

"She doesn't refuse to see us," said James calmly, "she'll come and see us, all right. She simply has other things to think about."

"She shouldn't have other things to think about," said Millicent pettishly, quite aware of her tone and position, "she hasn't been to see us in over a year. She hasn't seen the baby walk or talk." She rinsed herself and stood up, a column of pearly pink marble, a Venus of the bathtub. Botticellian.

Her husband regarded her admiringly, in spite of himself. "She must have three hundred pictures of Jassy," he said, turning to finish his interrupted shave. Millicent tossed her head, threw on her housecoat, and sidled past him into their bedroom. He was obliged to wipe the steam off the shaving mirror a second time. Millicent habitually filled the tub to the brim with steaming-hot water.

"Pictures aren't the same," he heard her complain from the bedroom, "and I wonder what she's doing in Montreal."

He began to laugh cheerfully; he was looking forward to their evening out. "I'm sure I know," he said lewdly.

Millicent was as usual scandalized by the hint.

When Millicent Holman's father, Doctor Lawson Bird, had died three years before, he had been the best-known dentist in eastern Ontario, and among the best technically. He had not been trained as a specialist but had acquired a very considerable proficiency in oral surgery over the years, and had cases referred to him from a hundred miles away. But much more than his professional attainments, which were quite real and valuable, his hobbies and activities had made him widely known.

He had, for example, played semi-pro hockey every winter until he was past forty, and it was widely rumoured that as a younger man he had turned down professional offers and might have played for the Maple Leafs if his career hadn't intervened. This was not strictly true. He had never been a fast enough skater to be a professional but he played excellent Senior-B hockey with locally sponsored teams. He was a stocky, rough defenceman, known on the sports pages of many small eastern Ontario weeklies as "the denting dentist" or "the extract," in reference to his habit of scoring crucial last-period goals.

He had founded the Stoverville Camera Club and was an excellent amateur photographer who had sold news and candid shots to the Toronto papers. He owned two boats, a launch for trolling and a one-design sloop which he raced, and in the summer was on the Saint Lawrence at every moment that could be spared from his extensive practice. He belonged to an exclusive hunting lodge owned by several rich friends of his in Stoverville, which is a town with money in it. He played a fair game of golf, collected records—his taste running as high as Brahms—and was in short a man of solid professional worth and many graceful and attractive personal accomplishments. When he was alive, the people who came to the Birds' home were either his friends or relatives—he belonged to an enormous and enormously ramified old family—or his former classmates at Stoverville Collegiate Institute.

Mrs. Bird seemed to prefer to stay in the background. Her husband was so popular, so widely known, so genuinely loved and admired, and her daughter—their only child—such a vivid, gay girl, that the Birds' friends and relations hardly remembered that Mrs. Bird was around the house at all, except, of course, at mealtime.

She had been trained as a nurse before her marriage and spent long hours nursing the dozen elderly invalids who composed the senior stratum of Doctor Bird's family connection, suffering many disappointments and rebuffs in this charitable and kindly activity. These old people were hard—immensely hard—to please. Some of them were absolute monsters of senile rancour; she was accused regularly of theft, sometimes of intrigue, and it was made plain to her that she was only a Bird by marriage.

One ancient aunt of Doctor Bird's, after Mrs. Bird had spent ten years in caring for her during her decline, actually, specifically, and by name, cut her out of her will, charging that she was an unworthy wife for Doctor Lawson.

Mrs. Bird said nothing to this; she knew what the old and sick can imagine as they lie in bed with nothing to do but stoke the fires of their resentment. She knew that she had been kindness itself to the old aunt.

She didn't let herself be daunted; everyone in the family must know that what Aunt Sarah asserted was false, or if they didn't they certainly should have. The one great reward that Mrs. Bird looked for was the opportunity to take care of Lawson, really at last to be able to do something for him, if his health should fail before hers.

But she was denied the chance. Three years ago Doctor Bird suffered a coronary attack while trolling on the river. By the time his companion could get him ashore he was beyond help. He died during the night in the Stoverville General, quite literally mourned by everyone who had known him.

He had served as Chairman of the Board of Education for several years and the Stoverville schools were closed on the day following his death and on the following Monday, the day of the funeral.

He was only fifty-four years old and had just begun to earn more than he spent, which was a lot. He had always lived on a large scale, had been a free and generous spender, and the cost of his multitudinous hobbies and interests had been very great. He had, for example, just bought an enormous outboard motor, paid cash for it, and never used it. When it finally came to be sold, it brought Mrs. Bird about one-fifth what the Doctor had paid for it. It was, by this time, a last year's model, and it was hard to find a buyer.

It became evident very speedily that Ruthie, as Mrs. Bird was known in the family, was going to be left with very little. When the final balance came to be set, what was left was a few thousand in cash and the value of the outstanding accounts at the office. Mrs. Bird felt no surprise or disappointment on the score of her inheritance. She had known vaguely that her husband's insurance program was not in satisfactory shape. He had alluded to it once or twice in passing, saying that he had bought his insurance in the late thirties, and that while it had seemed like enough at the time, it certainly wasn't these days. He had been meaning to do something about it but had gone along putting it off.

It was a stroke of good fortune that Millicent's wedding had taken place a few months before the Doctor's death instead of afterwards. It had cost him thousands, money which came from current income and from the sale of a piece of riverfront property he had been hanging on to for years; he had intended to build a combination boathouse, cottage, and hunting lodge on it. But he gladly spent the money on the wedding instead. After the ceremony James and Millicent had moved to the United States to live and they were not in Stoverville when the Doctor died.

When they heard, in the middle of the night, they were surprised and shocked. In the morning they started up from Connecticut by car, arriving in time to attend the beginnings of the solemn family council which began the evening after Doctor Lawson died and continued at intervals for over a year. All were perplexed at "poor Ruthie's" situation, and they grew more perplexed and reluctant to make any positive cash commitments as the facts concerning the Doctor's estate grew clearer.

"Of course you can come and live with me, Ruthie," said old Aunt Cleila, her eyes moist and glittering, "Lawson would want you to."

"No, I don't believe I will," said Mrs. Bird positively, with an unfamiliar briskness. The old aunts and uncles were a trifle taken aback at her brusquerie. They had been so used to her habitual self-effacement that it came as a surprise to them to see her make a choice of her own.

She told her son-in-law much later that Aunt Cleila had discharged her housemaid as soon as she heard about Lawson, meaning to have "poor Ruthie" supply the gap.

"What do they think I am?" she asked James, strictly privately. "Do they imagine that I don't know what a housemaid gets paid these days?"

James grinned. "I won't invite you to Hartford," he said. "I don't want you thinking such things about us."

"Gracious," she said, with the faintest touch of asperity, "I know I can come to you at any time, James." She smiled at him kindly, almost, he suspected, patronizingly. "You must lead a pretty quiet life these days," she hazarded.

"We do," he assented, wondering what she was really thinking.

The aunts and uncles, and Doctor Bird's cousins and connections, who between them dominated Stoverville society—for there is "society" even in Stoverville—were aghast at Ruthie's cavalier dismissal of Aunt Cleila's offer. They decided amongst themselves that she must be holding out for something more comfortable. She had, they estimated, enough money to live on for about two years. When that was exhausted her independence would be much reduced. They could hardly contain themselves for so long.

"Come to us and care for the children. We'll pay you a small honorarium and you'll have your nights free," said Cousin Roger, the Cadillac dealer.

"Oh, Roger, don't you see," she smiled inflexibly, "it's been fifteen years since I had anything to do with young children." Cousin Roger, who knew a thing or two about the management of staff, domestic and business, felt that he had met his match.

Finally Uncle Maurice came to see her one night, in all the weight of his seniority as the oldest male member of the family. He had always liked Ruthie, and found her pale and uninteresting, though a good nurse. He was at this time Mayor of Stoverville.

"Now, look here, Ruthie," he told her kindly, "You won't be able to stay in this house much longer. After all, it doesn't belong to you."

It was true. It belonged to some Toronto cousins who meant to spend their retirement in Stoverville; they had let Doctor Lawson have it for a nominal rent while he lived. Now their retirement was approaching and they wanted the house.

"Grover and Pauline will be moving down here this summer," said the Mayor. "You don't want to be in their way when they come."

"Of course not, Uncle Maurice," said Ruthie with alacrity. The old man felt encouraged, and went on.

"I'm prepared to find you a good job downtown," he said. "I heard today that there's an opening for a saleslady in the Mode Shoppe."

"I don't think I'd like waiting on the people in Stoverville," said Mrs. Bird with a faint smile.

It was on the tip of Uncle Maurice's tongue

to tell her that she had no choice; but something in her manner warned him and he held his peace.

"Won't you tell me," he said at length, in great puzzlement, "what you think you'd like to do?"

"Of course," she said pleasantly and with a funny composure. "I'd like to find something that will get me out of Stoverville for a while."

"Do you fancy anything in particular?" asked Uncle Maurice dryly. He had a glimmer of what was going through her head.

"Why, yes," she said, "I believe I'll have a try at real estate."

"Real estate?"

"Yes."

"I see," he said in amazement, "well...if I can help you in any way, Ruthie, I hope you'll let me know." He was really a nice old fellow, was Uncle Maurice.

"Perhaps you can swing some business my way," said Mrs. Bird cheerfully, as she showed him to the door.

Without waiting for the news of her decision to spread around town, Mrs. Bird placed the accounts receivable from the dental practice in the hands of a collection agency (an act which infuriated a great many of the late Doctor's clients), took what cash she had with her, and left for Toronto without saying good-bye to anyone. She caught on as a trainee with a big-time real-estate broker, and for nine months made no sales, although she trailed hundreds of clients through development houses in the far-ranging Toronto suburbs.

She wrote to James and Millicent now and then, recounting her hilarious adventures and misadventures. A fifty-year-old Hungarian with extensive rooming-house properties was pursuing her (she was herself a year or two under fifty), escorting her to the Csardas Café for the two-dollar goulash dinner. He proposed marriage and the investment of her accounts receivable in more rooming houses for more immigrants. He also had a project for a Hungarian daily which he hoped she might back.

The manager of the branch office was swiping her clients as soon as she got them interested in anything, and closing with them.

"I don't mind that," she wrote, "because he knows I can turn him in to the Real Estate Board any time, so he gives me extra training. I didn't expect to make any money while I'm learning the tricks; it's like an apprenticeship. Anyway, it shows that I can soften a prospect up for the kill pretty well."

When James Holman read this, he laughed immoderately, in a way that made his wife very angry.

"I don't know what you're laughing at," Millicent said in the tones of extreme vexation; "that horrible man's simply taking advantage of her."

"Sure he is," said James, laughing, "and she knows it. She's terribly sharp. She knows they wouldn't dream of paying her while she's learning the business. This is all just experience. You wait!" and he paused to savour the prospect. "She'll go back to Stoverville and lay it waste."

Mrs. Bird passed the examinations which qualified her as a realtor with inordinately high marks. Then, her certificate in her bag and her training indelibly stamped in her mind, she descended on the Stoverville real-estate market like a shrike upon doves. She took a bachelor apartment on the east side of town, got herself accepted as a saleswoman by the newest and most alert broker in town, and began to prowl all over town in her car, late into the evenings, making notes on the houses and affairs of all the people she knew, and on the prospects of their households breaking up. She knew the town and its inhabitants so well that she was better qualified than any of the other salesmen in the office.

None of the other people were Stoverville natives; they had all been shipped in from the home office in Toronto. None had so close a grasp of the local context, not even the branch manager, who came to cherish her mightily. She knew which middle-aged couple was only waiting eagerly to marry off the last plain daughter before fleeing to Florida, what pair of rich youngsters had gone through three houses already and were seeking a fourth that might conform more closely to their notion of a love nest. She could gauge precisely the size of the fading old family fortunes which held the valuable riverfront properties along King Street, East, and understood before they did themselves which dowagers would soon be obliged to sell their huge houses in order to shut off the tax drain.

She anticipated all marriages, divorces, births, and deaths, and knew more vital statistics than the County Registrar. Soon she was making more sales than anyone in the office, even the manager; she was the first lady realtor that Stoverville had ever seen, a kind of albatross or Moby Dick, a "lusus naturae," a mysterious natural phenomenon.

Aunt Cleila deplored the turn of affairs because, although she herself was very comfortably fixed, holding much acreage out in the back concessions as well as her King Street house, her income was fixed and rather small. She guessed that "poor Ruthie" with only her tiny bachelor apartment to maintain would soon have more loose money to dispose of than she herself. She made a series of querulous phone calls around the family circle but obtained small sympathy.

Cousin Roger was wiser. He did his level best to sell Mrs. Bird a Cadillac, telling her that her new position virtually dictated the purchase.

"You can take six people out to see a house at once," he said, "and think of the impression you'll create."

She stared at him thoughtfully. "What do you think of these Volkswagen station wagons?"

Cousin Roger retired in chagrin.

Of them all, Uncle Maurice pursued the wisest course. He made no overture to Mrs. Bird, figuring that when she wanted to come and see him she would without being asked. Soon she was in and out of his office frequently, conferring with him on the financial backgrounds of her clients. Between them, she and Uncle Maurice knew enough about Stoverville equities to jail half the town.

In Hartford, Conn., Millicent and James were left to themselves almost completely. Mrs. Bird came to see them very briefly when Jassy was born and then hastened back to Stoverville pleading the excuse of a pending big deal. They asked her back repeatedly but her replies were evasive until finally they saw that it was useless and stopped asking her.

Just before she climbed into the bathtub, Millicent had been reading her mother's latest evasive note. She and James had had to hire a sitter in order to enjoy one of their rare evenings out. She thought irritatedly of other people's mothers and the quantity of free babysitting they afforded. In her letter, Mrs. Bird mentioned that she would be spending the next two weeks in Montreal, first at a realtors' convention, then in investigating the finances of a suspicious subdivider.

She was paying for the trip with the proceeds of her next-to-last big sale. She had succeeded in moving a famous old Stoverville white elephant, a forty-room riverfront mansion that had been unoccupied for ten years and was impoverishing the owners with upkeep and tax charges. She had sold it to an order of teaching sisters as the nucleus of a convent boarding school. Her commission had been thirteen hundred. She was taking the manager of her office to dinner that night in Montreal; they had important matters to discuss.

Millicent began to shed tears, not of sorrow but of sheer annoyance. "I'm hopeless, I know," she wailed in extreme irritation, "but I can't understand mother at all."

James thought to himself that he had no complaints; they would certainly be Mrs. Bird's heirs, which, though a small, mean, and distant consolation for the denial of Mrs. Bird's company, was nevertheless a consolation. Unless, that is, he pondered, unless . . . he was not certain of her age but thought it sufficient.

"We'll be seeing her," he said, content to wait, "sooner or later. She's not interested in us. Why should she be? She has other fish to fry," and he thought of the two realtors conferring over dinner at Café Martin.

"Well, I think it's unnatural," complained Millicent.

"It's the most natural thing in the world," said James. He repeated it with satisfaction. "The most natural thing in the world."

He began to laugh to himself in a way which, he knew, always antagonized his wife.

PRODUCTION NOTES

As in the other television scripts, selected scenes can be chosen for classroom presentation. The scenes with two or three characters would work best. These can be performed either by themselves or grouped together to make the story line flow or to emphasize the change in Mrs. Bird's character.

The person playing Mrs. Bird must suggest an inner strength from her first scene. At the same time, her friends and relations must see something of a woman who can be manipulated by circumstances and by themselves. Her big scenes (Fourteen, Sixteen, and Eighteen) should be played with a great deal of honesty—she is aware of her strengths as well as of her situation.

Cousin Stanley shouldn't be played as too much of a villain, nor should Sampson Willey. Both are, in a sense, converted by the end of the play to see Mrs. Bird's worth.

If your school has video equipment, you might consider taping a scene or two, using different points of view. How would this change the nature of a scene—for example, the initial one between Mrs. Bird and Sampson Willey?

Scene Sixteen, the one in which Mrs. Bird receives the real-estate award, offers the widest range of characterizations. It would be the most lively scene to do in the classroom.

STILL STANDS THE HOUSE

Gwen Pharis Ringwood

PLAY SUMMARY

A young farmer on the prairies during the Depression has a chance to sell his farm and move closer to town. His wife, expecting their first child, longs for such a move, but the man's sister refuses to let him sell their father's house—a house where she spent her youth caring for her father. The decision is finally made to sell; the sister takes a violent revenge.

ABOUT THE AUTHOR

A prolific and popular playwright, Gwen Pharis Ringwood has written plays that are favourites for both amateur and professional companies. Mrs. Ringwood studied at the universities of Alberta and North Carolina. She received her first break as a writer by being offered a contract to write radio plays. Now in her seventies, she is still energetically overseeing productions of her plays and continues to write.

LEVEL OF DIFFICULTY

The actual vocabulary used in the play is not difficult, but some of the words are rather dated. The character who will offer the most difficulty is Hester—not only in her motivation and her actions, but occasionally in her lines. Her speeches are sometimes paraphrases of biblical lines or images; a knowledge of these references will add depth to what she is saying. Much of her motivation is unclear even to herself; subconscious desires and memories are an important part of the character we see. Alert the students to watch for Hester's actions and words—there might be more to both than there appears on the surface.

PRE-READING ACTIVITIES

1. Discuss the dangers of winter storms. Recall for the students the worst storm that you can remember or some harrowing storm incident that you read about. Encourage the students to recount incidents from their own experiences. This discussion will help to establish the atmosphere in which the play may be most effectively read.
2. Read aloud excerpts from Sinclair Ross's story "The Painted Door" (found in *Tigers of the Snow*, ed. MacNeill and Sorestad). The reading will evoke atmosphere and supply information to those not familiar with a prairie blizzard.
3. Have students research what it was like for farmers on the prairies during the Depression, what hardships they had to endure, and how some of them survived. This will establish a social context for the play. Students might also look at a book like John Steinbeck's *The Grapes of Wrath* for something of the same historical and social background.
4. Discuss fantasies and hallucinations by way of review of *Come Away, Come Away* or *Saint Joan*. Relate the discussion to *Still Stands the House*, showing how people can be isolated from others either mentally or physically and can develop hallucinations.

VOCABULARY

1. *sideboard* (p. 65) a piece of dining-room furniture with drawers and shelves for cutlery and linen as well as space on top for dishes. "(Along the left wall...is a mahogany *sideboard*.)"
2. *dryland* (p. 66) having no water or source of irrigation. "Five thousand dollars and an irrigated quarter is a good price for a *dryland* farm these days."
3. *Wedgwood* (p. 68) a kind of fine china with a raised design, originated in the eighteenth century by the English potter Josiah Wedgwood. "(She takes an old *Wedgwood* bowl from the sideboard...)"
4. *chintz* (p. 68) a cotton cloth printed with colourful patterns. "(Ruth returns to the sideboard, taking some bright *chintz* from the drawer.)"
5. *shroud, winding sheet* (p. 69) a cloth in which a dead person is wrapped for burial. "He called it a moving *shroud*, a *winding sheet* that the wind lifts and raises and lets fall again."
6. *separator* (p. 69) a machine that separates cream from milk. "Did you get the *separator* put up?"
7. *coulee* (p. 73) a deep ravine that is often dry in the summer. "I've ploughed that southern slope along the *coulee* every summer since I was twelve."
8. *harrow* (p. 73) to use a harrow, a machine with iron teeth, to break up the soil on ploughed land. "...the dirt I'd ploughed and *harrowed* and sowed to grain..."
9. *jasmine* (p. 74) a perfume made from jasmine blossoms. "Your body anointed with *jasmine* for his pleasure."

10. *fallow* (p. 76) a piece of land that is left unseeded for a season. "The snow lies deep on the summer *fallow* ..."

COMPREHENSION

A

1. The conflict of the play is established early on. Who are the characters in conflict and what is the issue?

2. Why is Hester so unwilling to leave the farm? Explain the reasons for her close attachment to her father.

3. What foreshadowing exists in the play?

4. Why did Hester never marry?

5. Why does Bruce not accept the offer for the farm? What elements of character do his reasons reveal?

6. What prompts Bruce finally to decide to sell? What decision does Hester make in response?

B

1. What differences of character exist between Ruth and Hester?

2. To which of the three main characters do you find yourself most sympathetic? Why?

3. Hester says, "We could always stand alone, the three of us." Which three does she mean?

4. What devices does the playwright use to suggest Ruth's nature?

5. What is the sort of struggle that Bruce must go through during the course of the play?

LITERARY TECHNIQUE

1. The early exposition of the play sets the action in time and space. Although the reader of the play has the opening stage directions, an audience would not. What information, including foreshadowing, are we given about the setting in the first six speeches?

2. What can we expect Hester to be like even before we meet her? Would this kind of knowledge be helpful to an actress portraying Hester? Explain.

3. Look up the meaning of the word "melodrama." Decide if this play is a melodrama and be prepared to defend your decision.

4. Can you see any significance to Hester's unravelling her knitting as Bruce leaves to get the mare?

5. Does the author prepare us for the ending? If so, how?

FOLLOW-UP ACTIVITIES

1. Hester speaks of herself late in the play as "the wise virgin," referring to the New Testament parable of the wise and foolish virgins. Have the students read this biblical selection and see how it relates to the play.

2. Other segments of the play have biblical references— some of Hester's accusations toward Ruth are based on sections of the Song of Solomon. Divide students into groups and see if they can trace any of the biblical paraphrases in the play. How appropriate are the uses of biblical sections? The two female characters have biblical names. (Hester is a form of Esther.) Why? What are the parallels or contrasts that are set up?

3. Have the students devise a scene from Hester and Bruce's youth, when their father was still alive. Some of the events of this early scene can prepare for the characters of the brother and sister in *Still Stands the House*.

4. Direct the students in preparing a model of the set for the play. The opening stage directions are detailed enough to give many specific ideas. The students might also prepare some drawings of costume sketches for the three main characters; the production photos in the anthology will give them some suggestions.

PRODUCTION NOTES

Because this play is melodrama, there are very few subtleties of character. Everyone in the play is virtually one-dimensional. This does not mean, though, that the characterizations are easy. One must, for instance, play Hester so as to elicit some sympathy for her, even though she is the "villain" of the piece. Similarly, Ruth should be a bit more than the traditional heroine.

Costumes and set should be as naturalistic as possible, depending upon limitations of space, resources, and purpose.

It is useful early on to set up a dramatic contrast between Ruth and Hester—in their looks, their speeches, their tones, their manner of address. Be careful not to make Hester too vehement early on in the play—it will detract from her later actions. Try to show Ruth as a woman with her own form of determination even while she's concerned for Hester's welfare.

It will be difficult to show Hester's gradual recession from reality, her move into her own world of the past. You might ask several students to play the final scene between Ruth and Hester; each pair might contribute a different interpretation of the scene.

This is an extremely popular festival play for highschool actors because of the relatively uncomplicated nature of the characters, the conflict, and the action.

UNIT 2: WRAP-UP QUESTIONS

1. Write an essay that shows how a character in both plays has to make a "life-or-death" decision.

2. How does the setting for each play add to its mood, tone, and theme?

3. Which characters in the two plays are the most sympathetic for you? Why? Could you give some evidence to show that even the most unsympathetic characters have some redeeming qualities? If so, why does the playwright create such a "mixed" character?

4. Discuss how the visual aspects of each play add to its themes.

5. Discuss how, in each play, the past is an important determiner of the present.

6. In most narrative works of literature, a central character grows in some way from the beginning of the work to the end. Compare how Mrs. Bird and Hester "grow" during their respective plays.

Unit 3: Follies and Foolery

The Ugly Duckling/A. A. Milne (stage play)
Showdown at Sand Valley/Ken Mitchell (stage play)

This unit examines the human condition through the medium of laughter. By holding certain popular foibles up to mild ridicule, the playwrights help us to laugh at similar weaknesses we ourselves might have. Both *The Ugly Duckling* and *Showdown at Sand Valley* use established types of writing—the fairy tale and the western, respectively—to poke fun at the form and also to comment on some personal qualities that many of us share. Though *Showdown at Sand Valley* has a light touch throughout, *The Ugly Duckling*'s humour contains a kernel of seriousness.

It is always healthy to be able to laugh at our own all-too-human weaknesses. Laughter is a kind of medicine that reminds us not to take ourselves too seriously.

Though comedy can be used as a serious weapon to attack certain aspects of society, it can also be used gently to show us our own foibles and foolishness. This sort of mild satire may use a standard form of writing—the fairy tale, let's say, or the western—as the vehicle for the comedy. But it is the human side of the characters with which we identify, thus seeing the humour in our own lives.

The Ugly Duckling, a sort of anti-fairy tale by A. A. Milne, is the story of a plain princess whom no one wants to wed. But a special prince discovers her own sort of beauty so that the two can "live happily ever after." Ken Mitchell's *Showdown at Sand Valley* plays with the image of the Wild West desperado to demonstrate that even a feared gunslinger might be nothing but bluster.

THE UGLY DUCKLING

A. A. Milne

PLAY SUMMARY

This is a one-act version by A. A. Milne of the Andersen fable in which the ugly duckling is actually a beautiful princess. Her father, the King, tries his hardest to find a husband for his seemingly homely daughter and finds the perfect mate in a prince whom everyone considers dull.

ABOUT THE AUTHOR

A. A. (Alan Alexander) Milne (1882-1956) was a British author, most famous for his creation of the classic Winnie the Pooh stories, ostensibly for children. He has also written other books for children as well as novels, short stories, and plays for adults. For a time, Milne also served as an assistant editor of *Punch*, the British humour magazine.

LEVEL OF DIFFICULTY

This is one of the easiest plays in the anthology. Because of its fairy-tale heritage, the play will appeal to almost anyone. The humour of the piece depends a great deal upon preconceptions of what the fairy-tale princess and prince should be like. The only aspect of the play that might cause some slight problem is occasional "British" diction. During the reading have students watch for the elements of the story that are being satirized and have them come up with a statement of the play's "moral" or "message."

PRE-READING ACTIVITIES

1. Have the students generate a list of fairy tales they may remember. Have one or two tell briefly the plot of a fairy tale a student has named.

2. Ask for names of fairy-tale writers. The students may suggest the Brothers Grimm, Aesop, or Hans Christian Andersen. If the students do not suggest it, you should mention Andersen's "The Ugly Duckling." Have someone who knows it recount the story, or you might read the students a version of the tale.

3. Ask the students to define satire and add whatever elements are necessary to complete the definition. Mention that satire is a function of the preconceived ideas and stereotypes that people have.

4. Discuss the common elements in fairy tales. Students may suggest beautiful maidens (often princesses), handsome princes, fairy godmothers, magic charms, a "moral," "living happily ever after," and so on. Have the students suggest possible ways that this standard fairy-tale format might be altered to satirize the form and style.

VOCABULARY

1. *cryptic* (p. 82) having a hidden meaning. "You know what she said." "It was *cryptic*."

2. *besetting* (p. 82) constantly bothering. "Great-Aunt Malkin's *besetting* weakness."

3. *surreptitiously* (p. 82) secretly; stealthily. "(The King snaps his fingers *surreptitiously* in the direction of the Chancellor.)"

4. *ruse* (p. 83) a trick or scheme. "...a harmless *ruse*, of which you will find frequent record in the history books..."

5. *waft* (p. 84) to wave gently, as with a light breeze. "... you must, as it were, *waft* me into a seat by your side."

6. *battlements* (p. 86) walls for defence built around a castle. "That beech tree, and then a swing and a grab for the *battlements* ..."

COMPREHENSION

A

1. How is Prince Simon to be the King's last hope to marry off his daughter?

2. Describe the unusual events of the last Tournament of Love and offer a reason for the strange behaviour of the contestants.

3. How is Dulcibella to be involved in the King's plot?

4. How does Simon, alias Carlo, get into the castle? Why is it an especially brave feat for him to perform?

5. How does Simon save the day at the time of the riddle?

B

1. Explain Great-Aunt Malkin's words at Camilla's christening, "Where ignorance is bliss, 'Tis folly to be wise."

2. Explain the wisdom of Great-Aunt Malkin's christening gift.

3. Why is Camilla "a new and strangely beautiful Camilla" when she meets Simon?

4. Discuss the characters of the King and Queen and the nature of their relationship.

5. The King thinks that physical appearance is the most important thing in the world. What does Camilla think is most important? Who is closer to the truth, in your opinion?

LITERARY TECHNIQUE

1. The basis for the humour and meaning of this play lies in the fairy-tale, stereotyped roles of King, Queen, Fairy Godmother, Beautiful Princess, and Handsome Prince, and the very definitely unstereotyped personalities who inhabit these roles. The characters, however, still feel obliged to play the game by the rules—that is, fulfil the stereotypes. Discuss both the stereotypes and the individual personalities in the play.

2. How could the change in Camilla's appearance, from plain to beautiful, be accomplished on the stage?

3. See if the students can find a line, either spoken by or about a character, that reveals the nature of each of the main characters: the King, Camilla, and Simon.

4. How does the author make use of irony throughout the play? List the instances.

5. What physical features would a director look for in actors when the play is being cast?

6. Ask the students to look at the parts of the play that they found to be most humorous. What makes them funny? Is it characterization, dialogue, incidents, irony? Is it something else? Discuss.

FOLLOW-UP ACTIVITIES

1. Have the students improvise one of the "unwritten" scenes of the play—for example, the christening of Camilla, the Tournament of Love, or an episode from the life of Prince Simon.

2. Have the students write their own versions of a well-known fairy tale, either in satiric form or in a modern setting, with contemporary characters speaking modern dialect. Have this new version presented to the class.

3. Have the students write a newspaper account of the wedding of Princess Camilla and Prince Simon. What unexpected events might occur in such an account? How would the King and Queen react?

PRODUCTION NOTES

The Ugly Duckling is probably the most playable of all the works in this collection. Properties are minimal, costuming very simple, and characterizations obvious, yet the whole work is interesting and varied. It might be presented as readers' theatre—that is, with no visual production at all. The students sit on stools or chairs at the front of the classroom and read the script in character. Yet the students will probably find it fun to stage the play in a full production.

The role of the King allows for the most comedy in the play. The actor chosen for the part must be versatile and not self-conscious. The episode between the King and Dulcibella can be very funny, especially if the actor playing the King can persuade the audience that he is remembering his "lost youth."

Camilla is among the more difficult roles in the play. Be careful that she does not become pompous and stuffy in her self-assurance. The scene between her and Simon should allow the two performers to demonstrate a gradual affection growing between the characters.

This play presents some excellent two-player scenes: the King and the Chancellor; the King and Camilla; the King and Dulcibella; Camilla and Simon. Let the actors have fun with these scenes, exploring the verbal and situational humour.

SHOWDOWN AT SAND VALLEY

Ken Mitchell

PLAY SUMMARY

This humorous play is set in Saskatchewan's pioneer days. News that a wild desperado from the American Wild West is heading for Sand Valley sets the small town's inhabitants on their ears. He turns out, however, to be "wee Willy," the son of the former schoolteacher; his reputation far exceeds his bravado, especially where his mother is concerned.

ABOUT THE AUTHOR

A poet, novelist, actor, and playwright, Ken Mitchell lives in Regina and teaches at the University of Regina. Mitchell has had a long association with the Globe Theatre of Regina, which produced his play *Heroes*. Another of his plays, *Cruel Tears*, a country-and-western version of Shakespeare's *Othello*, was produced by Saskatoon's Persephone Theatre. Mitchell has also written screenplays for the National Film Board of Canada.

LEVEL OF DIFFICULTY

The students will have few comprehension problems with this selection; it was written to be performed by and for students. The only problem might be the use of local, old-fashioned dialect and Scottish dialect. The playwright has used simplified phonetic spelling to cue the reader in to the pronunciation of slang or idiomatic expressions—for example, "t'day" for "today" and "izzen" for "isn't." You might write some of these words on the chalkboard before the students read the play and ask them to guess what the words mean; suggest that they might figure out the meanings if the words were pronounced aloud.

PRE-READING ACTIVITIES

1. Review the definition of satire with the students. Give examples or have the students give examples to support the definition. Mention, as you did in discussing *The Ugly Duckling*, that satire is a function of the preconceived ideas and stereotypes that people have.

2. Have the students discuss the image of the Wild West that comes from American western movies and novels.

3. Have the students write a short story using stereotypical elements of a Wild West tale.

4. Have the students research what a small town in Saskatchewan would be like at the turn of the century. Would it be full of dangerous desperadoes and gunslingers?

5. Discuss the fact that some people speak different dialects and pronounce words differently. Write some of the dialect sentences from the play on the chalkboard and ask for volunteers to read them out loud. Discuss what each means. Why does the writer use such unusual spellings? Where might each speaker have come from? What kind of person might speak such sentences? Then have the students play with dialect on their own—using the patterns that you have put on the board, the students can make up several sentences and write them in some form of dialect. Have other students work out what the dialect sentences mean.

VOCABULARY

1. *reeve* (p. 93) the elected head of a rural town council. "Horace B. Lankitt—the *reeve* of Sand Valley."

2. *braces* (p. 94) suspenders. "Sit down, Perc. Loosen yer *braces*."

3. *temperance* (p.94) abstinence from all alcoholic drinks. "Mrs. Jennifer McAllister,... president-elect of the Ladies' *Temperance* League."

4. *burr* (p. 95) a type of pronunciation in which *r* sounds are prominent. "(speaking with a thick Scots *burr*)"

5. *birkie* (p. 95) a Scottish dialect word for "man." "What's the name of this *birkie*?"

6. *dehydyuhrated* (p. 96) a dialect form of "dehydrated," dried out. "Man can't face a gang a cutthroats with his brain *dehydyuhrated*."

7. *Boor War* (p. 96) the Boer War, fought at the end of the nineteenth century between the British and the Boers (descendants of the Dutch) in South Africa. "Ain't bin a revolver in Sand Valley since Doc Wages came back from the *Boor War* . . ."

8. *dugout* (p. 96) on the prairies, a large hole used to hold water collected from rainfall or spring thaw. ". . . and chucked his iron into Oscar Bergson's *dugout*."

9. *stubble-jumpers* (p. 96) a derogatory phrase. "Sure, coulda bin them crazy *stubble-jumpers* up in Shakespeare."

10. *Boot Hill* (p. 97) the traditional cemetery in a Wild West town. "We could all be in—*Boot Hill* by tonight!"

11. *breeks* (p. 99) a dialect form of "breeches," trousers. "You're not so big I can't take down your *breeks* and lay a willow switch a few times across your bare bummy."

12. *O.C.* (p. 101) Officer in Charge; commanding officer. "...contravening a direct order from *O.C.*, F. Division..."

COMPREHENSION

A

1. What are the townspeople preparing for? Are the preparations appropriate to the event? Why or why not?

2. Why does Montana Bill look "kinda familiar" to Sam?

3. What is Gompers's plan for Montana Bill's arrival?

4. What is Montana Bill's story about why he is on the run?

5. Why did Montana Bill leave home in the first place?

6. Why does the Mountie not "get his man"?

B

1. Which of the men in the town is the most organized? The bravest? The most cowardly?

2. What do we learn of Mrs. McAllister in her first scene?

3. What is Montana Bill's true character? How does this add to the humour of the story?

4. Who is the person most in control of the situation at the end of the play? Give reasons for your choice.

5. What type of man is Corporal Wretched-Smith? Is he a traditional Mountie? Why or why not?

LITERARY TECHNIQUE

1. Why does the author use a narrator in his play? Is it effective or necessary?

2. What stereotype of the Wild West does the author make use of?

3. What do the names of people and places in the play tell us about the setting?

4. Find an instance of foreshadowing in the early part of the play.

5. How does the author prepare us for the appearance of the Mountie? Are our expectations met by Corporal Wretched-Smith?

6. How do the preparations for the arrival of the gunslinger contribute to the humour of the play?

7. In your opinion, what lines, characters, and events contribute most to the comedy of the play? Give reasons for your choices.

FOLLOW-UP ACTIVITIES

1. Have the students dramatize a scene between "wee Willy" and his mother before he leaves home. The scene might show, in fact, why he goes to the United States.

2. Have the students watch a western show on television and write a short paper about its stereotypical elements. Then have them write a brief parody of the same show, satirizing those stereotypical elements. Alternatively, you might start this exercise by showing them a film in class or playing them a recording that deals with Wild West themes.

3. Have the students create sound effects for a performance of the play.

PRODUCTION NOTES

This play was first performed in 1975 by a group of theatre students from the University of Regina. They had received a grant to tour the province and needed a play that was entertaining, was capable of being performed outdoors, and was portable. *Showdown at Sand Valley* turned out to be a success in parks, county fairs, and community halls.

Author Ken Mitchell has written the following about the show: "The actors, under the direction of Robert Clinton, presented all the required props and sets in mime: chairs, doors, horses, even a sewing machine. It was a fast-paced, comic, and highly visual production. One hot night in July, the actors found themselves placed in the midway of the Swift Current Exhibition on a flat-bed trailer, competing for attention with ferris wheels, strippers, Black Angus cattle, and midway barkers. That they not only attracted but held a large crowd was a fine testimonial to their performance and, perhaps, to the entertainment value of *Showdown at Sand Valley*."

Follow the author's directions in terms of simplicity of set. Divide the set in two, with Main Street and the hotel on one side and Mrs. McAllister's house on the other.

Since this is a play based on stereotypes, encourage the students to develop stereotyped accents for the characters. Don't worry too much about authenticity.

Since the narrator is a link between the play and the audience, it is vital that the student playing the narrator speak directly *to* the audience, establishing eye contact with them. If the number of available actors is limited, consider using one of the townspeople as narrator. The student could come downstage during the narration sequences and make eye contact with the audience.

Since the play has only one female character, you might make some of the townspeople into women—

Samantha Gompers, for instance, instead of Stanley Gompers.

Because the humour of the play is broad and farcical, toy rifles and six-shooter cap guns with holsters would be more appropriate than real-looking firearms.

UNIT 3: WRAP-UP QUESTIONS

1. Both *The Ugly Duckling* and *Showdown at Sand Valley* are satires on the human condition. They poke fun at the weaknesses and foolishness of people. By making specific reference to the plays, explain what follies or weaknesses are satirized.

2. These two plays are examples of comedy. Comedy in the theatre need not mean that the play is funny, merely that it is not of a serious nature. Are there, in fact, any truly funny moments in either play? Explain.

3. If these two plays are not of a serious nature, then is the message they convey unimportant? Tell why or why not and describe the theme of each play.

4. There is often a thin line between comedy and tragedy. The elements of tragedy lie just beneath the surface of comedy. For example, in slapstick comedy, the clown performs a pratfall, a deliberate, comic, sit-down fall to the ground. We are quite aware that the clown is not hurt. But what if the clown were hurt? Then we have tragedy. What tragic elements lie beneath the surface of *The Ugly Duckling* and *Showdown at Sand Valley*?

Unit 4: Winners and Losers

Cyclone Jack/Carol Bolt (musical play)
Ride to the Hill/Ron Taylor (television play)

This unit highlights the struggle to win that goes on in each person's life. Winning, though, might not be seen in external or objective terms, but rather as internal and subjective; perhaps it can be defined as one's personal growth. The first reading of *Cyclone Jack* might suggest that the central figure is a winner because of his racing victories, but a closer reading points out that he is not treated as a winner by those around him. In a contrasting play, the young protagonist in *Ride to the Hill* loses a central possession in her life, though she wins an important battle in her move toward adulthood.

WINNERS AND LOSERS

Though of course the outcome of such a conflict is important, the growth that comes as a result of the struggle can be the most rewarding part of the "contest of life." The dramatists in this unit demonstrate that ultimately it is the central character who decides whether he or she is a winner or loser. It is the subjective viewpoint that determines success.

In Carol Bolt's musical play *Cyclone Jack*, the Canadian runner Tom Longboat succeeds as an athlete but is exploited as a person by those around him. *Ride to the Hill*, a television play by Ron Taylor, shows a protagonist who learns something about maturing and human nature when she must give up her most prized possession, a pinto pony.

Some writers see life as a continual contest. A person struggles for success in all aspects of his or her life—be it at school, at home, with peers, or in the work world. Some see this sort of struggle as the major spark that keeps us going: without the stress that goes along with struggle, we would simply cease to function.

CYCLONE JACK

Carol Bolt

PLAY SUMMARY

The play details some of the highlights and problems of the career of the great native Canadian long-distance runner Tom Longboat. He was a successful runner in the early decades of this century. Longboat's love of running and the exploitation and condescension surrounding his victories make up the main episodes of the work.

ABOUT THE AUTHOR

Carol Bolt was born in Winnipeg and began writing while attending the University of British Columbia. Her work has been produced in theatres across Canada as well as on CBC. She is one of the founding members of the Playwrights' Co-op in Toronto and has been active in a number of community theatre programs. *Cyclone Jack* was written as a commission for Toronto's Young People's Theatre.

LEVEL OF DIFFICULTY

This is one of the more difficult plays in the anthology. It is made up of a number of vignettes or scenes that don't necessarily have a straight narrative flow. You might begin a study of the text by looking at individual vignettes for theme, characterization, and so forth. The play also contains music; the lyrics are printed in italics. The students might discuss what the songs add to the play; you might spend one class on the lyrics alone. Some of the characters' motivations are not overtly presented in the text; the students can discuss what some of these might be.

PRE-READING ACTIVITIES

1. Discuss long-distance running with your class. Some of the students might be runners or joggers. Have them tell why they run, how they feel during and after a long run. Is there something competitive in running against yourself? Why?

2. Any good encyclopedia will give winning times and distances achieved in Olympic Games as far back as 1896. Give your students a copy of this information and discuss how each effort was bettered in succeeding games. Discuss why this is so.

3. Have the students do research on the Olympic Games or the Boston Marathon. They might also look at recent media coverage of either of the events or of a local running competition.

4. Invite a local long-distance runner, or possibly a physical-education teacher from your school, to talk to the class about running—how an athlete prepares physically and psychologically, the pressure of a running competition, and so on.

5. Read to the class excerpts from *Chariots of Fire* or *Flanigan's Run* to establish interest in and atmosphere for the play.

6. Tell the story of the American Olympic athlete Jim Thorpe. Pay particular attention to the revoking of his medals by the Olympic Committee. Detail briefly the requirements of an athlete who wishes to participate in the Olympic Games. Note that Jim Thorpe's medals were returned recently to his family.

VOCABULARY

1. *Onondaga* (p. 107) one branch of the Iroquois people. "Said I'm not the fastest *Onondaga* marathoner..."

2. *one, two* (p. l08) first and second place. "Going to make it *one, two*, Charlie?"

3. *raucous* (p. 110) harsh-sounding and noisy. "(There is *raucous* and rowdy cheering...)"

4. *hostel* (p. 110) a building that provides overnight accommodation. "A *hostel* for sportsmen..."

5. *amo amas amat amateur* (p. 110) an invented conjugation of the Latin verb "to love." Flanagan suggests both that Tom loves running and that he is an amateur rather than a professional runner.

6. *catechism* (p. 113) a series of questions and answers about religion, used to teach religious doctrine. "That I should drink my milk and learn my *catechism* ..."

7. *tape* (p. 114) in a race, a tape is stretched across the finish line; the first runner to cross the finish line breaks the tape and wins the race. "(...as Tom breaks the *tape* and exits...)"

8. *Massey Hall* (p. 116) a Toronto concert hall, the former home of the Toronto Symphony. "I guess you thought we were having the reception at the Grand Central Hotel. No sir, Tom. *Massey Hall*."

9. *snake-oil salesman...flim-flam, flash four-flusher* (pp. 116-117) all phrases that refer to a deceptive, untrustworthy, cheating person.

COMPREHENSION

A

1. Why does Tom Longboat race?
2. What is the attitude of Tom's managers toward Tom?
3. Tom has some difficulty establishing his amateur status. What is the problem? What happens in the end?
4. What are Tom Longboat's competitors' opinions of him?
5. What incident shows that Tom is indeed a great sportsman?
6. Describe the celebration of Tom's wedding to Lauretta Maracle.
7. What happens at the Toronto reception after Tom wins the Boston Marathon?

B

1. There are suggestions in the play that Tom not only does not train but seems to become involved in bouts of self-destruction. Locate these references and comment on them.
2. Throughout the play there are suggestions that Tom is being exploited by some people and actively discouraged by others. Describe the exploitation and the reasons for it. Why would some people try to prevent Tom from competing?
3. What is the nature of the relationship between Tom and Charlie Petch? Discuss.
4. How does Flanagan use both Tom and Lauretta? Tom and Charlie Petch?
5. Tom experiences prejudice and condescension from a number of people. Explain and quote lines to support your answer.

LITERARY TECHNIQUE

1. How has the playwright captured the attention of the audience at the start of the play? Give at least two means by which she holds the audience's attention in other parts of the play.
2. The playwright must introduce the main characters and action as quickly as possible. What do we learn of Tom Longboat and his problem(s) within the first few minutes of the drama? What method has the playwright used to present Tom's biography?
3. Quote lines that the characters deliver throughout the play to inform us of time and setting.
4. Characterization is developed through what the characters say and do and through what others say about them. Making direct reference to the play by either quoting lines or referring to incidents, describe the following characters: Tom Longboat; Chuck Ashley; Tom Flanagan; Lauretta Maracle.
5. Quote three instances where characters deliver lines that tell the audience what action is taking place as well as where and when the action is occurring. What does such a technique tell us about the nature of drama?
6. In what ways does this play differ from some of the more traditional plays you have read? (For example, *Cyclone Jack* lacks scene divisions.) Discuss the advantages or drawbacks of these different techniques.

FOLLOW-UP ACTIVITIES

1. Have the students research and write a brief biography of Tom Longboat. They might consult the entry in the *Encyclopedia Canadiana* or an article by F. Cronin in the February 4, 1956, issue of *Maclean's* magazine, "The Rise and Fall of Tom Longboat." How has the playwright used biographical incidents in her work?
2. Have the students improvise a scene in which Tom and Lauretta discuss how Flanagan is treating them.
3. Discuss how the song lyrics add to the theme and characterizations of the play. Do they advance the action or bring it to a stop? Obtain a copy of the music (see the caution at the end of the play) and see how music and lyrics fit together.

PRODUCTION NOTES

The episodic nature of the script lends itself to readers' theatre, with the cast sitting on stools at the front of the room and reading the play in character.

If you stage the play, there are no restrictions of time and space. In keeping with the author's approach, costuming and sets need only be representational and suggestive. All actors might have a basic costume of dark sweater and jeans and then add articles of clothing (numbers for racers, hats, ties, and so on) to create another character.

It is a good idea to begin working on a staging of the play by rehearsing individual scenes. Before you go on to another scene, see that the students understand the characters and why the characters behave as they do.

Tom is a complex figure, especially toward the end of the play. Discuss his actions with the student playing the role; why, for instance, does Tom laugh at anything in the last few scenes?

Be sure student actors know who is involved in a scene and who is talking to whom. It is also useful to work with them on the tone of many of the lines.

RIDE TO THE HILL

Ron Taylor

PLAY SUMMARY

Pauline, a young girl about to enter adulthood, suffers from fears about her height and awkwardness. Combined with the teasing to which she has been subjected is her father's insistence that she give up her beloved small pony and begin riding an animal more suited to her size. The play is the story of her transition from child to adult.

ABOUT THE AUTHOR

Ron Taylor is a Canadian playwright who was born in Toronto in 1931. He went to New York and trained as an actor, but he returned to Toronto where he combined driving a taxi with a writing career. He has written several television, radio, and stage plays.

LEVEL OF DIFFICULTY

The lines of the play are quite easy to understand. Students might have some difficulty with the fact that much of the play is visual—many of the scenes are without dialogue at all. Encourage students to try to "see" a scene as they read it. They might also want to think of what is going on in a character's mind when there is no dialogue to reveal such thoughts.

PRE-READING ACTIVITIES

1. Have the students discuss what they believe to be the qualities of a mature person. They might mention such attributes as responsibility, independence, good will, the ability to distinguish the real from the imagined, integrity, adaptability, and co-operativeness. As part of this discussion, the students might also note some qualities of the immature person, who responds in a childish fashion to the challenges of life. This discussion will help to prepare the students to recognize the protagonist's growth toward maturity.

2. Discuss the idea of characterization with the students. Show through literary examples (short stories, novels, some of the plays in this anthology) how the author develops characters through what the characters say or do or through what others say about them.

3. Have the students research how a person cares for a riding horse. They might consider making a field trip to a local stable to watch how a horse is saddled, groomed, and so on.

4. Discuss with the students the leaving behind of old possessions and concepts that they have outgrown. You might encourage them to share personal experiences that might be analogous with Pauline's in the play.

5. Have the students watch a television program and write about those scenes in which no dialogue is used. What do the author and director do to put a point across? Would the same scene have worked better with dialogue?

VOCABULARY

1. *hand* (p. 119) a unit of measure used to give the height of a horse; approximately ten centimetres. "(...a small, brown-and-white pinto about twelve *hands* in height.)"

2. *currycomb* (p. 119) a brush with metal teeth used for grooming a horse. "(He carries a *currycomb* and a brush.)"

3. *perspective* (p. 120) the appearance of objects, buildings, and so on, as determined by their distance from the viewer. "(...we get a full *perspective* of the hill.)"

4. *pastoral* (p. 120) having to do with the countryside and nature. "(...we follow their ride back to the corral in a series of beautiful *pastoral* shots...)"

5. *gregarious* (p. 121) fond of being with others. "(He is a likable, *gregarious*, just turned fifteen-year-old...)"

6. *stance* (p. 123) in games like baseball, the position of a player's feet. "(He picks up another stone, takes his *stance*, checks the imaginary bases...)"

7. *flat-out* (p. 125) at maximum speed or effort. "(It is a wild, *flat-out* ride...)"

8. *canter* (p. 125) a gentle gallop. "(She moves him into a *canter*, then stops.)"

COMPREHENSION

A

1. What is the conflict in the play?

2. Why does Pauline have to give up Stanley, her pinto?

3. What sort of fantasy does Pauline have about seeing Stanley some day in the future?

4. How does Martin show that he is sensitive to Pauline's moods and feelings? Make references to incidents in the play.

5. How does Martin hurt Pauline without his being aware of it until it is too late?

6. What accident happens to make Pauline accept her new horse?

B

1. "Two of the purposes of fiction are to help set standards of behaviour in solving problems and to give us an understanding of the problems of others." Discuss the effectiveness of *Ride to the Hill* in achieving these goals.

2. Do you think that Pauline has genuine cause to be upset over the loss of her horse and the circumstances surrounding that loss, or is she being immature? Explain. What have the adults of Pauline's world done to make her feel as she does?

3. How does Martin stop Pauline from being angry with him?

4. Pauline's last speech reads, "You freak. You stupid freak. You ugly, stupid freak. You big, gangling, gawky, stupid, ugly freak!" Although she addresses the horse, what underlying meaning do her words convey? What does the closing action of the drama reveal about her feelings toward the horse? Toward herself?

5. What is the significance of the title in relation to the rest of the play?

LITERARY TECHNIQUE

1. MOTIVATION refers to the deliberate inclusion by the playwright of reasons why the characters do what they do. In short, motivation is the reason behind the characters' actions or statements. How does the playwright suggest or explain the following actions or statements:

   - the selling of the pinto pony
   - Martin's telling about the electric-train incident
   - Pauline's statement, "Do you mean that we'd look funny walking down the street together..."
   - Pauline's not riding to the top of the hill at the end of the play

2. Playwrights develop characters by having them say and do particular things or by having others say something about them. Describe the characters of the following through what they say and do or from what others say about them: Pauline; Martin; Martin's father; Pauline's father.

3. How does the playwright make his point in scenes that have no dialogue? Would some of these scenes be improved if they had a character speaking?

FOLLOW-UP ACTIVITIES

1. If your school has video equipment, make a video of Scene Seven, the meeting of Pauline and Martin. See if different points of view for the camera might give a different sense of the scene.

2. Invite a television camera operator or director in to speak to the class about the importance of camera angles and television work in general. If possible, arrange a field trip to a local television station and let the class learn about the production of a television show.

3. Have the students illustrate some of the visual scenes in the play. Remind them to look for the point of view that the script gives to the camera.

4. Have the students write a scene that occurs after the end of the play—Martin and Pauline meet in school, or perhaps they meet while each is out riding. Imagine several different ways that such a scene might progress.

PRODUCTION NOTES

Although written as a television script, *Ride to the Hill* has some excellent scenes for classroom presentation. For example, Scene Seven is the centre of the play; it contains the most dialogue and is the longest scene. You might consider combining Scenes Two, Five, and Six.

Of course, the horses need not be in the presentation; they could easily be mimed in the dialogue sections.

Point out how, in Scene Seven, the leadership or control of the scene passes between Martin and Pauline. Use different staging techniques such as position on the stage, sitting or standing, as well as shifting emphasis of the delivery of words to move the control back and forth. The student playing Pauline should try to convey a hurt quality beneath her anger at the beginning of the scene. The student playing Martin should be somewhat cocky, but not so much that he becomes unlikable.

UNIT 4: WRAP-UP QUESTIONS

1. Both *Cyclone Jack* and *Ride to the Hill* are representative of a universal human situation—winning and losing. But something may be gained with each loss, just as something may be lost with each victory. Explain what is gained and lost in each drama. Who could be categorized as winners? As losers? Why?

2. Would you categorize these plays as tragedies—that is, as plays in which the main characters suffer great misfortune? Why or why not?

3. PLOT in a drama is the rising sequence of events which are outlined as follows:

   - BEGINNING: The playwright plunges the audience immediately into the action of the drama.

   - PROBLEM: The protagonist (main character) is faced with some difficulty which he or she attempts to solve.

   - CONFLICT: The protagonist becomes involved in a struggle to solve the problem.

   - CRISIS: The high point of the drama, at which time the problem must be solved.

   - RESOLUTION or DENOUEMENT: This element is the outcome of the drama.

   Analyse the two plays in this unit according to their plots.

4. TONE is the playwright's attitude toward her or his characters and subject. What attitudes toward the main characters in each play are expressed by the playwrights? Quote key lines to support your answers. What behaviour exemplifies winners? What behaviour exemplifies losers?

5. The basis for *Cyclone Jack* is historical, while *Ride to the Hill* is fictional. Create a brief one-act play from an incident in history or from a favourite short story.

Unit 5: Courtroom Justice

Saint Joan/George Bernard Shaw (stage play - excerpt)
Riel/John Coulter (stage play - excerpt)

This unit focusses on two historical figures who fought their last battles in the courtroom. The trial scenes from *Saint Joan* and *Riel* both show the heated arguments and tensions as the respective protagonists seek legal acquittal for their actions. Though Joan is a fifteenth-century French figure and Riel is a nineteenth-century Canadian one, the two face the forces of church and state that want to condemn them; the parallels make for interesting comparisons.

The witnesses give testimony, the two sides present their arguments, the jury leaves the room for the eagerly awaited decision—there is perhaps no more theatrical and dramatic situation than a courtroom scene. Often the choices in the courtroom are not of a clear-cut, black-and-white nature.

This unit examines two historical figures who were put on trial for their beliefs. Though hundreds of years apart in time, both Joan of Arc and Louis Riel sought to change the societies in which they lived. Both figures were caught up in a clash of cultures and were worshipped by their followers for what they were attempting to do. The trial setting concentrates the arguments of the central characters and those who opposed them. At the same time, the setting creates tension for the viewer as to the outcome of the struggle.

In the excerpt from George Bernard Shaw's *Saint Joan*, we watch the young Joan defend herself against the forces of both church and state as they try to crush her with charges of blasphemy and witchcraft. A selection from John Coulter's *Riel* uses the actual transcript of Riel's 1885 trial for treason to show the court battle that surrounded a figure from our own history.

SAINT JOAN (excerpt)

George Bernard Shaw

PLAY SUMMARY

In the trial scene from George Bernard Shaw's *Saint Joan*, the forces of church and state make a concerted effort to condemn Joan both for reputed blasphemy and witchcraft and for the danger she offers to the politics of the time. She is finally condemned because she will not give up her personal liberty. She is then burned at the stake. Her story does not end, however, with her death.

ABOUT THE AUTHOR

It has been said that the world would have been a duller place without George Bernard Shaw (1856-1950). The controversial but brilliant Irish playwright, social reformer, and critic created many of the best pieces of writing in the past hundred years, including *Pygmalion* (later adapted into the musical comedy *My Fair Lady*), *Caesar and Cleopatra*, and *Saint Joan*, called by many his greatest play. Shaw received the Nobel Prize for literature in 1925.

LEVEL OF DIFFICULTY

This excerpt is one of the more difficult selections in the anthology. There are a number of religious and legal terms that are part of the trial process. Joan's dilemma, however, is clearly presented from the start. It is her almost constant single-mindedness that is the most memorable aspect of the excerpt. Help the students to sort out the various forces that stand in opposition to Joan; each churchman and political figure has a different reason for wanting to see Joan executed, and each has his own defining character. Some historical background will certainly be needed—the political situation between England and the warring dukedoms of France in the 1400s; the attitude of the Roman Catholic church toward heresy and witchcraft; the widespread belief of the people of the time that miracles can and do happen.

PRE-READING ACTIVITIES

1. Discuss heroes and heroines who have devoted their lives to their country in some way—people such as Gandhi, Louis Riel (see the following play in the anthology), Florence Nightingale. What characteristics do these people have in common? Discuss the nature of heroism and sacrifice for a larger goal than self.

2. Have the students research attitudes toward witchcraft in the middle ages. What sorts of people were likely to be accused? What were their punishments?

3. Discuss the title of the play. What sort of person does it suggest will be at the centre of the work? What kind of person is a saint? What sorts of things do saintly people do?

VOCABULARY

1. *Inquisition* (p. 129) a court established by the Roman Catholic church in the thirteenth century to punish heretics. "(...the court being the bishop's court with the *Inquisition* participating...)"

2. *assessors* (p. 129) people with technical knowledge called in to advise a court on specialist matters. "(...the canons, the doctors of law and theology, and the Dominican monks, who act as *assessors*.)"

3. *scribes* (p. 129) public clerks or secretaries. "(In the angle is a table for the *scribes*...)"

4. *sits* (p. 130) is officially begun. "The court *sits*."

5. *obdurate* (p. 131) stubborn; unyielding. "That is what happens to the *obdurate*."

6. *wantonly* (p. 131) without reason or excuse. "It must not be applied *wantonly*."

7. *cloth-of-gold* (p. 131) material made of silk or woollen threads woven with gold threads. "If I had not worn my *cloth-of-gold* surcoat in battle like a fool..."

8. *surcoat* (p. 131) an outer coat, such as a garment previously worn by a knight over his armour. "If I had not worn my cloth-of-gold *surcoat* in battle like a fool..."

9. *Burgundian* (p. 131) from the region of Burgundy in eastern France. "...that *Burgundian* soldier..."

10. *Church Militant* (p. 132) the church seen as fighting the forces of evil. "...will you submit your case to the inspired interpretation of the *Church Militant*?"

11. *the Maid* (p. 133) another name for Joan. "...you are *the Maid*'s best advocates."

12. *trumpery* (p. 133) worthless; useless. "Does he press these *trumpery* matters?"

13. *excommunication* (p. 133) a formal expulsion from the church. "...the doom of *excommunication*..."

14. *remonstrances* (p. 133) protests; complaints. "...our most earnest *remonstrances* and entreaties..."

15. *creed* (p. 134) a statement of faith or religious belief. "The blessed St. Athanasius has laid it down in his *creed*..."

16. *recantation* (p. 135) a taking back formally or officially, as an oath. "You must sign a solemn *recantation* of your heresy."

17. *abjure* (p. 136) to swear to give up. "All of which I now renounce and *abjure* and depart from..."

18. *J-e-h-a-n-e* (p. 136) Ladvenu says the letters of a French form of Joan's name as he helps her to write them.

19. *antiphonally* (p. 138) sung or chanted in alternate parts. "(They rise solemnly and intone the sentence *antiphonally*.)"

20. *relapsed* (p. 138) slipped back to a former state. "We decree that thou art a *relapsed* heretic."

21. *sundered* (p. 138) cut off from. "*Sundered* from her body." (that is, the church)

22. *feint* (p. 139) a movement intended to deceive. "(He makes a *feint* of retiring.)"

23. *diocese* (p. 139) the region over which a bishop has authority. "It is not in your *diocese*."

24. *mystery* (p. 141) a trade or craft. "I am the Master Executioner of Rouen; it is a highly skilled *mystery*."

COMPREHENSION

A

1. The stage directions say that the setting is "...a great stone hall in the castle, arranged for a trial-at-law, but not a trial-by-jury...." What is the difference?

2. What does Joan say in her first few speeches that, first of all, catches the immediate attention of the audience and, second, gives a clear idea of her predicament?

3. Joan displays a spirited common sense and intelligence in her first argument with D'Estivet. Explain how Joan wins this brief argument.

4. What argument does Joan present for not wearing woman's clothing?

5. Whose voices does Joan claim to hear?

6. What does Joan fear worse than being burned at the stake?

7. Who is Joan's main defender at the end of the play?

B

1. Joan says to the Inquisitor in relation to telling the whole truth, "He who tells too much truth is sure to be hanged." What does she mean? Does she tell "too much truth"? Explain.

2. Essentially, Joan defies the society of her day. Is she right in doing so? Why or why not?

3. Analyse Joan's impassioned speech about freedom. Why does she say at the end of that speech, "I know that your counsel is of the devil, and that mine is of God"?

4. Why won't de Stogumber sit down when he is told to do so? How is he finally made to take his seat?

5. In the end the Inquisitor states that Joan is quite innocent, "...crushed between these mighty forces, the Church and the Law." These grimly cynical words suggest the real issue, the one not stated in Joan's trial. What is the issue?

LITERARY TECHNIQUE

1. The playwright must give as much information about the characters, the situation, and the setting as quickly as possible. What does the audience learn about these three matters within the first hundred or so lines?

2. Characterization is developed both through what a character says and does and what is said about him or her. The playwright has developed contrasting characters among Joan's accusers—the intelligent and the dull, the vengeful and the merciful, the leaders and the followers, the bigoted and the enlightened. Write two or three paragraphs about the character of each of the accusers. Why has Shaw contrasted them?

3. Shaw has created the character of Joan in such a way that we are sympathetic toward her. What is there about her that attracts our sympathy?

4. A symbol is something that stands for something else; for example, a flag might stand as a symbol for a country. Explain the symbolism in the line, "Her heart would not burn, my lord; but everything that was left is at the bottom of the river."

5. How does Shaw keep Joan at the centre of the play even after she has left the stage?

FOLLOW-UP ACTIVITIES

1. Encourage some students to read the entire play and its preface. You might want to read and discuss parts of the preface with the students, since it may be difficult for them.

2. Have the students read and stage the first scene of the Shaw play, which gives the audience its first view of Joan. It is a simpler scene than the trial scene. Just as the French captain Robert de Baudricourt must be won over by Joan's argument, so must the audience. Discuss the techniques that Shaw has used to do this.

3. In his preface to *Saint Joan*, Shaw says about Joan of Arc, "...she refused to accept the specific woman's lot, and dressed and fought and lived as men did.

"As she continued to assert herself in all these ways with such force that she was famous throughout western Europe before she was out of her teens (indeed she never got out of them), it is hardly surprising that she was judicially burnt, ostensibly for a number of capital crimes which we no longer punish as such, but essentially for what we call unwomanly and insufferable presumption. . . . As her actual condition was pure upstart, there were only two opinions about her. One was that she was miraculous: the other that she was unbearable."

Discuss the meaning of this statement with the students. Then have them research Joan of Arc's life. In addition to entries in encyclopedias such as the *Encyclopaedia Britannica* and *The McGraw-Hill Encyclopedia of World Biography*, they might consult a book such as Nancy W. Ross's *Joan of Arc*. W. S. Scott's *Jeanne D'Arc: Her Life, Death, and the Myth* contains a clear biography as well as a good history of the times. *Joan of Arc: The Legend and the Reality*, by Frances Gies, contains a good deal of information on the trial as well as a summary of thought about Joan over the past five centuries.

Have the students write a brief essay in which they discuss Shaw's statement (above) in view of what they know about Joan. You might have them discuss their essays in class.

4. Play a recording of the trial scene. (There are several available, one featuring the fine actress Siobhan McKenna.) Let them comment on the personalities of the different characters as they are created by the performers.

5. Discuss the short scene between the Earl of Warwick and Peter Cauchon, the Bishop of Beauvais. What is the source of the hostility between them? Have the students research the relationship between the church and the state at this time.

6. Form two teams and have the opposing sides argue the question "Is Joan a heroine?" Let those members of the class who are not on one of the teams judge which team wins.

PRODUCTION NOTES

The real power of the play comes in Joan's defence before her accusers. The actress playing Joan must be chosen with care, for the role is difficult to do convincingly. The actress must go through rapid swings of mood and move from the depths of despair to the hottest of angers. It might be worth having several students work on Joan's long speech about liberty to see how different people interpret the lines.

Sets can be as simple as chairs; nothing more is needed. Costuming can be black choir robes (if available) or any dark dress for the Inquisitor, magistrates, and priests. Joan's costume should be rough and ill-fitting, perhaps burlap, but *not* comical in any way.

Distinction should be made between the characters of Joan's opponents. All are against her, but some show pity and compassion for her while others merely want her dead.

Though the tone of the piece is generally serious, there is some opportunity for comedy in the early actions of a character like de Stogumber. He should be used as a contrast to the darker forces of the play; this will also allow his breakdown after Joan's death to be more meaningful.

RIEL (excerpt)

John Coulter

PLAY SUMMARY

This excerpt from John Coulter's play *Riel* shows the courtroom scene in which the title character stands trial for treason against the Crown. The two sides, Crown and Defence, call witnesses and examine them; Riel himself finally testifies. After several short scenes outside the courtroom, we learn that the jury finds Riel guilty; the judge orders him to be hanged. The trial material is pieced together from the actual transcript of Riel's trial in Regina in 1885.

ABOUT THE AUTHOR

John Coulter (1888-1980) was born in Belfast, Northern Ireland, and received an art education in Belfast and Manchester before he moved to Canada. He became a writer early in life and has written a biography of Sir Winston Churchill, a novel, some poetry, and two operas in addition to his plays. His work has been performed on CBC. *Riel* is his best-known play, largely because of its annual summer presentation in Regina.

LEVEL OF DIFFICULTY

As with the *Saint Joan* excerpt, this excerpt has legal terminology that should be explained to the students. There is also a theatrical, non-naturalistic way of handling the action in the courtroom—the use of areas of the stage and spotlights to establish groups of characters for the audience. This should be pointed out to the students before they begin reading the text. The argument of each of the witnesses is clear; alert students to watch the way the two attorneys can lead witnesses to areas that the Crown or Defence thinks important. Riel's speeches are impassioned but also well argued. They are the emotional centre of the excerpt. Have the students pay close attention to what he says when he finally gets on the witness stand.

PRE-READING ACTIVITIES

1. Have the students view the CBC production *Riel* as historical background to the excerpt from Coulter's play.

2. Read the historical account of Louis Riel's trial and hanging in *Strange Empire* by Joseph Kinsey Howard. (There is a paperback edition of this book available.) Review the material with your students.

3. Review the historical events of 1885 leading up to the Rebellion of 1885 and eventually to Riel's trial and execution. Discuss these events with your students.

   There are a number of books that the students might consult. *Revolt in the West*, by Edward McCourt, is an intermediate text with many illustrations; it tells the historical events in a narrative form. Another such text with illustrations is *The Last War Drum*, by Desmond Morton. *The Life of Louis Riel*, by Peter Charlebois, is also full of illustrations. Both it and E. B. Osler's *The Man Who Had to Hang Riel* are pro-Riel accounts. Frank W. Anderson's *Riel's Manitoba Uprising* is a short account of the historical events. *The Riel Rebellion*, compiled by Nick and Helma Mika, offers contemporary newspaper accounts of the events. Finally, H. Bowsfield's *Louis Riel: Rebel of the Western Frontier or Victim of Politics and Prejudice?* is a collection of various opinions about Riel, from the nineteenth century to the present; it is a difficult but worthwhile book for some students to investigate.

4. Invite a lawyer or judge to speak to your class about the various parts of a trial and how a trial is run. You might plan a field trip to see a local trial in operation.

5. Have the students draw a map marking the key locations of the Rebellion of 1885.

VOCABULARY

1. *oyez* (p. 143) hear; attend; a call uttered three times before a court commences its duties.

2. *bench* (p. 143) the seat where judges sit in a law court. "(. . .Judge Richardson is standing before the raised seat which is the *bench*.)"

3. *dock* (p. 143) the place where an accused person stands in a law court. "(. . .Riel stands behind a rail which is the *dock*.)"

4. *arraign* (p. 144) to bring before a court for trial. "*Arraign* the prisoner."

5. *tenacity* (p. 144) stubbornness; persistence. "He managed to inspire his men with almost fanatical bravery and *tenacity*."

6. *Gatling gun* (p. 144) an early type of machine gun. ". . . the superior firepower of our *Gatling gun*."

7. *mangy* (p. 146) shabby; dirty. ". . .so many hungry, *mangy* coyotes. . ."

8. *peremptorily* (p. 149) in a manner that allows no denial. "(*peremptorily*) Now stop."

9. *cassock* (p. 149) a long outer garment, often worn by a clergyman. "(He is a noticeably unkempt bearded man in a greasy *cassock*.)"

10. *Oblat* (p. 149) a form of "oblate," a Roman Catholic who belongs to a secular group devoted to religious work. "Alexis André, *Oblat*."

11. *megalomania* (pp. 150-151) a sort of mental illness characterized by delusions of grandeur, wealth, or greatness. "...the mental disease by which the prisoner was afflicted...*megalomania*."

12. *Mahomet* (p. 152) another name for Mohammed, a prophet and the founder of Islam. "...then they became great prophets and great men; *Mahomet*, for instance."

13. *telling his beads* (p. 152) to count one's rosary beads one by one while saying prayers. "His little statue of St. Joseph stands on the table, and when he's *telling his beads* I've noticed that he holds it in his hand and hugs it."

14. *apologia pro vita sua* (p. 153) Latin, a defence of one's life; a formal defence of a cause or one's beliefs or actions. "A sort of *apologia pro vita sua*."

15. *"putting an antic disposition on"* (p. 153) pretending to be mad. "Ah, but was not Hamlet '*putting an antic disposition on*'?"

16. *Pilate* (p. 157) the Roman ruler of Judea who ordered the crucifixion of Christ. "...I've been thinking we know a little more now of the considerations *Pilate* had to weigh..."

17. *Easter tragedy* (p. 157) the crucifixion of Christ. "...how anxious the prisoner is to identify his own predicament with the—*Easter tragedy*?"

18. *black cap* (p. 158) the cap worn by a judge when passing a death sentence. "(The Judge puts on the *black cap*.)"

COMPREHENSION

A

1. At the opening of the play we are given the setting and the problem with which the characters are faced. Describe the setting and the problem.

2. We get some idea of Riel's ability as a leader from what Middleton says about the fight at Batoche. Explain.

3. What are some of Riel's views on religion?

4. What is the relationship between Charles Nolin and Riel?

5. According to Nolin, how does Riel act in battle? Does he fight as a soldier?

6. Whom does Riel consider to be his mothers?

7. In the second scene, why does the woman want to speak to the judge and jury?

B

1. Describe clearly in two separate paragraphs the following: Riel's conflict with the government; Riel's conflict with the church.

2. Was Riel's struggle with the church and state sane and just? Why or why not?

3. In *Saint Joan*, Joan says, "He who tells too much truth is sure to be hanged." How does this statement apply to Louis Riel?

4. What view does the witness Charles Nolin present of Louis Riel? Why does Riel interrupt during Nolin's testimony?

5. What are the views of Riel presented in Scene Four? How do they differ from those presented in the courtroom? Why is there a difference?

6. Why does the judge take so harsh a view of Riel in the final scene?

LITERARY TECHNIQUE

1. Does the playwright seem more interested in the events or the characters? Explain, using instances from the play to support your answer.

2. From the bare statements of fact delivered in dialogue we are eventually able to glimpse Louis Riel's complex character. In these instances we discover Riel from what others say about him. Select what you believe to be the highlights of his character and support your opinion with lines from the play.

3. How does the division of the stage into various areas, defined in part by spotlights, contribute to the scenes in the courtroom?

4. What does Scene Two contribute to our view of Louis Riel?

5. What does Scene Four contribute to our view of Louis Riel?

FOLLOW-UP ACTIVITIES

1. Encourage some students to read all of Coulter's play *Riel*. Does the work as a whole offer a different view of the character than we have in the scenes in the anthology?

2. Form two teams and have the opposing sides argue the question "Was Louis Riel justified in his actions?" Let those members of the class who are not on one of the teams judge which team wins.

3. Ask the students to name some modern and historic heroes. What qualities do they share? Is Riel a hero?

4. Have some students examine the transcripts of Riel's trial. How are they different from what Coulter has presented? Do we get a different view of Riel from the play than we do from the transcripts? Why?

PRODUCTION NOTES

The first scene is a long one for class presentation, but it offers some good contrasts of characterization. Middleton, for instance, could be the brusque, no-nonsense military man, while Nolin could be less firm in his statements. The two actors who play the Crown and the Defence are the ones who lead the action in this scene, so they should be strong performers who are able to take the testimonies in the directions that are useful to them.

The court setting need not be as complex as it is described in the play. A single chair could be placed in the centre of the acting area, to be used either as a focal point for the audience or for the witness on the "stand" to sit on.

Riel is the most complex role in the play. Choose carefully the actor who will play him. In his long speeches, be careful not to make the man sound smug. A sense of sincerity is at the core of all his statements. Although Riel's speeches when he is on the witness stand can be found in several different scenes, one student actor could take all the defence speeches and present them to the class, as Riel did to the court, as a monologue.

Because of the quickness of the scene changes, it might be easier in a classroom setting to deal just with the actual trial in one production.

On the other hand, do not neglect Scenes Two and Four. Each adds something to our view of the central figure. You might stage them during a different class period and ask the students what the scenes contribute to the play. Scene Four especially offers not only a different view of Riel but also of the two lawyers and the professional witnesses, the two doctors.

UNIT 5: WRAP-UP QUESTIONS

1. Both Joan of Arc and Louis Riel, centuries apart, took up arms against the government of the time. There is a close parallel between these two in terms of their idealism, in the fact that they resorted to violence to redress wrongs as they saw them, in their claims that they heard celestial voices, and so on. Write an essay in which you compare the circumstances which caused each figure to rebel. Discuss the cause of their defeat, the similarity of their personalities, the circumstances of their trials, the accusers who opposed them, and the circumstances of their deaths. (The teacher might choose several of these specifics for the students to concentrate on.)

2. Discuss the question of the sanity of both Joan of Arc and Louis Riel.

3. Both Louis Riel and Joan of Arc had a goal. What was it in each instance? Was each goal a justifiable one in terms of right and good? What did the people of the time think of the goals? What would people today think of the goals?

4. Compare life in prison—both as they describe it in the plays and as they envision it in their futures—for Louis Riel and Joan of Arc. Do they have similar worries or fears about a lifetime of imprisonment?

5. Could both Joan of Arc and Louis Riel be described as martyrs? If so, to what cause? Would they have seen themselves in this context?

6. At the conclusion of *Saint Joan*, the Executioner says, "You have heard the last of her." Is this statement true of either Joan or Riel? Explain and discuss the irony of the statement.

Unit 6: The Unexpected

Feathertop/Maurice Valency (television play)
Visit to a Small Planet/Gore Vidal (television play)

This unit uses fantasy and science fiction to comment on aspects of our everyday lives. Both *Feathertop* and *Visit to a Small Planet* have a protagonist who steps into human society as an outsider, someone whose values are different from ours. In *Feathertop*, this outsider is benevolent, hoping to help improve our lot. In *Visit to a Small Planet*, he is amoral, hoping to pursue his own ends by playing on what he sees as the human need for war.

A good dramatist can make us believe that even the most unrealistic situation is a fact. This is especially true in the case of fantasy and science fiction. We might end up in the most unexpected of worlds, with the most unusual of characters, but the writer must first have established a "normal" setting or framework for the events that follow.

Fantasy and science fiction are also means for commenting on human nature. Although a situation may have something of the supernatural about it, the people within that situation are human beings with the same feelings, fears, and aspirations that we have. Bringing in a character from another world—either literally or figuratively—allows the dramatist to bring into sharp focus the other characters.

In Maurice Valency's *Feathertop*, a witch brings a scarecrow to life and sends it out into the world to encounter real-life straw men. Gore Vidal's *Visit to a Small Planet* shows what happens when a stranger from another planet arrives on earth with the goal of ruling the world and starting a global war.

FEATHERTOP

Maurice Valency

PLAY SUMMARY

Feathertop is a play adapted from a nineteenth-century story by Nathaniel Hawthorne. Feathertop is a scarecrow brought to life by the witch, Mother Rigby, and sent out into the world to make a fool of a rich, pompous man. Feathertop falls in love with the rich man's daughter but gives her up when he realizes that he is, after all, only a scarecrow.

ABOUT THE AUTHOR

Maurice Valency is an American playwright who was born in New York in 1903. He began a career as a lawyer but changed vocations to become a teacher, critic, and dramatist. He has adapted many French plays for presentation on the American stage and has written librettos for New York's Metropolitan Opera.

LEVEL OF DIFFICULTY

The play is easy to comprehend. Its scene changes are smooth and almost strictly narrative; the reader should have no problem knowing when the playwright moves us to a different playing area. All the characters are easily recognizable types. You might point out to the students that though there is a comedic tone running through the play, there is also something of the wistful and melancholic. Have them watch for this aspect of the drama. Some archaic terms might create some small problems.

PRE-READING ACTIVITIES

1. Check an encyclopedia for a few details on witchcraft in New England during the eighteenth century. Review these details with your class. This brief historical review will help to give some perspective to the play and perhaps explain why this particular setting has been chosen for the action.

2. Read to the class Washington Irving's short story "The Legend of Sleepy Hollow." What are some of the characteristics of the tale? How does the supernatural fit into it? How did the people of the time (close to that of the play *Feathertop*) think about the supernatural? Are figures like ghosts and witches thought of differently today?

3. Discuss with the students the changes that are most needed in the world today. In the play, Feathertop states

his ambition as follows: "... I shall help them. I shall heal them. I shall make all men equal and all men good. I shall exalt the humble. I shall abase the proud. I shall feed the hungry. Aye, the world will be the better for me." Do any of the students' statements agree with the character's goals?

Ask the students whether it is possible to make broad, sweeping changes in the world today. Discuss the consequences if we don't.

Finally, discuss the statement that one good deed, even if it is done unwillingly, is more than most people can boast. Have the students keep this point in mind, since this is, in effect, what Mother Rigby says in her last speech.

This discussion will help to get the students thinking along the lines of the play's theme.

4. Have the students think about bringing various inanimate objects to life. What characteristics would these new beings have, based on their inanimate characteristics? What would a grandfather clock be like, for instance, or a shiny new Cadillac?

VOCABULARY

1. *astrolabe* (p. 161) an astronomical device for measuring the altitude of stars. "(On the wall hangs an old brass *astrolabe* ...)"

2. *ramshackle* (p. 161) loose; likely to come apart. "(... a *ramshackle* grandeur...)"

3. *tiewig* (p. 161) a wig tied at the back with a ribbon. "(An old *tiewig* gives the figure a cockiness...)"

4. *yestreen* (p. 161) an abbreviation of "yester evening." "Late, late *yestreen* I saw the new moon..."

5. *a leg up* (p. 162) some help in succeeding. "Well, I shall give him *a leg up* ..."

6. *homespun* (p. 163) not polished; simple; plain. "Bit *homespun* still."

7. *Knight of the Garter* (p. 165) the oldest and most important order of knighthood in Great Britain. "There! You're a *Knight of the Garter*. Lord Feathertop!"

8. *Windsor chair* (p. 166) a type of wooden chair with a rounded spindle back and a flat or slightly hollowed seat. "(*Windsor chairs* are drawn up to the fire.)"

9. *George III* (p. 166) the king of England at the time of the play. "(... a portrait of *George III* on the wall.)"

10. *pikestaff* (p. 166) the shaft or staff of a spear. "Come now, 'tis plain as a *pikestaff*."

11. *Hessians* (p. 166) German mercenary soldiers who fought in the British army in the eighteenth century. "Here he threatens to send his *Hessians* to sack a farm…"

12. *selectmen* (p. 166) members of a local board in a New England town. "The *selectmen* are perjurers."

13. *figure dance* (p. 169) a dance, such as the minuet, in which the dancers follow some pattern of movements on the dance floor. "(Several couples take places to dance a *figure dance* of the minuet variety.)"

COMPREHENSION

A

1. How does Mother Rigby bring Feathertop to life? For what purpose is he brought to life?

2. What advice does Mother Rigby give Feathertop in order for him to live a successful life? Do you agree with her? Why or why not?

3. Who does Gookin think Feathertop is? Why does Gookin think he has come? What does Feathertop do and say which confirms Gookin's opinion?

4. What do Bell and Whitby tell Feathertop?

5. Feathertop tells Polly that his understanding of the world becomes clear when he looks at her. He says, "Then all is clear.…What it [the world] is, and what I am, and what I have to do." What becomes clear to Feathertop and what does he do?

6. What causes Polly to faint? What does Feathertop do then? How does Mother Rigby react?

B

1. Describe the first scene with Feathertop. How does he change? Why does he change?

2. Why is what Feathertop looks like, both physically and in dress, important?

3. How do Gookin, Bell, and Whitby treat each other? Explain. Does each character always express the same opinion of the others?

4. Why is a mirror important in the climactic scene of the play?

LITERARY TECHNIQUE

1. How do the stage directions, particularly the opening stage directions, show us what the play is about?

2. IRONY is a literary technique that involves opposites of expectations. VERBAL IRONY develops through what someone says. SITUATIONAL IRONY develops through happenings or incidents. Give examples of both types of irony in this play.

3. Playwrights sometimes prepare the audience for the drama's outcome. This technique is known as FORE-SHADOWING. Give at least one example of foreshadowing in *Feathertop*.

4. The playwright must give as much information to the audience as quickly as possible. What do you learn of the overall plot in Mother Rigby's opening monologue?

5. What function does Bob Endicott have in the play?

FOLLOW-UP ACTIVITIES

1. Read the students the original Nathaniel Hawthorne short story on which Maurice Valency's play is based. How has the dramatist changed the short story? Why? How successful is the adaptation, in your opinion?

2. Have the students write a newspaper report of Gookin's party. How would the party end?

3. Have the students draw Mother Rigby's room as it is described in the first scene of the play. Alternatively, let them bring in some props that might fit into the scene. What might they add to the set that is not mentioned in the script but would be appropriate?

4. Select a familiar story, possibly a children's story, and, using the adaptation of *Feathertop* as a model, turn the story into a brief drama. You might suggest to the students that they use the original setting and write it as a play for children. You might alternatively suggest that they change the setting and give the story a more modern, adult twist, like *The Ugly Duckling*.

PRODUCTION NOTES

Because of the cutting technique in television plays, some parts of *Feathertop* are not especially playable in the classroom. Some form of classroom production can be made, however, using selected scenes that have been rearranged and joined together.

All of the characters are straightforward in their presentation, except perhaps Feathertop himself. He must be seen gaining more and more confidence in himself until he actually believes he is capable of solving all the problems of the world. This attitude must be sharply contrasted with the dejection he feels when he is forced to remember that he is only a scarecrow.

Gookin, Bell, and Whitby are good figures of comedy. Gookin especially must be played by a versatile actor who can change from a man of charm to a "tattletale" very quickly. He is perhaps the most humorous figure in the play.

Mother Rigby is the source of knowledge in the work. Her first and last speeches are important in establishing the author's theme. You might consider having several students read her part and offer different interpretations of the role. She might, for example, be somewhat distanced and disinterested in what she does, or vengeful, or mischievous.

VISIT TO A SMALL PLANET

Gore Vidal

PLAY SUMMARY

Kreton, a charming stranger from another planet, arrives on earth with the goal of ruling the world and manipulating the nations into making global war. This plan is about to succeed when another visitor arrives to take Kreton back to his home planet, where he is considered to be mentally retarded.

ABOUT THE AUTHOR

Gore Vidal is a popular American novelist and playwright with more than fifty published works to his credit. Born in 1925, he came into prominence as a writer after World War II. It is said that he had not watched television until he decided to write television scripts. His most successful script for television is *Visit to a Small Planet*, which was first performed in 1955, with Cyril Ritchard as Kreton. A motion-picture adaptation, filled with a good deal more slapstick comedy, starred Jerry Lewis.

LEVEL OF DIFFICULTY

The script is of average difficulty. The characters are relatively straightforward in their thoughts and feelings, so that student readers do not have to guess at their motives. Only Kreton, the central figure, keeps his thoughts to himself—and that is the element of surprise in the play. Since this play is an early work for television, it is restricted to a small set—several rooms in a house. The stage directions are quite clear as to where the action is occurring. Students should find very few vocabulary problems, since characters are—except in the case of the two visitors—contemporary figures who think and speak like the rest of us. The plot, not at all complex, is developed along strict narrative lines.

PRE-READING ACTIVITIES

1. Discuss with the students the attempts by various leaders to conquer the world. Examples of such people might be Julius Caesar, Napoleon, and Hitler. Talk about the motives of all or one of them. Discuss how close each came to his goal. Tell how each was stopped and how dangerous each was to the world of his time.

   This discussion will help the students understand the reality that underlies this play, that there is more to it than mere fantasy.

2. Have the students either watch a film or read a book about a visitor (or visitors) from another planet coming to earth. Is the visitor friendly or hostile? How do the earth people react? Some recent movies that treat this subject are *E.T.* and *Close Encounters of the Third Kind*; students have probably seen them both. Some books that students might read are H. G. Wells's *War of the Worlds* and Robert A. Heinlein's *Stranger in a Strange Land*.

3. A constant fear in the world today is global destruction. A global ambition is the exploration of space. Discuss these two preoccupations in terms of the relationship of one to the other and in terms of their effects upon the students' lives.

   The purpose of this exercise is to focus the attention of the students on two vital aspects of the play—war and outer space—in terms of what could happen in our contemporary world.

4. Read the students a short science-fiction tale by a popular writer, perhaps Ray Bradbury. Talk about the elements of the story, what makes it science fiction. Bring into the conversation the fact that no matter how much marvellous technology is in the story, no matter how many millions of kilometres away from earth the tale is set, it must have some recognizable human figures in it in order to hold our interest.

VOCABULARY

1. *unctuous* (p. 173) persuasive; having an oily charm. "(He is middle-aged, *unctuous*, resonant.)"

2. *patronizing* (p. 176) acting in a haughty, condescending manner. "I do hope I don't sound *patronizing*."

3. *gad about* (p. 179) to travel around looking for pleasure or excitement. "However, *I* am a hobbyist. I love to *gad about*."

4. *fission bomb* (p. 182) an atomic bomb that gets its force from the splitting of atoms. "Do we have the general's permission to try a *fission bomb* on the force field?"

5. *swarthy* (p. 183) having a dark skin. "(A *swarthy* man in uniform...)"

6. *lurid* (p. 185) terrible; startling; sensational. "...those *lurid* emotions."

7. *dividers* (p. 186) a mechanical instrument used for measuring distances, drawing circles, and so on; compasses. "(He has a pair of *dividers* . . .)"

8. *kibitzer* (p. 187) a person who gives unwanted advice; a meddler. "I am simply a . . . a *kibitzer*."

9. *touché* (p. 187) an acknowledgment that a remark has been accurate. "You'll sacrifice us all for the sake of your . . . your vibrations!" "*Touché* . . ."

10. *Hussar* (p. 188) a member of a European cavalry regiment from the nineteenth century, known for elegant dress. "(Kreton, dressed as a *Hussar* with shako, enters.)"

11. *shako* (p. 188) a tall, cylindrical military hat of the nineteenth century, often with a plume. "(Kreton, dressed as a Hussar with *shako*, enters.)"

COMPREHENSION

A

1. What is Mrs. Spelding's main concern after Kreton arrives?

2. What is General Powers's initial attitude toward Kreton? Does his attitude change during the play?

3. What powers does Kreton have that convince the earth people that he can do anything he wants?

4. What uniforms does Kreton prefer to General Powers's uniform? Why?

B

1. What do the characters' names suggest? For example, Kreton, General Powers?

2. The first few pages of the play give indication of character for the central figures. Describe Roger Spelding's character as it is revealed in the first three pages of the play. Does his character change? If so, how?

3. List the differences between Kreton and humans. Which is the most significant? Why?

4. What is martial law? Why does General Powers impose it on the house?

5. What is Kreton's real attitude toward humans? Give lines that show what he really thinks of us.

6. Kreton thinks that our entire existence in society is violent. What evidence in the world today suggests that he is wrong?

7. Is there any way that the humans can foil Kreton's plans?

8. Can you think of other, real people who have tried to take over the world? Why did they not succeed?

LITERARY TECHNIQUE

1. Is Kreton's purpose simply "a visit to a small planet"? When do we learn that he has other motives? Where does this point come in the structure of the play? Why?

2. Can you think of a reason why the author has Kreton repeat phrases such as "I couldn't begin to explain" when he is asked to describe how things work?

3. The end of Act One gives us new information about Kreton. What does the end of Act Two give us?

4. What is the meaning of the word *cretin*? How has the author made use of that word's meaning? How has he prepared us through incidents in the play for this revelation of Kreton's real nature?

5. What elements of the play contribute to the fantasy aspect? What elements contribute to the aspect of satire?

6. Why does the playwright make Kreton so attractive and likable a person until we learn the truth of his visit?

FOLLOW-UP ACTIVITIES

1. Kreton suggests that most people usually assume that strangers are hostile. Have the students search for examples in literature—short stories, poems, plays, or novels—that either support or do not support Kreton's position. The students might choose one work and write an essay that either supports or does not support Kreton's statement. Alternatively, form two teams and have the opposing sides argue the question "Do most people assume that strangers are hostile?" Let those members of the class who are not on one of the teams judge which team wins.

2. Have the students write their own science-fiction stories. Discuss with them some of the elements of such a tale—human characters at its centre, advanced technology of some sort, setting, and so on.

3. Invite a local scientist or science teacher to speak to your class about space travel or the possibility of life on other worlds. If possible, suggest that the speaker read *Visit to a Small Planet* first so that he or she can make reference to it in the discussion.

4. Have the students write a scene that shows what happens when Kreton returns with the second visitor to his own world. What is his world like? Alternatively, students might draw or paint pictures of Kreton's world.

PRODUCTION NOTES

All or parts of this play can be produced in a classroom or on a stage, with a few minor adjustments for technical problems, such as floating guns.

All of the characters are clearly presented and, with the exception of Kreton, are exactly as they appear. Kreton is the most complex. The actor playing the part must show the character passing through three stages of development—he must be charismatic, demonic, and childish. The transition from one of these stages to the next must be motivated by dialogue and actions. He can be sweet-tempered but can turn petulant quickly. The actor should not let on too early that Kreton has dark purposes here on earth.

Since it is Ellen who finally confronts Kreton and calls him to task for what he is doing, she should have a sense of self-assurance from the beginning of the play, when she argues with her father over her choice of a husband.

General Powers can be played rather broadly as a typical military man, concerned only with following his duty. Later in the play, when he is Kreton's assistant, there should be an icy reserve when he follows the visitor's orders.

Scene and time changes can be accomplished through lighting (perhaps blackouts) or by using different parts of the playing area.

Have the students think about ways to stage "magical" aspects of the play, such as the exploding vase or the floating guns. Possibly they can come up with similar ideas that are equally startling but that can be staged in the classroom.

UNIT 6: WRAP-UP QUESTIONS

1. Both *Feathertop* and *Visit to a Small Planet* have a main character who views the human condition as an outsider—someone who is not one of us. What human characteristics do both Feathertop and Kreton find? How do their assessments of humanity differ?

2. Playwrights, like other writers, must create in the audience something that Coleridge called "a willing suspension of disbelief"—that is, the audience must be able to imagine that the story is really happening, that the actors are actually the characters they portray, no matter how unlikely the circumstances. Do you think that these two plays are written in such a way as to bring about "a willing suspension of disbelief"? Why or why not?

3. The THEME is the main idea expressed in a play. It is the playwright's judgment about or a particular feeling toward his or her subject matter.

   A statement of the theme is more than a simple, moralistic, one-sentence comment; too often such a statement is an oversimplification of the playwright's purpose. However, a brief, two- or three-sentence summary of the playwright's view of the truth, or commentary on life or people, can help the students formulate a tentative understanding of theme. What is the universal truth expressed in each play in this unit? Should there be lines of dialogue that overtly state the theme? Why or why not? Are there such lines in these plays?

4. Write an essay comparing Kreton and Feathertop. What does each want to do with the human race? Do their purposes ever overlap?

FRONT ROW

FRONT ROW

An Anthology of Plays

Edited by

James A. MacNeill
R. Garnet Colborne
Jonathan Kaplan

NELSON CANADA

Published in 1984 by
Nelson Canada,
A Division of International Thomson
Limited
1120 Birchmount Road
Scarborough, Ontario
M1K 5G4

ISBN 0-17-602054-3

Canadian Cataloguing in Publication Data

Main entry under title:
Front row : an anthology of plays

ISBN 0-17-602054-3

1. Canadian drama (English)—20th century.*
2. American drama—20th century.
I. MacNeill, James A., 1933-
II. Colborne, R. Garnet.
III. Kaplan, Jonathan, 1947-

PS8307.F76 1983   C812'.5   C84-098014-0
PR9196.3.F76 1983

Printed and bound in Canada
by John Deyell Company

1234567890/JD/0987654

Table of Contents

Design: Paul Kaufhold
Typesetting: Trigraph Inc.
Printing: John Deyell Company

Illustrations
David Bathurst: 34, 39, 172, 190; Sharon Smith: 77, 92.
Photographs
Cover (left to right): courtesy of the Canadian Opera Company/Robert C. Ragsdale, photographer; courtesy of the Shaw Festival/David Cooper, photographer; Canada Wide/Hugh Wesley. Text: courtesy of Young People's Theatre/Birgitte Nielsen, photographer: 7-10; courtesy of The National Broadcasting Company, Inc.: 12, 23; courtesy of the Canadian Broadcasting Corporation: 46, 55, 62; courtesy of the Gwen Pharis Ringwood Papers, University of Calgary Libraries, Special Collections Division: 64; courtesy of the Soho Rep Theatre, New York: 78, 85; courtesy of Phil Lapides, photographer: 111; courtesy of the City of Toronto Archives: 104; Canada Wide/Hugh Wesley: 118; courtesy of the Shaw Festival/David Cooper, photographer: 128, 133, 137; courtesy of the Canadian Opera Company/Robert C. Ragsdale, photographer: 148, 154; File #NA-1081-3, courtesy of the Glenbow-Alberta Institute: 142; © Beth Bergman, courtesy of The Juilliard School: 160, 169.
In accordance with the rules of Canadian Actors' Equity Association and the Association for Canadian Television and Radio Artists (ACTRA), the following performers have agreed to allow their photographs to appear in this book. Mary Ann McDonald: 9 (centre); Donna Goodhand: 9 (bottom); Barry MacGregor: 10 (top); Brent Carver: 10 (middle); Maxine Miller: 45, 46, 55, 62; Jack Mather: 45; Frank Perry, 46, 55, 62; Stan Lesk: 111; Richard Kelley: 111; Nora McLellan: 128, 137; David Hemblen: 133 (left); Herb Foster: 133 (centre); Tom McCamus: 137.

Acknowledgments
Permission to reprint copyrighted material is gratefully acknowledged:

A Storm in Summer copyright © 1970 by Rod Serling. Reprinted by permission of International Creative Management, New York.

Come Away, Come Away by Mavor Moore. Reprinted by permission of Canadian Speakers' and Writers' Service, Toronto.

Friends and Relations by Hugh Hood. Reprinted by permission of the author.

Still Stands the House by Gwen Pharis Ringwood. Reprinted by permission of Samuel French Ltd., New York.

The Ugly Duckling by A. A. Milne. Reprinted by permission of Samuel French Ltd., London, England.

Showdown at Sand Valley by Ken Mitchell. Reprinted by permission of Bella Pomer Agency, Inc., Toronto.

Cyclone Jack by Carol Bolt. Reprinted by permission of Great North Agency, Ltd., Toronto.

Ride to the Hill by Ron Taylor. Reprinted by permission of the author.

Saint Joan by George Bernard Shaw. Excerpt reprinted by permission of the Society of Authors, London, England.

Riel by John Coulter. Excerpt reprinted by permission of John Robert Colombo.

Feathertop by Maurice Valency. Reprinted by permission of Dramatists Play Service, New York.

Visit to a Small Planet from *Visit to a Small Planet and other Television Plays* by Gore Vidal, copyright © 1956 by Gore Vidal. By permission of Little, Brown and Company.

Half-Hour, Please

In a professional theatre production, the half-hour before the play begins is the time that the stage technicians and performers prepare for that magical moment when the curtain goes up. Here's what happens behind the scenes at Toronto's Young People's Theatre just before a performance of Warren Graves's play *The Prisoner of Zenda*.

The costume shop, now quiet, shows signs of recent activity. On the sewing-machine table are a wig and hat from the show and a model of the set.

The sound technician makes sure that all of the audio equipment is in working order. He is responsible for the production's music and sound effects.

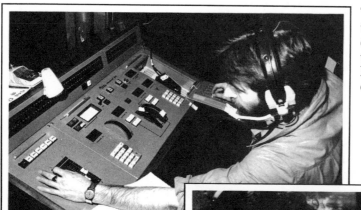

The lighting technician checks to see that his equipment is ready. A computerized lighting board such as the one in front of him allows for hundreds of different lighting effects on the stage.

The stage manager (*left*) is in charge of the overall running of the play. She co-ordinates the technical aspects of the show, such as lights and sound, and makes sure that everything goes smoothly.

The view (*below*) from the stage manager's booth at the back of the theatre, high above the heads of the audience.

The assistant stage manager (*above*) makes sure that all the props are in their proper places before the curtain goes up.

Mary Ann McDonald (*right*), the heroine of the play, is helped into her costume by her dresser. Since the play is a costume drama set in Europe at the end of the last century, the dress is elaborate.

Donna Goodhand, another actress, checks her wig and make-up a last time before she leaves the dressing room. Every detail must give the impression that she is a nineteenth-century noblewoman.

Barry MacGregor (*right*), who plays the villain in the show, wears a formal military uniform.

Brent Carver (*below*), the hero of the play, puts on the final touches of his costume and make-up in the dressing room.

The hero and villain rehearse their sword fight backstage. Though every move is carefully planned, the fight must appear spontaneous and exciting to the audience.

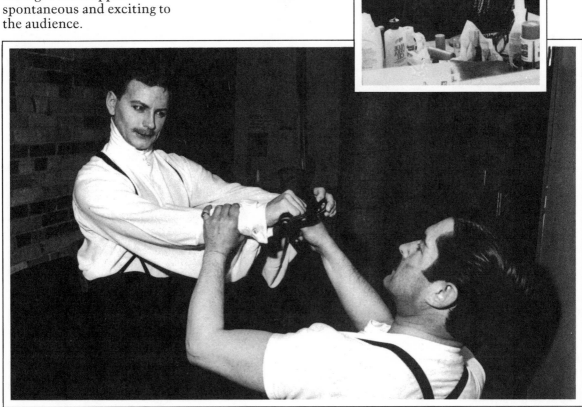

YOUTH AND AGE

Most people think of youth and old age as being at opposite ends of the human spectrum, but the young and the old can and do share a great deal.

A playwright can show these similarities and differences in a dramatic way, setting up characters who speak and interact right before our eyes. Through the use of com-

parison and contrast, the writer can demonstrate that despite the so-called generation gap, the young and the old have the same fears and hopes, the same needs for human warmth and consideration.

A Storm in Summer, an award-winning television play by Rod Serling, is the story of a lonely and bitter old man and an equally bitter young boy from the ghetto. In Mavor Moore's radio play *Come Away, Come Away*, a small girl acts as a catalyst for an old man and helps him to come to grips with the conflicts in his life.

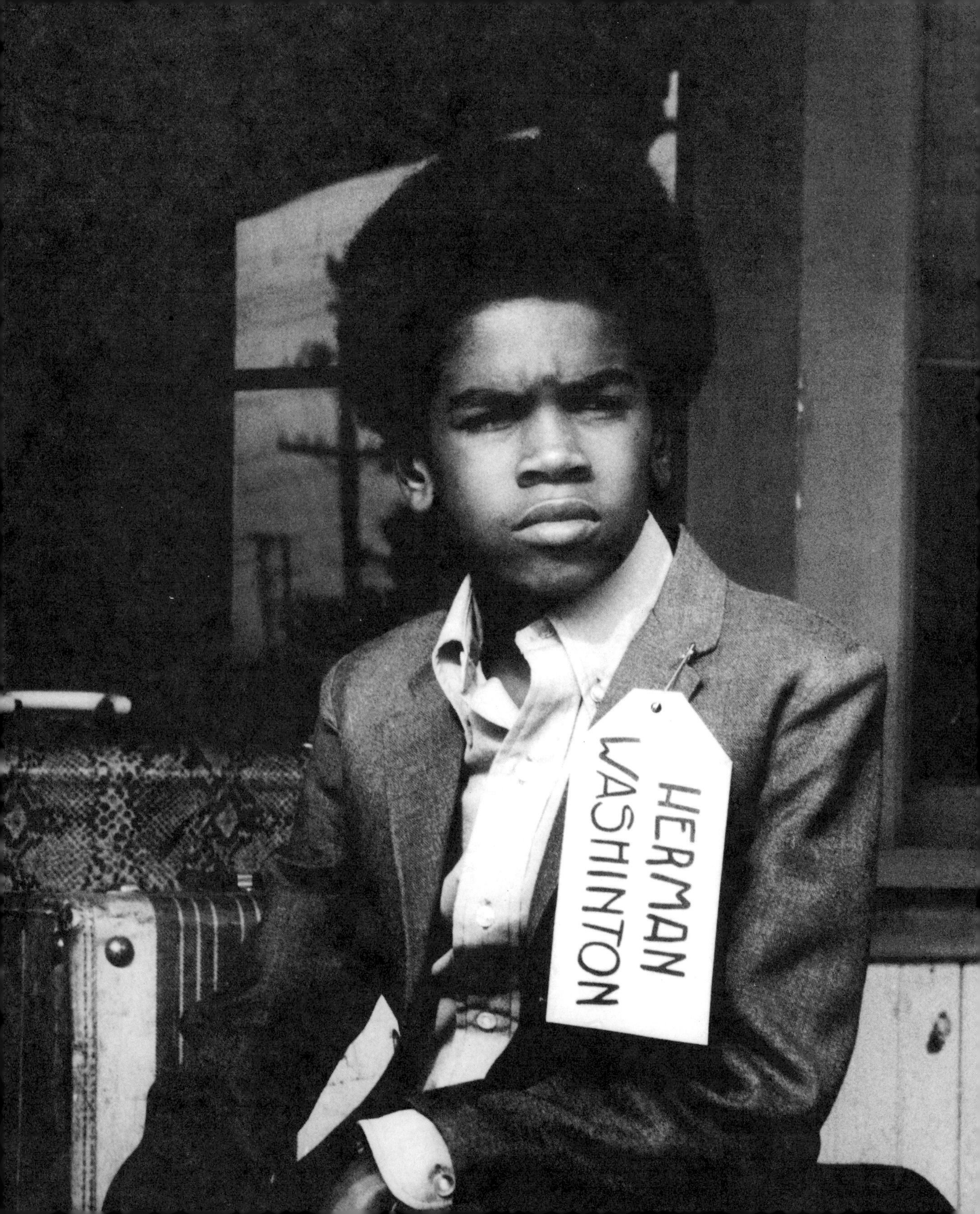
HERMAN
WASHINTON

A Storm in Summer
Rod Serling

CHARACTERS

Abel Shaddick—an elderly shopkeeper in a small town in upstate New York

Stanley Banner—his fast-talking and unreliable nephew

Herman Washington—a black boy from a New York City ghetto

Gloria Ross—a society woman who spends her summers in the town

Harriet—her friend

Mrs. Parker—a conservative member of Gloria's country club

Mrs. Gold—one of Shaddick's customers

Two Hot Rodders—two local teen-age bullies

Maitre D'—at Gloria's country club

A Policeman

Setting—a vacation community in upstate New York

> *"That's the worst thing about prejudice, Herman. The haters turn the victims into haters. You line up the two teams . . . and who's to tell them apart."*

TEASER

(Shaddick, inside his delicatessen, is just in the process of putting away the various items for the night—chickens, trays of cold cuts, and so on. He then moves out through the front door and starts to crank up the awning.

A police car pulls up and a policeman gets out, checks the store alongside, then notices Shaddick.)

Policeman: How are you tonight, Mr. Shaddick?

Shaddick: A day older since you last asked me.

Policeman: Another hot one, huh?

Shaddick: Why not? You wanna know something? *(He jerks his thumb skyward.)* Up there—in the Kingdom of Heaven—is a spe-cial department. A Celestial Bureau dedicated to the harassment of Abel Shaddick. It is staffed by a hundred fallen angels, blue-printing my ultimate destruction.

Policeman: *(grins)* Somebody up there doesn't like you much, huh?

Shaddick: I can see the staff meetings now. Monday, we'll give him prickly heat. Tuesday, two bum cheques he'll get and a breakdown in the refrigeration. On Wednesday, the bank will call one of his notes and on Thursday, his nephew Stanley will come to stay with him. And on Friday—which is today—they'll send down a heat wave—with humidity, yet—so he'll have insomnia and have to lie in bed all night worrying about something worse than Friday.

Policeman: *(grins)* What's worse than Friday?

Shaddick: Saturday!

ACT ONE

(It is a bright sunny morning. Shaddick starts to lower very old awning, letting it squeak slowly down. At one point while he's turning handle it sticks—this is obviously an everyday occurrence. He gives handle a slap with his hand to free it, then awning continues down into place.

The scene changes to inside the deli. Shaddick enters with some crates.)

Shaddick: Morning, Benjy. *(The phone rings and Shaddick puts down crates to answer it.)* Yes? *(takes pencil and pad of paper)* One pint pickled herrings. Yes. Loaf of corn rye. You want that sliced? All right. *(pause)* Yes, lady—I'm writing it down! *(continues to scribble down order)* Yes. Two dozen eggs. That it? *(pause)* No, lady—I don't deliver. I'm too poor for a truck and too old for a bicycle! *(Pause, then he furiously scratches out everything he's written.)* So suit yourself. You wanna come in and pick it up— come in and pick it up. *(pause)* That's right, lady—independent! *(He slams down phone, stares at it, shakes his head, then aloud to himself.)* Deliveries yet. Food stamps. Lucky numbers. Name the president. Hit...the jackpot. A black year on the twentieth century! *(He goes behind counter, moves over to picture of his son, looks at it.)* So, Benjy— the hot spell continues. Your cousin Stanley has been here for six days—oh, I told you yesterday. And your cousin Stanley, as I also told you, has all the charm of an untipped waiter. He commutes between his mattress and the country club. And should I have failed to mention it, Benjy—your cousin Stanley is not my glass of tea.

(A Cadillac convertible pulls up in front of the deli. An attractive woman, Gloria Ross, gets out of car, looks a little dubiously at store front, and then enters. As she opens the door, a bell rings.)

Shaddick: Can I help you, lady?

Gloria: *(brittle smile—half nervous, half condescending)* Good morning...does a Mr. Banner live here?

Shaddick: Mr. Banner? Oh, yes, Mr. Banner. Formerly Mr. "Bloom." Strictly speaking, he doesn't *live* here. He just drops in on occasion in between his big deals. Mr. Banner, formerly Mr. Bloom, is my nephew.

Gloria: *(smile persists)* You must be Mr. Shaddick.

Shaddick: I must be....Now what can I get you?

(She removes papers from her purse.)

Gloria: I'm Gloria Ross, Mr. Shaddick. I met your nephew at the club last night. *(Slight pause as Shaddick glares at her. Her smile fades slightly.)* The country club. Perhaps Mr....Mr. Banner mentioned it.

Shaddick: By the time my nephew with the new name returned to his mattress early this morning, I'd already had five hours of sleep and two sizable nightmares—one having to do with an avenging angel knocking on my door and telling me that Stanley Banner, formerly Bloom, would live with me for the rest of his life. *(pause)* No, lady—I have not talked to my nephew since early yesterday.

(The bell rings again as a little old lady enters. She is Mrs. Gold, a "professional shopper," a chicken feeler, pickle analyst, an all-around pain.)

Mrs. Gold: Morning, Shaddick.

(Shaddick mumbles. Mrs. Gold starts feeling vegetables, then heads toward a hanging line of plucked, scrawny chickens and immediately begins to feel them, one by one. Shaddick throws her one icy look, then turns back toward Gloria. Her smile persists but it's wearing around the edges.)

Gloria: You've no doubt heard of the Fresh Air Vacation Plan—

Shaddick: *(another look at Mrs. Gold fingering chickens)* The Fresh Air Vacation Plan.

Gloria: *(eagerly)* We bring childen in from the

city to spend two weeks here with families in the community. *(Shaddick mumbles.)* But of course... well... we make it a policy to check on the nature of the homes that the children are entering. It's just a... a standard procedure. You know, just to make certain of... of compatibility.

Shaddick: So how much does my nephew Stanley owe for the raffle tickets?

Gloria: *(frowning a little)* No, there aren't any raffle tickets, Mr. Shaddick. You see, when a family volunteers to take a child—

Shaddick: *(interrupting by turning away, pointing toward Mrs. Gold)* Mrs. Gold—you here to purchase or just fondle?

Mrs. Gold: *(coldly)* I don't buy anything but the fresh. *(pointing to chickens)* These are fresh?

Shaddick: They were until you played with them.

Mrs. Gold: You want my business or don't you, Mr. Shaddick?

Shaddick: Your business I would welcome, Mrs. Gold—but your daily rubdown of my poultry I can do without.

Mrs. Gold: I'll take this one. *(She brings it to Shaddick.)*

Shaddick: A prize winner... lucky chicken... I found a home for you. *(He throws it on scale. Mrs. Gold peers over counter to check weight.)*

Mrs. Gold: Just the chicken, Mr. Shaddick— I'm not buying your thumb.

(Shaddick throws her an icy look, scoops chicken off scale, tosses it on some brown paper, wraps it up, ties it up, bites off string, tosses it on counter.)

Shaddick: A dollar ninety-one.

(Mrs. Gold laboriously counts out change, puts it on counter, takes chicken, stares back at Shaddick.)

Mrs. Gold: If it's no good, you'll hear from me.

Shaddick: *(nodding)* I won't sleep until your decision is handed down.

(Mrs. Gold walks haughtily toward door, mumbling, moves out, slamming it behind her.)

Shaddick: *(nodding, hot with anger, tight-lipped)* Some way to start a day—protecting the honour of a plucked chicken. *(turns to Gloria)* Nu.

(Gloria is nervous, flustered, ill at ease.)

Gloria: Do you think I could speak to Stanley—?

Shaddick: The big shot? Like I told you—he's in bed.

Gloria: *(taking the bit in her teeth)* The child is supposed to arrive today, Mr. Shaddick—

Shaddick: What child?

Gloria: I've been trying to explain it to you. Mr. Banner—Mr. Bloom—your nephew Stanley—he volunteered—

Shaddick: *(interrupting her)* He volunteered? A child is coming here because my nephew Stanley volunteered?

Gloria: You still don't understand, Mr. Shaddick.

Shaddick: *(throwing up his hands, his voice loud)* What, what, what? Tell me. What don't I understand?

Gloria: *(almost recoiling)* The idea was that you'd be, in a sense, cosponsors of the child. Stanley assured us that he'd be staying with you through the summer—

(He whirls around, picks up a cleaver off chopping block. Gloria hurriedly moves back. Shaddick whirls around toward her, holding cleaver.)

Shaddick: Lady from the country club—do yourself a favour! The next time my bigshot nephew shows up at one of your pishy-poshy Junior League affairs, just show him the door.

Gloria: Really, Mr. Shaddick—

Shaddick: *(overlapping her)* That way you'll save yourself embarrassment and very likely a bum cheque. Good-bye, lady.

(The woman stands there, blinking, and it takes a moment for anything to come out.)

Gloria: What . . . what about the boy? He's probably on a train by now.

Shaddick: Then take him *off* the train.

(For the first time, anger overcomes fear on Gloria's face.)

Gloria: Mr. Shaddick, a little child is coming here out of the slums—

Shaddick: *(disgusted)* Please, lady—that's where *I* came from and I still don't get enough fresh air. *(jerks his thumb in direction of stairway)* All I got is that freeloader in the summer tuxed up there—half-sponge, half-mouth!

Gloria: Mr. Shaddick . . .

Shaddick: You go back and tell your members that I got no time for children, no sympathy for their social charities, and no place for my nephew Stanley Banner! This is my final word! Again—good-bye, lady! *(turns his back on her, walks away)*

Gloria: You've put me in a dreadful position, Mr. Shaddick. I'm going to be on the phone half the day trying to . . .

Shaddick: Lady, please, enough already.

(He stands there listening to her footsteps as she leaves. We hear the bell on the door ring and then the door closing.
Gloria exits from the delicatessen and walks over to her convertible. Another debutante-type (Harriet) sits alongside driver's seat. She looks expectantly toward Gloria, who comes around and enters through driver's door. We then see Gloria and Harriet in car.)

Harriet: What's he like?

(Gloria turns on ignition.)

Gloria: Scrooge! *(Throws car into gear.)* You put some poor unsuspecting little kid in with that old goat, he'd be scarred for life.

Harriet: That kid may be on a train now.

Gloria: I'll put in a call to New York.

(Harriet takes piece of paper out of purse, looks up.)

Harriet: The kid's name is Washington.

Gloria: As in George.

(Harriet, with a little smile, shakes her head.)

Harriet: Not according to this. As in Booker T.

(Car zooms away from curb.
We move back inside the deli. Stanley starts down the steps. He is a smooth manipulator. He comes down the steps imitating Fred Astaire, singing and finger snapping—and once down, moving over to the hotplate and a mug of coffee. The dance steps and the singing continue. Shaddick looks skyward at the invisible God.)

Stanley: Morning, Unc . . .

Shaddick: *(to himself)* Tell me something—I deserve this?

Stanley: Nice affair at the club last night.

(Shaddick just glares at him, then turns his back.)

Stanley: Gonna be hot today. New York'll be murder. *(pause)* I gotta be there by lunchtime. *(Another pause. Still no response from Shaddick.)* Guy I know got a discotheque in Atlantic City. He's looking for a manager. Could be three hundred a week. Listen, I could be gone for quite some time—

Shaddick: I'm very upset.

(Stanley shakes his head, grins at him.)

Stanley: I'll bet. Well, I'll send you a post card from Atlantic City—

Shaddick: I already know Atlantic City. And your post cards usually cost me two cents to cover the insufficient postage. Do me a favour, Stanley—if by some miracle you get the job and the three hundred a week, and you find yourself with an extra ten bucks, please use 'em to buy some flowers for your mama's grave.

(Stanley looks at him, smile fading.)

Stanley: You got a thing about death, don't you, Unc?

Shaddick: You don't, huh, Stanley? You're immortal. You don't die.

(Stanley tilts his head at him—half bewildered, half not really liking the old man or understanding him.)

Stanley: How long has Ben been gone? Nineteen forty-four, wasn't it? That's almost twenty-five years ago. You keep his picture around...his effects...like he was killed on Thursday.

Shaddick: Mr. Bloom—son of my late sister—my bed you can borrow. My telephone you can use. My food, feel free to eat...but how I mourn my child...and for how long...that's *my* business. Understand?

Stanley: *(with exaggerated shrug)* All right, all right! *(looks at his watch, whistles)* Oh, look at the time! I wanna catch the eleven o'clock train. *(pause)* Stay loose, Unc. *(He starts through door. Shaddick holds up a hand.)*

Shaddick: A moment, please, Mr. Rockefeller. An item of unfinished business. Namely, your last philanthropy.

(Stanley turns to him from door and frowns.)

Stanley: What're you talking about?

Shaddick: The slum child you're going to entertain for two weeks. A lady was here earlier. Miss Ross.

(Stanley slaps his palm against his forehead.)

Stanley: I forgot all about that. *(pause)* I'll call her from the station.

Shaddick: You do that, Stanley. Your bad debts I'll meet—your indiscriminate charities... no!

Stanley: Relax! Will you relax? *(thin little smile)* I had a little too much to drink last night. They had this booth where they were signing up kids—they had one more to place—well, you know how it is.

Shaddick: *(not smiling)* I know how it is with *you*. A good deed must be accompanied by a brass section and a photographer!

Stanley: How is it with you, Unc?

Shaddick: Yeah...explain the question.

Stanley: I don't know how you survive.

Shaddick: I manage.

Stanley: What do you manage? Seven days a week, hating everything you do and doing the same thing. Up at eight, open the cases, hang up the chickens, scream at somebody on the phone. Nine o'clock at night you lock it all up and next morning you start all over again.

Shaddick: In the language of the time, Stanley, that's what's known as making a living. Easy it's not. Enjoyable it's not. But it's what ancient idiots like me do to stay alive. I wouldn't expect *you* to understand it. Anyone who could change a name like they change their shirt—this kind of person wants the rose without the thorn. Life isn't like that! Life is misery. But *I* made a pact with it.

Stanley: You made a pact with it, you love it. Because that's the way you're built, Unc. You'd rather be caught dead than smiling.

Shaddick: You wanna see me smile, Stanley? In heaven, you'll see me smile. When they read out my will and they get to that part where it says how much I leave to my nephew, Stanley Banner. One blank page.

(Stanley shakes his head back and forth and has to smile.)

Stanley: I can't top you, Unc. I'll go pack. *(starts toward stairs)* Wish me luck.

Shaddick: *(shrugs)* What I wish for you, I apologize to God for.

(The scene changes to the town's small train station. Train is just pulling out. Room is mobbed with fresh-air kids, all tagged and identified, and one by one being led away by waiting foster parents. Herman Washington sits by himself. He is a grim little gnome—a tiny man-child. Stanley enters, moves over to ticket cage, buys ticket, turns, spots Herman sitting alone. He moves to Herman, looks briefly at name tag, and sees his own name underneath.)

Stanley: Whadd'ya say?

(Herman looks at him very soberly.)

Herman: You the man what they call the sponsor?

Stanley: *(wetting his lips a little nervously)* I'm Stan Banner. You're... *(reads from tag)* ...Herman Washington.

(Herman nods.)

Herman: Where we goin'?

Stanley: *(nervous laugh)* We got a little problem— *(Herman waits patiently.)* Like here I've been waiting for you all along—and suddenly I get this special hurry-up call to get to New York. *(Herman again just waits and doesn't respond.)* But I tell you what you do. You go down to the delicatessen—it's just down the street—turn right out there and you'll run right into it. A little tiny place on the other side of the street. My uncle's there. He'll look after you until I get back.

Loudspeaker Voice: Eleven-oh-eight to New York now arriving.

Stanley: That's my train, kid. *(sticks out his hand)* You have a ball, Herm. I'll be seeing you later. *(Herman looks at hand, then very slowly lets his eyes rise up to Stanley's face, making his own very special judgment. Stanley moves to ticket window.)* New York... *(turns to Herman)* Don't let my...my uncle turn you off. He's not a bad egg. Just a little...a little old and...set in his ways....But you go over there and tell him who you are. *(Herman picks up his battered suitcase, looks toward door, then back to Stanley. Stanley is hung-up, guilty, and anxious.)* I'm awful sorry I gotta cut out on you like this, Herm. I mean it.

Herman: Your uncle like you?

Stanley: *(blinks)* You don't dig me?

Herman: *(after slow head shake)* You talk too much and you talk too loud.

(Herman turns and moves to door, leaving Stanley there just blinking at him. He leaves the station and starts a slow walk down side-walk toward heart of town.

The scene changes to inside the deli. Shaddick finishes arranging trays inside display case, then looks up toward window. Standing on sidewalk, staring back at him, is Herman—the undersized black militant with a grim, set, determined, challenging look on his face.

There is no question that he's right out of a ghetto. This moment finds him out of it for the first time. He has to exercise his own special brand of courage to combat his little-boy fear. After a moment he straightens his little bony shoulders, moves into delicatessen, reading from paper in his hand as he does so.

Shaddick at this point doesn't make the connection at all between his nephew and the child.)

Shaddick: *(after long, waiting pause)* Nu?

(Herman blinks, frowns, looks down at himself.)

Herman: You mean the suit?

Shaddick: I mean—what can I get you?

(Herman puts down suitcase.)

Herman: What do you got?

(Shaddick studies him for a moment.)

Shaddick: What do you want?

Herman: Got a Coca Cola?

Shaddick: For a Coca Cola, you go to the drug-store.

Herman: I'll take a glass of water.

Shaddick: A glass of water. *(He shrugs, moves over to sink, rinses out glass, fills it, carries it back over to counter, puts glass on top of it.)* With customers like you I could go bankrupt in a week. Here you are...

(Herman reaches up for glass, takes it, drinks it thirstily, returns glass to top of counter, stands there, unsure of himself for a moment, then fingers large hand-painted badge on his lapel which reads "Herman D. Washington.")

Herman: I'm Herman D. Washington.

Shaddick: I'm Abel Shaddick...

Herman: I come on the train. Just a coupla minutes ago.

(Shaddick scratches his head, leans on counter.)

Shaddick: I came on a boat fifty-five years ago. So what else should we talk about?

Herman: This here is the address I was supposed to go to, so I'm your kid.

Shaddick: Mr. Washington, do you get the same impression that I do—that there is occurring a breakdown in our communication?

Herman: *(studying him)* Don't you dig, man? *(pause)* I'm supposed to stay here two weeks. *(He looks down at piece of paper.)* Stanley Banner. *(He looks up.)* He's what they call my sponsor. He was at the train station. He sent me here. *(Shaddick begins to understand.)* My Gramma got this phone call late last night. Lady say I should be on the train at eight o'clock. So that's what I do. *(He holds up paper in his hand.)* And they give me this here thing to tell me who was gonna meet me. And where I was supposed to go. *(pause)* That Stanley cat—the one I met—he say I should come over here and see you.

Shaddick: *(hesitates)* Mr. Washington...the man you accurately described as the Stanley cat, Mr. Banner, has left town and in the process left both of us on a limb. I'm afraid that...that...well, there is nobody here to look after you.

(Herman nods. His brief eight years have obviously been a parade of disappointments. He absorbs them like food. He reaches into his pocket, his little face sober, takes out a train ticket, puts it on counter.)

Herman: Is this what I use to go back to New York?

(Shaddick turns it around and looks at it, nods.)

Shaddick: That's right. It's the return part of your ticket. Don't lose that now. *(looks up at clock on wall)* The next train is about three hours from now. You've missed the eleven o'clock.

Herman: Okay. *(He looks fascinated at counter.)*

Shaddick: *(very reluctantly)* You want some breakfast? *(pause)* I asked you a question. Do you want some breakfast? You want something to eat?

(Herman, after studying Shaddick with his own special intensity, shakes his head.)

Herman: I jus' go back on the train. I don't wanna stay here.

(Shaddick shrugs. He's vaguely disturbed. He's not sure why.)

Shaddick: So go back on the train. But first— the least I could do is offer you something to eat. *(pause)* See anything you like?

(Herman takes a slow walk down length of counter, looking into display case.)

Herman: *(pointing)* What's that there?

Shaddick: Show me.... That's pastrami. You want a nice pastrami sandwich?

Herman: What's pastrami?

Shaddick: It's corned beef. Highly seasoned. It's...it's Jewish.

(Herman looks up at him with his sombre little face.)

Herman: You Jewish? Guy who own our building—he Jewish. Man, he pretty bad cat. Nobody likes him. I ain't hungry. *(turns toward door)*

Shaddick: So where are you going?

Herman: To the train station.

Shaddick: You got a three-hour wait. You might as well stay here. *(Herman shakes his head.)* Why not?

Herman: 'Cause I don't like you.

(Shaddick again has the sense of being disturbed and again is unable to put his finger on why.)

Shaddick: So you don't like me. So go sit in a hot train station and broil for three hours.

Herman: What you care?

Shaddick: I don't care. I really don't care. Between a bankrupt business and bum nephew, I don't need a three-foot-tall Ethiopian anti-Semite! You, I don't need. *(He deliberately turns his back on boy. Herman looks through glass of display case to a tray of fish. Shaddick turns toward him.)* Nu? What keeps you?

Herman: *(pointing toward fish)* Them are fish.

Shaddick: That's what them are.

Herman: *(looks up at him)* I never been fishin'. They told me that's one of the things you done when you got sponsored. People take you fishin'. *(looks down at fish)* I ain't never been fishin'.

(Shaddick moves down counter, leans on it, looking across and down at boy.)

Shaddick: Where do you live?

Herman: Hundred Thirty-Sixth Street.

Shaddick: *(softly)* No lakes on Hundred Thirty-Sixth Street, huh?

(Herman shakes his head, then looks up.)

Herman: You got a lake here?

Shaddick: Yeah, I got a small lake.

Herman: You ever fish in it?

Shaddick: My son and I used to. My son. Now there was a fisherman. *(moves over to picture, holds it up)* That's him there...Benjy.

Herman: Soldier.

Shaddick: Second lieutenant. A bombardier.

Herman: Where is he now?

Shaddick: *(with a soft little smile)* He was killed on a raid over a place called Stuttgardt.

Herman: I got a brother. His name's Bill. He's in Vietnam. A sergeant. Man, he's a tiger. He sent me a picture of him carryin' a gun. He's a real tiger. *(looks intently at picture, then into Shaddick's face)* You say he's dead?

Shaddick: *(nods)* He was nineteen. *(looks at picture)* This was twenty-four years ago.

Herman: What about your mama? *(then frowning)* I mean, *his* mama.

Shaddick: His mama died many years ago, when he was a baby. I raised him.

Herman: *(studies Shaddick intently)* Who is this cat, Stanley?

Shaddick: Don't ask. *(looks long at the boy)* Thanks to him you took a train ride for nothing.

Herman: Where this here lake?

Shaddick: You want to see the lake? It's one mile south. You take a left on Main Street. Lake Wanateeshie.

Herman: *(repeating it but stumbling)* Wanatee-shie. *(frowns)* That Jewish?

Shaddick: Jewish—Indian. While you're gone I'll call the lady here in town who's responsible for you. She can phone your grandmother. *(turns away, busying himself behind counter)* All right, go along then and... don't drown.

Herman: When my brother come back—he gonna take me fishin'. He promise me. My brother—when he say somethin', you gotta believe him.

Shaddick: *(nods)* Without question. It's a trait that runs in your family. Honour and invincibility. *(Herman remains standing there. There is a pause.)* So what do you wait for now—the Messiah?

Herman: This here lake I'm goin' to—nobody give me trouble...will they? I mean...I mean...I black.

Shaddick: Who could give you trouble? Who would dare? You're the only ten-year-old kid on earth who sounds like Humphrey Bogart. *(Then he turns to Herman, who still stands there, unsure, irresolute.)* Now what?

Herman: Nothin'.

Shaddick: Nothin'. That means *something*.

Herman: That mean *nothin'*.

Shaddick: You're afraid to tell me?

Herman: Afraid? No way, baby. No how.

Shaddick: Then speak your mind, why don't you?

(pause)

Herman: Don't *you* ever go fishin'?

Shaddick: Not since my Benjy was killed have I put a worm to hook. *(pause)* Why?

Herman: Nothin'.

Shaddick: Nothing, meaning why don't you and I go fishing? *(Herman shrugs but doesn't say anything. Shaddick looks at Benjy's photo.)* Benjy...an inspiration! *(He whirls around, pounds a fish on cash register to ring up a "NO SALE.")* Since the first of the month I haven't taken in enough to pay the electric bill—and this fisherman from a Hundred Thirty-Sixth Street thinks I got nothing better in life to do than play Huckleberry Finn.

(Herman stares at him. Shaddick returns the look.)

Herman: What that thing you say goes runnin' in the family?

Shaddick: *(frowning)* A trait.

Herman: *(nods)* Whatever you call it. You got the same thing goin' between Stanley and you.

Shaddick: *(mockingly)* The philosopher. So tell me. What is the trait that binds me with my nephew Stanley?

Herman: *(emotionlessly)* You're the same kinda cats. He get on a train. You hide behind the pastrami.

(Shaddick gnaws slightly on his lower lip, studying the boy, then the delicatessen, then he looks up toward the clock.)

Shaddick: You know what an Achilles heel is? *(Herman shakes his head.)* It's an infected boil on the soul. *(Again he looks up toward clock. He starts to remove apron.)* For maybe an hour I'll go with you. But for no longer than an hour.

Herman: Maybe we catch some big fish, then you can sell 'em.

Shaddick: Mr. Washington...with my luck I will catch one minnow, one sunstroke, and a summons from the game warden. *(He heaves a gigantic sigh, moves to door, opens it, and hangs "CLOSED" sign on door. Herman stands in door holding his suitcase.)* A question: in your luggage there—you got worms? *(Herman shakes his head.)* Then why are you taking it with us? *(Herman leaves suitcase inside by door. Shaddick looks down at Herman, who gives him a quizzical look.)* Nu? You got something to say?

Herman: You forgot somethin'.

Shaddick: Enlighten me.

Herman: Fishin' poles. We ain't got no fishin' poles. When you go fishin' you gotta have fishin' poles.

(Shaddick nods seriously, as if responding to some incredibly deep philosophy.)

Shaddick: I give you this, Herman. You have all the gaiety of an undertaker—but you are a very discerning boy. Very discerning. So you know what we'll have to do? We'll have to stop at the hardware store, and we'll buy—what was it?

Herman: Fishing poles.

(We next see the two of them walking down the street. Every now and then Herman looks a little secretively at Shaddick. They stop at a light before crossing the street.)

Shaddick: Ah...I need this. *(Shaddick reaches down to take the boy's hand. Herman pulls it away.)* That's to cross the street.

Herman: *(quite seriously)* I been crossin' streets since I was two years old.

Shaddick: *(looks down at him)* I don't suppose it ever occurred to you that maybe *I* needed help crossing the street?

Herman: *(nods very seriously)* That's different, man. *(He looks up at Shaddick's hand, frowns with that intense, inquisitive little look.)* What you say your name was?

Shaddick: Shaddick. Abel Shaddick. *(Herman*

looks very thoughtful.) You don't like it?

Herman: *(shrugs)* Make no difference to me what they call you. *(The signal light turns green. Herman reaches up, takes Shaddick's hand.)* Let's go, Shaddick.

Shaddick: *(for first time smiling)* I'm right with you, Washington.

(They walk across the street, hand in hand.)

(Fade out)

ACT TWO

(Shaddick and Herman are perched on large, jutting rock that overhangs a small lake shaded by a couple of giant elms. They both have fishing poles. Shaddick is explaining how to use them.)

Shaddick: Now this is what you have to do, Herman. Keep your eye on that bobbin. The bait we are using, Herman, is what the fish want.

Herman: Why?

Shaddick: *(blinks at him for a moment)* Because...because a wise fish knows what he wants. Every once in a while give the line a little pull.

Herman: *(imitating him)* Like this?

Shaddick: Just a little bit...that's it. If we're lucky, this will attract their attention. Now when the fish nibbles, the bobbin will begin to shake. And when that happens don't get excited. When he's got the hook in his mouth he'll pull the bobbin way underwater. Then you give it a good tug and that sets the hook. You understand me? *(Herman nods. Both of them sit on rock with lines.)* Now I, myself, have conquered this thing only in theory. But my son, Benjy...there was a fisherman. He had a nose for it.

Herman: A nose?

Shaddick: An instinct. *(He shakes his head back and forth.)* Right from the start I never had to teach Benjy anything. *(During this speech the camera moves to Herman, whose*

eyes suddenly go wide. He's not listening to Shaddick, he's just watching. Shaddick continues to talk, unaware of what's going on.) I remember one summer—lessee—it must have been around '37, '38...in that area but a little further down...Benjy caught a bass at this very lake.... *(Herman tugs at him.)* Such a bass— *(pauses, shuts his eyes, still oblivious to boy tugging at him)* All I know is that this was a fish among fish— *(Herman is tugging. A fish is hooked on Shaddick's line. Shaddick is completely unaware of it.)*

Herman: *(exploding)* You got somethin', man! You got a fish! Somethin's pullin'—

Shaddick: What did I tell you to do?! Remind me!

(Shaddick is suddenly aware of what is going on, rises, and topples forward with a yell into shallow water below. He sits in water, drenched—water up around his neck.
Herman has gotten his own bite and is pulling furiously on line, reeling in as he pulls. A large bass emerges on Herman's line—he pulls it off hook and then holds it, squirming, in his hand.)

Herman: Look! Look! I gotta fish! Look at this one! This here is a fish! And I got it! Look at this fish!

(The camera moves back to Shaddick sitting in water, his rod and reel floating nearby. He looks up at Herman on rock, wipes his wet face with a sleeve—tries to interrupt Herman.)

Shaddick: I see the fish....Mr. Washington—a favour? *(Herman, still clutching fish, looks down at him.)* You have one more minute to exult in pulling in the fish. After that, be so kind as to pull in this ancient mariner.

(Herman carefully puts fish in cheap basket alongside him, then climbs down from rock, wades out to where Shaddick is, and helps the old man to shore.
The scene changes to the delicatessen. The clock on the wall reads 7:30. Shaddick enters from bedroom. Herman is asleep on the bed, dead to the world. Also visible is a plate of partially eaten food and an empty glass. Shaddick

picks up plate and glass, turns, and walks out of room with them. Shaddick starts to wash dishes, looks at picture.)

Shaddick: Benjy—today, a revelation! I now know what ultimately destroys old men. It is not hardening of the arteries, as has been thought—but a softening of the brain. Inside my bedroom, sleeping, is a small, dark shadow with a chip on his shoulder the size of a loaf of pumpernickel! And you know what I've been doing today, Benjy? I've been fishing on the lake with this boy. Where you and I used to go. Five and a half hours in the hot sun—much of it spent underwater—because your cousin Stanley has got a mouth like a whale and the instincts of a shark!

(He turns as we hear a car coming to a stop. Through window we see Gloria Ross get out of convertible, leaving an attractive young man on front seat. She walks toward door, opens it. The bell on the door rings.)

Gloria: I received a message you'd called, Mr. Shaddick—

Shaddick: It was so long ago, I'd forgotten.

Gloria: *(with courteous apology)* I'm so sorry. It was the golf tournament—

Shaddick: Miss Ross, for each day of your life I wish you a hole in one. But at the moment, I've got a few problems of my own.

Gloria: I understand from your message that the little boy arrived and he's here with you.

Shaddick: *(with a jerk of his thumb toward bedroom)* He's asleep.

Gloria: Didn't your nephew—

Shaddick: *(interrupting)* Don't mention that name, please. Now did you find someone else in town who can take the child off my hands?

Gloria: That's why I'm here, Mr. Shaddick. I'm going to have to take the child myself.

Shaddick: He'll make a good caddy.

Gloria: Well, he obviously can't stay here.

Shaddick: For once, we're in agreement.

Between a seventy-two-year-old Jew and a ten-year-old black boy, Miss Ross, there is not what you would call a mutuality of interest.

Gloria: He can stay with me tonight and I'll arrange to send him home in the morning.

Shaddick: Home? Are you telling me that on the membership rolls of that pishy-poshy club of yours, isn't there one lousy family willing to take him?

Gloria: Given time, we'd find many. *(an apologetic smile)* But we want the boy to feel comfortable. And under the circumstances—well...you know—

Shaddick: *(intensely)* Enlighten me.

Gloria: Well, for a black child to move into—

Shaddick: A black child.

Gloria: Now wait a minute...

Shaddick: The cardinal sin.

Gloria: *(tightly)* Don't make me out a bigot—

Shaddick: *(overlapping her speech)* Then don't make *me* out an idiot! I'm a long time on this earth, lady—and I'm an expert on bigotry.

Gloria: *(struggling for composure and patience)* Mr. Shaddick, I want that little boy to enjoy himself. I don't care what colour he is. But you don't take a child off a Harlem street, stick him in the swimming pool at the country club, and expect him to make an adjustment between breakfast and lunch!

Shaddick: Since when is swimming such an adjustment?

Gloria: This is a sociological problem.

Shaddick: Mazeltov to all the sociological problems in the world. I got a feeling about you, Miss Ross...you'll forgive me in advance...that you dabble in good deeds the way a person would reach for a pickle in a barrel. Tentatively and gingerly.

Gloria: I think that will be quite enough, Mr. Shaddick.

Shaddick: Not quite. You're a little like my nephew. You're so busy dressing up for the charity ball—you forget what the charity is! An act of kindness, Miss Ross, is not such a big deal when it comes in fashionable spasms during the social season! You understand?!

Gloria: I'll take the boy now, Mr. Shaddick.

Shaddick: Miss Ross, you shouldn't give yourself such trouble. The boy. . .stays here. Maybe two days. . .maybe a week.

Gloria: (*letting it all out*) That's very nice, Mr. Shaddick. Well, let me tell you something. You don't like my good deeds—I don't like yours. They're grudging, rotten-tempered afterthoughts, using a child you couldn't care less about as a gesture to those of us you loathe. And I gather you loathe a lot of us, Mr. Shaddick.

Shaddick: Which is my right, Miss Ross?

Gloria: Yes, it is, Mr. Shaddick. And it proves the point. You don't have to go to a country club to find a bigot—sometimes they're in delicatessens.

(*Shaddick's head goes down for a moment as the words hit him; then he looks up, half smiles.*)

Shaddick: So we each drew a little blood—Miss Ross? (*He pauses, then looks back toward curtained partition, then back to Gloria.*) But the boy stays here. . .and we'll do a little fishing. . .a little hiking. . .maybe even compare notes on ghettos. I am not the most gracious of men, Miss Ross—as you have pointed out. But in my life I have made some friends.

(*pause*)

Gloria: Good night, Mr. Shaddick.

(*She nods, turns, moves to door, and exits; the door slams and the bell tinkles loudly.*
Herman enters through the curtained partition, rubbing his eyes with one hand, holding the fish in the other.)

Shaddick: Nu? (*points to fish*) You got plans for that?

Herman: (*nods*) What did the lady want?

Shaddick: She wanted to divest herself of responsibility. This is the national pastime, Herman. The great American sport. This year's slogan: "Let George do it."

Herman: Who's George?

Shaddick: George. Tom, Dick, and Harry. Somebody else. The other guy. I play the game too.

Herman: (*cocking his head at him*) You sure do talk funny.

(*pause*)

Shaddick: What are you going to do with that?

Herman: I gonna get it stuffed. And then I gonna put one of them metal things with writing on it underneath—

Shaddick: A plaque.

Herman: (*delighted*) Yeah, a plaque. And I gonna say on it, "This fish caught by Herman D. Washington in honour of his brother, Bill, Sergeant in the Green Berets. . .with love from his brother, Herman D. Washington." (*looks up, suddenly concerned*) Can I get that all in there?

Shaddick: In small print.

Herman: (*holds up fish*) Big, ain't she?

Shaddick: Enormous. (*moves over to fish, takes it from Herman*) But we'll put it on ice so that by the time it reaches your brother he'll be able to stand close enough to read the small print. (*Shaddick carries fish to cooler, opens it, puts fish on shelf, looks at boy.*) Herman—I want to ask you something. You have a choice. You can leave on the train tomorrow morning or you can stay here with me for a few days.

Herman: Why?

Shaddick: What do you mean, why?

Herman: Why you want me to stay?

Shaddick: Did I say I wanted you to stay? I gave you a choice. I said you could stay if you wanted to or you could go home tomorrow.

(Herman, as always, is analysing in his little-old-man way—and dead serious.)

Herman: I stay a coupla days.

Shaddick: *(with a gesture)* I'm overwhelmed. *(pause)* Now go wash your face and hands in that sink there...been touching fish.... Then we'll go see what's playing at the movies. And then after that we'll have a soda. And after that we'll come back here and I'll lie awake half the night wondering why I'm going to all the trouble.

(There is a pause. Shaddick watches Herman, amused.)

Herman: *(looking at Shaddick)* You lookin' at me all smiley. Why you look at me smiley?

Shaddick: You prefer rage?

Herman: You know what my brother Bill say? He say he don't care if Mister Charlie hates him...and he sure don't care if Mister Charlie likes him. He say that Mister Charlie should just get his foot offa him. That what my brother Bill say.

Shaddick: *(reacting)* Have I put my foot on you?

Herman: I just wanted to tell you. I'm stayin' because it hot in New York. And here I can go fishin'. That why I'm stayin'. *(Herman moves to bedroom. Shaddick follows him.)* Too bad you ain't black.

Shaddick: Why?

Herman: I seen all the people lookin' at us this afternoon while we was fishin'.

Shaddick: So they looked at us.

Herman: I know what they thinkin'.

Shaddick: Enlighten me.

Herman: They thinkin'...they thinkin', "What that li'l black boy doin' with the old Jew?"

(Shaddick's face turns grim and cold. He walks over to Herman.)

Shaddick: Listen, as one former ghetto dweller to another—a lesson maybe both of us should learn, Herman. Once two people go fishing together...or to the movies...all they should care about is that they enjoy. This is fundamental.

Herman: *(looks up at him)* We equal, huh?

Shaddick: More than we both realize.

Herman: There's rats where I live. Great big ones. And the johns stink. You smell 'em all over the building. If we equal—how come I gotta live there? *(Again his little mind obviously gallops ahead.)* When my brother come back, we gonna move outta there. We gonna move out to the country. *(Herman stares straight at Shaddick.)* And we gonna spit right in that landlord's eye.

(Shaddick winces at this.)

Shaddick: *(voice soft, almost a whisper)* Mazeltov. But for the time being...with *this* Jew...you'll go to the movies.

Herman: *(shrugs)* Okay.

Shaddick: The good fortune of Abel Shaddick. A hundred and seventy million people I could have as a house guest...and I get him!

(Herman follows Shaddick to door. Shaddick flicks a light switch, then opens door. Herman goes out. Herman reaches for "CLOSED" sign, hangs it on doorknob outside. Shaddick closes door and locks it.

The scene changes to an ice-cream parlour, later that night. Through front window we're looking at Shaddick and Herman sitting in a near-empty room, finishing up two sodas. The camera's point of view then moves inside the ice-cream parlour. Herman's piping little voice is continuous as we move in toward table.)

Herman: ...but when the cat with the machine gun give it to that other bad cat, how come the FBI leave the back door open and them other two bad cats able to get out? Man, anybody know you gotta guard the back door when you got two bad cats up in a building and you know they got tommy-guns too.

(Shaddick finishes last slurp of his soda, pushes it aside.)

Shaddick: Herman, there are multiple areas

which I know nothing about. One is tommy-guns, the other is bad cats, and still another is the FBI.

Herman: But they crazy not to guard the back door.

Shaddick: Are they...yes, I agree. *(Waitress hands Shaddick check.)* Thanks.... *(He points to Herman's soda.)* You finished?

Herman: *(nods)* If it was me, man, I'd'a guarded that back door—

Shaddick: So we'll write to Hollywood and we'll put the question to them? Would that satisfy you?

Herman: *(scratches his head, continues to sit there)* Maybe we do that. I'll give you the words—what do they call that?

Shaddick: *(taking some money out of his pocket)* You'll dictate the letter. *(He rises from table.)*

Herman: Yeah, I think I do that.

Shaddick: *(mumbles)* ...back door...

(Shaddick pays cashier. Herman moves past him, exits.
Out in the street Herman meets two hot rodders, who block his path.)

Hot Rodder No. 1: Jus' don't stand there, baby...aren't you gonna get outta the way of two big dudes like us?

Hot Rodder No. 2: Yeah, kid, let's see you do it.

(Shaddick comes out, stands alongside Herman. The hot rodder sticks an unlit cigarette in his mouth, lounges against car. He points at Shaddick.)

Hot Rodder No. 2: Get a load of this...what a combination. Whadda ya say, old man?

(Shaddick, taking Herman's arm, starts to move down sidewalk. Shaddick faces hot rodders, who block his path.)

Shaddick: The name is Shaddick. *(nods toward Herman)* That name is Washington. What's the matter, cowboys. You bored...is that it? You got to go after an old man and a little boy...is that it? *(Shaddick backs away*

to stand next to Herman and looks warily from one to the other.) You know who these are...two night crawlers in search of proof of manhood!

Hot Rodder No. 2: Manhood!

Shaddick: Such courage, Herman, such courtesy.

(At this point Hot Rodder No. 2 advances on Shaddick, lashes out, pushing him against the wall of the building, holding up one clenched fist as if to strike. Herman takes a knife out of his pocket and starts to run toward them. Hot Rodder No. 1 sticks out his foot, tripping Herman. The knife falls to the sidewalk.)

Herman: *(shouting)* Get the knife, Shaddick! Use the knife! *(Herman moves toward it on his hands and knees, scrabbling for it as Hot Rodder No. 1 pulls him back by the legs. He is screaming now.)* Use the knife, Shaddick!

(Suddenly the whole scene is engulfed in light as a police prowl car comes around corner—a spotlight alongside driver's seat is aimed at them. Car moves over to scene—two policemen get out.)

Policeman: What's the trouble here?

Hot Rodder No. 1: No trouble, man...no trouble at all. We're just on our way out.

Policeman: Hold it. *(He moves over to Shaddick.)* Mr. Shaddick. You okay?

Shaddick: In the pink.

Policeman: *(to hot rodders)* Take off. *(Hot rodders get in car, drive off.)* You want a ride home?

Shaddick: My friend and I will walk.

(The policeman looks from one to the other, then suddenly sees the knife still on sidewalk, walks over to it, picks it up, closes blade, then pops it open.)

Policeman: Who belongs to this?

Shaddick: *(quickly)* That's mine.

Policeman: Yours?

Shaddick: Definitely mine.

(The policeman closes blade again, moves over to Shaddick, hands it to him.)

Policeman: That's quite a weapon, Mr. Shaddick. Be careful with it. *(pause)* Give a yell if we're needed. Good night.

(He turns, moves back into police car, guns the engine. The car pulls away.
Shaddick turns to look at the boy, then looks down at the knife in his hand. He hands it to Herman.)

Shaddick: Good night. *(very softly)* Put this in your pants and don't let me see it again. *(Boy soberly takes knife, looks at it briefly, puts it in his pants pocket. Then the two of them exchange a look.)* If it ever reaches a point where I must cut into another man's stomach, I will have lived too long.

(Again, here we get a reading into the incredible telescoped maturity of the kid.)

Herman: Where you been? You let some cat back you up against a wall and you don't do nothin' about it—you ain't gonna live long enough!

Shaddick: *(after a pause)* You'd have used it?

Herman: *(nods)* If I had to.

Shaddick: *(looks off thoughtfully down empty street)* Which is perhaps the worst thing about prejudice, Herman. The haters turn the victims into haters. You line up the two teams...and who's to tell them apart. *(pause)* So let's go home.

(The scene changes to the delicatessen. Herman and Shaddick enter.)

Shaddick: *(with look at clock on wall)* Look at the time. Past midnight. *(He locks the door.)* You got a toothbrush? All right...go. *(Herman nods, moves toward bedroom.)* Herman...an invitation from Miss Ross for you to swim in the country-club swimming pool. Reeking of perfume...and misplaced contrition. *(He sticks invitation under Herman's nose. Herman moves away.)*

Herman: You talkin' crazy again.

Shaddick: Want to go swimming...shall we accept?

Herman: Yeah.

Shaddick: Sure....All right, go to bed now.

(Herman moves into bedroom. Shaddick follows him.)

Herman: What you do before I come here?

Shaddick: What did I do?

Herman: I mean...you don't go fishing. You don't go to the movies. You don't drink no sodas.

(Shaddick looks off thoughtfully.)

Shaddick: You know...you're right. This is the first movie I've seen since Myrna Loy. I used to love Myrna Loy. And I'd forgotten how good a soda could taste. *(looks at the little boy)* At the risk of leaning on you, Herman—you seem to have opened up my life a little bit.

Herman: *(very tightly)* You make a mistake if you lean on anybody. That what Bill say. He say never count on the other guy and don't ever turn your back. That what it all about.

Shaddick: And if someone leans on you?

Herman: *(very simply)* Break his arm.

(Shaddick, after a long silence, walks to Herman, looks deep into the little boy's face.)

Shaddick: Listen, my little boychik—even if you think it—don't say it—all right? I have tasted more hate in my lifetime than I have wine.

Herman: *(softly)* Man—don't you think I ain't?

(Shaddick turns, goes through partition into the other room, goes to coffee pot and begins cleaning it. After a moment the curtain parts a little and the little boy is standing there.)

Herman: Shaddick? *(Shaddick turns to him.)* It don't make no difference—but you ain't chicken.

Shaddick: I'm not?

Herman: No. You're a tiger.

Shaddick: Then you tell me something. Why is

my mouth dry and my heart still beating like it had been trying to get across the road ahead of me?

Herman: *(with a little shrug)* You an *old* tiger.

Shaddick: *(with a smile)* Old tiger.... You remind me of that the next time I go crazy and think I'm Moyshe Dayan.

Herman: *(shaking his head)* Maybe you not crazy—but you talk crazy.

(Shaddick waves him off. He disappears into the curtained room again. Shaddick moves around counter, pausing by photograph of his son, looks at it.)

Shaddick: Good night, Benjy.

(He takes a slow, shuffling walk to stairway, flicks light, and starts to move upstairs.)

(Fade out)

ACT THREE

(The scene is the dining room in the country club. Herman and Shaddick enter, go to table. They look out window from table.)

Shaddick: See Miss Ross?

(Mrs. Parker, a formidable dowager at another table, calls over maitre d', whispers to him. He casts glances toward Shaddick, listens to woman, and walks to Shaddick's table.)

Herman: Next time I'm gonna go off that high board feet first...

Maitre D': Excuse me, sir...I didn't see you come in.

Shaddick: You're forgiven.

Herman: But I ain't gonna hold my nose or anything like that.

Shaddick: He is available for lifeguard duties after lunch. Please inform the members.

Maitre D': *(a little nervously)* The...ah...the pool and club house are open only to members and guests.

(Shaddick looks at him.)

Shaddick: A fact?

Maitre D': I'm afraid so.

Shaddick: We are guests of a member.

Maitre D': A member?

Shaddick: Miss Gloria Ross.

Maitre D': I see. Well...thank you very much.

(pause)

Shaddick: *(to Herman)* Do you see anything you like?

(The maitre d' turns and moves back over to the table where Mrs. Parker is staring at them with a cold, arrogant hostility; then he turns back toward Shaddick.)

Maitre D': I wonder if I might have your name, sir.

Shaddick: Shaddick. Abel Shaddick. And Herman D. Washington.

Maitre D': I'll take your order in just a minute, sir.

(The maitre d' nods and continues over to Mrs. Parker's table. We see them gesturing. Shaddick studies this scene for a moment, then looks at Herman.)

Shaddick: Our enemies are multiplying, Herman.

Herman: *(looks up, reading from the menu)* Hey, Shaddick—what's "ground steak garnished with delicacies, served in sizzling splendour"?

Shaddick: Hamburger...overpriced! *(Again he looks toward the woman beyond them who is staring at them with explicit displeasure. Shaddick leans over toward Herman, his voice lower.)* Herman—I got an idea! Let's go fishing at the lake. On the way is a diner where hamburgers are hamburgers and they cost a quarter. (Herman studies him for a moment, quickly looks toward Mrs. Parker.)*

Herman: She's gettin' to you?

Shaddick: I'm afraid we're getting to her.

(Herman shrugs, rises.)

Herman: I get my clothes from the locker.

(Herman exits.
Gloria enters from another room, moves toward Shaddick's table. Mrs. Parker approaches her.)

Mrs. Parker: Gloria? *(Gloria stops.)* Are they your guests?

Gloria: They're my guests.

Mrs. Parker: Well, my dear, I don't want to start anything...

Gloria: Then don't.

(Gloria continues over to Shaddick's table.)

Shaddick: Ah...Miss Ross...

Gloria: How are you, Mr. Shaddick?

Shaddick: Fine, thank you. And appreciative of the invitation. Herman enjoyed his swim—

Gloria: You're not leaving?

Shaddick: *(with a look toward Mrs. Parker)* We're going to the lake to fish. Here it is a little difficult to breathe.

(Maitre d' approaches Gloria.)

Maitre D': Telephone call for you, Miss Ross...long distance.

Gloria: I'll be right there. Please wait—please... *(She goes to the telephone and speaks into it.)* Yes? *(She frowns.)* Who? I'm afraid I don't hear you. Could you speak louder? Who? *(pause)* Mrs. Washington? Mrs. Washington—could you...could you control yourself? I don't understand you. *(pause)* That's right. Please. *(pause)* Now tell me that again, would you? *(The camera moves in on a closer shot of her face. She speaks into phone, very softly.)* I see. I'm... I'm terribly sorry. Do you...do you want us to tell the boy? *(pause)* All right. Will you be there the rest of the afternoon? I'll see that somebody gets on the train with him back to New York. *(pause)* Yes, I'll call you later and tell you what train. That's all right. *(pause)* And Mrs. Washington—I'm...I'm truly very sorry. *(She puts the receiver down, walks across the room over to the door where Shaddick is just about to walk out.)* Mr. Shad-dick—that call was from Herman's grandmother.

Shaddick: Oh...

Gloria: *(a pause as she struggles a little)* It seems he had a brother in Vietnam.

Shaddick: *(smiles)* You should hear Herman talk about that brother! Lawrence of Arabia and Joe Louis rolled into one.

Gloria: *(softly)* He's dead, Mr. Shaddick. The grandmother just received the telegram. He was killed on Monday.

(Shaddick stands motionless. His eyes close for a moment, his head goes down. Then he looks up, tears in his eyes. He nods, gnaws on his lip, and just nods.
Through the window we see Herman walking along the pool, now clothed in shorts and T-shirt, with his bathing suit wrapped in a towel.)

Shaddick: *(turning to Gloria)* Who tells him?

Gloria: His grandmother suggested that we do.

Shaddick: We do? *(He takes a deep breath, closes his eyes again.)* We do.

Gloria: I...I don't know how.

Shaddick: It's very easy. *(pause)* You just stick a hole in the little boy's heart, and then you stand back and watch him bleed.

Gloria: *(her eyes glistening)* What can I do, Mr. Shaddick?

(Shaddick shrugs.)

Shaddick: What can any of us do... *(He looks toward the window.)* ...except to start the bleeding process and then...then hope that there's enough iron in that little black frame to withstand the blow.

Gloria: Are you going to tell him now?

Shaddick: No...no...not here.

(They stand there waiting as Herman enters.)

Herman: *(to Gloria)* Thanks for letting me swim.

Gloria: That's all right, Herman.

Herman: *(to Shaddick)* You sick?

Shaddick: No, Herman, I'm not sick.

Herman: We goin' to the lake now?

Shaddick: Why not?

Herman: We gotta stop at the delicatessen and get the fishin' poles.

Shaddick: If that's what you want.

Herman: *(looks at him)* You sure you ain't sick?

Shaddick: No . . . perhaps just a little.

Gloria: I'll see you both later . . .

(Shaddick and Herman move toward door. Herman carefully eyes her.)

Herman: Bye. *(to Shaddick)* She looks a little sick, too.

(Gloria stands there silently and motionlessly for a moment after they leave. Mrs. Parker rises, moves over to Gloria.)

Mrs. Parker: Gloria, my dear—I don't want to make a thing about this—and this is hardly personal.

Gloria: *(in a soft, whispered voice)* Isn't it?

Mrs. Parker: There are certain lines that have to be drawn. I mean . . . to invite that old man—

(Gloria's face freezes, and it's the look on her face that stops Mrs. Parker cold.)

Gloria: That old man and that soon-to-be wounded little boy . . . are the only honest-to-God human beings anywhere near this swimming pool. And that, Mrs. Parker, is meant to be extremely personal.

(The scene changes to the lake. Herman and Shaddick are on the rock, fishing. There's a dead silence—Herman engrossed in his fishing, Shaddick looking pale and old and waiting for the right moment. And finally, because he can wait no longer, he turns to the boy.)

Shaddick: Herman . . . I have something to tell you now. Something . . . something very serious.

Herman: *(without looking at him)* What?

Shaddick: Look at me, Herman.

(The camera shows us Herman's face as he turns to look at Shaddick.)

Shaddick's Voice: There was a call from your grandmother. It's about your brother Bill.

(At this point bobbin is suddenly grabbed by a fish and pulled under the water. We watch it spiral in descent down into the depths, carrying a fishing pole with it. A pan back over to the rock. Shaddick is there alone, looking after a running little boy.

The scene changes to the front of the delicatessen. The bright afternoon has turned into a cloud-laced sky, darkening by the moment, the sound of distant rolling thunder, and after a moment heavy drops of rain.

Shaddick walks slowly toward the delicatessen. He stops for a moment, reacts, then continues to walk.

Herman stands by the front door of the delicatessen. Shaddick moves to him, says nothing—just inserts the key in the lock, opens the door. Herman enters, walks the length of the counter, and disappears into the bedroom. Shaddick stands near the front door, then closes it

Inside the store, Shaddick pauses for a moment, then walks slowly over to the bedroom, stands at the curtains, then calls out.)

Shaddick: *(calling)* Herman? May I come in?

(There is a silence. Shaddick parts the curtains, moves into the bedroom.

Herman has his suitcase on the bed and is thrusting in the few tiny remnants of what he owns. Shaddick takes his suit off the hanger, lays it on the bed along with a shirt and tie. We hear distant thunder.)

Shaddick: The train leaves in about an hour. We have plenty of time.

(Herman nods, finishes jamming the stuff into the suitcase, starts to close it, turns, looks up at Shaddick.)

Herman: You know the fish?

Shaddick: The enormous one.

Herman: You keep it. Eat it or sell it. I ain't gonna need it.

Shaddick: What if I... what if I had it mounted? On a gold plaque? Your name on it?

(Herman shakes his head.)

Herman: Don't want it. I caught it for Bill.

(With the speaking of the name, the cold-steel defence of the boy gets dented. He lets out one tiny sob that catches in his throat. Shaddick sits at table, hands folded in front of him.)

Shaddick: If I said something, Herman... would you listen?

(Herman nods.)

Shaddick: A long time ago—almost twenty-five years ago—in this very room—I got a telegram. You know, Herman—the telegrams don't change. The wars change. The enemy changes. But the words used to tell the living about the dead... they don't change. *(pause)* "We regret to inform you that your son, Second Lieutenant Benjamin Shaddick, was killed in action, June 14th, 1944, while on a bombing mission over Stuttgardt, Germany." *(pause)* I read that telegram, Herman, maybe a hundred times. I read it until the words seemed to float in the air in front of my eyes. *(He reaches across the bed to touch Herman's hand.)* Do you know what I thought then, Herman? I thought my life had ended. I thought there had been stripped from me some... some vital part of my body—that from that moment on I would never again be able to smile... to laugh... to enjoy anything on earth. I felt as you must feel now. *(All of what the old man is saying does not reach Herman, but something of its truth and its understanding does reach him.)* You think at the time that the sorrow and the anguish is unbearable... and that the tears will never stop. But Herman... the tears do stop. Somehow... some way... there is an end to the crying.

Herman: *(very softly, thoughtfully)* One time... long time ago... I jus' a li'l kid then. I got roller skates, see? And I start down the steps... and I fall. And man, it hurt real bad. And Bill come out and he go down the steps and he pick me up and he look at me and he

say, "Hermie... Hermie—don't you cry." *(pause)* I don't cry, Shaddick. Not me. I never gonna cry.

(Shaddick rises from the bed, moves to the curtained partition, his back to the boy.)

Shaddick: You are a very brave boy, Herman. You are really incredibly brave. *(pause)* You stay here... go on with your packing. I'll call you when it's time to go. *(He comes out through the curtains, walks behind the counter, stops, his head down. Softly, under his breath, he speaks.)* Let this old Jew cry, Herman. I'll cry for the two of us.

(Shaddick moves to the window. The rain now comes down in torrents against the pane. The camera shows Shaddick's face—the tears roll down the ancient, lined cheeks much as the rain drops on the window.

Herman comes into the room carrying his suitcase. He moves to Shaddick. Shaddick turns to him, wiping his face.)

Herman: Why you cry? He nothin' to you. You never even know my brother. So why you cry, man?

Shaddick: *(very softly)* I cry because I'm an old man, Herman. And sometimes... that's all that's left to old men. They cry at the irony of things. That the fine young men die... and the old men go on.

(Gloria's car pulls up outside. Gloria gets out, rushes through the rain to the front door, and enters.)

Gloria: I thought I'd drive Herman to New York, Mr. Shaddick.

(Shaddick looks at Herman.)

Shaddick: It's for him to decide. The weather is so bad...

Gloria: It's begun to rain. I'll drive you, Herman. Is that all right?

(Herman nods silently, unemotionally.)

Herman: That all right.

Gloria: Herman... I'm truly sorry.

(Herman again nods but says nothing.)

Shaddick: Do you want me to drive in with you, Herman?

(*Herman turns to him. There is a moment's pause.*)

Herman: No. No, you stay here. (*He picks up his suitcase.*) I ready. (*Gloria opens the door, steps aside to let him pass. Herman moves to the door, then turns very slowly to look at Shaddick. He speaks very directly and with no emotion.*) G'bye.

(*Shaddick takes a step toward the boy, wanting to say more, do more, show more, but he can't bring himself to try to scale the fortress that surrounds this kid. He puts his hand up in the way of a wave. Herman turns, follows Gloria out and into the car.*

The engine starts, then suddenly the passenger's door opens. Herman comes out, runs through the rain to the front door of the delicatessen, and then enters. He moves very close to the old man and looks up at him, then very slowly reaches up. Shaddick puts out his own hand and the two of them clasp.)

Herman: I jus' wanna say somethin' to you— Don't you cry no more. Understand? (*The camera shows us Herman's little face, and for the first time we see tears.*) We gonna make out. You'n me. We gonna make out—

(*And then he starts to cry. Shaddick takes the little boy to him, hugs him fiercely, protectively, then very slowly they separate.*)

Shaddick: When you come back we can go fishing again.

Herman: I come back. I really gonna come back.

(*Herman turns, moves out the door and into the car. The car door closes and the car pulls away.*

Shaddick turns from the window, moves down the length of the counter, pausing—just to stand there, looking at nothing.)

Shaddick: Benjy... (*The phone rings. Shaddick turns, moves toward the phone, picks it up as if it were a heavy weight.*) Yes? (*pause*) Who? (*pause*) A collect call. A collect call

from who—I shouldn't ask. (*He closes his eyes, nods.*) Mr. Banner. All right, I'll take it. (*We hear a torrential pouring of words at the other end of the receiver. Shaddick simply stands there, shoulders bent, eyes half closed. He waits for the outpouring of words to dry up.*) Hello, Stanley...what—I am sorry that the thing blew up. Yeah, you, you may come back and stay for as long as you want. (*Another outpouring of words, then Shaddick looks up, studies the curtained room.*) No...not there. That room is reserved, for Herman. (*pause*) That's right—Herman Washington. He's a friend of mine. A very close and personal friend. That room will be saved for him. Upstairs, Stanley. (*pause*) Think nothing of it, Stanley...bye. (*He replaces the receiver, looks briefly toward the curtained room again, then takes a slow walk over to the counter and moves behind it to look down at the picture of his dead son.*) The dead, my son, come in all colours. You must know this. We, unfortunately, are still learning. (*He turns and looks down the length of the counter toward the window.*) It's raining quite hard, Benjy. A real summer storm. And this, I guess, will end the heat. End the heat...and cleanse the earth. (*A silence; he closes his eyes tightly.*) How we need it!

(*He moves down the length of the counter back to the window to look out at the falling rain.*)

(*Fade out*)

Caution:
Enquiries regarding the performance of this play, amateur or professional, should be directed to Mr. Jed Mattes, International Creative Management, 40 West 57 Street, New York, New York 10019.

Come Away, Come Away

Mavor Moore

CHARACTERS
An old man
A young girl

"Forgetting's hard, hardest thing there is."

(*The scene is a park.*
Music: *In the far distance, a mournful, unrhythmic guitar.* **Sound:** *Birds—not many, varied, and at different distances. The burble of a nearby stream rises and falls. Dried leaves rustle.*)

Girl: Hi.

Old Man: Mm? Oh, hello there.

(*pause*)

Girl: I'm collecting leaves.

Old Man: Yes, I can see that.

(*pause*)

Girl: They're all dead.

Old Man: Yes. Used to be green; then they turn red and stay on the tree for their picture and then they die.

Girl: That's when they fall down.

Old Man: Oh, yes, that's what happens.

(*pause*)

Girl: What are *you* doing?

Old Man: Me? Well, I was thinking.

Girl: Hmph.

Old Man: It may not sound like much, but there's a good deal to thinking.

Girl: Is it harder 'n reading?

Old Man: Oh, much. Reading, somebody else gives you the ideas. Thinking, you have to come up with them yourself.

Girl: How do you?

Old Man: Well, at first you have to have a lot to think about. That means you have to have done a lot.

Girl: You mean lived?

Old Man: Yes, that's it. Then you have to remember it. Now that's not easy, remembering.

Girl: I remember lots of things.

Old Man: Oh, well, that's because you haven't got all that much to work on yet. I have boxes and boxes and files and cabinets and shelves and cupboards—right here in my head. Yes. Someday I'll get them all sorted out, you know. . . but right now I flip open my mind, and out pops a thought—then another. You put one thought up against the next and they dance together, and the two of them make you think of another—and pretty soon there's a whole roomful of thoughts, all shapes and sizes, a whole fancy-dress ball— and you lose sight of the thought you started with, because all you can see is the pattern they make, like a crazy quilt, only moving, moving.

Girl: Like leaves?

Old Man: Yes. *(pause)* Only it's one after the other, you see. Like notes that make a tune, and pretty soon you've forgotten the notes and only remember the tune. And the tune comes back and back, and you forget where it started. Echoes.

Girl: Hmph.

(pause)

Old Man: Then you have to start remembering again.

Girl: What're you remembering?

Old Man: Oh, times.

Girl: Hmph.

(pause)

Old Man: You all alone?

Girl: Sure.

Old Man: You live near here?

Girl: Nope.

Old Man: Far away?

Girl: *(moving offstage)* Quite a way.

Old Man: Why'd you come so far?

Girl: *(off)* I told you. The leaves.

Old Man: Oh, yes. *(pause)* You come here often?

Girl: *(off)* Sure. Do you?

Old Man: Sometimes. I've never seen you before.

Girl: *(off)* I've seen you.

Old Man: My eyes aren't as good as they used to be.

Girl: *(off)* Does it make you remember, coming here?

Old Man: Yes. But no; not really. Nothing ever happened to me here. I mean, I never came here when I was a kid, like you. I had another place, far away. I used to climb trees, swing on the branches and the vines, chase chipmunks. Oh, I was a great tree climber!

Girl: *(off)* Why d'you come here?

Old Man: Oh, I don't know. . . this place: gives me new things to think about—new things that're really old too, like streams and pebbles and flowers, only in new patterns. You need to smell things growing, changing. Things getting ready to happen—right on the brink, not over and done with. Otherwise. . . you see, it's wondering—wondering what's going to happen—that keeps you alive. Touching things, young people, wondering. *(pause)* Old people talk too much.

Girl: *(off)* Hey!

Old Man: What?

Girl: *(coming onstage)* Look—I found something! In the leaves, all covered with leaves!

Old Man: What's that you've got?

Girl: A dead bird.

Old Man: What's it, a sparrow?

(pause)

Girl: It won't ever fly again.

Old Man: Best put it down.

(Sound: *Slight crinkle of brown-paper bag.)*

Girl: I'll put him in my bag.

Old Man: Better bury him when you get home.

Girl: He's all stiff.

Old Man: Yes. You get like that. Yes. *(pause)* You know that fellow who plays the guitar?

Girl: Sure. He plays it all the time.

Old Man: Sometimes I hear him, sometimes I don't. My ears aren't all that good now.

Girl: He makes it up.

Old Man: Yes. *(pause)* Is he a young fellow?

Girl: No. He's sad.

Old Man: Still...how do you know?

Girl: He told me.

Old Man: You talk to everybody?

Girl: If they like to.

Old Man: You're not scared?

Girl: Nope.

Old Man: You're not scared of me?

Girl: Nope.

Old Man: Well, now. *(pause)* That's nice, that's very nice. *(pause)* What're you doing now?

Girl: Sorting the leaves.

Old Man: That'll take a long time.

Girl: I know.

Old Man: And you don't mind talking to me?

Girl: Nope.

Old Man: Your mother never tell you not to talk to strangers?

Girl: Why not?

Old Man: Well...old men. Lonely old men.

Girl: How old are you?

Old Man: Oh, I'm pretty old.

Girl: How old?

Old Man: Over eighty. How old are you?

Girl: Why d'you want to know?

Old Man: *(mock umbrage)*) I told you *my* age!

Girl: Guess.

Old Man: Well, I'd say...about seven. And a half.

(pause)

Girl: How old are the leaves?

Old Man: These ones? Oh, maybe six months.

Girl: Hmph.

Old Man: So you see you're older than they are, and I'm a lot older than you are—and we can all talk together, and nobody's scared of anybody else! *(He suddenly laughs.)* Say, it does me good to talk to you! Think of all you've got ahead of you! I like you! What's your name?

Girl: Oh, people call me different things.

Old Man: What do you call yourself?

Girl: All depends.

Old Man: Depends on what?

Girl: What I'm doing.

Old Man: What do you call yourself when you're out sorting and cheering up an old man?

Girl: Mort.

Old Man: Mort? That's a boy's name!

Girl: Not just.

Old Man: I never heard of a girl called Mort. *(sighs)* I don't know—I like girls' names better. I had a granddaughter, name of Millie. *(pause)* Crying. That fellow used to hit her. No good. Still, what could anyone do? I told him, right out. Said, you're piling up grief. Blamed everybody but himself. Tears streaming down her face. Do you love him, Millie? It killed her. *(He groans.)*

Girl: You got something wrong with you?

Old Man: Mm? Something wrong?

Girl: Old people always have something wrong with them.

Old Man: Oh, that.

Girl: Then what?

Old Man: Oh, well...I'm not too bad.

(pause)

Girl: Do you hurt?

Old Man: Not so's you'd notice.

Girl: Don't you hurt *somewhere?*

Old Man: Well, now and then.

Girl: Where?

Old Man: Places.

Girl: All over?

Old Man: Sometimes.

Girl: That what happens when you get old?

Old Man: That's about it. That's about it.

(**Music:** *The guitar in the distance stops.*)

Girl: Has it stopped now?

Old Man: What?

Girl: The hurt.

Old Man: Some.

Girl: You were remembering, weren't you!

Old Man: Yes. *(pause)* That's what happens, you see. I was thinking about you...

Girl: When I came over?

Old Man: Just now...

Girl: I saw you looking at me.

Old Man: I was, and then...

Girl: I saw you look away. You didn't even see the water or the trees or anything.

Old Man: That's what happens. There's a difference, what you see and what you're looking at.

Girl: How come?

Old Man: Well, you now, you think of what you're doing, you look at what you're seeing, at leaves. I think of what I'm looking at on the inside of my head. That's because I'm old.

Girl: You short-sighted?

Old Man: A funny thing, that. When you get old, you grow four eyes.

Girl: Four?

Old Man: Yes. The two you started with get weaker, but then you grow two more that get stronger.

Girl: Show me.

Old Man: Oh, you can't see them. One's on the inside, so's you can see your whole life, like movies, the best bits and the scary bits...get you all excited again...so you can be sure they really happened or couldn't have happened...

Girl: Where's the other eye?

Old Man: It's outside somewhere, away out, at the end of a long arm, like a periscope, looking back at you, so you see yourself and everything you're doing and can't stop yourself doing.

Girl: Like what?

Old Man: Oh, talking. You hear other old people talking your ear off, and you swear you won't be like that, but you talk. And crying for no reason. Putting your feet where you don't want them to go. Telling people you love to go to blazes. Throwing things out you want to keep and keeping things you want to throw out. Remembering. Most of all, remembering.

Girl: Don't you like remembering?

Old Man: Some things. Oh yes, some things you...but once it starts to work, you see, you can't turn it off...things come piling in... *(He shivers.)*

Girl: Things you want to forget?

Old Man: Yes. You think forgetting's easy?

Girl: Sure. I forget all the time.

Old Man: That's because you haven't all that much to remember. Forgetting's hard, hardest thing there is.

Girl: Harder than thinking?

Old Man: Oh, yes. Because to think you have to forget an awful lot. An awful lot, to think straight. It's gone, you see—all gone. Nothing you can do about it, any of it: the people, the times, the places...good, bad, or indifferent...they're gone. And you can't live in the past. You have to look around you, what's happening now. There's an ache...you can't ache it over again. You need...new aches... to be alive.

(pause)

Girl: Is that what you got now?

Old Man: Talking to you?

Girl: You got an ache?

Old Man: *(chuckling)* No! No, you make me feel better.

Girl: I made you think how old you were, didn't I?

(A long pause; the old man is deeply hurt.)

Girl: You got an ache now?

Old Man: Yes, I . . . is that why you wanted to talk to me?

Girl: I just wondered.

Old Man: *(gradually recovering, chuckling)* That's it! That's better! Wondering! Full of wonder! By George! Wonder—that's the cure! That's life—not to know what's coming next and to care, to wonder! Listen, my name's Fred. We're good friends now, aren't we!

Girl: Maybe.

Old Man: Oh, I can tell you lots of things! I can show you things—

Girl: What did you used to do, before?

Old Man: *(eagerly)* Oh, lots of things. I was a soldier once.

Girl: You get wounded?

Old Man: Oh, yes.

Girl: Where?

Old Man: You can't see it.

Girl: Show me.

Old Man: I'll show you once. *(rolling up his sleeve)* Here, in my left arm.

(pause)

Girl: What made it?

Old Man: A bullet.

Girl: Hmph. Who were you fighting?

Old Man: Germans. It was a long time ago. In the Great War.

Girl: You kill any of them?

Old Man: Oh, yes. I got a medal for that.

Girl: Why?

Old Man: Well, they were trying to kill me.

Girl: Why?

Old Man: I forget. But they started it.

Girl: You didn't do anything?

Old Man: I don't think so. Not right then. Not first.

Girl: Did you hate them?

Old Man: Oh, yes.

Girl: Was that why you killed them?

Old Man: I guess so.

Girl: You have to hate somebody to kill them?

Old Man: Oh, yes. Otherwise...

Girl: Did the man who shot at you hate you?

Old Man: I guess he must've.

Girl: You always hate someone who kills you?

Old Man: Well, it's too late after. You have to hate them first.

Girl: But why?

Old Man: I don't know.

Girl: If someone killed you now, would you have to hate them first?

Old Man: Oh, yes. But no; it all depends. It depends on when.

Girl: Now.

(pause)

Old Man: I don't know.

Girl: But you're old now. It wouldn't matter.

(pause)

Old Man: It's not the ones you hate who die.

Girl: Look at this leaf! You ever see one so beautiful?

Old Man: How could he lie there in the mud and not see a tank plough over him? Over his head. She couldn't face the thought. Fifty years. Fifty years later, she still...don't you think *I* dream about it? You think it helps to know you can't forget? He's gone, we're here. Our own lives to live. Making love, how *can* you with a ghost behind the eyes?

Girl: Why does the red turn yellow?

Old Man: He's my son, not his. My head. *(pause)* For what it's worth. It's not the ones you hate who kill you.

Girl: Who, then?

Old Man: And it's not the ones you hate who die.

Girl: Who, then?

Old Man: The ones you love. One after the other.

Girl: You ever kill someone you love?

Old Man: Oh, yes. *(pause)* Once you find where it hurts...

Girl: What hurts?

(pause)

Old Man: Well, children hurt. Growing hurts. Knowing hurts. The world hurts.

Girl: Show me.

Old Man: How?

Girl: Show me the other wounds.

Old Man: Oh, not mine...I can't show you mine, but I don't mean them, the ones I carry. It's the ones I...the ones others... *(pause)* And they're all gone, you see. You can't ever make it up.

(pause)

Girl: How come, with everybody getting killed and dying, you got to be so old?

Old Man: Oh, well! *(He laughs and brightens.)* I was lucky, you see—and careful.

Girl: What'd you do?

Old Man: Didn't do anything for the lucky part, except be prepared. But careful? Oh, I tell you, I used to keep in shape! I was a good athlete. Spring and fall I used to run—track and field, broad jump, all that. Summers I swam. Oh, I was a strong swimmer, still am. Still go down to the Y, you know. . . every now and then. Badminton, too. And deck tennis, with a quoit. . . you ever play that?

Girl: No.

Old Man: Oh, that's a great game. Tough— have to be tough for deck tennis if you play it right. . . not that namby-pamby kind. And water polo, that's even tougher. . . have to swim with your legs, keep your hands free for the ball. That was summers, you know. Then winters, snowshoeing. Nobody does that now. . . all this skiing's what they do now. . . but I used to snowshoe. Miles and miles, up north. Only way you could get some places. Oh, that's a muscle builder! *(pause)* Couldn't do that now. *(pause)* Every morning, winter and summer, used to do deep breathing, fresh air. Oh, that sets you up. *(pause)* Can't do that today.

Girl: Is it hard breathing, when you're old?

Old Man: No, sir, not that, it's not me, it's the world. No more fresh air. You can't breathe that muck. I'm in pretty good shape—but the world. . .

(pause)

Girl: That all you did?

Old Man: Oh, no, that was just. . . I went to college, after the war. Learned to be a lawyer. Everybody needs a lawyer, you see, because you have to have laws and nobody else can make 'em out. Oh, I was a good lawyer! Used to do my homework. You do your homework?

Girl: Sure.

Old Man: Good for you. Well, I used to do my homework. Then I'd get up in court. "Objection, my lord! Objection sustained!" *(pause)* Sometimes, of course, I wasn't sustained. But I always put up a good fight. One fellow,

bank robber, oh, he was a tough customer—I thought they'd hang him sure. But I was able to get him the benefit of the doubt. Big fellow he was, with blond hair and hands like a blacksmith. By George! *(pause)* Later on, he killed his wife with a crowbar. Nice girl.

(pause)

Girl: You didn't help her much.

Old Man: No. But I helped lots of good people. One fellow, a piano tuner, hands mangled in a car accident. He'd never've got a cent, but I took it all the way up on appeal. Never charged him a nickel. Said, that's okay, Billy— I'm not in it for the money. Justice. *(pause)* Of course, most of it's the quiet stuff. Dog work. Routine, going in and coming out. Paper: "Whereas the aforesaid" and "inasmuch as notwithstanding" and "do hereby jointly and severally" and "the party of the first part and the party of the second part". . . and then bang—the seal. You never know. *(pause)* I did *not* work too hard! How can you say that? I'm home as much as most other men. Weekends, I take the children out. I don't gamble. I don't drink that much. What do you expect of a man?

(pause)

Girl: The sun's going down.

(pause)

Old Man: Yes. She used to say that. Summers, we'd be sitting there, after dinner, and she'd say look, the sun's going down. *(pause)* Hadn't you best be getting home?

Girl: I'm not through yet.

Old Man: It'll come up tomorrow. Now let's you and me talk about tomorrow. Forget all that stuff that happened long ago. Let's think about tomorrow.

Girl: All right.

Old Man: *(vigorously)* Tomorrow morning, I'm going to get up early.

Girl: What's early?

Old Man: Six o'clock. I'll eat a good breakfast, my usual.

Girl: What's that?

Old Man: Oatmeal. Always have my bowl of hot oatmeal. Then I'll get dressed and shave and bring in the paper and read all the day's news. You read the paper?

Girl: No.

Old Man: Oh, you ought to read the paper! I'm surprised at you not reading the paper. Nothing like it for keeping on top of things. TV, of course, and the radio for background, but they're more companions. The paper's got it all down, the whole story, not just snippets. Oh, the paper's a great thing for knowing what's going on in the world. I read it all— "continue on page eight," all that—financial pages, sports section, women's doings, comics, bridge... all except the horoscope—that's nonsense. That's the whole point about the future, not to know it, not to know what's coming up the next day. News! How could it be news if you already knew what was coming? Every day's different. Tomorrow, who knows?

Girl: Then what?

Old Man: After the paper? *(He falters, afraid.)* Well, that's... after the paper, I have to decide. Up to the paper, it's the same every day. The paper's the same every day, you know.

Girl: I thought you said it was different.

Old Man: Oh, the details change! The details are never the same from one day to the next, for goodness's sake! That keeps you guessing. I mean, there's always a war but each time it's someplace else. Women are always changing their clothes, but you never know what next. *That* never changes! Every day, so far, up to the paper, every day's about the same. Then I... then I have to decide what to do. *(pause)* What to do. What to do.

Girl: You won't be here tomorrow.

Old Man: Well, I don't know. I haven't made up my mind. Maybe I'll see what's going on in the world.

Girl: You said the world hurts.

Old Man: Did I?

Girl: A while back.

Old Man: Oh, that's only sometimes. *(firmly)* Actually, I have a great deal to do.

Girl: Like what?

Old Man: Responsibilities.

Girl: You got a family?

Old Man: Grandchildren, you know. They... they sometimes need me. *(pause)* Oh, yes, I'm needed... now and then. One of them calls me up... every so often. *(pause)* 'Course, we don't talk much, in a movie... can't say much in a movie, you know... but they like the movie. I'm... *(pause)* Actually, I'm pretty busy even for that. Lot of demands on my time.

Girl: What for?

Old Man: Well, things to be sorted. Books, papers, that sort of thing. Boxes and filing drawers, all that. I have to go back over it, sort it out. Important papers.

Girl: What about?

Old Man: Oh, business, legal, family stuff.

Girl: What good's it?

Old Man: Well, it has to be sorted. Catalogued, you know.

Girl: That why you kept it?

Old Man: No, no. It's important.

Girl: What for?

Old Man: For me. That's my whole life. It has to be sorted. Nobody else to do it. Photographs, newspaper cuttings, letters, old letters, all that. Letters... terrible.

Girl: Why'n't you throw them out, then?

Old Man: They have to be sorted. Some of them... *(pause)* They have to be sorted.

(pause)

Girl: Maybe you won't get 'round to it.

Old Man: Oh, yes. Tomorrow morning. I'll do it tomorrow. I've been putting it off.

Girl: Why?

(pause)

Old Man: Digging.

Girl: What?

Old Man: It's digging. Digging in the . . . digging up memories. That's hard.

Girl: Harder than forgetting?

Old Man: Oh, yes.

Girl: How come?

Old Man: Well, it's not just memories, you see—you can forget memories if you try. But with these, there they are; not just what you remember, but what they were . . . what you wrote, what she actually looked like . . . the places. What the words said, what the faces say. Holding things. Happy. *(pause)* There it is. *(pause)* How could I have done that to you? *(pause)* Houses. I never meant . . . *(pause)* I didn't say it right. If I could have seen you, talked to you. *(pause)* What lies! By George, that boy would've made a fortune as a storyteller! "I was robbed in Times Square last night by three thugs: please send me a hundred bucks." "The girl's father will let me off if I donate a thousand bucks to the cause." "Helen says she'll keep quiet about the drugs if you'll give her the house." What lies! *(pause)* What do you do? What do you do with a boy like that—let him go to jail? *(pause)* "To be divided among my children *per stirpes* . . ." *Per stirpes.* Who gives a damn! *(Pause; then he groans.)*

Girl: Are you okay?

Old Man: Have to sort those papers. Get at it tomorrow, first thing.

Girl: How long will it take?

Old Man: I don't know. I'm the only one can do it, though.

Girl: Before you die?

(pause)

Old Man: I'll make time.

Girl: How d'you know?

(pause)

Old Man: I'll feel better tomorrow.

Girl: Hmph.

(Pause. **Music:** *The faraway guitar begins to play again.)*

Old Man: So, I'd better be going. Sun's almost down.

Girl: I can still see.

Old Man: Haven't you finished sorting those leaves?

Girl: Nearly.

Old Man: You'd better come with me, let me see you on your way.

Girl: Sure. We'll go together.

(pause)

Old Man: That fellow with the guitar's at it again.

Girl: I know.

Old Man: Sad. A lament. Why doesn't he play something lively?

(pause)

Girl: You afraid to die?

Old Man: Me? Why do you . . .

Girl: Just wondering.

Old Man: There, you see—wondering! You just wonder, keep on wondering, and you'll be all right.

Girl: Well, *are* you?

Old Man: Oh, no. Most of my friends are gone. Only I'd like it to be unexpected. Don't want to dry up gradually, like some of them; faculties going, one by one . . . limbs failing . . . eaten away inside . . . knowing it's coming. Just turn the page one day and find it there.

Girl: What's it like, d'you think?

Old Man: Dying? *(jovially)* Well, an old fellow in a white nightshirt comes along, toting a scythe over his shoulder. He taps you with a bony finger and says here I am. It's time.

Girl: How d'you know?

Old Man: Oh, I hear tell. But I'm going to give him a run for his money.

Girl: He might surprise you.

Old Man: Oh, I hope he will! You only die when you join the past, become a memory like the rest of them, forget. Surprise! That's life! You remember that, now.

Girl: Sure.

(pause)

Old Man: You're a funny kid. Collecting dead leaves, a dead bird. *(pause)* But you've certainly cheered me up! Talking to you... Come on now—pick up your bag, let's get on our way. *(He rises with effort.)* Oh, I'm so stiff!

Girl: *(rising)* Are you feeling okay?

Old Man: I—feel—wonderful! I never felt better in my life, if you want to know. Are you my friend?

Girl: Sure.

Old Man: If I came back tomorrow, would you be here?

Girl: Maybe.

Old Man: What would you like to do tomorrow? We could—

Girl: Climb trees?

Old Man: That's what we'll do!

Girl: *(going toward offstage)* Like this one?

Old Man: Just like that!

Girl: Show me!

Old Man: It's getting dark!

*(**Music:** The guitar becomes more rhythmical and excited.)*

Girl: That doesn't matter!

Old Man: You want me to climb this tree?

Girl: Try! Try that one there!

Old Man: All right! *(He attempts to climb.)* I'll show you how it's done! When I was a boy...! If I can just...! Now...! *(He groans and falls.)*

*(**Sound:** His body hitting the leaf-covered ground. **Music:** There is a long pause in the guitar music; then the mournful lay starts gently up again. It begins to move in closer.)*

Old Man: *(painfully)* I couldn't...I fell...

Girl: *(close, gently)* You don't hate me, do you?

Old Man: What?...

Girl: For coming now.

Old Man: A little girl...

Girl: Who knows?

Old Man: ...with a brown-paper bag...

Girl: It was time, that's all.

*(**Music:** The guitar moves much closer now and then dies.)*

DECISIONS

Everyone faces decisions countless times a day. The decision might be as small as choosing what to have for breakfast or what clothes to put on in the morning. It is almost as if these were practice for the larger decisions in our lives, such as what career we want to pursue or what sorts of relationships we want to establish with others.

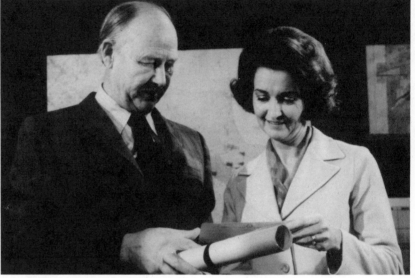

These larger decisions are the stuff of which good drama is made. A "life-and-death" decision puts a great deal of responsibility on the person with the alternatives. The repercussions might affect not only the decision-maker but also other people. It is in these moments of conflict and tension that a good play can give us insight into how we ourselves might solve our own conflicts.

In Hugh Hood's *Friends and Relations*, a widow has to decide whether she will follow the societal role assigned to her or establish a life of her own and explore her "personhood." Gwen Pharis Ringwood's *Still Stands the House* shows a family in conflict, with each of its three members making choices that involve the other two. Should the family unit change or should it go on as it has for decades?

Friends and Relations

Hugh Hood

CHARACTERS

Mrs. Ruth Bird—a recent widow whose life has until now been devoted to her family

Christine Fletcher—her married daughter

Jim Fletcher—Christine's husband

Cousin Stanley—a relative of the late Mr. Bird and a car dealer

Uncle Lou—another relative and the town mayor

Sampson Willey—a successful real-estate agent

Larry Godfrey—the office manager of the Stoverville branch of Langbourne Associates, a real-estate agency

Mrs. Naomi Solomons—a friend of the Bird family

Mrs. Claude Harkness—another family friend

Andras Szekely—a businessman who buys housing property

"Ruth, grow up! This isn't your nice big old home on Charleston Road. This is the world!"

ACT ONE

(SCENE 1: We are looking at a recent grave, banked with flowers, still perhaps rimmed by the artificial turf sometimes used by undertakers. Around and behind the grave are weeds and tall grass. There is no sound but that of a faint breeze. We see weeds and grass move with the light motion of the air. We move in to a close shot of the fresh flowers and the new headstone with its freshly chiselled inscription: "Lawson Bird, M.D. Born 1920. Died 1974." The sound of the breeze drops and there is a brief silence. Then, while we are still looking at the headstone, we begin to hear the sound of conversation, not too animated, at the post-funeral reception in the Bird house in Stoverville. We can hear clinking glasses and then we can distinguish voices for the opening two lines of dialogue.)

Mrs. Solomons: Are you going right back to Montreal, Christine?

Christine: Jim's leaving on Monday but I'm staying for a while, till Mother gets settled.

(SCENE 2: The after-funeral reception in the Bird home in Stoverville. We are in the dining room by the door to the hall. The living room, hall, and dining room, where a buffet lunch is displayed, should all be visible. The house has a strong conservative atmosphere. Mrs. Solomons is speaking to Christine Fletcher. We can see Jim Fletcher standing beside them.)

Mrs. Solomons: Chris, it's a shock...to lose somebody you've lived with for thirty years.

Christine: She's going to have a very difficult adjustment.

(Mrs. Solomons shows signs of getting ready to leave, putting on her gloves, etc. She moves into the hall.)

Mrs. Solomons: Sam is in obstetrics in Montreal...I guess you know.

Christine: I've been intending to phone him.

Mrs. Solomons: I wish you would. You and Jim are the only Stoverville people he knows in Montreal.

Christine: I'd love to see Sam. He's kind of like an old boyfriend...but...you aren't leaving?

Mrs. Solomons: I think I will. It's a big turnout and the noise might tire Ruthie.

Christine: Everybody's been so thoughtful. I mean...look at all the food...those pies. *(She gestures widely at the range of dishes on the buffet. We should see various guests helping themselves.)*

Mrs. Solomons: There wasn't a better-known or better-liked man in Stoverville than your father. I guess you know that. I'll say good-bye now, Christine.

(Mrs. Solomons is seen exiting as Christine calls after her.)

Christine: Oh, good-bye, good-bye, and thanks for everything.

Jim: Isn't she nice? We'll have to be sure to phone Sam. Old boyfriend or not.

(Jim and Christine chuckle soberly together as Mrs. Claude Harkness appears.)

Mrs. Harkness: My dears, I simply had to come...

Jim: It's very kind...

Mrs. Harkness: *(not about to be interrupted)* ...to go off just like that. Makes you think, doesn't it? A coronary, they said. That was it, wasn't it, Chrissie?

Christine: I'm afraid so.

Mrs. Harkness: I just want to say, if there's anything Claude can do now, any little thing. Just refer the patients to Claude.

Christine: Thank you.

Mrs. Harkness: *(moving out of sight)* He looked so natural, like he was asleep. *(Her voice fades away.)*

Jim: Who was that?

Christine: Wasn't it Doctor Harkness's wife? She's aged since I saw her. I imagine things like this are kind of a diversion for her.

(Jim and Christine remain talking together as the camera pans slowly across to where Cousin Stanley and Uncle Lou are chatting in the dining room.)

Cousin Stanley: ...well, I literally begged him, Uncle Lou. I said, "Lawson, why don't you pay cash for this car? You can afford it."

Uncle Lou: Surely he had the payments insured.

Cousin Stanley: No thanks to him. It was me that put it in the contract. Lawson always thought he'd live forever.

Uncle Lou: He had a good life, Stan. He never had a care in the world. He was playing Senior "B" hockey when he was past forty.

Cousin Stanley: Yeah, and he had a heart attack that killed him before he was fifty-five.

(Jim Fletcher comes over to join them.)

Uncle Lou: Hello, Jim. We were talking about your mother-in-law's prospects. She isn't going to be any too well off, do you realize that?

Jim: Of course, if she absolutely *had* to she could always come and live with us in Montreal.

Cousin Stanley: She'll need a lot of help, Mr. Fletcher. Somebody to lean on.

Uncle Lou: Yes, it's a shame. The doctor was a great man in his way. He'll be missed. I don't quite know how poor Ruth will survive.

Cousin Stanley: You know, Mr. Fletcher... Jim...she doesn't know what a safety-deposit box *is*? Nobody ever saw her. What with the doctor so popular and Christine so pretty, you hardly realized poor Ruthie was in the house.

Jim: She's upstairs, resting.

(SCENE 3: On the staircase landing, Mrs. Bird stands with a photograph in her hand. The guests catch sight of her. Crowd noises.)

Cousin Stanley: Here she is now, everybody.

Mrs. Harkness: She hasn't been crying, anyway. She's been brave through it all.

Uncle Lou: Brave, yes. And pretty quiet.

Mrs. Bird: I was looking for this. Heavens, what a pile of junk in that attic.

(We see a photograph of Doctor Bird in his old hockey uniform.)

Mrs. Bird: Chris, darling, first thing Monday we'll have to get into the attic and throw things out. And some of the junk we can sell. Lawson's snowshoes. He bought them the winter we were married. Never used them that I can remember. *(looks at photo)* This is how I think of him, full of get-up-and-go. *(Mrs. Bird begins to move downstairs.)*

Uncle Lou: He could have been a pro, Ruthie.

Mrs. Bird: No, I don't believe so, Uncle Lou. He wasn't a good enough skater and he'd never have left Stoverville. But me...I've never really given up the notion of being a city girl. *(As she says this she moves briskly down the last of the stairs and crosses the dining room toward a big window. People swirl around her and make way for her.)*

Christine: Mother, you can just pack up and come to Montreal.

Mrs. Bird: But Christine, your apartment's so pokey, and in a while there'll be children...

Jim: You're very welcome, Mrs. Bird, any time at all.

Mrs. Bird: Maybe for weekends.

Cousin Stanley: You might do some baby-sitting for us, Ruthie. You adore the children.

Mrs. Bird: At a safe distance, Stanley. I haven't dealt with young children for twenty years.

Cousin Stanley: You'll have to work out something, Ruth. Lawson didn't leave much.

Mrs. Bird: *(to Uncle Lou)* I suppose that's right, isn't it, Uncle Lou, or should I say "Your Worship"?

Uncle Lou: Oh, goodness, Ruth. It just happens to be my turn to be mayor...look here, how would it be if I came along over to see you? What about tomorrow morning? I handled Lawson's insurance, you know, and some other matters.

Mrs. Bird: I wish you would. Come along any time, please. I'll be here. *(She turns and addresses the crowd generally.)* And now won't you all have something to eat and perhaps a drink? Lawson would want you to enjoy yourselves. *(to Cousin Stanley)* What about you, Stanley? You'd be more comfortable with something to drink. *(She goes to the dining-room buffet table and begins to pour drinks.)*

(SCENE 4: The living room, next morning. Much more sunshine is showing. We see Mrs. Bird at a small writing desk, adding up figures. We hear footsteps on the porch and the doorbell rings.)

Mrs. Bird: I'll get it. I'll get it. *(She gets up and goes to the front door, where she greets Uncle Lou.)* Good morning, Uncle Lou. Are you on your way to the office?

Uncle Lou: No, Ruthie, I want to take the whole morning to go over things with you.

Mrs. Bird: I wouldn't want you to lose a prospect.

Uncle Lou: They can look after prospects while I'm out of the office...at least I hope they can. And I want to take time to help you, Ruth. In a way I feel responsible. I feel that I allowed Lawson to neglect his affairs.

Mrs. Bird: He was half asleep most of the time. He made house calls at all hours, day or night. He had the right to spend his money as he pleased, and I'm glad he did because he enjoyed his life. I'm not apologizing for Lawson in any way.

Uncle Lou: Of course not, Ruth. But I should have kept after him all the same. I had policies waiting for his signature that he just never got around to. This house isn't yours, you know, and you couldn't afford to run it anyway. Eventually you'll have to go into an apartment.

Mrs. Bird: How much does it all add up to?

Uncle Lou: Let's see now, the car is free and clear . . . and you'll be getting eighteen thousand in insurance money, from policies Lawson bought around 1950. About two thousand in a couple of bank accounts . . . comes to around twenty thousand, plus the car. The other big item is the accounts receivable at the office. Plenty of people owe you money. Lawson doesn't seem to have been very good about sending out bills.

Mrs. Bird: As long as there was enough coming in for us to get along, he didn't care about bills.

Uncle Lou: He was a funny guy . . .

(Tight close-up of Mrs. Bird's face. She speaks reflectively.)

Mrs. Bird: Yes . . . a funny guy.

(This is Lawson's epitaph, in a way. They are silent for a moment.)

Uncle Lou: Anyway, there's around ten thousand owing. You might get half of it.

Mrs. Bird: Is that all?

Uncle Lou: Hardest thing in the world, to collect a dead doctor's bills. Hardest thing in the world . . . there isn't the same sense of obligation.

Mrs. Bird: Five thousand, maybe?

Uncle Lou: With any luck. *And* it'll take six months and more to get them all in, *and* you'll have to go to a collection agency for some of them. That would give you around twenty-five thousand to invest and you could get a safe eight, eight-and-a-quarter per cent interest, say two thousand a year.

Mrs. Bird: I'll have to work.

Uncle Lou: The way prices are going you need to earn another three to four thousand a year just to keep yourself.

Mrs. Bird: I'm fifty. I'll have lots of time to work. *(She doesn't seem too displeased about this, either.)*

Uncle Lou: I've taken the liberty of making a few inquiries. I think they'd pay you eighty a week at the Emmeline Shoppe. You must know a lot about ladies' wear.

Mrs. Bird: I wouldn't like waiting on my friends.

Uncle Lou: Have you had any ideas yourself?

Mrs. Bird: I believe I'll try real estate. I think I could sell homes—especially to women.

Uncle Lou: You wouldn't need much capital and you already own a car. I think that's a very good idea.

Mrs. Bird: Yes, I've thought of all that. *(She shows Uncle Lou to the door. She has a very pleased look. They both laugh in a friendly way through the last two lines.)*

Uncle Lou: As I say, if there's anything I can do to help . . . any good advice.

Mrs. Bird: Why, Your Worship, I'll be coming in all the time, to pick your brains.

(SCENE 5: The living room in the Bird house. Christine and Jim are talking quietly.)

Jim: I don't want to be a fink, Chris, but I really don't see how we could fit her in permanently.

Christine: The thing is, we made her an offer.

Jim: It would be awfully squeezed if . . . I mean if . . .

Christine: *(briskly)* If I'm pregnant.

Jim: That's it. Would she have enough to get by on, do you think?

Christine: I doubt it. Apparently Dad spent everything as it came in. He probably thought he was good for another thirty years.

Jim: Do you think we're going to have to take care of her?

Christine: I think she'd sooner starve, if you really want to know. You can go back to Montreal with a clear conscience.

Jim: I have to go back. You know that.

Christine: I've got a funny feeling about Mother. I don't know why.

(SCENE 6: The living room in the Bird house. Mrs. Bird is talking to Sampson Willey, a real-estate agent.)

Mrs. Bird: . . . and I asked you to come, Sampson, because you and Lawson were so close, and you were in the boat with him when it happened.

Sampson Willey: If we could have got him to shore faster, he might have been all right.

Mrs. Bird: I don't think so. It was a massive attack.

Sampson Willey: I can't help feeling responsible, all the same.

Mrs. Bird: Then perhaps you'll help me. I want to come into your office as a trainee, Sampson. I want to learn the real-estate business from scratch.

Willey: There's never been a woman realtor in Stoverville that I know of.

Mrs. Bird: I'll be the first. And you won't have to install a desk for me or anything. And I'll buy my own filing equipment and keep it in my apartment, when I find one.

Willey: The office isn't *that small*. We could fit in a filing cabinet.

Mrs. Bird: I figure with good luck I can qualify for a salesman's certificate over the winter.

Willey: There's an awful lot to learn . . . property evaluation . . . the local tax situation.

Mrs. Bird: How to prepare an offer. Legal connections.

Willey: All that. How to manage a closing. And all the practical things like how to brush off somebody who's just looking.

Mrs. Bird: All those practical things. That's what I need to know.

Willey: *(eying her speculatively)* You're sure you're not thinking of going out and opening your own office later on?

Mrs. Bird: Nothing at all like that. I just want to sell houses to women. I think I'd understand what a woman wants in a property. Cupboards. Closets. Storage space. The wife has a big say in the choice of a house, right?

Willey: Too big a say, in my opinion.

Mrs. Bird: Besides, I'm kind of an expert on Stoverville. I've had nearly thirty years to watch who's getting married or separated. Who died. Who might be thinking of selling their house or buying one. Give me a try, Sampson. It won't cost you a thing.

Willey: I don't see why I shouldn't; you might bring in some new prospects. Tell you what, come along into the office on Monday, and we'll give it a try.

(Fade out)

ACT TWO

(SCENE 7: About five months has elapsed and it is now early spring. We are at the doorway to the big veranda of the Bird house in bright sunshine. Christine, now about five months pregnant, is at the door, talking to Cousin Stanley.)

Christine: I know she's here some place, Stanley. She just popped in from the office. Come on in and sit down.

(She leads him into the living room. He sits down and Christine goes off in search of her mother. Some changes in the set decor may be made here, to clear away junk and make the room look less cluttered. Mrs. Bird has spoken of moving into an apartment, but now almost half a year has gone by and she is still hanging on in her big old house. The point is not underlined in the dialogue, but the decor might make it quite subtly and agreeably. Cousin Stanley fans himself moodily with a piece of paper he holds in his hand.)

Cousin Stanley: Some nerve she's got. And only a Bird by marriage at that. Never in thirty years. Not till this minute. Never!

(Mrs. Bird enters very briskly.)

Mrs. Bird: Good morning, Stanley, and what can I do for you? Can I sell you a house?

Cousin Stanley: *(angrily)* I'm quite pleased with the house I've got, thank you all the same. I've been living in it since long before *you* ever came here.

Mrs. Bird: It's still heavily mortgaged, isn't it?

Cousin Stanley: How do you know?

Mrs. Bird: It's my business to know.

Cousin Stanley: You know more than you need to know. You never should have got mixed up with Sampson Willey. He's got more twists than a corkscrew. Did he put you up to this? *(He flourishes his piece of paper angrily.)*

Mrs. Bird: This what?

Cousin Stanley: In thirty years I never had a bill from Lawson, and now this. Nine hundred and fifty-seven dollars. I'm disappointed.

Mrs. Bird: Let's be accurate, Stanley. You've been billed every three months for years, at a very modest scale, less than a quarter of what another doctor would charge. It's just that you got into the habit of ignoring them.

Cousin Stanley: Maybe they went to the office and I didn't see them.

Mrs. Bird: They've always been sent to your home. And now I expect you to close the account; otherwise I'll have to take the usual steps.

Cousin Stanley: But half of Stoverville owed Lawson money, and *all* the family.

Mrs. Bird: The family *is* half of Stoverville. I can't write off all those accounts. You aren't related to me except by marriage.

(We see a quick close-up of Christine, who is in the hall listening to this with much pleasure.)

Cousin Stanley: I won't pay. I can't pay.

Mrs. Bird: You'll have to come into court to explain why. I tell you, Stanley, this money is half of what Lawson left me, and I intend to preserve it and pass it on to Christine and her husband. And their children. If you want to know, it was Uncle Lou who advised me to take the matter into court. He paid Lawson's bills the same day he got them.

Cousin Stanley: Very well, I'll pay, but that's the last you'll ever see of me.

(He stomps out of the room, to the front door, flings it open, and leaves. We see bright shafts of sunshine through the wide doorway.)

(SCENE 8: Christine and Mrs. Bird hugging each other in the hallway with sunlight falling on them.)

Christine: Hooray, oh boy, hooray. I've been waiting for that for years. It'll get around, too.

Mrs. Bird: It just wasn't fair, Christine. Your father treated Stanley's family for years and never got paid one cent for his pains. I'll collect that money, you just wait and see.

Christine: Don't worry about passing it on to us, either. Spend it on yourself.

Mrs. Bird: I'd like for you and Jim and your children... *(We see a shot of mother and daughter. We get a strong sense of their resemblance and their love for one another.)* ...to have something from your father and me. Perhaps a down payment on a house....

Christine: Mother, are you trying to sell me a house?

(They are both laughing.)

Mrs. Bird: It would keep the commission in the family.

Christine: I see I can go back to Montreal without worrying. You're going to be all right.

Mrs. Bird: Better than all right. Much, much better than just "all right." I'm going to have my life.

(SCENE 9: A montage sequence of several shots that make up a distinct picture. Brisk "doing-business" music. No dialogue. Only natural sounds of mallet, footsteps, car, voices in distance. We see Mrs. Bird's hands and forearms holding a realtor's sign which says "SAMPSON WILLEY REALTY, STOVERVILLE. FOR SALE." She plants the sign in the ground by its sharpened stake end and pounds the flat end energetically with a mallet. Then we see Mrs. Bird escorting a young couple up the walk of the house in whose front lawn the sign is standing. Then we get a shot of Mrs. Bird sitting at a desk in an office with a typewriter in front of her. She is wearing a hat and picking out letters on the typewriter slowly, then faster, then faster still. Finally we see a car bumping along very quickly over a back road. It turns in to a farmhouse gate, stops, and Mrs. Bird gets out. Passing some stray chickens and the farmhouse dog, she disappears into a barn. She has a second realtor's sign under her arm. In a moment she emerges from the barn with an elderly farmer trotting along behind her.)

(SCENE 10: The office of Willey Realty. There are a couple of desks and filing cabinets. Through an open door we can see a receptionist's desk. General air of modest but consistent success; the office is a small but going concern. Mrs. Solomons is talking with Mrs. Bird.)

Mrs. Solomons: . . . and I got a letter from Sam this morning. He likes it better in Montreal now, but I guess you know all about that because he's Christine's obstetrician. When's the baby due, by the way?

Mrs. Bird: I think about two months.

Mrs. Solomons: Don't you know for sure?

Mrs. Bird: I've been rushed to death in the office. You know, Naomi, there's an awful lot to learn in this business. I've been at it since last fall and I haven't actually closed a sale.

Mrs. Solomons: What, not even one?

Mrs. Bird: Not actually closed one by myself, no, but I've passed my exam, and I'm a certified salesperson.

Mrs. Solomons: When will you start actually earning money?

Mrs. Bird: Pretty soon now, I think. You're the first prospect I've had that looked like really doing business. You don't need that big place any more, now the children are grown up. If I can sell it for you and find you a smaller home, you'll be my first sale, and that'll get me rolling.

Mrs. Solomons: I didn't realize you were counting on us so much. I'm sorry I've taken up so much of your time with looking.

Mrs. Bird: That's what I'm here for, Naomi. Now, let's do some business. What about that town house in the east end? I tell you what, dear, I really think that's the house for you. Perfect for an older couple, and you could always use the second bedroom for a guest room. Suppose I put my hat on, and we go over and take another look.

Mrs. Solomons: I don't need to see it again, Ruth.

Mrs. Bird: Didn't you like it at all?

Mrs. Solomons: Oh, yes, Ben and I both just loved it.

Mrs. Bird: It's perfect for you, in my opinion.

Mrs. Solomons: We're going to take it.

Mrs. Bird: Why, that's marvellous. My first sale. I'll fill out an offer.

Mrs. Solomons: We've already made an offer.

Mrs. Bird: No you haven't. I didn't file an offer for you.

Mrs. Solomons: Well . . . actually . . . Mr. Willey came by on Saturday and talked it over with us. He said there was no point in waiting any longer, so he took us over to the development office and we made an offer on the spot. Twenty-six thousand.

Mrs. Bird: But you were my customer.

Mrs. Solomons: He just pushed us into it.

You'll share the commission, isn't that right?

Mrs. Bird: Not if Sampson writes the offer and handles the closing. I guess I'm right out of it.

Mrs. Solomons: Oh, Ruth, I'm really sorry. I'll have Ben speak to Mr. Willey about the commission.

(SCENE 11: The Willey Realty office, as Mrs. Bird talks to Willey.)

Mrs. Bird: . . . my first customers that looked anywhere ready to buy and you stole them away from me . . . and I've had others not so far along that you took over. I didn't mind at first because I thought you were trying to help me close the deal. But you've never once put my name on the offer. Am I just in the office to find prospects for you? I have to clothe myself, Mr. Willey, please remember that, and run my car and pay for my advertisements. I haven't cost you a cent, and you've made plenty of money from my getting out and digging. I want you to share the commission on the Solomons sale with me.

Willey: You want to know something, Ruth? Ben and Naomi were fed up with being shown house after house. They were ready to deal, but you had them all confused. They'd seen a dozen houses and according to you every one was the best buy in Stoverville.

Mrs. Bird: When I'm showing a house I try to feel it's the best property in town. You told me to do that yourself.

Willey: I know I did, but you haven't got the feel of it yet. You have to make it like a story, like a little play. You have to sense how close the prospect is to a commitment. I've seen you waste two or three days on prospects I knew weren't serious.

Mrs. Bird: But the Solomons were serious and I knew it.

Willey: You were losing them. You were letting them off the hook.

Mrs. Bird: No, I was trying to be—

Willey: Don't interrupt me; let me finish or you'll never be a good real-estate agent. Every sale has its own rhythm and its own pace and story. You have to know exactly when to move in. You've got to sock it to them and make them like it. If you lose the rhythm, you'll lose your confidence and you'll never make the sale.

Mrs. Bird: The fact remains that you stole my client.

Willey: You were *losing* them. In a week they'd have gone to somebody else. I was a pal of Lawson's, sure, but in this office I'm doing business, and I won't let you cost me a chance to do business.

Mrs. Bird: That's heartless. It's mean.

Willey: Ruth, grow up! This isn't your nice big old home on Charleston Road. This is the world!

(We see a close-up of Mrs. Bird.)

Mrs. Bird: It's hard. It's hard.

Willey: Life is hard. Next time I see you backing off on a sale, I'll grab it just the same.

Mrs. Bird: I could take you before the real-estate board.

Willey: They'll tell you exactly what I've just told you. Be careful not to make yourself into a joke.

Mrs. Bird: Right. Right! As long as I'm working out of this office, I'll keep my clients out of your way. If I get a chance to steal any of yours, I'll do it.

Willey: *(big grin on his face)* You're welcome to try, but you haven't got a chance. And if you think I'm crooked, wait till you run up against the other guys in town. They'll skin you alive.

Mrs. Bird: Not after this they won't.

(Fade out)

ACT THREE

(SCENE 12: Jim and Christine's apartment in Montreal. We hear very occasional baby cries and gurglings through this scene. Jim and Christine read over a letter from Mrs. Bird.)

Jim: Quick, what does she say? Where are we going to put her? I was hoping she wouldn't come till we get the baby off the two a.m. feeding. I hate having him in our room.

Christine: He can go into the living room.

Jim: But then it's such a mess in the morning. What does she say?

Christine: *(reading)* "...and I left Willey because he was cheating me over every sale. What a bandit! But Mr. Langbourne was down from London last week, and I talked him into taking me into the Stoverville branch. They have branches all over Ontario, so it looks like a real opportunity. I expect to make my first independent sale this week. You've got to sock it to them and make them swallow it. You can't let them off the hook."

(Jim and Christine stare at each other.)

Jim: That doesn't sound like your mother.

Christine: *(still reading)* "...this man Szekely came to Stoverville about a year ago. There are a number of people from Hungary working up at the plant and all over town. He buys houses and fixes them up for rooming houses and flats and rents them to the Hungarians. I brought him into the office..."

Jim: Doesn't she say anything about the baby?

Christine: Not one word.

Jim: That's not like her either.

Christine: She never used to miss a chance to see us.

(SCENE 13: *A large, modern real-estate office. The office has a wide plate-glass window out front with lettering: "LANGBOURNE ASSOCIATES: REAL ESTATE: MORTGAGES! TORONTO, LONDON, PETERBOROUGH, STOVERVILLE." We should be able to watch mimed action through this window. At the beginning of the scene, however, we are inside the office watching Mrs. Bird on the phone.*)

Mrs. Bird: (*energetically, into the phone*) ... no, no. No! No, I tell you, there's not the slightest use your coming into the office unless you've got some money. It's a waste of both our time.... You do?...Oh, you do?... How much? Where did you get it?...What do you have to pay on it?...What?...You can't carry a second mortgage on your salary.... What? Oh, I see. Yes, if you could arrange that, we might talk business. If he didn't charge you interest. Then you could carry the first mortgage. You could handle it that way, but otherwise we can't do a thing for you. All right. That's right. Call me back.

(*During this speech the office manager, Larry Godfrey, enters. He stands watching Mrs. Bird closely. She waves her pencil back and forth at him as she talks. He speaks when she hangs up.*)

Godfrey: Hitchcock?

Mrs. Bird: He says his grandfather might put up the down payment.

Godfrey: I thought for sure you were wasting your time over the place. It's been listed for two years.

Mrs. Bird: His wife keeps bugging him. She's a friend of my daughter's. She can see the intangibles.

Godfrey: Do you think they'll go for it?

Mrs. Bird: They'll have to get the money from the old man. Then we'll see.

Godfrey: You know, when I was transferred from Toronto I was depressed about it. I didn't know eastern Ontario at all, and no matter how much you go out looking at properties you just can't get to know the region in a couple of years.

Mrs. Bird: I can tell you all you need to know. Before I got into this business, I did nothing but study this town and the people.

Godfrey: If you can make this Hitchcock sale, you'll have me convinced.

Mrs. Bird: That reminds me, I've got to call the trust company about the Hitchcock mortgage. We really should have our own mortgage department.

Godfrey: We do, in Toronto, London, and Peterborough. I guess Mr. Langbourne thinks we aren't quite ready.

Mrs. Bird: We're losing clients that way. Why should the trust company collect interest, instead of us?

Godfrey: Do you think we're doing a big enough volume?

Mrs. Bird: If we aren't now, we soon will be. Anyway, the mortgage department can wait. After I phone the trust, I've got to write up the new Szekely papers. He's going to offer for all three properties in a package deal... (*Cousin Stanley slinks into the office, looking somewhat abashed. Godfrey is clearly not much impressed by his appearance or manner.*) ...Why, hello there, Stanley, have you met our new manager? Mr. Godfrey— Mr. Bird.

Godfrey: How do you do, Mr. Bird. Can we interest you in anything?

Cousin Stanley: Not today, thanks. I'm not in the market. In fact, I'm selling.

(Godfrey smiles politely and exits.)

Mrs. Bird: Did you want to see me about something, Stanley?

Cousin Stanley: *(embarrassed, as well he might be)* The fact is, Ruth, I've got to do something about my mortgage. I've always used the house equity to finance inventory at the showroom, but now the payments have gotten out of hand.

Mrs. Bird: I told you that months ago, Stanley. What you really should do is get rid of that big place and take a low-rent apartment. That would reduce your upkeep costs and expenses close to five hundred a month.

Cousin Stanley: But how would it look?

Mrs. Bird: You can't keep up appearances in bankruptcy court, Stanley. Why don't you put yourself in my hands? I've got an idea about that place of yours. We just might move it to an institution or a funeral director.

Cousin Stanley: No possible way. The zoning forbids it.

Mrs. Bird: The zoning is not a serious problem. *(There is a pause while they eye each other warily.)* Come on now, Stanley, aren't you going to try to sell me a car?

Cousin Stanley: Lawson got a real good deal on the car you've been driving.

Mrs. Bird: I've had good use out of it, Stanley, there's no denying.

Cousin Stanley: Now you need a new car, I hope you'll come to me. I've got a steel-gray demonstrator that would just suit you.

Mrs. Bird: No, I'll tell you what I have in mind. A pick-up.

Cousin Stanley: A pick-up?

Mrs. Bird: An extended-cab pick-up, one of the big ones with the picture rear window and four-wheel drive. I get over some mighty rough back roads. I'll try to work you in on the sale if I can. Maybe you can unload my present car...

(SCENE 14: We are in the Langbourne office quite late at night. Mrs. Bird and Szekely are talking business. There is a single pool of light over the desk Mrs. Bird uses, and we have the sense of plenty of dark space around her. There is a conspiratorial air to the whole scene. It is a key scene, and Mrs. Bird's long speech at the end is the most important speech in the play. The speech should be delivered haltingly, almost dreamily.)

Mrs. Bird: Put your signature there, and there, Andras, and I'll get it into the Seymour office first thing tomorrow. You'll make money on this purchase.

Szekely: I know.

Mrs. Bird: You don't leave much to chance.

Szekely: Chance is a luxury I cannot afford. Long before I tried to get out of Hungary I had funds to my credit in Switzerland. It wasn't easy to transfer the money. One man who carried drafts for me is still in prison. Another has been searching for his wife and children all over Europe for a decade. I try not to leave anything to chance.

Mrs. Bird: You must have seen some very sad things.

Szekely: I have...children starving...men shot for no reason...I won't go on with it, but, you see, I like a little security. Property in my name. Friends who can count on me. I've done well since I came to Canada. I've got tenants ready to fill these houses. *(He indicates the papers he is in process of signing.)* I'll make money while I'm paying for them, and I'll amass more capital for investment. You have to care for yourself in this world; nobody will do it for you.

Mrs. Bird: My husband took pretty good care of me.

Szekely: I've heard he left you only a small inheritance.

Mrs. Bird: It wasn't enough to live on, but it was money. I've been able to add to it. Now it's a respectable sum. I might do something with it in mortgages.

Szekely: You mean you've got between twenty and twenty-five thousand.

Mrs. Bird: A very good guess.

Szekely: I don't guess, Mrs. Bird.

Mrs. Bird: No, I suppose not.

Szekely: Twenty thousand dollars...or a bit more...is not a big sum, but it isn't negligible. There are things one could do with it, maybe by adding it in with other holdings. I'm not a great capitalist myself.

Mrs. Bird: How much have you to spare?

Szekely: Ah, that would be telling...but you are welcome to guess.

Mrs. Bird: Free at this moment and ready to put into new properties? I'd say around thirty-five thousand or a shade more.

(They both laugh; they enjoy each other's company.)

Szekely: That's why I like doing business with you, Ruth. You don't waste time over inessentials. So...what about it?

Mrs. Bird: What about what?

Szekely: Should we go in together? We can do much more with sixty thousand than we could separately. You want to sell me that enormous house of your cousin Stanley, correct?

Mrs. Bird: I think we could do something with the property that Stanley hasn't the initiative to see. It's a perfect location.

Szekely: For a riverfront hotel, perhaps?

Mrs. Bird: And a marina, that's an essential.

Szekely: It would require more capital than I can manage at present. Why not come in with me...as a permanent arrangement?

Mrs. Bird: What sort of arrangement?

Szekely: The usual one. A marriage contract.

Your property would be completely safe-guarded.

Mrs. Bird: You mean you'd like us to get married?

Szekely: It's the best way to manage this affair.

Mrs. Bird: That's very sensible of you, Andras, and very kind.

Szekely: Kindness has very little to do with it.

Mrs. Bird: I think it has. I'll tell you something, Andras, that I wouldn't say to anyone else. Lawson was a very selfish man. Yes, he was. An extremely selfish man. Everybody thought he was a darling, but he had all the life and I had none. I stayed home and listened to the neighbours and all our friends and relations singing his praises...my own family was off at the other end of Ontario and in time they died and I had no family but his...and to them I was always an outsider... *(She takes a bit of a pause here. Camera comes in for a close-up on her face.)* But I'll tell you something strange, Andras. Lawson was selfish and inconsiderate and foolish and improvident, but I loved him. I can't explain that. I just did. *(There should be the feeling of great loneliness and loss in her face here.)* In many ways he was an impossible man; sometimes he didn't seem to know I was a living person...he never talked to me very much. But he wasn't deliberately unkind. He just went ahead and did what he thought was right. He was not a great doctor, but his patients had confidence in him and they mostly got well. They took their life from him, and when they called for him, he always came...and then he was such a kind father. I don't know how it is. A lot of women these days aren't interested in being married; they're afraid of just that kind of servitude. Perhaps rightly. I can't say. When you've been married, the way I was married, it marks you, and you can't do it a second time. I couldn't ever feel married to anybody else, even on a business basis.

Szekely: Very well, if that's how you feel, perhaps we can work out something else almost as suitable.

Mrs. Bird: You're not too upset?

Szekely: *(smiles)* I'm past fifty, Ruth. I've been disappointed before.

(Fade out)

ACT FOUR

(SCENE 15: We open with a shot through the plate-glass window of the Langbourne office, watching Mrs. Bird—in mime—scolding Cousin Stanley energetically. Then we appear to move in through the window to hear their conversation.)

Mrs. Bird: Stanley, Stanley, what's going to become of you? I've told you a thousand times there's nothing to be gained by coming back at me with this. When you owned the house, you had exactly the same opportunity to develop it.

Cousin Stanley: Where would I ever get the money that's gone into renovations and promotion and equipment? Electric signs! You and Szekely cheated me out of the chance, Ruth.

Mrs. Bird: Nonsense! All you ever did with the house was live in it and use it to secure loans. Why, you begged me to sell it for you.

Cousin Stanley: It was your idea to sell it, not mine. Why didn't you ask me to go in with you?

Mrs. Bird: You just said yourself you had no money. It had to be done by somebody like Andras Szekely, with drive and motivation. He's got a gold mine there. "PANNONIA MARINE WONDERLAND. FINE FOOD. OVERNIGHT ACCOMMODATION. MARINA. THOUSAND ISLANDS TOURS..."

Cousin Stanley: There's something else that annoys me. What is this Pannonia stuff, anyway?

Mrs. Bird: That's just the Latin word for Hungary.

Cousin Stanley: Latin, Hungary. I saw a car with an Arkansas plate parked there this morning, and it's your fault. You let that house go out of the family.

Mrs. Bird: Not right out. I'm holding a one-third interest.

Cousin Stanley: Why you lucky... woman!
(He spits this last word out.)

Mrs. Bird: Luck had nothing to do with it; it was planning. Thanks to Andras and me a lot of people will make money out of it. It's just a small operation now, but we're going to put the earnings back into expansion. We'll add another motel wing and increase the overnight accommodation. We'll extend the marina. Maybe in a couple of summers we'll set up our own yacht club.

Cousin Stanley: You've had to cut some pretty sharp corners. I wouldn't want it on my conscience.

Mrs. Bird: You mean the zoning regulations? Why, for years the town has been wailing about low assessments in the east end. Now we're assessed at four times what you were. When we appeared before the zoning committee, they had the good sense to see it— Uncle Lou, Jack Sniderman, and one or two others.

Cousin Stanley: But you did your renovating and applied for a liquor licence *before* you went to city council. How come you were so sure you were going to be rezoned?

Mrs. Bird: Stop acting like a prosecuting attorney, Stanley. I wouldn't do anything wrong, and you know it. All we did was check on what property the councilmen owned. Then we showed them how increased assessment could work for all of us in Stoverville.

Cousin Stanley: What's good for Andras Szekely is good for Stoverville.

Mrs. Bird: There's plenty of truth in that. We could use more like him.

Cousin Stanley: I've never been really fond of strangers.

Mrs. Bird: You're acting mighty tiresome today, Stanley. Did you come in just to gossip and pass backchat?

Cousin Stanley: I came to do business. In some ways, I'm glad you got me out of that house, although I wish I'd been in on the renovation. Still, I've been able to cut back expenses, like you said, and I'm not in the hole I've been in the last couple of years. This year's models are going well... fairly well, anyway.

Mrs. Bird: So now you want to go into a new house, have me find you a top-quality deal, waive my commission, and get you the best possible mortgage terms.

Cousin Stanley: How did you know?

Mrs. Bird: Stanley... Stanley... Stanley...

Cousin Stanley: All right, all right. *(laughing grudgingly)* But will you do it?

Mrs. Bird: I'll tell you what I'm going to do. I'll find you a good solid, small house, nothing undignified—you can count on that—and I'll get you a mortgage that doesn't drive you into the ground.

(She is being quite nice to him. She is very willing to try to get along with people like Stanley. He is rather overwhelmed by this.)

Cousin Stanley: That's thoughtful of you, Ruth, and I appreciate it.

Mrs. Bird: When the time comes for me and Andras to look for fresh capital, if you've got a few thousand you want to risk at that time, I'll work you in, so you won't feel your old house has gone right away from you. *(smiling)* I don't want to cheat you, Stanley, or be your enemy. I just want to be your equal.

(SCENE 16: We are in the Langbourne office. This is Mrs. Bird's big triumphal scene, with plenty of comic undertones. Uncle Lou, Sampson Willey, and Larry Godfrey are in conversation. Office workers are busy in background with typewriters and phones.)

Godfrey: *(to Willey)* Stop peeking at the filing cabinets, Sampson; you'll get nothing out of them.

Willey: What have you got in here now, eight salesmen?

Godfrey: Ten, not counting myself and Ruth Bird. She's technically the office manager. I'm the branch manager, but we both spend most of our time selling. We've got a woman on the switchboard and a couple of clerks, too.

Willey: You must be as big as the other Langbourne branches, right?

Godfrey: Not as big as Toronto or London, but I think we're about even with Peterborough.

Uncle Lou: What is it, three years you've been here now?

Godfrey: We came here just about the time Sampson let Ruth go.

Willey: *(sharply)* I didn't let her go. She quit on me.

Uncle Lou: That makes it four years since Lawson Bird died. It doesn't seem that long.

(Willey keeps prowling around looking at stuff. He spots a wall chart.)

Willey: I was in the boat with him when he died... what's this, your sales graph?

Godfrey: Keeps going up.

Willey: And you're doing mortgage financing, too?

Godfrey: That was Ruth's idea.

Willey: Ruth, Ruth, Ruth. I never thought I'd be coming over here with this. *(He takes an envelope and a scroll from his briefcase.)*

Godfrey: Who's making the presentation?

Willey: *(to Uncle Lou)* You are, you're the mayor.

Godfrey: How does the mayor come into it?

Willey: Well, you have to figure that real estate is tied up with Stoverville's development. The realtors really shape the town, *(giving Uncle Lou a sidelong look)* sometimes in ways you might not expect.

Uncle Lou: *(deliberately)* Like that deal of yours with the supermarket chain from Ottawa.

Godfrey: An occasional stretching doesn't hurt anybody. If you're too inflexible about building regulations, you get a stagnant climate.

(We see Mrs. Bird through the window. She enters the office from the street. She calls as she comes in.)

Mrs. Bird: Okay, if you want to go to lunch, Larry.

Godfrey: I'll just stick around for the ceremony.

Mrs. Bird: *(eying Willey)* What ceremony? What are you doing here, Sampson? At this very moment you're supposed to be in Bert Leventritt's office, telling him the frontage I proposed isn't enough and that you've got a better spot out by Highway 401.

Willey: How do you know?

Mrs. Bird: I just came from there. He said you were coming in at noon. I'm afraid you'll be out of luck there, Sampson. We fixed it up before lunch.

Willey: Well, I'll be... *(There is a pause. The other men try to restrain their laughter.)* I tell you guys, this woman is capable of anything. *(to Mrs. Bird)* I suppose you've got the whole scheme set up by now.

Mrs. Bird: Just about wrapped up.

Willey: *(severely)* Ruth, that was my customer.

Mrs. Bird: Where have I heard that tune before?

Willey: I ought to report you to the grievance committee.

Mrs. Bird: Wouldn't do you a bit of good.

Willey: I know.

Mrs. Bird: *(to Godfrey)* I hope you haven't been letting Sampson snoop around, Larry.

Godfrey: I've been keeping an eye on him.

Uncle Lou: *(hilarious)* Ruthie, you're a terror.

Willey: All right, let's cut out the joking and get on with it.

Mrs. Bird: This is where we really have to watch him, Larry.

Willey: Cut it out, now, or I won't give you the money.

Mrs. Bird: What money? Oh, oh... I see. The award. I'm afraid I haven't been keeping track of the listings lately. Too much on my mind.

Willey: How many times a day does she check them, Larry?

Godfrey: Never more than fifty.

(The three men take a more formal attitude.)

Willey: About what I figured. *(to Mrs. Bird)* You know, I'm president of the real estate board this year, Ruth, and Lou is mayor, so you can see for yourself why we're here. This is the end of the second quarter—April, May, June, the best months of the year. In aggregate sales for this quarter, your name leads all the rest. You're well out in front. Larry is in third spot, and I'm right back of him. We've had our differences, Ruth, and I'll grab your clients whenever I've got the chance... but all the same...

Godfrey: I'm keeping my eye on him from now on, Ruth.

Willey: ...and much as I hate to admit it, you're a born salesman... or should I say salesperson... anyway, whatever, you're it.

Mrs. Bird: Any hard feelings, Sampson?

Willey: Just a few. It's those lost commissions. But as this year's president, I'm here to present you with our bonus-listings award for the second quarter, a cheque for five hundred dollars, and this handsomely lithographed scroll. I'm not going to claim it makes me very happy because it doesn't; it's costing me money. But there it is; you won it.

Mrs. Bird: That speech does you credit, Sampson.

Uncle Lou: *(giving Ruth a hug and a kiss)* At this point I usually say a few words, but I'll

skip it this time. It's five hundred dollars in found money, Ruth, and I hope you spend it on yourself.

Mrs. Bird: I'm so pleased I don't know what to say.

Godfrey: You've got a great future.

Mrs. Bird: Imagine! A fifty-five-year-old widow with a great future.

(SCENE 17: In Jim and Christine's Montreal apartment, Jim watches Christine open a letter. She takes out a small slip of paper.)

Jim: I hope that's what it seems to be.

Christine: It's a cheque, all right . . . for five hundred dollars.

Jim: A present for us? What does she say?

Christine: *(reading the letter)* "Dear kids: I'm sorry I won't get to see you while I'm in Montreal. The convention runs three days and it's taking all my time, and I still haven't met my grandchild. I know it's awful, but these days I have to attend strictly to busi-

ness. Tomorrow night I'm going to dinner at Chez Bardet with Mr. Godfrey, and in the afternoon I'm addressing the convention on the subject of 'The Woman Realtor.' I hope the enclosed cheque will help make my apologies. From now on, I'll be able to help you more than I ever hoped. Meanwhile, take care of yourselves and the baby. Your loving Mom."

(Jim looks hungrily at the cheque.)

Jim: She's in Montreal, and she isn't coming to see us?

Christine: *(a little sadly)* So she says.

Jim: I never heard of such a thing.

(SCENE 18: Mrs. Bird and Godfrey are in a fancy Montreal restaurant. Mrs. Bird wears a very tasteful, obviously expensive, cocktail dress and has a new coiffure. Her clothes have been gradually changing throughout the play. Now she looks wonderful. The whole point of the scene can be made visually.)

Godfrey: *(very confidential, leaning on the heavily laden table)* I could see you were going to be one of the great ones as soon as Langbourne brought you into the office, and there's no reason at all why he should get a cut from everything we do. Have you ever thought of opening your own office? Godfrey and Bird? Or else Bird and Godfrey, if you like that better. We could go a long way together.

Mrs. Bird: Oh no, not you too.

Godfrey: What?

Mrs. Bird: Nothing…nothing…I was thinking out loud.

Godfrey: Let me give you some more wine. *(They drink.)* I never heard a better address than the one you gave this afternoon. I'm going to propose a toast…to future prospects.

Mrs. Bird: *(raising her glass)* To future prospects.

Godfrey: We can take the whole office staff with us. They all feel the same way.

Mrs. Bird: But we won't do anything mean… or disloyal…will we?

Godfrey: I should say not! Here, tell you what we do. There's a good storefront on King Street, just needs a certain amount of paint, plenty of staff room. We'll move in there as soon as we can arrange things…

(His voice fades slowly. The camera moves back as they continue their planning, until we have a wide view of this splendid room.)

(Fade out)

Still Stands the House

Gwen Pharis Ringwood

CHARACTERS

Bruce Warren—a prairie farmer

Ruth Warren—his wife, raised in the town

Hester Warren—his sister, devoted to the family homestead

Arthur Manning—an agent who wants to buy the Warren farm

"We could always stand alone, the three of us."

(Scene—a living room.

The icy wind of a northern blizzard sweeps across the prairie, lashes about the old Warren farmhouse, and howls insistently at the door and windows. But the Warren house was built to withstand the menace of the Canadian winter and scornfully suffers the storm to shriek about the chimney corner, to knock at the door and rattle the windows in a wild attempt to force an entrance.

The living room of this house has about it a faded austerity, a decayed elegance that is as remote and cheerless as a hearth in which no fire is ever laid. The room has made a stern and solemn pact with the past. Once it held the warm surge of life; but as the years have gone by, it has settled in a rigid pattern of neat, uncompromising severity.

As if in defiance of the room, the frost has covered the window in the rear wall with a wild and exotic design. Beside the window is an imposing leather armchair, turned toward the handsome coal stove in the right corner. A footstool is near the chair. A door at the centre of the rear wall leads to the snow-sheeted world outside. Along the left wall, between a closed door to the bedroom (now unused) and

an open door to a kitchen, is a mahogany sideboard. Above it is a portrait of old Martin Warren, who built this house and lived in it until his death. The portrait is of a stern and handsome man in his early fifties, and in the expression of the eyes the artist has caught something of his unconquerable will.

An open staircase, winding to the bedrooms upstairs, extends into the room at right. There is a rocking chair by the stove with a small table beside it. A mahogany dining table and two matching chairs are placed at a convenient distance from the sideboard and the kitchen door. The figured wallpaper is cracked and faded. The dark rug, the heavy curtains, and the tablecloth show signs of much wear, but there is nothing of cheapness about them.

Two coal-oil lanterns have been left beside the kitchen door. Blooming bravely on the table, in contrast to its surroundings, is a pot of lavender hyacinths.

Ruth Warren is standing near the outside door, talking to Arthur Manning, who is about to leave. Ruth is small, fair-haired, and pretty, twenty-five or twenty-six years of age. There is more strength in her than her rather delicate appearance would indicate. She wears a soft blue housedress, with a light wool cardigan over it. Manning is a middle-aged man of prosperous appearance. He wears a heavy overcoat over a dark business suit. His hat, gloves, and scarf are on the armchair.)

Ruth: Do you think you'd better try to go back tonight, Mr. Manning? The roads may be drifted.

Manning: It's a bad blizzard, all right, but I don't think I'll have any trouble. There's a heater in the car, and I've just had the engine checked over.

Ruth: You'll be welcome if you care to spend the night.

Manning: Thank you, but I'm afraid I've got to get back to town. I'd hate to try it in an old car, but this one of mine can pull through anything.

Ruth: I've never seen a storm come up so quickly.

Manning: These prairie blizzards are no joke. One of my sheepherders got lost in one last year, just half a mile from the house. He froze to death out there trying to find his way.

Ruth: How frightful!

Manning: One of the ranch hands found him the next morning. Poor old fellow—he'd herded for me for twenty years. I never knew how he came to be out in a storm like that.

Ruth: They say when a person gets lost he begins to go round in a circle, although it seems straight ahead.

Manning: Yes, I've always heard that. The winters are the one thing I've got against this country.

Ruth: *(wistfully)* I used to like them in town. We went skating on the river and tobogganing. But out here it's different.

Manning: If Bruce sells the farm and takes this irrigated place near town, you won't notice the winter so much, Mrs. Warren.

Ruth: No. I hope he does take your offer, Mr. Manning. I want him to.

Manning: He'll never get a better. Five thousand dollars and an irrigated quarter is a good price for a dryland farm these days.

Ruth: If only we didn't have to decide so soon.

Manning: I talked it all over with Bruce in town a couple of weeks ago, and I think he's pretty well made up his mind. All he needs to do is sign the papers.

Ruth: I thought he'd have until spring to decide.

Manning: I've got orders to close the deal before I go south next week. You tell Bruce I'll come by tomorrow or the next day, and we can get it all settled.

Ruth: I'll tell him. I hope he does take it, Mr. Manning.

Manning: I know you do and you're right. I think all he needs is a little persuading. He's had a hard time here these dry years.

Ruth: I don't know what Hester will say.

Manning: I understand she's very much attached to the place. Is it true that she never leaves the farm?

Ruth: Not often.

Manning: She'd be better off where she could get out more.

Ruth: I don't know.

Manning: I suppose all those years out here, keeping house for Bruce and her father, were pretty hard on her.

Ruth: The house has come to mean so much to her. But maybe she won't mind. *(smiling hopefully)* We'll see.

(The door to the bedroom, left, is opened quietly, and Hester Warren enters the room. She closes and locks the door behind her and stands looking at the two in the room with cold surmise. Hester is forty years old. She is tall, dark, and unsmiling. The stern rigidity of her body, the bitter austerity of her mouth, and the almost arrogant dignity of her carriage seem to make her a part of the room she enters. There is bitter resentment in her dark eyes as she confronts Ruth and Manning. She holds a leather-

bound Bible close to her breast.)

Ruth: *(startled)* Why, Hester! I thought you never unlocked that door.

Hester: *(quietly)* No. I keep Father's room as it was.

Ruth: Then why were you—

Hester: I was reading in Father's room. I heard a stranger.

Ruth: You know Mr. Manning, Hester.

Manning: *(with forced friendliness)* I don't suppose you remember me, Miss Warren.

Hester: *(without moving)* How do you do?

Manning: *(embarrassed at her coldness and anxious to get away)* Well, I'll be getting on home. I'll leave these papers for Bruce to sign, Mrs. Warren. Tell him I'll come by tomorrow. He'll find it's all there, just as we talked about it. *(He lays the document on the table.)*

Ruth: Thank you, Mr. Manning.

Manning: *(turning to go)* Take care of yourselves. Good night. *(to Hester)* Good night, Miss Warren.

(Hester barely nods.)

Ruth: You're sure you ought to try it in the storm?

Manning: Sure. There's no danger if I go right away. *(He goes out.)*

Ruth: *(calling after him as she shuts the door)* Good night.

(Hester watches Manning out and, as Ruth returns, she looks at her suspiciously. There is a silence which Hester finally breaks.)

Hester: What did he want here?

Ruth: *(uncomfortable under Hester's scrutiny)* He just left some papers for Bruce to look over, Hester. He was in a hurry so he didn't wait to see Bruce.

Hester: I see. What has Arthur Manning got to do with Bruce?

Ruth: It's something to do with the farm, Hester. I'll put these away. *(She starts to take up*

the document on the table, but Hester is before her.)

Hester: *(after a long look at the document)* A deed of sale. *(turning angrily upon Ruth)* So this is what you've been hiding from me.

Ruth: *(quickly)* Oh, no! Nothing's settled, Hester. Mr. Manning made an offer and Bruce wants to think it over. That's all.

Hester: *(her eyes betraying her intense agitation)* Bruce isn't going to sell this place!

Ruth: It's just an offer. Nothing has been decided.

Hester: Your hand's in this! You've been after him to leave here.

Ruth: *(trying to conciliate her)* Let's not quarrel. You can talk to Bruce about it, Hester.

Hester: You hate this house, I know that.

Ruth: No. *(facing Hester firmly)* But I think Bruce ought to sell.

Hester: You married him. You made your choice.

Ruth: *(quietly)* I've not regretted that. It's just that we're so cut off and lonely here; and this is the best offer we could get. But let me put these away. *(indicating the deed of sale)* We'll talk about it later, the three of us.

Hester: *(allowing Ruth to take the papers)* You may as well burn them. He isn't going to sell.

Ruth: Please, Hester—we'll discuss it when Bruce comes. *(She places the document on the sideboard, then crosses to the stove.)* I'll build up the fire.

Hester: *(takes the Bible to the sideboard and places it under her father's portrait. She stands looking up at the portrait.)* This house will not be sold. I won't allow it.

Ruth: *(puts some coal on the fire and shivers)* It's so cold it almost frightens me. The thermometer has dropped ten degrees within the hour.

Hester: I hope Bruce knows enough to get the stock in. They'll freeze where they stand if they're left out tonight. *(She moves to the* *window and takes her knitting from the ledge.)*

Ruth: He'll have them in. *(crossing to the table)* Look, Hester, how the hyacinths have bloomed. I could smell them when I came in the room just now.

Hester: Hyacinths always seem like death to me.

Ruth: *(her voice young and vibrant)* Oh, no. They're birth, they're spring! They say in Greece you find them growing wild in April. *(She takes an old Wedgwood bowl from the sideboard, preparing to set the pot of hyacinths in it.)*

Hester: *(in a dry, unfriendly tone)* I've asked you not to use that Wedgwood bowl. It was my grandmother's. I don't want it broken.

Ruth: I'm sorry. *(Replacing the bowl, she gets a plain one from inside the sideboard.)* I thought the hyacinths would look so pretty in it, but I'll use the plain one.

Hester: You've gone to as much trouble for that plant as if it were a child. *(Hester sits in the rocking chair by the stove.)*

Ruth: *(placing the hyacinths in the bowl)* They're so sweet. I like to touch them.

Hester: They'll freeze tonight, I'm thinking.

Ruth: Not in here. We'll have to keep the fire up anyway. *(Leaving the bowl of hyacinths on the table, Ruth returns to the sideboard, taking some bright chintz from the drawer. She holds it up for Hester to see.)* I've almost finished the curtains, Hester.

Hester: *(tonelessly)* You have?

Ruth: Don't you think they'll make this room more cheerful?

Hester: The ones we have seem good enough to me.

Ruth: But they're so old.

Hester: *(coldly)* Old things have beauty when you've eyes to see it. That velvet has a richness that you can't buy now.

Ruth: *(moving to the window)* I want to make the room gay and happy for spring. You'll see how much difference these will make.

Hester: I've no doubt. *(Hester rises and goes to the table to avoid looking at the curtains.)*

Ruth: *(measuring the chintz with the curtains at the window)* I wonder if I have them wide enough. *(The wind rises. As if the sound had quelled her pleasure in the bright curtains, Ruth turns slowly away from the window. A touch of hysteria creeps into her voice.)* The wind swirls and shrieks and raises such queer echoes in this old house! It seems to laugh at us in here, thinking we're safe, hugging the stove! As if it knew it could blow out the light and the fire and— (getting hold of herself)* I've never seen a blizzard when it was as cold as this. Have you, Hester?

Hester: *(knitting)* Bruce was born on a night like this.

(Throughout this scene Hester seldom looks at Ruth but gives all her attention to her knitting. She seems reluctant to talk and yet impelled to do so.)

Ruth: I didn't know.

Hester: Father had to ride for the doctor while I stayed here with Mother.

Ruth: Alone?

Hester: Yes. I was rubbing Father's hands with snow when we heard the baby crying. Then we helped the doctor bathe him.

Ruth: You were such a little girl to do so much.

Hester: After Mother died I did it all.

Ruth: I know, but it was too hard for a child. I don't see how you managed.

Hester: Father always helped me with the washing.

Ruth: Not many men would stay in from the field to do that.

Hester: No. *(Her knitting drops to her lap, and for a moment she is lost in the past.)* "We'll have to lean on one another now, Daughter." Those were his words. And that's the way it was. I was beside him until—I never left him.

Ruth: *(at Hester's side)* You've never talked of him like this before.

Hester: *(unconscious of Ruth)* He always liked the snow. *(Her eyes are on the portrait of her father.)* He called it a moving shroud, a winding sheet that the wind lifts and raises and lets fall again.

Ruth: It is like that.

Hester: He'd come in and say, "The snow lies deep on the summer fallow, Hester. That means a good crop next year."

Ruth: I know. It's glorious in the fall with the wheat like gold on the hills. No wonder he loved it.

Hester: *(called out of her dream and abruptly resuming her knitting)* There hasn't been much wheat out there these last years.

Ruth: That isn't Bruce's fault, Hester.

Hester: You have to love a place to make things grow. The land knows when you don't care about it, and Bruce doesn't care about it any more. Not like Father did.

Ruth: *(her hands raised to touch the portrait above the sideboard)* I wish I'd known your father.

Hester: *(rising and facing Ruth with a sudden and terrible anger)* Don't touch that picture. It's mine.

Ruth: *(startled, she faces Hester)* Why, Hester—

Hester: Can't I have anything of my own? Must you put your fingers on everything I have?

Ruth: *(moving to Hester)* Hester, you know I didn't mean—What is the matter with you?

Hester: I won't have you touch it.

Ruth: *(gently)* Do you hate my being here so much?

Hester: *(turning away)* You've more right here than I have now, I suppose.

Ruth: *(crossing over to the stove)* You make me feel that I've no right at all.

Hester: *(a martyr now)* I'm sorry if you don't approve my ways. I can go, if that's what you want.

Ruth: *(pleading)* Please—I've never had a sister, and when Bruce told me he had one, I thought we'd be such friends—

Hester: *(sitting in the chair by the stove)* We're not a family to put words to everything we feel. *(She resumes her knitting.)*

Ruth: *(trying to bridge the gulf between them)* I get too excited over things: I know it. Bruce tells me I sound affected when I say too much about the way I feel, the way I like people—or the sky in the evening. I—

Hester: *(without looking up)* Did you get the separator put up? Or shall I do it?

Ruth: *(discouraged, turning away and sitting down at the table with her sewing)* It's ready for the milk when Bruce brings it. I put it together this morning.

Hester: The lanterns are empty.

Ruth: I'll fill them in a minute.

Hester: When I managed this house, I always filled the lanterns right after supper. Then they were ready.

Ruth: *(impatiently)* I said I'd fill them, Hester, and I will. They're both there in the corner. *(She indicates the lanterns at the end of the sideboard.)*

Hester: Bruce didn't take one, then?

Ruth: No.

Hester: You'd better put a lamp in the window.

Ruth: *(lights a small lamp on the sideboard and takes it to the window)* I wish he'd come. It's strange how women feel safer when their men are near, close enough to touch, isn't it? No matter how strong you think you are. *(As she speaks, Ruth drapes some of the chintz over the armchair.)*

Hester: I can't say that I need my strength from Bruce, or could get it if I needed it.

Ruth: That's because he's still a little boy to you. *(A pause. Then Ruth speaks hesitantly.)* Hester—

Hester: Yes?

Ruth: Will you mind the baby in the house?

Hester: *(after a silence, constrainedly)* No, I won't mind. I'll keep out of the way.

Ruth: *(warmly, commanding a response)* I don't want you to. You'll love him, Hester.

Hester: *(harshly)* I loved Bruce, but I got no thanks for it. He feels I stand in his way now.

Ruth: *(suddenly aware that Hester has needed and wanted love)* You mustn't say that. It isn't true.

Hester: When he was little, after Mother died, he'd come tugging at my hand—He'd get hold of my little finger and say, "Come, Hettie—come and look." Everything was "Hettie" then.

Ruth: *(eagerly, moving to Hester)* It will be like that again. This baby will be almost like your own.

Hester: *(as if Ruth's words were an implied reproach)* I could have married, and married well if I'd had a mind to.

Ruth: I know that. I've wondered why you didn't, Hester.

Hester: The young men used to ride over here on Sunday, but I stopped that. *(a pause)* I never saw a man I'd let touch me. Maybe you don't mind that kind of thing. I do.

Ruth: *(involuntarily; it is a cry)* No! *(attempting to put her arms around Hester)* What hurt you?

Hester: *(rising)* Don't try your soft ways on me. *(She moves behind the armchair; her hand falls caressingly on the back of the chair.)* I couldn't leave Bruce and Father alone. My duty was here in this house. So I stayed. *(Hester notices the chintz material draped over the chair and, taking it up, turns to Ruth angrily.)* What do you intend to do with this?

Ruth: I thought—there's enough left to make covers for the chair to match the curtains—

Hester: *(throwing the chintz down)* This is Father's chair. I won't have it changed.

Ruth: I'm sorry, Hester. *(with spirit)* Must we keep everything the same forever?

Hester: There's nothing in this house that isn't good, that wasn't bought with care and pride by one of us who loved it. This stuff is cheap and gaudy.

Ruth: It isn't dull and falling apart with age.

Hester: Before my father died, when he was ill, he sat here in this chair where he could see them threshing from the window. It was the first time since he came here that he'd not been in the fields at harvest. Now you come—you who never knew him, who never saw him—and you won't rest until—

Ruth: Hester!

Hester: You've got no right to touch it! *(Her hands grip the back of the old chair as she stands rigid, her eyes blazing.)*

(Bruce Warren enters from outside, carrying a pail of milk. He is tall and dark, about thirty years old, sensitive and bitter. His vain struggle to make the farm pay since his father's death has left him with an oppressive sense of failure. He is proud and quick to resent an imagined reproach. He has dark hair, his shoulders are a little stooped, and he moves restlessly and abruptly. Despite his moodiness, he is extremely likable. He is dressed warmly in dark trousers, a sweater under his heavy leather coat; he wears gloves, cap, and high boots. He brushes the snow from his coat as he enters.)

Bruce: *(carrying the milk into the kitchen)* Is the separator up, Ruth?

Ruth: Yes, it's all ready, Bruce. Wait, I'll help you. *(She follows him into the kitchen.)*

(Hester stands at the chair a moment after they have gone; her eyes fall on the table. Slowly she goes toward it, as if drawn by something she hates. She looks down at the lavender blooms for a moment. Then with a quick, angry gesture, she crushes one of the stalks. She turns away and is winding up her wool when Bruce and Ruth return.)

Ruth: You must be frozen.

Bruce: *(taking off his coat and gloves)* I'm cold, all right. God, it's a blizzard: thirty-eight below, and a high wind. *(He throws his coat over a chair at the table.)*

Ruth: *(with pride)* Did you see the hyacinths? They've bloomed since yesterday.

Bruce: *(smiling)* Yes, they're pretty. *(Touching them, he notices the broken stalk.)* Looks like one of them's broken.

Ruth: Where? *(She sees it.)* Oh, it is! And that one hadn't bloomed yet! I wonder—it wasn't broken when I— *(Ruth turns accusingly to Hester)* Hester!

Hester: *(returning Ruth's look calmly and responding coldly)* Yes?

Ruth: Hester, did you—

Bruce: *(going over to the fire)* Oh, Ruth, don't make such a fuss about it. It can't be helped.

Hester: I'll take care of the milk. *(She takes the small lamp from the window.)*

Ruth: I'll do it.

Hester: *(moving toward the kitchen)* You turn the separator so slow the cream's as thin as water.

Ruth: *(stung to reply)* That's not true. You never give me a chance to—

Bruce: *(irritably)* For God's sake, don't quarrel about it. *(He sits in the chair by the stove.)*

Hester: I don't intend to quarrel. *(She goes into the kitchen.)*

(Ruth follows Hester to the door. The sound of the separator comes from the kitchen. Ruth turns wearily, takes up the pot of hyacinths, and places them on the stand near the stove. Then she sits on the footstool.)

Ruth: It's always that way.

Bruce: *(gazing moodily at the stove)* Why don't you two try to get along?

(a silence)

Ruth: Did you put the stock in? *(The question is merely something to fill the empty space of silence between them.)*

Bruce: Yes. That black mare may foal tonight. I'll have to look at her later on.

Ruth: It's bitter weather for a little colt to be born.

Bruce: Yes.

(Another silence. Finally Ruth, to throw off the tension between them, gets up and moves her footstool over to his chair.)

Ruth: I'm glad you're here. I've been lonesome for you.

Bruce: *(putting his hand on hers)* I'm glad to be here.

Ruth: I thought of you out at the barn, trying to work in this cold.

Bruce: I was all right. I'd hate to walk far tonight, though. You can't see your hand before your face.

Ruth: *(after a look at the kitchen)* Hester's been so strange again these last few days, Bruce.

Bruce: I know it's hard, Ruth.

Ruth: It's like it was when I first came here. At everything I touch, she cries out like I'd hurt her somehow.

Bruce: Hester has to do things her own way. She's always been like that.

Ruth: If only she could like me a little. I think she almost does sometimes, but then—

Bruce: You think too much about her.

Ruth: Maybe it's because we've been shut in so close. I'm almost afraid of her lately.

Bruce: She's not had an easy life, Ruth.

Ruth: I know that. She talked about your father almost constantly today.

Bruce: His death hit us both hard. Dad ran the farm, decided everything.

Ruth: It's been six years, Bruce.

Bruce: There are things you don't count out by years.

Ruth: He wouldn't want you to go on remembering forever.

Bruce: *(looking at the floor)* No.

Ruth: You should get free of this house. It's not good for you to stay here. It's not good for Hester. *(Getting up, she crosses to the sideboard and returns with the deed of sale, which she hands to Bruce.)* Mr. Manning left this for you. He's coming back tomorrow for it, when you've signed it.

Bruce: *(takes the papers, annoyed by her assurance)* He doesn't need to get so excited. I haven't decided to sign yet. He said he wouldn't need to know till spring. *(He goes over to the lamp at the table and studies the document.)*

Ruth: His company gave him orders to close the deal this week or let it go.

Bruce: This week?

Ruth: That's what he said.

Bruce: Well, I'll think about it.

Ruth: You'll have to decide tonight, Bruce. No one else will offer you as much. Five thousand dollars and an irrigated farm a mile from town seems a good price.

Bruce: I'm not complaining about the deal. It's fair.

Ruth: *(urgently)* You're going to take it, aren't you, Bruce?

Bruce: I don't know. God, I don't know. *(He throws the document on the table.)* I don't want to sell, Ruth. I think I'll try it another year.

Ruth: Bruce, you've struggled here too long now. You haven't had a crop, a good crop, in five years.

Bruce: I need to be told that!

Ruth: It's not your fault. But you've told me you ought to give it up, that it's too dry here.

Bruce: We may get a crop this year. We're due for one.

Ruth: If you take this offer, we'll be nearer town. We'll have water on the place. We can have a garden and trees growing.

Bruce: That's about what those irrigated farms are—gardens.

Ruth: And, Bruce, it wouldn't be so lonely there, so cruelly lonely.

Bruce: I told you how it was before you came.

Ruth: *(resenting his tone)* You didn't tell me you worshipped a house. That you made a god of a house and a section of land. You didn't tell me that!

Bruce: *(angrily)* You didn't tell me that you'd moon at a window for your old friends, either. *(He stands up and throws the deed of sale on the table.)*

Ruth: How could I help it here?

Bruce: And you didn't tell me you'd be afraid of having a child. What kind of a woman are you that you don't want your child?

Ruth: That's not true.

Bruce: No? You cried when you knew, didn't you?

Ruth: Bruce!

Bruce: *(going blindly on)* What makes you feel the way you do, then? Other women have children without so much fuss. Other women are glad.

Ruth: *(intensely angry)* Don't speak to me like that. Keep your land. Eat and sleep and dream land, I don't care!

Bruce: *(turning to the portrait of his father)* My father came out here and took a homestead. He broke the prairie with one plough and a team of horses. He built a house to live in out of the sod. You didn't know that, did you? He and Mother lived here in a sod shanty and struggled to make things grow. Then they built a one-room shack; and when the good years came, they built this house. The finest in the country! I thought my son would have it.

Ruth: *(moving to him)* What is there left to give a son? A house that stirs with ghosts! A piece of worn-out land where the rain never comes.

Bruce: That's not all. I don't suppose you can understand.

Ruth: *(turning away from him, deeply hurt)* No. I don't suppose I can. You give me little chance to know how you feel about things.

Bruce: *(his anger gone)* Ruth, I didn't mean that. But you've always lived in town. *(He goes to the window and stands looking out for a moment, then turns.)* Those rocks along the fence out there, I picked up every one of them with my own hands and carried them with my own hands across the field and piled them there. I've ploughed that southern slope along the coulee every year since I was twelve. *(His voice is torn with a kind of shame for his emotions.)* I feel about the land like Hester does about the house, I guess. I don't want to leave it. I don't want to give it up.

Ruth: *(gently)* But it's poor land, Bruce.

(Bruce sits down, gazing gloomily at the fire. Hester comes in from the kitchen with a small lamp and places it on the sideboard. Then she sits at the table, taking up her knitting. As Bruce speaks, she watches him intently.)

Bruce: Yes, it's strange that in a soil that won't grow trees a man can put roots down, but he can.

Ruth: *(at his side)* You'd feel the same about another place, after a little while.

Bruce: I don't know. When I saw the wind last spring blowing the dirt away, the dirt I'd ploughed and harrowed and sowed to grain, I felt as though a part of myself was blowing away in the dust. Even now, with the land three feet under snow, I can look out and feel it waiting for the seed I've saved for it.

Ruth: But if we go, we'll be nearer other people, not cut off from everything that lives.

Bruce: You need people, don't you?

Hester: Yes. She needs them. I've seen her at the window looking toward the town. Day after day she stands there.

(Bruce and Ruth, absorbed in the conflict between them, had forgotten Hester's presence.

At Hester's words, Ruth turns on them both, flaming with anger.)

Ruth: You two. You're so *perfect!*

Hester: *(knitting)* We could always stand alone, the three of us. We didn't need to turn to every stranger who held his hand out.

Ruth: No! You'd sit in this husk of a house, living like shadows, until these four walls closed in on you, buried you.

Hester: I never stood at a window, looking down the road that leads to town.

Ruth: *(the pent-up hysteria of the day and the longing of months breaking through, tumbling out in her words)* It's not for myself I look down that road, Hester. It's for the child I'm going to have. You're right, Bruce, I am afraid. It's not what you think, though, not for myself. You two and your father lived so long in this dark house that you forgot there's a world beating outside, forgot that people laugh and play sometimes. And you've shut me out! *(There is a catch in her voice.)* I never would have trampled on your thoughts if you'd given them to me. But as it is, I might as well not be a person. You'd like a shadow better that wouldn't touch your house. A child would die here. A child can't live with shadows.

Bruce: *(much disturbed, rising and going to her)* Ruth! I didn't know you hated it so much.

Ruth: I thought it would change. I thought I could change it. You know now.

Bruce: *(quietly)* Yes.

Ruth: *(pleading)* If we go, I'll *want* this child, Bruce. Don't you see? But I'm not happy here. What kind of a life will our child have? He'll be old before he's out of school. *(She looks at the hyacinth on the stand.)* He'll be like this hyacinth that's broken before it bloomed.

Bruce: *(going to the table and looking down at the deed of sale, his voice tired and flat, but resolved)* All right. I'll tell Manning I'll let him have the place.

Hester: *(turning quickly to Bruce)* What do you mean?

Bruce: I'm going to sell the farm to Manning. He was here today.

Hester: *(standing up, her eyes blazing)* You can't sell this house.

Bruce: *(looking at the deed of sale)* Oh, Ruth's right. We can't make a living on the place. *(He sits down, leafing through the document.)* It's too dry. And too far from school.

Hester: It wasn't too far for you to go, or me.

Bruce: *(irritably)* Do you think I want to sell?

Hester: *She* does. But she can't do it. *(Her voice is low.)* This house belongs to me.

Bruce: Hester, don't start that again! I wish to God the land had been divided differently, but it wasn't.

Hester: Father meant for us to stay here and keep things as they were when he was with us.

Bruce: The soil wasn't blowing away when he was farming it.

Hester: He meant for me to have the house.

Ruth: You'll go with us where we go, Hester.

Hester: *(to Ruth)* You came here. You plotted with him to take this house from me. But it's mine!

Bruce: *(his voice cracking through the room)* Stop that, Hester! I love this place as much as you do, but I'm selling it. I'm selling it, I tell you. *(As he speaks, he gets up abruptly and, taking up his coat, puts it on. Hester sinks slowly into the chair, staring. Ruth tries to put her hand on Bruce's arm.)*

Ruth: Bruce! Not that way! Not for me. If it's that way, I don't care enough.

Bruce: *(shaking himself free)* Oh, leave me alone!

Ruth: Bruce!

Bruce: *(going to the door)* I'll be glad when it's over, I suppose.

Ruth: Where are you going?

Bruce: *(taking his cap and gloves)* To look at that mare.

Ruth: Bruce!

(But he has gone. Hester gets up, goes to her father's chair, and stands behind it, facing Ruth; she moves and speaks as if she were in a dream.)

Hester: This is my house. I won't have strangers in it.

Ruth: *(at the table, without looking at Hester)* Oh, Hester! I didn't want it to be this way. I tried—

Hester: *(as if she were speaking to a stranger)* Why did you come here?

Ruth: I've hurt you. But I'm right about this. I know I'm right.

Hester: There isn't any room for you.

Ruth: Can't you see? It's for all of us. *(Hester comes toward Ruth with a strange, blazing anger in her face.)*

Hester: I know your kind. You tempted him with your bright hair.

Ruth: Hester!

Hester: Your body anointed with jasmine for his pleasure.

Ruth: Hester, don't say such things!

Hester: Oh, I know what you are! You and women like you. You put a dream around him with your arms, a sinful dream.

Ruth: *(drawing back)* Hester!

Hester: You lift your white face to every stranger like you offered him a cup to drink from. *(Turning from Ruth, as if she had forgotten her presence, Hester looks fondly at the room.)* I'll never leave this house.

Bruce: *(opens the door and comes in quickly and stormily. He goes into the kitchen as he speaks.)* That mare's got out. She jumped the corral. I'll have to go after her.

Ruth: *(concerned)* Bruce, where will she be?

Bruce: *(returning with an old blanket)* She'll be in the snowshed by the coulee. She always goes there when she's about to foal.

(Hester sits in the chair by the stove, her knitting in her hand. She pays no attention to the others.)

Ruth: But you can't go after her in this storm.

Bruce: I'll take this old blanket to cover the colt, if it's born yet. Where's the lantern? *(He sees the two lanterns by the kitchen door and, taking one of them to the table, lights it.)*

Ruth: It's three miles, Bruce. You mustn't go on foot. It's dangerous.

Bruce: I'll have to. She'd never live through the night, or the colt either. *(He turns to go.)* You'd better go to bed. Good night, Hester.

Ruth: Let me come with you.

Bruce: No. *(Then, as he looks at her, all resentment leaves him. He puts down the lantern, goes to her, and takes her in his arms.)* Ruth, forget what I said. You know I didn't mean—

Ruth: *(softly)* I said things I didn't mean, too—

Bruce: I love you, Ruth. You know it, don't you?

Ruth: Bruce!

(He kisses her, and for a moment their love is a flame in the room.)

Bruce: Don't worry. I won't be long.

Ruth: I'll wait.

(Bruce goes out. Ruth follows him to the door, and, as it closes, she stands against it for a moment. There is a silence. Hester is slowly unravelling her knitting but is unaware of it. The black wool falls in spirals about her chair.)

Hester: *(suddenly)* It's an old house. I was born here. *(then in a strange, calm voice that seems to come from a long distance)* You shouldn't let Bruce be so much alone. You lose him that way. He comes back to us then. He'll see you don't belong here unless you keep your hand on him all the time. *(Ruth looks curiously at Hester but does not give her all her attention. Hester suddenly becomes harsh.)* This is my house. You can't

change it. *(Ruth starts to say something but remains silent.)* Father gave it to me. There isn't any room for you. *(in a high, childlike tone, like the sound of a violin string breaking)* No room. *(She shakes her head gravely.)*

Ruth: *(aware that something is wrong)* Hester—

Hester: *(as if she were telling an often-recited story to a stranger)* I stayed home when Mother died and kept house for my little brother and my father. *(Her voice grows stronger.)* I was very beautiful, they said. My hair fell to my knees, and it was black as a furrow turned in spring. *(proudly)* I can have a husband any time I want, but my duty is here with Father. You see how it is. I can't leave him.

Ruth: *(going quickly to Hester and speaking with anxiety and gentleness)* Hester, what are you talking about?

Hester: That's Father's chair. I'll put his Bible out. *(She starts from her chair.)*

Ruth: *(preventing her)* Hester, your father's not here—not for six years. You speak of him as if you thought—Hester—

Hester: *(ignoring Ruth but remaining seated)* When I was a girl I always filled the lanterns after supper. Then I was ready for his coming.

Ruth: *(in terror)* Hester, I didn't fill them! I didn't fill the lanterns! *(She runs to the kitchen door and takes up the remaining lantern.)*

Hester: *(calmly)* Father called me the wise virgin then.

Ruth: Hester, Bruce took one! He thought I'd filled them. It will burn out and he'll be lost in the blizzard.

Hester: I always filled them.

Ruth: *(setting the lantern on the table)* I've got to go out after Bruce. If he gets down to the coulee and the lantern goes out, he'll never find the way back. I'll have to hurry! Where's the coal oil?

(Ruth goes to the kitchen and returns with a can of coal oil and pair of galoshes. Hester watches her closely. As Ruth comes in with the oil, Hester slowly rises and goes to her.)

Hester: I'll fill the lantern for you, Ruth.

Ruth: *(trying to remove the top of the can)* I can't get the top off. My hands are shaking so.

Hester: *(taking the oil can from Ruth)* I'll fill it for you.

Ruth: Please, Hester. While I get my things on! *(Giving Hester the oil can, Ruth runs to the footstool and hurriedly puts on her galoshes.)* I'm afraid that lantern will last just long enough to get him out there. He'll be across the field before I even get outside. *(She runs up the stairs.)*

Hester: *(standing motionless, the oil can in her hand)* You're going now. That's right. I told you you should go.

(Ruth disappears up the stairs. Hester moves a step towards the lantern, taking off the top of the coal-oil can. She hesitates and looks for a long moment after Ruth. With the strange lucidity of madness, slowly, deliberately, she places the top back again on the can and, moving behind the table, sets it on the floor without filling the lantern. Ruth hurries down the stairs excited and alarmed. She has on heavy clothes and is putting on her gloves.)

Ruth: Is it ready? *(Hester nods.)* Will you light it for me, Hester? Please. *(Hester lights the lantern.)* I'll put the light at the window. *(She crosses with the small lamp and places it at the window.)* Hurry, Hester! *(with a sob)* Oh, if only I can find him!

(Hester crosses to Ruth and gives her the lantern. Ruth takes the lantern and goes out. A gust of wind carries the snow into the room and blows shut the door after her. Hester goes to the window.)

Hester: *(her voice like an echo)* The snow lies deep on the summer fallow—the snow is a moving shroud—a winding sheet that the wind lifts and raises and lets fall again. *(turning from the window)* They've gone. They won't be back now. *(With an intense excitement, Hester blows out the lamp at the window and pulls down the shades. Her eyes fall on the bowl of hyacinths in the corner. Slowly she goes to it, takes it up, and, holding it away from her, carries it to the door. Opening the door, she sets the flowers outside. She closes the door and locks it. Her eyes blazing with excitement, she stands with her arms across the door as if shutting the world out. Then softly she moves to the door of her father's bedroom, unlocks it, and goes in, returning at once with a pair of men's bedroom slippers. Leaving the bedroom door open, she crosses to the sideboard, takes up the Bible, and, going to her father's chair, places the slippers beside it. She speaks very softly.)* I put your slippers out. *(She draws the footstool up to the chair.)* Everything will be the same now, Father. *(She opens the Bible.)* I'll read to you, Father. I'll read the one you like. *(She reads with quiet contentment.)* "And the winds blew, and beat upon the house; and it fell not: for it was founded upon a rock."

(The wind moans through the old house as the curtain falls.)

FOLLIES AND FOOLERY

It is always healthy to be able to laugh at our own all-too-human weaknesses. Laughter is a kind of medicine that reminds us not to take ourselves too seriously.

Though comedy can be used as a serious weapon to attack certain aspects of society, it can also be used gently to show us our own foibles and fool-ishness. This sort of mild satire may use a standard form of writing—the fairy tale, let's say, or the western—as the vehicle for the comedy. But it is the human side of the characters with which we identify, thus seeing the humour in our own lives.

The Ugly Duckling, a sort of anti-fairy tale by A. A. Milne, is the story of a plain princess whom no one wants to wed. But a special prince discovers her own sort of beauty so that the two can "live happily ever after." Ken Mitchell's *Showdown at Sand Valley* plays with the image of the Wild West desperado to demonstrate that even a feared gunslinger might be nothing but bluster.

The Ugly Duckling

A. A. Milne

CHARACTERS

The King

The Queen

Princess Camilla—their daughter

The Chancellor

Dulcibella—Princess Camilla's waiting
maid

Prince Simon

Carlo—Prince Simon's attendant

---

*"It is our little plan that at the first
meeting she should pass herself off as
the princess—a harmless ruse, of which
you will find frequent record
in the history books."*

---

*(The scene is the throne room of the palace. It
is a room of many doors, or, if preferred, cur-
tain-openings: simply furnished with three
thrones for Their Majesties and Her Royal
Highness the Princess Camilla—in other words,
with three handsome chairs. At each side is a
long seat: reserved, as it might be, for His Majesty's council (if any), but useful, as today, for
other purposes. The King is asleep on his
throne with a handkerchief over his face. He is
a king of any country from any storybook, in
whatever costume you please. But he should be
wearing his crown.)*

An Offstage Voice: His Excellency the Chancellor!

*(The Chancellor, an elderly man in horn-
rimmed spectacles, enters, bowing. The King
wakes up with a start and removes the handkerchief from his face.)*

King: *(with simple dignity)* I was thinking.

Chancellor: *(bowing)* Never, Your Majesty,
was greater need for thought than now.

King: That's what I was thinking. *(He struggles into a more dignified position.)* Well,
what is it? More trouble?

Chancellor: What we might call the old trouble, Your Majesty.

King: It's what I was saying last night to the
Queen. "Uneasy lies the head that wears a
crown," was how I put it.

Chancellor: A profound and original thought,
which may well go down to posterity.

King: You mean it may go down well with posterity. I hope so. Remind me to tell you some time of another little thing I said to Her Majesty: something about a fierce light beating on a throne. Posterity would like that, too. Well, what is it?

Chancellor: It is in the matter of Her Royal Highness's wedding.

King: Oh...yes.

Chancellor: As Your Majesty is aware, the young Prince Simon arrives today to seek Her Royal Highness's hand in marriage. He has been travelling in distant lands and, as I understand, has not—er—has not—

King: You mean he hasn't heard anything.

Chancellor: It is a little difficult to put this tactfully, Your Majesty.

King: Do your best, and I will tell you afterwards how you got on.

Chancellor: Let me put it this way. The prince will naturally assume that Her Royal Highness has the customary—so customary as to be, in my own poor opinion, slightly monotonous—has what one might call the inevitable—so inevitable as to be, in my opinion again, almost mechanical—will assume, that she has the, as *I* think of it, faultily faultless, icily regular, splendidly—

King: What you are trying to say in the fewest words possible is that my daughter is not beautiful.

Chancellor: Her beauty is certainly elusive, Your Majesty.

King: It is. It has eluded you, it has eluded me, it has eluded everybody who has seen her. It even eluded the court painter. His last words were, "Well, I did my best." His successor is now painting the view across the meadows from the west turret. He says that his doctor has advised him to keep to landscape.

Chancellor: It is unfortunate, Your Majesty, but there it is. One just cannot understand how it can have occurred.

King: You don't think she takes after *me*, at all? You don't detect a likeness?

Chancellor: Most certainly not, Your Majesty.

King: Good...Your predecessor did.

Chancellor: I have often wondered what happened to my predecessor.

King: Well, now you know.

(There is a short silence.)

Chancellor: Looking at the bright side, although Her Royal Highness is not, strictly speaking, beautiful—

King: Not, truthfully speaking, beautiful—

Chancellor: Yet she has great beauty of character.

King: My dear Chancellor, we are not considering Her Royal Highness's character, but her chances of getting married. You observe that there is a distinction.

Chancellor: Yes, Your Majesty.

King: Look at it from the suitor's point of view. If a woman is beautiful, it is easy to assume that she has, tucked away inside her, an equally beautiful character. But it is impossible to assume that an unattractive woman, however elevated in character, has, tucked away inside her, an equally beautiful face. That is, so to speak, not where you want it—tucked away.

Chancellor: Quite so, Your Majesty.

King: This doesn't, of course, alter the fact that the Princess Camilla is quite the nicest person in the kingdom.

Chancellor: *(enthusiastically)* She is indeed, Your Majesty. *(hurriedly)* With the exception, I need hardly say, of Your Majesty—and Her Majesty.

King: Your exceptions are tolerated for their loyalty and condemned for their extreme silliness.

Chancellor: Thank you, Your Majesty.

King: As an adjective for your king, the word "nice" is ill-chosen. As an adjective for Her Majesty, it is—ill-chosen.

(At which moment Her Majesty comes in. The King rises. The Chancellor bows low.)

Queen: *(briskly)* Ah. Talking about Camilla? *(She sits down.)*

King: *(returning to his throne)* As always, my dear, you are right.

Queen: *(to Chancellor)* This fellow, Simon— What's he like?

Chancellor: Nobody has seen him, Your Majesty.

Queen: How old is he?

Chancellor: Five-and-twenty, I understand.

Queen: In twenty-five years he must have been seen by somebody.

King: *(to the Chancellor)* Just a fleeting glimpse.

Chancellor: I meant, Your Majesty, that no detailed report of him has reached this country, save that he has the usual personal advantages and qualities expected of a prince and has been travelling in distant and dangerous lands.

Queen: Ah! Nothing gone wrong with his eyes? Sunstroke or anything?

Chancellor: Not that I am aware of, Your Majesty. At the same time, as I was venturing to say to His Majesty, Her Royal Highness's character and disposition are so outstandingly—

Queen: Stuff and nonsense. You remember what happened when we had the Tournament of Love last year.

Chancellor: I was not myself present, Your Majesty. I had not then the honour of—I was abroad and never heard the full story.

Queen: No; it was the other fool. They all rode up to Camilla to pay their homage—it was the first time they had seen her. The heralds blew their trumpets and announced that she would marry whichever prince was left master of the field when all but one had been unhorsed. The trumpets were blown again, they charged enthusiastically into the fight, and— *(The King looks nonchalantly at the ceiling and whistles a few bars.)* —don't do that.

King: I'm sorry, my dear.

Queen: *(to Chancellor)* And what happened? They all simultaneously fell off their horses and assumed a posture of defeat.

King: One of them was not quite so quick as the others. I was very quick. I proclaimed him the victor.

Queen: At the Feast of Betrothal held that night—

King: We were all very quick.

Queen: The Chancellor announced that by the laws of the country the successful suitor had to pass a further test. He had to give the correct answer to a riddle.

Chancellor: Such undoubtedly is the fact, Your Majesty.

King: There are times for announcing facts and times for looking at things in a broadminded way. Please remember that, Chancellor.

Chancellor: Yes, Your Majesty.

Queen: I invented the riddle myself. Quite an easy one. What is it which has four legs and barks like a dog? The answer is, "A dog."

King: *(to Chancellor)* You see that?

Chancellor: Yes, Your Majesty.

King: It isn't difficult.

Queen: He, however, seemed to find it so. He said an eagle. Then he said a serpent; a very high mountain with slippery sides; two peacocks; a moonlight night; the day after tomorrow—

King: Nobody could accuse him of not trying.

Queen: *I* did.

King: I *should* have said that nobody could fail to recognize in his attitude an appearance of doggedness.

Queen: Finally he said "Death." I nudged the King—

King: Accepting the word "nudge" for the moment, I rubbed my ankle with one hand, clapped him on the shoulder with the other, and congratulated him on the correct answer. He disappeared under the table, and, personally, I never saw him again.

Queen: His body was found in the moat next morning.

Chancellor: But what was he doing in the moat, Your Majesty?

King: Bobbing about. Try not to ask needless questions.

Chancellor: It all seems so strange.

Queen: What does?

Chancellor: That Her Royal Highness, alone of all the princesses one has ever heard of, should lack that invariable attribute of royalty, supreme beauty.

Queen: *(to the King)* That was your Great-Aunt Malkin. She came to the christening. You know what she said.

King: It was cryptic. Great-Aunt Malkin's besetting weakness. She came to *my* christening—she was one hundred and one then, and that was fifty-one years ago. *(to the Chancellor)* How old would that make her?

Chancellor: One hundred and fifty-two, Your Majesty.

King: *(after thought)* About that, yes. She promised me that when I grew up I should have all the happiness which my wife deserved. It struck me at the time—well, when I say "at the time," I was only a week old—but it did strike me as soon as anything could strike me—I mean of that nature—well, work it out for yourself, Chancellor. It opens up a most interesting field of speculation. Though naturally I have not liked to go into it at all deeply with Her Majesty.

Queen: I never heard anything less cryptic. She was wishing you extreme happiness.

King: I don't think she was *wishing* me anything. However.

Chancellor: *(to the Queen)* But what, Your Majesty, did she wish Her Royal Highness?

Queen: Her other godmother—on my side—had promised her the dazzling beauty for which all the women in my family are famous— *(She pauses, and the King snaps his fingers surreptitiously in the direction of the Chancellor.)*

Chancellor: *(hurriedly)* Indeed, yes, Your Majesty. *(The King relaxes.)*

Queen: And Great-Aunt Malkin said— *(to the King)* —what were the words?

King:

> I give you with this kiss
> A wedding-day surprise.
> Where ignorance is bliss
> 'Tis folly to be wise.

I thought the last two lines rather neat. But what it *meant*—

Queen: We can all see what it meant. She was given beauty—and where is it? Great-Aunt Malkin took it away from her. The wedding-day surprise is that there will never be a wedding day.

King: Young men being what they are, my dear, it would be much more surprising if there *were* a wedding day. So how—

(The princess comes in. She is young, happy, healthy, but not beautiful. Or let us say that by some trick of make-up or arrangement of hair she seems plain to us: unlike the princess of the storybooks.)

Princess: *(to the King)* Hallo, darling! *(seeing the others)* Oh, I say! Affairs of state? Sorry.

King: *(holding out his hand)* Don't go, Camilla. *(She takes his hand.)*

Chancellor: Shall I withdraw, Your Majesty?

Queen: You are aware, Camilla, that Prince Simon arrives today?

Princess: He has arrived. They're just letting down the drawbridge.

King: *(jumping up)* Arrived! I must—

Princess: Darling, you know what the drawbridge is like. It takes at *least* half an hour to let it down.

King: *(sitting down)* It wants oil. *(to the Chancellor)* Have *you* been grudging it oil?

Princess: We need a new drawbridge, darling.

Chancellor: Have I Your Majesty's permission—

King: Yes, yes.

(The Chancellor bows and goes out.)

Queen: You've told him, of course? It's the only chance.

King: Er—no. I was just going to, when—

Queen: Then I'd better. *(She goes to the door.)* You can explain to the girl; I'll have her sent to you. You've told Camilla?

King: Er—no. I was just going to, when—

Queen: Then you'd better tell her now.

King: My dear, are you sure—

Queen: It's the only chance left. *(dramatically to heaven)* My daughter! *(She goes out. There is a little silence when she is gone.)*

King: Camilla, I want to talk seriously to you about marriage.

Princess: Yes, father.

King: It is time that you learned of the facts of life.

Princess: Yes, father.

King: Now the great fact about marriage is that once you're married you live happy ever after. All our history books affirm this.

Princess: And your own experience too, darling.

King: *(with dignity)* Let us confine ourselves to history for the moment.

Princess: Yes, father.

King: Of course, there *may* be an exception here and there, which, as it were, proves the rule; just as—oh, well, never mind.

Princess: *(smiling)* Go on, darling. You were going to say that an exception here and there proves the rule that all princesses are beautiful.

King: Well—leave that for the moment. The point is that it doesn't matter *how* you marry, or *who* you marry, as long as you *get* married. Because you'll be happy ever after in any case. Do you follow me so far?

Princess: Yes, father.

King: Well, your mother and I have a little plan—

Princess: Was that it, going out of the door just now?

King: Er—yes. It concerns your waiting maid.

Princess: Darling, I have several.

King: Only one that leaps to the eye, so to speak. The one with the—well, with everything.

Princess: Dulcibella?

King: That's the one. It is our little plan that at the first meeting she would pass herself off as the princess—a harmless ruse, of which you will find frequent record in the history books—and allure Prince Simon to his—that is to say, bring him up to the—in other words, the wedding will take place immediately afterwards, and as quietly as possible—well, naturally in view of the fact that your Aunt Malkin is one hundred and fifty-two; and since you will be wearing the family bridal veil—which is no doubt how the custom arose—the surprise after the ceremony will be his. Are you following me at all? Your attention seems to be wandering.

Princess: I was wondering why you needed to tell me.

King: Just a precautionary measure, in case you happened to meet the prince or his attendant before the ceremony; in which case, of course, you would pass yourself off as the maid—

Princess: A harmless ruse, of which, also, you will find frequent record in the history books.

King: Exactly. But the occasion need not arise.

An Offstage Voice: The woman Dulcibella!

King: Ah! *(to the princess)* Now, Camilla, if you will just retire to your own apartments, I will come to you there when we are ready for the actual ceremony. *(He leads her out as he is talking; and as he returns calls out.)* Come in, my dear! *(Dulcibella comes in. She is beautiful but not intelligent.)* Now don't be frightened, there is nothing to be frightened about. Has Her Majesty told you what you have to do?

Dulcibella: Y-yes, Your Majesty.

King: Well now, let's see how well you can do it. You are sitting here, we will say. *(He leads her to a seat.)* Now imagine that I am Prince Simon. *(He curls his moustache and puts his stomach in. She giggles.)* You are the beautiful Princess Camilla whom he has never seen. *(she giggles again.)* This is a serious moment in your life, and you will find that a giggle will not be helpful. *(He goes to the door.)* I am announced: "His Royal Highness Prince Simon!" That's me being announced. Remember what I said about giggling. You should have a faraway look upon the face. *(She does her best.)* Farther away than that. *(She tries again.)* No, that's too far. You are sitting there, thinking beautiful thoughts—in maiden meditation, fancy-free, as I remember saying to Her Majesty once... speaking of somebody else...fancy-free, but with the mouth definitely shut—that's better. I advance and fall upon one knee. *(He does so.)* You extend your hand graciously—*graciously*; you're not trying to push him in the face—that's better, and I raise it to my lips—so—and I kiss it— *(kisses it warmly)* —no, perhaps not so ardently as that, more like this *(kisses it again)*, and I say, "Your Royal Highness, this is the most—er—Your Royal Highness, I shall ever be—no—Your Royal Highness, it is the proudest—" Well, the point is that *he* will say it, and it will be something complimentary, and then he will take your hand in both of his and press it to his heart. *(He does so.)* And then—what do *you* say?

Dulcibella: Coo!

King: No, *not* "coo."

Dulcibella: Never had anyone do *that* to me before.

King: That also strikes the wrong note. What you want to say is, "Oh, Prince Simon!"... Say it.

Dulcibella: *(loudly)* Oh, Prince Simon!

King: No, no. You don't need to shout until he has said "What?" two or three times. Always consider the possibility that he *isn't* deaf. Softly, and giving the words a dying fall, letting them play around his head like a flight of doves.

Dulcibella: *(still a little overloud)* O-o-o-o-h, Prinsimon!

King: Keep the idea in your mind of a flight of *doves* rather than a flight of panic-stricken elephants, and you will be all right. Now I'm going to get up, and you must, as it were, *waft* me into a seat by your side. *(She starts wafting.)* *Not* rescuing a drowning man, that's another idea altogether, useful at times, but at the moment inappropriate. Wafting. Prince Simon will put the necessary muscles into play—all you require to do is to indicate by a gracious movement of the hand the seat you require him to take. Now! *(He gets up, a little stiffly, and sits next to her.)* That was better. Well, here we are. Now, I think you give me a look: something, let us say, halfway between the breathless adoration of a nun and the freedom of a woman of the world; with an undertone of regal dignity, touched, as it were, with good comradeship. Now try that. *(She gives him a vacant look of bewilderment.)* Frankly, that didn't quite get it. There was just a little something missing. An absence, as it were, of all the qualities I asked for, and in their place an odd resemblance to an unsatisfied fish. Let us try to get at it another way. Dulcibella, have you a young man of your own?

Dulcibella: *(eagerly, seizing his hand)* Oo, yes, he's ever so smart, he's an archer, well not as you might say a real archer, he works in the armoury, but old Bottlenose, *you*

know who I mean, the captain of the guard, says the very next man they ever has to shoot, my Eg shall take his place, knowing father and how it is with Eg and me, and me being maid to Her Royal Highness and can't marry me till he's a real soldier, but ever so loving, and funny like, the things he says, I said to him once, "Eg," I said—

King: *(getting up)* I rather fancy, Dulcibella, that if you think of Eg all the time, *say* as little as possible, and, when thinking of Eg, see that the mouth is not more than partially open, you will do very well. I will show you where you are to sit and wait for His Royal Highness. *(He leads her out. On the way he speaks.)* Now remember—*waft*—*waft*—not *jerk*.

(Prince Simon wanders in from the back, unannounced. He is a very ordinary-looking young man in rather dusty clothes. He gives a deep sigh of relief as he sinks into the King's throne. Camilla, a new and strangely beautiful Camilla, comes in.)

Princess: *(surprised)* Well!

Prince: Oh, hallo!

Princess: Ought you?

Prince: *(getting up)* Do sit down, won't you?

Princess: Who are you, and how did you get here?

Prince: Well, that's rather a long story. Couldn't we sit down? You could sit here if you liked, but it isn't very comfortable.

Princess: That is the King's throne.

Prince: Oh, is that what it is?

Princess: Thrones are not meant to be comfortable.

Prince: Well, I don't know if they're meant to be, but they certainly aren't.

Princess: Why were you sitting on the King's throne, and who are you?

Prince: My name is Carlo.

Princess: Mine is Dulcibella.

Prince: Good. And now couldn't we sit down?

Princess: *(sitting down on the long seat to the left of the throne and, as it were, wafting him to a place next to her)* You may sit here, if you like. Why are you so tired? *(He sits down.)*

Prince: I've been taking very strenuous exercise.

Princess: Is that part of the long story?

Prince: It is.

Princess: *(settling herself)* I love stories.

Prince: This isn't a story really. You see, I'm attendant on Prince Simon, who is visiting here.

Princess: Oh? I'm attendant on Her Royal Highness.

Prince: Then you know what he's here for.

Princess: Yes.

Prince: She's very beautiful, I hear.

Princess: Did you hear that? Where have you been lately?

Prince: Travelling in distant lands—with Prince Simon.

Princess: Ah! All the same, I don't understand. Is Prince Simon in the palace now? The drawbridge *can't* be down yet!

Prince: I don't suppose it is. *And* what a noise it makes coming down!

Princess: Isn't it terrible?

Prince: I couldn't stand it any more. I just had to get away. That's why I'm here.

Princess: But how?

Prince: Well, there's only one way, isn't there? That beech tree, and then a swing and a grab for the battlements, and don't ask me to remember it all— *(He shudders.)*

Princess: You mean you came across the moat by that beech tree?

Prince: Yes. I got so tired of hanging about.

Princess: But it's terribly dangerous!

Prince: That's why I'm so exhausted. Nervous shock. *(He lies back and breathes loudly.)*

Princess: Of course, it's different for *me*.

Prince: *(sitting up)* Say that again. I must have got it wrong.

Princess: It's different for me, because I'm used to it. Besides, I'm so much lighter.

Prince: You don't mean that *you*—

Princess: Oh yes, often.

Prince: And I thought I was a brave man! At least, I didn't until five minutes ago, and now I don't again.

Princess: Oh, but you are! And I think it's wonderful to do it straight off the first time.

Prince: Well, *you* did.

Princess: Oh no, not the first time. When I was a child.

Prince: You mean that you crashed?

Princess: Well, you only fall into the moat.

Prince: Only! Can you *swim*?

Princess: Of course.

Prince: So you swam to the castle walls, and yelled for help, and they fished you out and walloped you. And next day you tried again. Well, if *that* isn't pluck—

Princess: Of course I didn't. I swam back and did it at once; I mean I tried again at once. It wasn't until the third time that I actually did it. You see, I was afraid I might lose my nerve.

Prince: Afraid she might lose her nerve!

Princess: There's a way of getting over from this side, too; a tree grows out from the wall and you jump into another tree—I don't think it's quite so easy.

Prince: Not quite so easy. Good. You must show me.

Princess: Oh, I will.

Prince: Perhaps it might be as well if you taught me how to swim first. I've often heard about swimming, but never—

Princess: You can't swim?

Prince: No. Don't look so surprised. There are a lot of other things which I can't do. I'll tell you about them as soon as you have a couple of years to spare.

Princess: You can't swim and yet you crossed by the beech tree! And you're *ever* so much heavier than I am! Now who's brave?

Prince: *(getting up)* You keep talking about how light you are. I must see if there's anything in it. Stand up! *(She stands obediently and he picks her up.)* You're right, Dulcibella. I could hold you here forever. *(looking at her)* You're very lovely. Do you know how lovely you are?

Princess: Yes. *(She laughs suddenly and happily.)*

Prince: Why do you laugh?

Princess: Aren't you tired of holding me?

Prince: Frankly, yes. I exaggerated when I said I could hold you forever. When you've been hanging by the arms for ten minutes over a very deep moat, wondering if it's too late to learn how to swim— *(puts her down)* —what I meant was that I should *like* to hold you forever. Why did you laugh?

Princess: Oh, well, it was a little private joke of mine.

Prince: If it comes to that, I've got a private joke too. Let's exchange them.

Princess: Mine's very private. One other woman in the whole world knows, and that's all.

Prince: Mine's just as private. One other man knows, and that's all.

Princess: What fun. I love secrets. . . . Well, here's mine. When I was born, one of my godmothers promised that I should be very beautiful.

Prince: How right she was.

Princess: But the other one said this:

> I give you with this kiss
> A wedding-day surprise.
> Where ignorance is bliss
> 'Tis folly to be wise.

And nobody knew what it meant. And I grew up very plain. And then, when I was about ten, I met my godmother in the forest one day. It was my tenth birthday. Nobody knows this—except you.

Prince: Except us.

Princess: Except us. And she told me what her gift meant. It meant that I *was* beautiful—but everybody else was to go on being ignorant and thinking me plain until my wedding day. Because, she said, she didn't want me to grow up spoilt and willful and vain, as I should have done if everybody had always been saying how beautiful I was; and the best thing in the world, she said, was to be quite sure of yourself, but not to expect admiration from other people. So ever since then my mirror has told me I'm beautiful, and everybody else thinks me ugly, and I get a lot of fun out of it.

Prince: Well, seeing that Dulcibella is the result, I can only say that your godmother was very, very wise.

Princess: And now tell me *your* secret.

Prince: It isn't such a pretty one. You see, Prince Simon was going to woo Princess Camilla, and he'd heard that she was beautiful and haughty and imperious—all *you* would have been if your godmother hadn't been so wise. And being a very ordinary-looking fellow himself, he was afraid she wouldn't think much of him, so he suggested to one of his attendants, a man called Carlo, of extremely attractive appearance, that *he* should pretend to be the prince and win the princess's hand; and then at the last moment they would change places—

Princess: How would they do that?

Prince: The prince was going to have been married in full armour—with his visor down.

Princess: *(laughing happily)* Oh, what fun!

Prince: Neat, isn't it?

Princess: *(laughing)* Oh, very... very... very.

Prince: Neat, but not so terribly *funny*. Why do you keep laughing?

Princess: Well, that's another secret.

Prince: If it comes to that, *I've* got another one up my sleeve. Shall we exchange again?

Princess: All right. You go first this time.

Prince: Very well... I am not Carlo. *(standing up and speaking dramatically)* I am Simon!—ow! (He sits down and rubs his leg violently.)

Princess: *(alarmed)* What is it?

Prince: Cramp. *(in a mild voice, still rubbing)* I was saying that I was Prince Simon.

Princess: Shall I rub it for you? *(She rubs.)*

Prince: *(still hopefully)* I am Simon.

Princess: Is that better?

Prince: *(despairingly)* I am Simon.

Princess: I know.

Prince: How did you know?

Princess: Well, you told me.

Prince: But oughtn't you to swoon or something?

Princess: Why? History records many similar ruses.

Prince: *(amazed)* Is that so? I've never read history. I thought I was being profoundly original.

Princess: Oh, no! Now I'll tell you *my* secret. For reasons very much like your own the Princess Camilla, who is held to be extremely plain, feared to meet Prince Simon. Is the drawbridge down yet?

Prince: Do your people give a faint, surprised cheer every time it gets down?

Princess: Naturally.

Prince: Then it came down about three minutes ago.

Princess: Ah! Then at this very moment your man Carlo is declaring his passionate love for my maid, Dulcibella. That, I think, is funny. *(So does the prince. He laughs heartily.)* Dulcibella, by the way, is in love with a man she calls Eg, so I hope Carlo isn't getting carried away.

Prince: Carlo is married, so Eg has nothing to fear.

Princess: By the way, I don't know if you heard, but I said, or as good as said, that I am the Princess Camilla.

Prince: I wasn't surprised. History, of which I read a great deal, records many similar ruses.

Princess: *(laughing)* Simon!

Prince: *(laughing)* Camilla! *(He stands up.)* May I try holding you again? *(She nods. He takes her in his arms and kisses her.)* Sweetheart!

Princess: You see, when you lifted me up before, you said, "You're very lovely," and my godmother said that the first person to whom I would seem lovely was the man I should marry; so I knew then that you were Simon and I should marry you.

Prince: I knew directly I saw you that I should marry you, even if you were Dulcibella. By the way, which of you *am* I marrying?

Princess: When she lifts her veil, it will be Camilla. *(Voices are heard outside.)* Until then it will be Dulcibella.

Prince: *(in a whisper)* Then good-bye, Camilla, until you lift your veil.

Princess: Good-bye, Simon, until you raise your visor.

(The King and Queen come in arm in arm, followed by Carlo and Dulcibella, also arm in arm. The Chancellor precedes them, walking backwards, bowing.)

Prince: *(supporting the Chancellor, as an accident seems inevitable)* Careful! *(The Chancellor turns indignantly round.)*

King: Who and what is this? More accurately, who and what are all these?

Carlo: My attendant, Carlo, Your Majesty. He will, with Your Majesty's permission, prepare me for the ceremony. *(The prince bows.)*

King: Of course, of course!

Queen: *(to Dulcibella)* Your maid Dulcibella, is it not, my love? *(Dulcibella nods*

violently.) I thought so. *(to Carlo) She* will prepare Her Royal Highness. *(The princess curtsies.)*

King: Ah, yes. Yes. *Most* important.

Princess: *(curtsying)* I beg pardon, Your Majesty, if I've done wrong, but I found the gentleman wandering—

King: *(crossing to her)* Quite right, my dear, quite right. *(He pinches her cheek and takes advantage of this kingly gesture to say in a loud whisper.)* We've pulled it off! *(They sit down; the King and Queen on their thrones, Dulcibella on the Princess's throne. Carlo stands behind Dulcibella, the Chancellor on the right of the Queen, and the prince and princess behind the long seat on the left.)*

Chancellor: *(consulting documents)* H'r'm! Have I Your Majesty's authority to put the final test to His Royal Highness?

Queen: *(whispering to King)* Is this safe?

King: *(whispering)* Perfectly, my dear. I told him the answer a minute ago. *(over his shoulder to Carlo)* Don't forget—"Dog." *(aloud)* Proceed, Your Excellency. It is my desire that the affairs of my country should ever be conducted in a strictly constitutional manner.

Chancellor: *(formally)* By the constitution of the country, a suitor to Her Royal Highness's hand cannot be deemed successful until he has given the correct answer to a riddle. *(conversationally)* The last suitor answered incorrectly and thus failed to win his bride.

King: By a coincidence he fell into the moat.

Chancellor: *(to Carlo)* I have now to ask Your Royal Highness if you are prepared for the ordeal?

Carlo: *(cheerfully)* Absolutely.

Chancellor: I may mention, as a matter, possibly, of some slight historical interest to our visitor, that by the constitution of the country the same riddle is not allowed to be asked on two successive occasions.

King: *(startled)* What's that?

Chancellor: This one, it is interesting to recall, was propounded exactly a century ago, and we must take it as a fortunate omen that it was well and truly solved.

King: *(to Queen)* I may want my sword directly.

Chancellor: The riddle is this. What is it which has four legs and mews like a cat?

Carlo: *(promptly)* A dog.

King: *(still more promptly)* Bravo, bravo! *(He claps loudly and nudges the Queen, who claps too.)*

Chancellor: *(peering at his documents)* According to the records of the occasion to which I referred, the correct answer would seem to be—

Princess: *(to Prince)* Say something, quick!

Chancellor: —not dog, but—

Prince: Your Majesty, have I permission to speak? Naturally His Royal Highness could not think of justifying himself on such an occasion, but I think that with Your Majesty's gracious permission, I could—

King: Certainly, certainly.

Prince: In our country, we have an animal to which we have given the name "dog," or, in the local dialect of the more mountainous districts, "doggie." It sits by the fireside and purrs.

Carlo: That's right. It purrs like anything.

Prince: When it needs milk, which is its staple food, it mews.

Carlo: *(enthusiastically)* Mews like nobody's business.

Prince: It also has four legs.

Carlo: One at each corner.

Prince: In some countries, I understand, this animal is called a "cat." In one distant country to which His Royal Highness and I penetrated it was called by the very curious name of "hippopotamus."

Carlo: That's right. *(to the prince)* Do you remember that ginger-coloured hippopota-mus which used to climb on to my shoulder and lick my ear?

Prince: I shall never forget it, sir. *(to the King)* So you see, Your Majesty—

King: Thank you. I think that makes it perfectly clear. *(firmly to the Chancellor)* You are about to agree?

Chancellor: Undoubtedly, your Majesty. May I be the first to congratulate His Royal Highness on solving the riddle so accurately?

King: You may be the first to see that all is in order for an immediate wedding.

Chancellor: Thank you, Your Majesty.

(He bows and withdraws. The King rises, as do the Queen and Dulcibella.)

King: *(to Carlo)* Doubtless, Prince Simon, you will wish to retire and prepare yourself for the ceremony.

Carlo: Thank you, sir.

Prince: Have I Your Majesty's permission to attend His Royal Highness? It is the custom of his country for princes of the royal blood to be married in full armour, a matter which requires a certain adjustment—

King: Of course, of course. *(Carlo bows to the King and Queen and goes out. As the prince is about to follow, the King stops him.)* Young man, you have a quality of quickness which I admire. It is my pleasure to reward it in any way which commends itelf to you.

Prince: Your Majesty is ever gracious. May I ask for my reward *after* the ceremony? *(He catches the eye of the princess, and they give each other a secret smile.)*

King: Certainly. *(The prince bows and goes out. To Dulcibella.)* Now, young woman, make yourself scarce. You've done your work excellently, and we will see that you and your—what was his name?

Dulcibella: Eg, Your Majesty.

King: —that you and your Eg are not forgotten.

Dulcibella: Coo! *(She curtsies and goes out.)*

Princess: *(calling)* Wait for me, Dulcibella!

King: (to Queen) Well, my dear, we may congratulate ourselves. As I remember saying to somebody once, "You have not lost a daughter, you have gained a son." How does he strike you?

Queen: Stupid.

King: They made a very handsome pair, I thought, he and Dulcibella.

Queen: Both stupid.

King: I said nothing about stupidity. What I *said* was that they were both extremely handsome. That is the important thing. (Struck by a sudden idea) Or isn't it?

Queen: What do you think of Prince Simon, Camilla?

Princess: I adore him. We shall be so happy together.

King: Well, of course you will. I told you so. Happy ever after.

Queen: Run along now and get ready.

Princess: Yes, mother. (She throws a kiss to them and goes out.)

King: (anxiously) My dear, have we been wrong about Camilla all this time? It seemed to me that she wasn't looking *quite* so plain as usual just now. Did *you* notice anything?

Queen: (carelessly) Just the excitement of the marriage.

King: (relieved) Ah, yes, that would account for it.

(Curtain)

Caution:
Enquiries regarding the performance of this play, professional or amateur, should be directed to Samuel French Limited, 52 Fitzroy Street, London, England W1P 6JR.

Showdown at Sand Valley

Ken Mitchell

CHARACTERS

Narrator

Stanley Gompers—owner of the general store

Horace B. Lankitt—the reeve of Sand Valley

Percy Nebbets—the station agent

Mrs. Jennifer McAllister—a former school-marm

Sam—a town hothead

Fester—operator of the hotel and bar

Montana Bill—a gun-slinger of the Ole West

Corporal Laurence Wretched-Smith—Mounted Policeman of British origin

---

*"There's a gunfighter headin' this way...
straight outta the Ol' Wild West!"*

(As few as six performers can present this play, by doubling up on parts. With more performers, Sand Valley can be populated with an assortment of townspeople.

As simple as possible, the set can be arranged with chairs and stools, or nothing at all. All of the action occurs along the main street of Sand Valley, with episodes on the street, in the home of Mrs. McAllister, and in the hotel. All of this can be done in mime. Music, using simple instruments such as harmonica and guitar, will enhance the "western" effects. The play might begin with a traditional western folk song.)

Narrator: In the early years of Saskatchewan, the boundless prairie was a peaceful setting for the growing of wheat. All was quiet in the Canadian West, except during election year, and the pioneers took up their tasks with dil- igence and enthusiasm. But one incident occurred that shattered this hopeful tranquility forever, and in the little town of Sand Valley, Saskatchewan, they still talk of the terrible day that—Montana Bill rode into town! *(music)* They called it— *(music)* Showdown at Sand Valley! *(pause)* It is two o'clock in the afternoon of August tenth, 1909. The main street in front of Stanley Gompers's general store is drowsy in the late afternoon sun, blissfully unaware of the blood-curdling scenes it will witness this day!

(Horace and Gompers appear.)

Horace: Wutcha whittlin' there, Gomp?

Gompers: *(pause)* Stick.

Horace: Zatta fact? Wutcha goin' whittle *out* of it?

Gompers: *(pause)* Little stick.

Horace: *(sighs)* Real scorcher t'day. *(No answer.)* Gonna burn the aitch outta them crops. Jis' like last year. *(Pause.)* Don'cha think?

Gompers: Uh-huh.

Horace: Ya don' *ack* worried. How's anybody goin' buy anythin' outta yer store if they got no crop?

Gompers: *(patient drawl)* Gotta eat, Hory. Everybody's gotta eat.

Percy: *(running on)* Hey, you guys! Hey! Have ya heard the news?

Horace: About Jackson's bull? *(scornfully)* They caught him last week. Say, why aren't you down at the station, stackin' cream cans? The train's comin' in tonight.

Percy: Then you ain't heard! It just came in by telegraph! Charlie Tackhammer sent it up from Bulkhead.

Gompers: *(delivering one of his sardonic observations)* How could we 'a heard if it just came over the wire, Perc?

Percy: *(irritated)* Say, you guys wanta hear it or not?

Horace: Okay, let's have it.

Gompers: Sit down, Perc. Loosen yer braces.

Percy: *(highly excited)* There's a gunfighter headin' this way! An American despera-do!

Horace: What?

Percy: Yeah! A real gun-slinger, straight outta the Ol' Wild West!

Gompers: Ha! Izzen this ol' West wild enough for yuh, Perc?

Percy: Darn it, Gomp, you know what I mean. Texas or Arizona or one a *them* places. Where they're always shootin' marshals and Indians and wicked saloon women. Don'cha read the magazines?

Horace: Well, what makes you think he's comin' tuh Sand Valley? What did Charlie say?

Percy: He was talkin' to the freight driver from Wooster Creek, and *he* says the fella came through *there* headin' for Sand Valley!

Horace: *(worried)* I dunno, Gomp. Charlie doesn't beat his gums to say nothin'.

Gompers: Charlie say he was a *gun-slinger*, Perc?

Percy: Said he had one a them old army pistols stuck in his belt. Said he was runnin' from the law across the border!

Horace: *(scared)* Sounds serious, Gomp!

Percy: *(shouts to someone off-stage)* Hey, Sam, have ya heard the news? No, it izzen about Jackson's bull—this is *excitin'* stuff. Just raise the hair on your neck! *(goes off)*

Horace: Well, arn'chuh gonna do somethin'?

Gompers: What do you suggest I do, Hory?

Horace: Well—round up a committee to take action. Call the Mounties in Regina! Lock up yer store!

Gompers: Can't lock up the store, Hory. It's a Friday afternoon.

Horace: But it's an emergency!

Gompers: You're the reeve, Hory. *You* form a committee.

Horace: What about the Mounties? We gotta wire Regina!

Gompers: Get Perc to send her through, 'fore he gets too far away—spreadin' the news.

Horace: Right! You're on the committee, Gomp. We'll meet over at the Prince Albert Hotel. In half an hour!

(They disperse. Music.)

Narrator: In the meantime, news of the danger spread through the town like wildfire. It rampaged up and down Main Street like a torrent, sweeping citizens off the board-walks, before flowing out into the side streets and finally lapping at the doorsill of the serene little cottage of Mrs. Jennifer McAllister, former schoolteacher of Sand Valley and president-elect of the Ladies' Temperance League.

Horace: *(knocking on door)* Miz McAllister! Miz McAllister!

Mrs. McAllister: *(speaking in a thick Scots burr)* Have patience, for heaven's sakes. I'm coming!

(She opens her door.)

Horace: *(near panic)* Miz McAllister! Lock your door! Close your windows.

Mrs. McAllister: Horace B. Lankitt! Where did ye learn your manners? Going about thumping on people's doors! I'm trying to get bread to rise!

Horace: Miz McAllister, don't start a lecture now! It's an emergency! There's a wild gunfighter coming to town!

Mrs. McAllister: Gunfighter! I'll gunfight *him* if he comes nosing around *my* wee hoose. What's the name of this birkie?

Horace: He's called—Montana Bill!

Mrs. McAllister: Oh, a *Yankee* ruffian, is he? Well, let him stick his drunken, rum-crazed toes across *my* doorsill, and he'll feel the clean prairie breeze whustlin' through his innards!

Horace: Don't worry, Miz McAllister! There's a committee to protect the town. We want you to go and stay at the Jordisons', so you won't be here alone.

Mrs. McAllister: I do not consider myself helpless, Horace. I'll stay in my own hoose.

Horace: But Miz McAllister, we can't spare a man to send over here—we need them all down at the hotel!

Mrs. McAllister: Don't you wurry aboot me. I've not required a man around the hoose these thurt-teen years, and I'll survive a *wee* while longer. And my Sandy (may he rest in peace) wouldna go aboot frightening respectable wumen with wild stories.

Horace: *(irritated by her response)* Is that so! Well, it's too bad his *son* didn't take after him! I still remember the time he put soap powder in the village pump!

Mrs. McAllister: Whussht! I'll not hear one word about it. My wee Wulliam may have played some pranks in his youth, but he's gone away now and there's an end to it. Good day.

Horace: Yeah, well—if you need any help, we'll be down at the Prince Albert Hotel—

Mrs. McAllister: Aye, I suspected as much! All of ye sprattling off to the liquor-bar at the first excuse for swulling down spirits.

Horace: But Miz McAllister, there's no other place we can meet to—

Mrs. McAllister: Leaving the women and children to the mercy o' gunfighters, while ye pay homage to the devil's whuskey! Ye drinkin', slatherin' pack o' cowards—!

(Horace goes out. Men gather at the Prince Albert Hotel bar, drinking and arguing.)

Percy: And here's the conclusion of our telegram! "The taxpayers of Sand Valley urgently demand RCMP officer to apprehend desperate criminal." *(pause)* "Please hurry." *(to crowd)* I thought I should add that. "Sincerely yours, Percy Nebbets, Station Agent." This reply came in ten minutes later. *(pause)* You wanna hear it?

Gompers: Go ahead!

Percy: *(clears throat)* "Percy Nebbets, Station Agent, Sand Valley. Dear Mr. Nebbets."

Gompers: *(growling)* Get on with it!

Percy: *(refusing to be hurried)* "Dear Mr. Nebbets. Your urgency is noted. Corporal Laurence Wretched-Smith of F Division will arrive evening train from Regina. He will assume all authority. For public safety, close all bars in town."

(astounded reaction from the crowd: gasps, snorts, curses)

Percy: "Sincerely, Colonel James B. Hogarth, Officer Commanding F Division!"

Sam: I'll be hog-tied to the correction line! Close the bar!

Fester: That's law and order for yuh! First good

day I've had since seeding, and they want to shut me down.

Percy: And they're only sending one man! How is he supposed to face down a mad-dog killer?

Sam: Jus' don't make sense. We ain't gonna be any use to him if we're all *dry!* Man can't face a gang a cutthroats with his brain dehy-dyuhrated.

Percy: *(terrified)* Gang? Hey, juh hear that? There's a gang comin' with him!

Crowd: *(shocked outburst)* Gang? Who said gang? Lemme outta here! Where's the door? I got some shopping tuh do!

Gompers: *(making himself heard over the uproar)* Sit down and shut up! *(silence)* There isn't any "gang." Probably no gun-fighter, either. *(pause)* Fes, top up that glass, will yuh?

Fester: Sorry, Mister Gompers, I gotta close the bar. Police orders.

Gompers: Awright, Fes, you close the bar, officially.

(Crowd mutters rebelliously.)

Gompers: Then fill that glass up *unofficially.*

(Crowd cheers.)

Sam: Attaboy, Gomp. Any crazy killer comes around here—we'll know how to handle him.

Horace: *(running in)* Sam, how did you make out with weapons?

Sam: Shore, we got all kinds a weapons. Nine shotguns. Six twenty-twos. Cavalry sword. Pitchforks, clubs. Slingshots. We got him out-gunned, awright.

Horace: No revolvers?

Sam: Ain't bin a revolver in Sand Valley since Doc Wages came back from the Boor War and chucked his iron into Oscar Bergson's dugout. Where *you* bin?

Horace: Aw, I was listenin' to Miz McAllister. The old battle-axe don't *want* pertection.

Gompers: Can't say as I blame her, with a militia like this one.

Horace: *(retorting)* Yeah, well I'll let *you* talk to her if she comes down here to close the bar, official or no official.

Percy: Take it easy, Hory. We're ready for him now!

Horace: You get all them telegrams away?

Percy: Yep, sent word to the agents at Bulk-head, Pavement Narrows, Toenail, and Wheat City. If he comes through any of them, they'll wire a warning to us!

Sam: Anybody ever find out why this here outlaw wants ta come ta Sand Valley anyway?

Horace: *(modestly)* Probably our reputation: barley capital a Saskatchewan. Folks heard of us far away as Meadowlark! Far as Moose Jaw!

Percy: Maybe folks in one a those towns kinda—sicked him on us. You know, jealous like.

Sam: Sure, coulda bin them crazy stubble-jumpers up in Shakespeare. They never forgive us fer beatin' them outta that baseball tournament down in Genesis.

Several: Shore, that's it. Them's the ones. What can yuh expect? *(etc.)*

Horace: *(making himself heard)* Well, he'll have ta shoot us all, then! Every man here played ball that day!

Percy: Right. One for all, and all for one!

Sam: United we stand! Deevided we fall!

(Roar of approval. Fester, who has been off-stage briefly, returns.)

Fester: Got a message here for yuh, Perc.

Several: Percy Nebbets! Hey, Perc! Message for yuh!

Percy: It's a telegram! From Charlie Tackhammer! Omigawsh! It says—

Several: Is he comin'? Where is he? *What's it say?*

Percy: It says, "Mr. Percy Nebbets, Station Agent...."

Several: Get to the message! Read it out! *What's it say?*

Percy: *(shocked)* It says—that Montana Bill—rode through Bulkhead fifteen minutes ago—headin' for Sand Valley!

(groans, gasps from the crowd)

Percy: *(laying on the punch line)* Armed to the teeth!

(Crowd breaks up in a panic, chairs flying. General scramble at the door, except for Horace and Gompers.)

Horace: Hold on, men! One for all, and all for one! You *decided!* United we stand—!

Sam: You'll look perty united with a bullet in yer liver!

Gompers: *(cutting into the uproar)* Gopher-bait!

(stunned silence)

Sam: Whu'ja say, Gomp?

Gompers: I said—"Gopher-bait!"

Several: Gopher-bait? What's gopher-bait?

Gompers: That's what you're *all* gonna be if you start stampedin' up and down the street trying to hide from this "hired killer." *If* he's a "hired killer."

Horace: You, uh, got some kin' a plan, Gomp?

Gompers: Yeah. *(pause)* I got a plan. *(pause)* You boys with the twenty-twos take 'em up on top of the general store. Mind my shingles. Sam, you take all the fellas with shotguns and get set up in the doorways along Main Street. Put up some feed sacks. Rest of you stay in here with me, and we'll rush into the street when we got the drop on him.

Sam: Hot diggety-dog! A real ambush!

Horace: *(impressed)* Where'd ya learn all that, Gomp?

Gompers: *(deprecating)* Read it in a Wild West mag. Keep 'em in the store.

Percy: Wild West. Holy smoke! We forgot about the Mountie comin' down from Regina.

Sam: Lot a good he's gonna do! Comin' in on the night train. Montana Bill's gonna be here in five minutes!

Fester: We could all be in—Boot Hill by tonight!

Horace: Right. We have to do it—take the law into our own hands. Okay, men, drink up and get out to your positions.

(They run out and line up along the street. Tense silence.)

Gompers: All set?

All: Yeah!

(silence)

Sam: What if he's got some—henchmen sneakin' around behind us?

Gompers: Don't start that stuff again!

Sam: Just thinkin'! *(pause)* Probably he'll hit the town shootin'!

Gompers: Will you shut up?

Horace: Quiet! You hear that?

(There is a sound of galloping in the distance.)

Percy: *(terrified)* Here he comes!

Several: That's him! Get ready, you guys!

Gompers: *(hoarsely)* Nobody shoot, 'less he shoots first.

(Galloping hits a crescendo as the men watch him ride into town amid unbearable tension. One or two might even faint away. Montana rides right past them, and the galloping recedes into the distance.)

Horace: *(unable to believe it)* He rode right past!

Percy: Right through town.

Fester: I don't git it.

Several: What's goin' on? What's he doin'?

Sam: *(furthest away, peering)* Turned down Elm Street. Headin' for Miz McAllister's.

Percy: Miz McAllister's!

Horace: *(agonized)* Oh, no! I warned her, too! She wouldn't lissen—crazy old teetotaller!

Fester: What's goin' on?

Horace: You heard! He's gone to Miz McAllister's.

Percy: Well, what for? *She* ain't no gun-slinger!

Fester: Maybe he's a drunk—hates temperance ladies.

Sam: Shore was a mean-lookin' brute. Big gun stuck in his belt. I thought we wuz all goners! *(pause)* Somepin funny, though.

Percy: Yeah. *(forces a laugh)* What?

Sam: He looked kinda familiar.

Horace: Well, what are we standin' *here* for? We gotta go help that poor old lady!

Percy: *(pause)* Wish that gol-dang Mountie would come.

Horace: We have to go and protect her.

Gompers: *(coming out of a daze)* You boys better stay away from that house.

Several: Why? Who? What is it, Gomp?

Gompers: I don't know Montana Bill—But that Montana Bill that rode past *me* wasn't Montana Bill. *(pause)* He was Miz McAllister's son, "Wulliam"!

All: Willie McAllister!

(Montana Bill knocks on Mrs. McAllister's door.)

Mrs. McAllister: Don't batter the door doon. I'm coming.

(She opens the door. Pause.)

Mrs. McAllister: Well, what is it?

Montana: *(surprised but pleased)* Maw, don't ya recognize me? It's Willie!

Mrs. McAllister: Wulliam!

Montana: Yeah, me. Ain't ya gonna gimme a big how-de-do?

Mrs. McAllister: *(waving him in)* Wipe your feet before ye come in, Wulliam.

Montana: Y-yeah, okay, maw. *(He scrapes his feet and closes door. They sit down. Montana clears his throat several times.)*

Mrs. McAllister: Ye didna write verra often.

Montana: I was busy, Maw!

Mrs. McAllister: Well, what did ye do to earn bread and butter?

Montana: Well, there was the money you sent once in a while. And I did sort of odd jobs—travellin' around.

Mrs. McAllister: Hmp! Avoiding wurrk, I imagine.

Montana: Aw, maw, don' git goin' on that. I thought you'd *like* ta see me again.

Mrs. McAllister: Aye, I am. *(pause)* I suppose *you* are this Montana Bill that has the whole toon in a state of terror?

Montana: *(with blushing modesty)* Yeah—Montana Bill. Name some of the boys down south up and give me. Monnn-tanna Bill. Has a kind a *swell* sound—donchuthink?

Mrs. McAllister: I think it's disgusting.

Montana: *(abashed)* Oh.

Mrs. McAllister: Don't ye see your coming here has embarrassed me in front of the toon? They believe ye some kind of gun-fighter.

Montana: Well, I *am* a gunfighter, maw! *(pause)* Sort of, anyway. *(thoughtfully)* Mebbe that's why all them guys were downtown with shotguns and ever'thin'. Near scared the pants off me. Looked like bank robbers—standing around on top of Gompers's store with a bunch of twenty-twos in the middle of the afternoon!

Mrs. McAllister: Yes, they're almost as addled as you.

Montana: Say, you don't suppose they'd come over here and start bullyin' at me, do ya, maw?

Mrs. McAllister: I suppose one of them would recognize you—even in that *ridiculous* costume.

Montana: Hey, these are my gunfighting duds, maw! They *all* dress like this!

Mrs. McAllister: Well, I won't have it. If you

plan to sleep in my hoose ye'll wear tweeds like everyone else. You do plan to stay here, William?

Montana: *(pause)* I'm—in trouble, maw.

Mrs. McAllister: Tell me all aboot it, laddie.

Montana: Well—I was in Billings, just walkin' down a back alley, mindin' my own business—checkin' around to see what I could see—when this fella came runnin' around the corner. Chased by another guy, shootin' at him! Well, the first one fell down dead at my feet and the other guy run off. There wasn't nobody else around, and I didn't have much to do, so I just kinda checked him over—well, I was standin' there not doin' anythin'. He had a wallet full of money, and this here pistol inside his jacket. I was standin' there lookin' at it, when the other fella showed up with a whole gang, hollerin', "That's him—there he is!" Well, I blasted a shot at 'em, over their heads like, and hit outta town for the border. Didn't stop till I got here.

Mrs. McAllister: *(sternly)* And now that you're here?

Montana: *(puzzled)* Well, I thought I might hide out. Sort of hole up for a while, till the heat's off.

Mrs. McAllister: There'll be no "heat off" in this hoose.

Montana: *(shocked)* Whuddaya mean, maw?

Mrs. McAllister: I mean you'll go back and turn yourself in to the American authorities. I'll have no cruminals or fugitives boarding at my table.

Montana: *(desperate)* But maw, I'm your own son!

Mrs. McAllister: Aye, and ye've not changed a whit since you left my hoose ten years ago. Ye were a brainless birkie then, and ye've not changed for the better. Your father would have gone and taken his consequences.

Montana: But they think I killed him! They'll hang me!

Mrs. McAllister: Whussht! They don't hang

men for thieving guns and wallets—not even silly Canadians prancing aboot in gunfighters' costume.

Montana: It'll hurt!

Mrs. McAllister: Ye've not a thing to fear if you trust in God—*and* leave the spirits in the bottle. They'll respect you if you're sober. Now go and surrender.

Montana: *(wailing)* Don't, maw! I'm too young to die!

Mrs. McAllister: Stop snivelling, Wulliam! Ye'll leave in the morning.

Montana: *(trying another tactic)* You don't love me any more!

Mrs. McAllister: Of course I love you, Wulliam, and I want to do what's best for ye. I'll tell you what—you go and take a bath—and I'll make you a nice bowl of porridge!

Montana: *Porridge!*

Mrs. McAllister: Yes. Oatmeal porridge.

Montana: But that's why I ran away! I couldn't stand it any more—oatmeal porridge!

Mrs. McAllister: Ye must eat what's best for ye, Wulliam.

Montana: No! I won't—I'll go out and—and rob Gompers's store! I'll get some baloney and bread and make some sandwiches.

Mrs. McAllister: Now whussht! You're not so big I can't take down your breeks and lay a willow switch a few times across your bare bummy.

Montana: That does it! *(stung to rebellion)* You've driven me to desperate actions, maw! I'm—I'm gonna—go straight downtown and shoot this town up. They always use tuh call me a momma's boy. I'll show 'em I can't be pushed around. I'm a gunfighter! Now they're gonna learn it the hard way. And you are too!

Mrs. McAllister: Whussht your prattling and sit doon whilst I boil the oatmeal.

Montana: *(taking a deep breath)* No! I'm going. *(He flings open the door.)*

Mrs. McAllister: Wulliam! Stop right there!

Montana: *(halting, resignedly)* What is it?

Mrs. McAllister: Is your face washed?

(Montana starts back, stops, starts walking out again.)

Mrs. McAllister: And straighten your tie if you're going to be meeting the public!

(Enraged, Montana stalks off. He puts his neckerchief crooked. He checks his gun and walks to the hotel. Meanwhile, the townsfolk are relaxing.)

Percy: Wee Willy McAllister! Haw! The terror of Sand Valley!

Sam: We should go over there and give him a good lickin' for scarin' us like that!

Horace: No need to. The old lady's doin' that for us right now!

(All laugh.)

Percy: *(hysterical)* Montana Bill!

(All laugh again. Drinks are poured.)

Horace: I just hope we can *explain* all this to that Mountie when he gets here.

Percy: Yup. Laurence Wretched-Smith, due in *(checks watch)* twenty-four minutes.

(Montana enters, swaggering.)

Sam: *(noticing Montana)* Why, if it ain't Wee Willy McAllister!

Fester: How ya doin', Willy?

Percy: Hey, Willy, let me buy ya a drink!

Sam: Need a chaser after a bowl of oatmeal porridge!

(He laughs. The others guffaw. Montana pulls out his gun and fires in the air. Percy squeals. Then, deathly silence.)

Montana: The name is Montana Bill, you stubble-jumpers, and you better *remember* it.

Horace: *(placating)* Su—Sure, Willy.

(The gun roars again. Percy whimpers.)

Montana: That's *Montana Bill!* The law's after me for killing a man in Billings, and I ain't

goin' back tied up like an old sow. Gimme a—a whisky, Fester.

Fester: Sure, Wil—*Montana.*

(He pours it.)

Montana: Cheers, you guys.

All: Cheers, Montana.

Montana: Why ain't *you* fellas drinkin'?

Gompers: Glasses are empty— *(grins)* Montana.

Montana: Fill 'em up, Fes. Fill 'em *all* up.

Fester: *(nervously)* You gonna—uh—*pay* for 'em—Mont—?

(Montana fires again.)

Fester: Comin' up, Montana!

Percy: *(edging out)* I'll pass, Fes. Just remembered I told the wife I'd be home early today—

Montana: You stay where you are. Nobody leaves.

Percy: But, Willy—!

(The gun fires.)

Montana: Unnerstood?

All: Yes, Montana!

(pause)

Gompers: So you got perty good with that gun down in the States, eh, Montana?

Montana: *(modestly)* I practised a bit. What uv it?

Gompers: Wanta make sure it's fair fight, that's all.

Montana: *(startled)* Fight? Who said anythin' about a fight?

Gompers: Oh, there'll be a fight, okay. Should be in about *(checks time)* five minutes— soon as the Mountie walks through that door.

Montana: What Mountie? There's no Mounties in Sand Valley! You guys are tryna bluff me.

Gompers: Why don't you show *Montana* here

that telegram you got from Regina, Perc?

Percy: *(rattling paper)* He—he—here it is.

Montana: *(snatching it)* Um. *(mumbles)* "Ur-gen-cy—Corporal Wretched-Smith—authority." *(suspicious)* Says here you're supposed to close the bar.

Sam: Fester thought it would be nice to stay open and let us have a drink with old Montana.

Montana: *(warming to this)* Well, that was right nice of you, Fes.

Percy: *(mistaking the tone)* Kin I go now, Montana?

(Another gunshot. Percy shrieks in terror. A train whistle is heard.)

Horace: The Mountie!

Gompers: There he comes, Montana.

Montana: Gimme another shot a whisky.

Sam: You gonna stay and fight it out?

Montana: *(swallowing)* Sometimes a man has tuh stand up for hisself. Can't let his mother run his life forever.

Horace: You can't fight that Mountie! That's resistin' arrest.

Montana: *(threatening)* Who says I can't?

Gompers: Nobody, Montana—nobody.

Sam: *(looking out the window)* Here he is!

Montana: Quick! Gimme another drink!

(Drink is poured. Montana swallows it noisily. The corporal enters.)

Corporal: *(British)* Aha! I thought you'd been ordered to close this bar *up?*

Several: Well, we thought—You see, he rode past—Didn't think it was—

Corporal: Well, my man, *that* will cost you a neat fine in district court—contravening a direct order from O.C., F Division, working under the authority of King George the Fifth, in times of dire emergency. Section 3, Paragraph A, sub-section (b) of the Statutes of Saskatchewan.

Fester: But you don't understand—this guy here's—

Corporal: May I enquire which of you is *(takes paper out of his pocket and reads it)* —Montana Bill?

All: There he is! That's him there! He's got a gun!

Montana: *I'm* Montana Bill.

Corporal: I see. I must warn you, of course, that anything you say here may be taken as evidence and used at your trial.

Montana: Trial? For what?

Corporal: Well, there are several possibilities: carrying an unregistered hand-gun, crossing the border illegally, threatening your fellow citizens, being intoxicated in a public place. Now would you step outside with me—?

Montana: I—I ain't goin'!

Corporal: Eh? What's that?

Montana: *(dramatically)* You'll have to take me out in a pine box, Mountie. I'll never swing!

Corporal: *(pause)* I see. What do you propose to do?

Montana: We're gonna have us a gunfight! Now get to the other end of the room!

(Crowd clears for cover. Corporal Wretched-Smith marches stiffly to far end. There is a tense silence.)

Montana: Go ahead—draw!

Corporal: *(primly)* You'll have to draw first. RCMP Ordinance Number 47.

Montana: Slap leather, Mountie!

(The suspense builds. Mrs. McAllister bursts in.)

Mrs. McAllister: Wulliam McAllister! *What* are ye doing?

Montana: Well, I was just—uh, havin' a kinduv a gun duel with uh—

Mrs. McAllister: Hand me that weapon!

Corporal: Be careful, madam. He's a dangerous criminal.

Mrs. McAllister: Dangerous my eye. He's my boy, Wulliam. Now, I'll relieve you of that pistol, young man.

Montana: *(writhing in embarrassment)* Aw, maw—!

Mrs. McAllister: Thank you. Now, oot the door! And leave the whusky where it is.

Corporal: You mustn't take him, madam. He's my prisoner!

Mrs. McAllister: *(pointing the gun)* Don't you tell me what *I* can do with him, ye scarlet little popinjay—or I'll confiscate yours, too.

(The corporal is stunned into silence.)

Mrs. McAllister: Now take this thing away with ye—before it goes off in my hand. Come, Wulliam.

Montana: *(meekly)* Where we goin', maw?

Mrs. McAllister: I'll never have any dignity in this town now—and it's plain you can't be trusted to look after yourself. We'll go somewhere where we aren't known.

Montana: But maw—!

Mrs. McAllister: Whussht! There's an end to it. I need my own son to comfort me in my old age.

(She takes him out.)

Montana: Aw, maw—

Gompers: Thought you boys had a reputation for always gettin' your man, Mr. Wretched-Smith.

Corporal: Highly irregular, you know. Blasted woman's a menace to law and order.

Sam: You said it. Now that *she's* gone—we can open the bar again! That is— *(looks him up and down)* if you're gonna take that tent off your head and drink like a man.

Corporal: I beg your pardon?

Gompers: Fester. Bring this boy a whisky!

Corporal: No! No, thank you. The O.C. would shoot—that is, it's against—uh *(thinks)* —Paragraph Nine, uh, sub-section— *(pause)* Would you have any dry gin? With lemon?

(Great cheer in the bar, as they crowd around and remove his hat. All laugh. Music.)

Narrator: And the afternoon light slants toward the prairie horizon, leaving the little town of Sand Valley in peaceful shadows once again. A cloud of dust rises from the westbound road out of town. It is Montana Bill and his mother riding off into the blood-red Saskatchewan sunset.

(Curtain)

Caution:
Enquiries regarding performing rights, professional or amateur, of this play should be directed to the Bella Pomer Agency, 22 Shallmar Boulevard, Ph. 2, Toronto, Ontario M5N 2Z8.

WINNERS AND LOSERS

Some writers see life as a continual contest. A person struggles for success in all aspects of his or her life—be it at school, at home, with peers, or in the work world. Some see this sort of struggle as the major spark that keeps us going: without the stress that goes along with struggle, we would simply cease to function.

Though of course the outcome of such a conflict is important, the growth that comes as a result of the struggle can be the most rewarding part of the "contest of life." The dramatists in this unit demonstrate that ultimately it is the central character who decides whether he or she is a winner or loser. It is the subjective viewpoint that determines success.

In Carol Bolt's musical play *Cyclone Jack*, the Canadian runner Tom Longboat succeeds as an athlete but is exploited as a person by those around him. *Ride to the Hill*, a television play by Ron Taylor, shows a protagonist who learns something about maturing and human nature when she must give up her most prized possession, a pinto pony.

Cyclone Jack
Carol Bolt

CHARACTERS

Tom Longboat—a native marathon runner from Brampton

Charlie Petch—a marathon runner from Hamilton

Tom Flanagan—a gambler and Tom Longboat's manager

Announcer

Emerson Coatsworth—the mayor of Toronto

Chuck Ashley—Tom Longboat's coach early in his career

Tom Shipman—a marathon runner from Montreal

Dorando—a marathon runner from Italy

Lauretta Maracle—Tom Longboat's wife

Lady Fan at the Boston Marathon

Secretary of the Canadian Olympic Committee

April—a woman from the West End Y, Toronto

NOTE: song lyrics are printed in italics.

"If the Olympic Committee stops him from running, the people of Canada are going to rise up in arms and have your nose for breakfast."

(The Caledonia Marathon. The cast are the runners.)

Voice: On your mark. Get set.

(A gunshot starts the race. Everyone except Tom sings.)

He's running like joy,
Like the joy of the wind in his face.
And the beat of his heart and his feet
Feels it's setting the pace
And his mind reaching out to what seems
Like a whole other space.

Reaching for, gasping for air,
When it just isn't there.
Aching, breaking, shaking, so why does he care?

If he goes twice as fast,
He might be getting somewhere.

(Tom Longboat wins the Caledonia Marathon, followed across the finish line by Charlie Petch and the rest of the cast. There is a huge cheer.)

Ah, vi vi vi
Vi vi vum
Let's get a rat-trap
Bigger'n a cat-trap
Vum vum vum
Vum vum vum
Cannibal vannibal
Bowlegged bah!
West End! West End!
Rah! Rah! Rah!

Charlie: *(to the audience)* Running twenty-five miles is running far enough to put yourself into another world. Until you get your second breath. Until that isn't enough. Your third breath. Till your body is foggy with pain but your mind is perfectly clear. Tom Longboat won the 1907 Caledonia Marathon, but he had some trouble on the way. Two Toronto gamblers drove right into him in their carriage. They said their horses went crazy. They forced him right off the road, but he won anyway.

Ashley: Congratulations, Tom. Now we can go down to Boston. You can run for Canada in the Boston Marathon.

Tom: Just as soon go back to Brantford.

Ashley: Charlie Petch from Hamilton wants to congratulate you, Tom. Good sportsmanship. He'll be going to Boston too.

Charlie: Congratulations, Mr. Longboat.

Ashley: You don't have to call him Mr. Longboat.

Tom: You can call me Cyclone Jack.

(The cast performs a lavish song-and-dance number.)

Cyclone Jack was Tom Longboat
Tom was only nineteen
His one big sin
He didn't run to win
No man is a running machine.

(Chorus—repeat first two lines of verse)

Said we wanted a runner
Was a marathon star
When he was twenty-one
We made him race the sun
But he didn't get very far.

(Chorus—repeat first two lines of verse)

Long as Tom wins races
He can do us no wrong
Since he takes first place
In every race
We're all singing Longboat's song.

(Chorus—repeat first two lines of verse)

What to do with a hero
A man like Cyclone Jack
When he was twenty-four
We sent him off to war
We didn't think he'd come back no more.

(Chorus—repeat first two lines of verse)

Tom came home from the trenches
Found his widow rewed
When he was twenty-five
We brought him back alive
He might as well have been dead.

(Chorus—repeat first two lines of verse)

Tom was finished running
Just plain finished as well
We couldn't celebrate
A has-been at twenty-eight
Not much there that we could sell.

(Chorus—repeat first two lines of verse)

No one wanted a loser
Tom was down on his luck
When he was thirty-five
We let him drive
A big Toronto garbage truck.

(Chorus—repeat first two lines of verse)

Just one place for a loser
Working on a garbage truck.

(At the end of this song, the scene changes to a train going to Boston. We see Tom and Chuck Ashley. Ashley talks with the physicality of an athletic coach. He pokes Tom a lot to make his point.)

Ashley: And I want you to train. Train? Well, you can't train on a train, Tom. But when we get back to the Y, you're a sportsman, you have to keep training. Early to bed and early to rise. You should be running twenty-five miles, three, four times a week.

Tom: I've always been a runner. I've never trained before.

Ashley: Ha, ha! Always kidding.

Tom: Ran from the Iroquois reservation at Brantford, all the way to Toronto and the West End Y. All the training I ever did.

Ashley: Discipline. Courage. Determination.

Charlie: *(singing to the audience)*
Long way from Brantford to Boston
Riding on the miles of railroad track
And on the way we lost Tom Longboat
We found Cyclone Jack.

Called him an Indian Iron Man
Called him an Indian Running Machine
Took him off the Brantford Reservation
To show him sights he'd never seen.

Tom was proud of his people
Of men who could run like deer
Said I'm not the fastest Onondaga marathoner
I'm the only Onondaga here.

Tom was young when they took him to the city
Showed him all the pretty ladies.
Gave him a big cigar.
It's no place for a marathoner runner
Sitting up sleeping in a railway car.

Ashley: Spunk. Grit. That's what makes this country great. That's what made my country great, anyway. I'm an American...look, Tom, look, out the window! The Stars and Stripes. *(sings)* Oh, say does that Star Spangled Banner still wave o'er the land of the free and the home of the brave. *(speaking)* That's an inspiration. That's a wonderful sight. Take your hat off, Tom, it's a mark of respect. Take your hat off! *(Tom does, but with no enthusiasm.)* You feel tired?

Tom: I can't sleep before a race.

Ashley: Sleepy! I knew you'd say that. Lights out. No cigars. You've got a race to win in the morning. Doesn't that look good. I got us a lower berth. We have to relax. Relax, Tom. Relax! Relax! We'll have your arms flinging out, like this. Your legs all tensing up and jumping out, like this. Call that muscle spasm. You remember our race strategy? We hold back at the start, let somebody else set the pace.

Tom: Charlie Petch.

Ashley: We can catch Petch in the stretch, Tom. We can show him that the North Side of Hamilton is nothing like the West End of Toronto.

Tom: There are four or five runners in Brantford...all of them faster than me.

Ashley: When we pass him...he won't be any good to anybody after that...Charlie Petch, he'll be eating nails, he'll be so mad when you pass him...

Tom: I run as fast as I have to to win.

Ashley: That's what I mean. That's strategy. Heh, heh, heh... *(Tom accidentally elbows Ashley.)* Oof! Tom...look, Tom...you've got your elbow in my ribs.

Tom: I can't sleep before a race.

Ashley: Well, that's why I got a lower berth. Lots of room on your side. *(Tom hits Ashley again.)* Ooof!

Tom: Sorry.

Ashley: Heh, heh. That's all right, Tom.

Tom: It's a muscle spasm.

(Tom elbows Ashley again.)

Ashley: Oooof!

Tom: I feel too strong for sleeping. You can get like that. *(He gives Ashley a last thrust to the ribs and Ashley rolls out of bed.)*

Ashley: Heh, heh, heh, you're always kidding, Tom. Don't worry about a thing. I'll just curl up here in the aisle.

Tom: *(singing)*
Marathon runner,
You're going to wait for the sun
Marathon runner,
You're going to wait for the sun
You've got all night long to sit through
Then you've got all day long to run.

Twenty-five miles,
That's too long to run without crying
Twenty-five miles
That's too long to run without crying
The nights you feel too strong to sleep
Why do you think you're dying?

You got to feel it,
All alone through the night
You got to feel it,
All alone all through the night

Reaching out for one more aching mile
Just waiting for the light.

Waiting for the race to start
Waiting with the pounding of my heart
Beat, beat, beat from my head to my feet
I'm waiting for the sun.

Ashley: *(waking up)* Big race today. How do we feel this morning? Good day for the race...

(The scene changes to the Boston Marathon track.)

Announcer: Good day for the race, ladies and gentlemen. April 19, 1907. Runners from all over America here for the annual Boston Marathon and some friends from Canada...

Shipman: *(offstage)* Where's my shoes?

Lady Fan: Who's that?

Announcer: Taking his position now, Charlie Petch from Hamilton, continuing Hamilton's great tradition of marathon runners.

(There are cheers for Charlie.)

Shipman: *(entering)* Anybody seen my shoes?

Lady Fan: Who is it?

Charlie: Tom Shipman, being from Montreal. He forgot his shoes.

Shipman: I can't run without my shoes. *(exits)*

Charlie: You weren't going to run very fast anyway, Shipman.

Announcer: The record for this course is two hours, twenty-nine minutes, twenty-three and three-fifths seconds, over the twenty-five mile distance.

Lady Fan: There goes Charlie. Char-lie Petch.

Shipman: *(offstage)* Going to make it one, two, Charlie? Petch is set for second place.

Announcer: Charlie Petch is in this race to win.

Lady Fan: I'd run twenty-five miles for Charlie Petch. He's only eighteen.

Announcer: Charlie Petch at the age of eighteen, running against the running machine. *(Tom enters to huge cheers. The fickle Lady Fan is particularly impressed.)* And here's the favourite, Tom Longboat. *(gunshot)* And they're off.

(Charlie takes an early lead.)

Tom: After you, Charlie.

(Lady Fan promenades through runners.)

Charlie: Nobody starts out to run twenty-five miles unless they think they can do it. Do it faster. I don't run twenty-five miles for nothing. I can win it. I can't even see him. He's too far behind me now.

Lady Fan: *(singing)*
Charlie Petch looks like a wreck
He has two left feet
But that Indian from Brantford
He's the man to beat
He's just like an Indian summer
You wonder where he's gone
The Onondaga runner
At the Boston Marathon.

Charlie Petch is out of breath
Dragging down the track
But the hero here in Boston
He's called Cyclone Jack
He's just like an Indian summer
You wonder where he's gone
The Onondaga runner
At the Boston Marathan.

(Tom is taking off his sweater. Ashley runs up beside him, or drives a car or a bicycle.)

Ashley: Throw it here, Tom. Throw it here, Tom. I'll catch it. Give me your sweater. That's what I'm here for. I'll catch it. *(Tom throws and Ashley misses the catch.)* Never mind, Tom. I'll get it. That's what I'm here for. *(Tom runs back, picks up the sweater, and tosses it to him. It hits him in the face.)* Thanks, Tom.

Charlie: *(exhausted)* Where is he? Where is he?

(Tom pulls up beside Charlie.)

Tom: You look tired, Charlie. Going to make it over the hill? Over the hill already? Your shoelace is untied. Petchie, Petchie, you can't catch me. Come on, Charlie, there's the finish line. Want to make it one, two?

(Tom makes a last dash ahead to cross the finish line, followed by Charlie. As Tom passes the finish line, he is draped in a Canadian flag and mobbed by April, a lady from the Y, Emerson Coatsworth, and Ashley.)

Charlie: He won. He doesn't race. He doesn't train. But he wins. I trained all winter for this race. I ran around Hamilton Bay with weights on my shoes. But I place nineteenth. Now we're going back to Toronto for a ceremony at the city hall. He'll get all the medals. He'll make all the speeches.

(A song bridges the action between Boston and Toronto.)

Long as Tom wins the races
He can do us no wrong
And since he takes first place
In every race
We're all singing Longboat's song
Long as Tom wins races
He can do us no wrong.

(Mayor Coatsworth stands at the podium at Toronto City Hall.)

Coatsworth: Five minutes off the record for the Boston Marathon. The amazing time of two hours, twenty-four minutes, twenty and four-fifths seconds. *(large cheer)* The old record, of course, was also held by a Canadian, Mr. J. J. Caffrey from Hamilton, and we have here with us Charlie Petch from Hamilton *(large cheers)* who came nineteenth. *(large groan of disappointment)*

Tom: *(to Ashley)* See this. I beat them. I don't have to do it your way any more. Take your hat off, Ashley.

Ashley: Always joking, always joking.

Tom: Take your hat off, Ashley.

Ashley: That's not good sportsmanship.

Tom: Take your hat off, Ashley.

Ashley: If you win or lose...

Tom: I won.

Ashley: He's just joking, Mr. Mayor, Mr. Coatsworth, sir.

Coatsworth: As mayor of the city of Toronto...

Ashley: Emerson Coatsworth is talking, Tom... *(Tom shouts with laughter.)* Quiet!

Coatsworth: This is a proud day for all of us. I know the citizens of Toronto are going to give these boys a fine welcome. We have medals to present. We have a scholarship for Tom Longboat. These boys don't want money or medals. They want you to cheer their victory. Hip Hip Hooray. Hip Hip Hooray. Hip Hip Hooray. Now here's Tom Longboat, to say a few words. *(cheers from everyone)* Keep it short, Tom.

Tom: I thank you very kindly, Mr. Mayor.

(A long pause. Tom beams, laughs. Everyone is uncomfortable, except for Tom and except for Charlie Petch, who sees his chance as the pause continues. And continues. And continues.)

Charlie: *(speaking at last)* Citizens of Toronto, I thank you for this great reception on this our return from our great effort in Boston. I cannot say too much for the way Mr. Longboat won the race. We tried to make it first and second, but we couldn't. Again, I thank you and remain, yours truly, Charlie Petch.

(Charlie sings.)

At City Hall
The whole soul control routine
Charlie Petch
Knows what I mean.
We'll dance, dance, dance, dance
If you want to do it then you got to get into it.

Indian Chief
Man with a thousand faces
Party like this,
What you get for winning races
Comedy team
Yeah, yeah, yeah, yeah
He's a running machine.

Dance, dance, dance, dance, dance, dance, dance

If you want to do it then you got to get into it.

Ashley: Good-bye, Tom.

Coatsworth: Good-bye, Tom.

Ashley: Don't do anything I wouldn't do.

Coatsworth: Does he?

Ashley: Be a good boy, Tom.

Tom: Yeah.

(Tom is now shaking the hand of April, the woman from the Y.)

Coatsworth: Let him go, April.

(But Tom persists until Charlie pulls him off.)

Tom: Some people call me Wildfire, but you can call me Cyclone Jack.

Charlie: They aren't used to cyclones at the Y, Tom. They don't even have a storm cellar.

(Charlie hustles Tom off.)

April: Is it true that he drinks? He's been seen with gamblers.

Ashley: You don't understand, ma'am. Tom doesn't like the city. He's like a kid when he's by himself. I'm with him all the time.

April: Except when he's with Tom Flanagan and Tim O'Rourke. They are gamblers.

Ashley: They're sportsmen, ma'am.

April: They like to bet on sports.

Ashley: He's a strange kind of boy. I mean, he's not at ease in the city, not at all.

April: He is not the sort of boy we need at the YMCA. He'll have to go.

Ashley: He needs to be managed, ma'am. You're going to drive him right into the arms of his gambler friends. Like Flanagan. Straight to the Grand Central Hotel.

(The scene changes to the Grand Central Hotel. There is raucous and rowdy cheering followed by a song and dance, led by Flanagan.)

Flanagan and Others:
My name is Tom Flanagan
O'Rourke and I
Are managers of the Grand Central Hotel
It's a haven for gentlemen

A hostel for sportsmen
For the man
Who is dapper and snappy and swell.

Are you the Tom Flanagan who keeps this hotel
Are you the same Flanagan they speak of so well
Are you the Tom Flanagan
Who's Tom Longboat's manager
Your man, again, Flanagan.
You're doing so well.

For fun and for frolic
For feasting and froth
The place that the vice squad quite often forgets
The whiskey is watered
The barmaid is beautiful
The boys in the backroom are placing their bets.

For rambling, for roving
For football and sporting
For drinking rye whiskey
As fast as you will

In all your days roving
There's none so jovial
As Flanagan of the Grand Central Hotel.

Flanagan: I have an appointment. I think I'm late.

(The scene changes to the Canadian Olympic Committee's office. Flanagan knocks.)

Flanagan: Would this be the Canadian Olympic Committee?

Secretary: And who shall I say is calling?

Flanagan: Flanagan. Tom Longboat's new manager.

Secretary: His manager. Oh. We can't see you. No.

Flanagan: We're discussing my runner's status in the Olympics.

Secretary: Well, no. This is the Olympic Committee. We deal with amateur sports. Only.

Flanagan: The boy is a natural runner. He loves to run. Amo amas amat amateur. From the Latin, to love.

Secretary: Well, no. Mr. Longboat has run in county fairs all over Ontario. For money.

Flanagan: An amateur never runs for money. Well, not unless it's offered to him.

Secretary: Mr. Flanagan! You take him from town to town with bands and carriages and silk hats. That is not sport. That is a freak show.

Flanagan: He loves to run. He hardly has time to run his cigar store.

Secretary: Well, no . . . the Olympic Committee is watching you, Mr. Flanagan.

Flanagan: We only bought him the cigar store so he could afford to run.

Secretary: He does not manage a cigar store. It is our information he has smoked all the cigars.

Flanagan: He does it for the love of it and if the Olympic Committee stops him from running, the people of Canada are going to rise up in arms and have your nose for breakfast.

Secretary: Well, no. The Olympics are for amateurs. The Italian, Dorando, an Olympian. The American, Hayes, an Olympian. Longboat is a professional.

Flanagan: The people want to see him run.

(Flanagan fires a gun which begins the Olympic Marathon. Dorando and Tom race in the background.)

Secretary: When you think of the marathon runner, you think of the Olympics, don't you? The torch coming into the stadium. The runner carrying the torch. Tom Longboat is a paid professional . . .

Flanagan: His prize money?

Secretary: Yes.

Flanagan: He gave it away. Every penny of it. Money means nothing to Tom Longboat. He simply loves to run.

Secretary: Longboat's friends corrupt him.

Flanagan: Every last dollar to a worthy cause. Distressed naval widows.

Secretary: Bets are being placed on the Olympic games!

Flanagan: The Humane Society. The Conservative Party of Canada.

Secretary: Tom Longboat is notorious. Silk hats. Card sharks. Pool halls.

Flanagan: Well, he's a sure thing, ma'am. Have you ever seen him run?

(Flanagan and the secretary turn and watch Tom. Dorando has exited.)

Secretary: Well, he does seem innocent enough in himself.

Flanagan: Some men will bet on anything.

Secretary: He's smiling. What a nice boy.

Flanagan: I've known men who'll bet you the sun won't rise tomorrow. It's a sickness with them.

Secretary: He breaks into a grin and . . . well, it's like the sun, smiling.

Flanagan: And you can't blame them. Because Longboat in the Olympics, that's a sure thing.

(Longboat collapses. As the finish line for the 1908 Olympics is arranged, Dorando staggers in. Lots of cheering. Dorando seems dazed. He is headed in the wrong direction, on the verge of collapse. He is pulled across the finish line.)

Flanagan: You dropped out. You were almost finished.

Secretary: They say he just spun around and then dropped senseless.

Charlie: Dorando took three hours something. Tom can do better than that.

Flanagan: *(to Tom)* I'm not in this for my health, you know.

Charlie: *(to the secretary)* They say Dorando was drugged.

Flanagan: *(to Tom)* Do you know what pays for your room at the Grand Central Hotel? All the cigars you can smoke? Money. Do you know where the money comes from? Winning races.

Charlie: Is he hurt?

Secretary: He just fell. As if someone shot him.

Flanagan: Nobody pays to watch you get tired of running, Tom.

Charlie: Tom doesn't get tired of running.

Flanagan: *(to Tom)* I don't need a loser.

Charlie: *(to Flanagan)* You had money on the marathon. So did a lot of other people. They paid you to make sure he didn't finish.

Secretary: Dropped senseless.

Charlie: Bribery.

Flanagan: Not Tom.

Tom: *(to Flanagan)* Where was your money?

Flanagan: Don't be silly.

Tom: Who did you bet on?

Charlie: I want you to know I think it's disgraceful, Mr. Flanagan.

Flanagan: He can beat Dorando.

Charlie: But he didn't.

Flanagan: He'll race Dorando, anybody.

Charlie: Tom Longboat is the greatest runner in the world. But it's four years to the next Olympics, Mr. Flanagan.

Flanagan: So?

Charlie: So he's going to spend the next four years running around Hamilton Bay. That's not running the best in the world.

Flanagan: He won't be wasting his time racing amateurs. Tom's a professional now. Well, he'll be a family man. Responsibility. Tom's going to be married, Charlie.

Charlie: Getting married?

Flanagan: To the lovely Lauretta Maracle.

(Lauretta enters as the others exit.)

Lauretta: *(singing)*
Indian girl in a mission school
Watching all the boys race horses
Trying not to think they're crazy
They think they can fly
See the boy against the horse
Run for miles and win, of course
Lazy boy in a mission school

Running, running, running by
City streets will hurt your feet
If you're flying high
Lazy boy in a mission school
Running, running, running by.

(She goes over to Tom, who is about to smoke a cigar.)

Tom: Don't tell me, Lauretta. You're going to tell me I should be in training. For Madison Square Garden.

Lauretta: I'm going to tell you I bought a new hat. A New York hat.

Tom: That I should drink my milk and learn my catechism...

Lauretta: That you shouldn't hang around with gamblers.

Tom: That it doesn't matter if I win or lose, as long as I win.

Lauretta: Flanagan runs you, Tom. I don't.

(Flanagan enters.)

Flanagan: Well, if it isn't the two lovebirds. Discussing Tom's training for the big race tonight, I have no doubt. Well, talk is fine and love is fine, but it doesn't win races at all, at all.

Lauretta: *(as Flanagan waves Tom out)* Will he win? Against Dorando?

Flanagan: He hasn't trained properly. After you're married, we'll change that, of course.

Lauretta: Did you bet much money on him?

(Flanagan begins to dress Lauretta up in carnival-like Indian gear—feathers and beads.)

Flanagan: No.

Lauretta: Did you bet against him? On Dorando?

Flanagan: Lauretta. What do you take me for?

Lauretta: Tom's manager, Flanagan.

Flanagan: This is just the beginning. We'll have other races. I'm booking a rematch with Dorando on New Year's Day, another race the week after that...

Lauretta: Will he finish this race?

Flanagan: He's finished if he doesn't. War paint?

Lauretta: Leave me alone. You make me look ridiculous.

(Flanagan puts on his own head-dress.)

Flanagan: That ain't the half of it, Lauretta.

Lauretta: We're a joke to you, aren't we? Like dancing bears.

Flanagan: *(applying his own war paint)* We're going into Madison Square Garden to watch Tom race. And we aren't going to win. So we're going to put on a show for them. So they'll come and see us again.

(The scene changes to Madison Square Garden.)

Flanagan: I've got a box right down in front. Could you do a war dance if the race slows down, Lauretta?

Lauretta: I'm going to war, Flanagan.

Flanagan: You're no help at all. There's Dorando. Boo! Boo! Boo!

Dorando: *(to himself)* Twenty thousand people here to watch me beat Tom Longboat. Fifteen thousand of them are smoking cigars. The air is dirty, heavy. Enough trouble breathing without thinking about the air. I was first across the finish line in the 1908 Olympics. I was so confused, I was running in the wrong direction. I'm afraid of this race.

Tom: Let you out of the old-folks home this afternoon, Dorando? You got your wheel chair waiting in the wings?

(A gunshot signals the start of the race.)

Flanagan, Lauretta, Charlie: *(singing)*
He's running like joy,
Like the joy of the wind in his face.
And the beat of his heart and his feet
Feels it's setting the pace
And his mind reaching out to what seems
Like a whole other space.

Reaching for, gasping for air,
When it just isn't there

Aching, breaking, shaking, so why does he care?
If he goes twice as fast,
He might be getting somewhere.

(At the finish Dorando collapses. Tom watches him fall. Tom looks like he doesn't know what happens next. He tries to help Dorando to his feet. Cheers build.)

Flanagan: Call him, Lauretta.

Lauretta: Tom! Tom!

(Tom finishes the race, running toward Lauretta.)

Flanagan: Come on, Tom, come on, Tom. *(as Tom breaks the tape and exits)* We won, Lauretta, we won!

Lauretta: Tom won't have to race in January.

Flanagan: But Dorando will want to.

Lauretta: It's too soon. You can't race him every week.

Flanagan: Madison Square Garden. Filled with people. They'd come to see him race tomorrow.

Lauretta: To see him collapse. Like Dorando.

Flanagan: They'd fight for tickets.

Lauretta: You dress me up like a fool. You run him to death.

Flanagan: We got a good thing going here, Lauretta.

Lauretta: Tom beat Dorando. He's the fastest. He doesn't have to prove anything.

Flanagan: The money, Lauretta.

Lauretta: He won't race.

Flanagan: He's a professional, Lauretta. That's his job.

Lauretta: He won't race.

Flanagan: Of course we'll race. How long do you think this is going to last?

Lauretta: Where's Tom?

(Flanagan and Lauretta exit. The scene changes to Dorando's hospital room. Tom is visiting Dorando.)

Tom: How are you, Dorando?

Dorando: Not bad. Look, the doctors say I strained my heart. What do they know? I feel fine.

Tom: Flanagan says we'll run again.

Dorando: Sure. It's all arranged. I'll be fine.

Tom: Do they drug you, Dorando?

Dorando: Look, if my brother comes in, don't talk about my heart. He's crazy, my brother.

Tom: Do you want to race again?

Dorando: Well, we have to, don't we?

Tom: Why?

Dorando: Because there's nowhere else to go and we have to get there fast.

Tom: Because you love it.

Dorando: For the money, Tom. While we can.

Tom: I don't think I race for the money.

Dorando: Sure you do.

Tom: I don't race at all. I just run.

Dorando: You're crazy.

Tom: All right.

Dorando: I'm older than you are. I don't have as long to race. You don't seem to care about running. You give away all your medals. But in four or five years, you'll be where I am. They'll say *you* strained *your* heart. You'll be worn out and Flanagan will sell you off. Or maybe he'll be long gone, because he'll get out before they drug you up like a workhorse to race. This is the top money. That's the kind of money that Flanagan wants.

Tom: Flanagan has nothing to do with me.

Dorando: He owns you.

Tom: Back in Brantford, we used to run faster, longer than horses. I guess that was crazy. It was fun, though.

Dorando: You're twenty-one years old. You've got maybe five years, maybe not that long. Get what you can while you can, Tom. Flanagan will.

Tom: Ever hear of Cyclone Jack?

Dorando: Oh, sure. He's Flanagan's Racing Machine.

Tom: Cyclone Jack has nothing to do with Flanagan. But he runs, Dorando. It's beautiful to run like that.

Dorando: Flanagan will burn you out. Ask him how long it will take.

(They exit. The scene changes to Flanagan's office. Flanagan enters, followed by Charlie. Tom enters to the side, unnoticed, and overhears them talk.)

Charlie: Mr. Flanagan, they say Tom's been missing for two days now.

Flanagan: Missing?

Charlie: What's wrong with him?

Flanagan: How's your running going, Charlie?

Charlie: Is he drinking?

Flanagan: Still in shape? You used to be pretty good. I've had my eye on you, Charlie.

Charlie: I'm just an amateur, Mr. Flanagan.

Flanagan: Can't keep a good man down?

Charlie: Is Tom down?

Flanagan: He's fine. He'll be fine. But you know how it is, Charlie. Tom's fast . . .

Charlie: Where is he?

Flanagan: There are times you want something to depend on. You've always been very dependable, Charlie.

Charlie: But I can't run like Tom does.

Flanagan: No, you're nothing like Tom, Charlie.

Tom: *(entering their scene)* That's the joy of it, isn't it?

Charlie: Tom!

Flanagan: You see, he's back. I told you he'd be back!

Charlie: Tom! We were worried . . .

Tom: I've been to see Dorando.

Flanagan: Now listen, Tom. I've got enough trouble with you winning races when you're not supposed to have a chance, losing races when you're a sure thing, without chasing you around New York.

Tom: You weren't chasing me.

Flanagan: No. I wasn't. I don't have the time.

Tom: You aren't a runner.

Flanagan: And neither are you. You're some kind of freak who races horses. Some kind of freak who wins races.

Charlie: He's been to see Dorando, Mr. Flanagan.

Tom: Dorando is a runner.

Flanagan: Some kind of brotherhood, is it? You and Dorando understand each other? You and Dorando and Charlie Petch. You're all runners and I don't belong.

Tom: That's right.

Flanagan: Look, Tom, you'd be far better off listening to me than some broken-down fugitive from a squirrel cage who hardly knows enough to put one foot in front of the other.

Tom: Do you mean Dorando?

Flanagan: Yes, I mean Dorando. Dorando the dummy.

Tom: They say he strained his heart.

Flanagan: That's too bad.

Tom: Well?

Flanagan: I said that's too bad. Dorando's past it.

Tom: When will I be past it?

Flanagan: You're always joking, aren't you? How old are you?

Tom: That's right.

Flanagan: You're twenty-one years old.

Tom: That's right.

Flanagan: That's right, that's right. What do you mean, that's right.

Tom: Four or five years left, Flanagan. Running for the big money, maybe not that long. You better start window shopping. You'll need another runner.

Flanagan: Tom! Tom! Tom. Tom. Tom. Tom. Tom. Tom. You're only twenty-one years old. You'll be married in two weeks. Your whole life ahead of you and you are the fastest man in the world. Look, about your wedding. I have a surprise for you.

Tom: What?

Flanagan: Guess. *(Tom begins to laugh. Anything will make him laugh. This mood continues to the end of the play.)* A hint. It's about your wedding reception. *(no reply except more laughter)* Guess where we're having the reception? I guess you thought we were having the reception at the Grand Central Hotel. No sir, Tom. Massey Hall. Massey Hall, Tom. We're going to put on a wonderful show. I'm arranging it. We've got it all ready. Just a minute. A preview. *(He exits.)*

Charlie: Why do you let him do it?

Tom: He lets me run.

Charlie: He uses you. He sells you up and down the country.

Tom: He lets me run.

Charlie: He runs you.

Tom: What does it matter where I'm running? If I'm running on the reservation at Brantford. If I'm running at Madison Square Garden. What's the difference? I love it, Charlie. Running. I don't run for Flanagan. I run for me.

Charlie: Flanagan asked me to race for him, Tom. To take over.

Tom: Did you believe him?

(Charlie laughs. So does Tom.)

Tom: You know Flanagan's a phony, Charlie.

Charlie: He's worse than that.

Tom: Sure. He's a fraud, he's a fake. He's a snake-oil salesman.

Charlie: A liar and a cheat.

Tom: He's a two-faced, double-dealing...

Charlie: Mealy-mouthed...

Tom: Flim-flam, flash...

Tom and Charlie: ...Four-flusher! *(They laugh.)*

Tom: Want to go to Flanagan's party, Charlie? At Massey Hall? Come on. It'll be fun.

(Tom exits to find Lauretta. The scene changes to Massey Hall.)

Charlie: Massey Hall, Cyclone Jack's wedding party held at Massey Hall.

(Lauretta and Tom enter in as much of a procession as can be arranged.)

Lauretta: There must be a thousand people here.

Tom: Sure there are. Well, thanks for coming.

(There follows a hymn of praise for Tom, sung by the cast.)

Long as Tom wins races
He can do us no wrong
Since he takes first place
In every race
We're all singing Longboat's song.

(Chorus—repeat first two lines of verse)

Cyclone Jack was Tom Longboat
Tom was only nineteen
His one big sin
He didn't run to win
No man is a running machine.

(Chorus—repeat first two lines of verse)

(This song should be staged as exuberantly as the original wedding reception, when tumbling acts and performers entertained. When the song is over, Tom finds himself alone on stage. There is a repeat of the two final verses from the song "Cyclone Jack," sung by everyone except Tom.)

Tom was finished running
Just plain finished as well
We couldn't celebrate
A has-been at twenty-eight
Not much there we could sell
Tom was finished running
Just plain finished as well.

No one wanted a loser
Tom was down on his luck
When he was thirty-five
We let him drive
A big Toronto garbage truck
Just one place for a loser
Working on a garbage truck.

(Curtain)

Ride to the Hill

Ron Taylor

CHARACTERS
Pauline
Mr. Hefferman
Martin

---

*"Look, I don't want the horse. I don't
even know how to ride one. So would
you please do me a favour and take
your horse back before I get killed."*

SCENE ONE

(Exterior. A side road. Day.

*A narrow side road leads down from the
main highway. Walking down the road is Pauline, a tall, angular fourteen-year-old, already
about one hundred seventy centimetres tall.
She wears jeans, a shirtlike blouse, and riding
boots. Her hair is long and straight, at times
half covering her face. She is not beautiful, and
only at certain moments can she even be called
pretty. Her movements are often awkward but
never clumsy. As she gets to the gate, she steps
off the road as a car, pulling an empty horse
van, passes her on the way out to the highway.
A lot of dust is thrown up by the van. Pauline
watches the van go. A sign on the gate reads:
"Horses Boarded." Pauline walks on toward the
stable.)*

SCENE TWO

(Exterior. A corral. Day.

*Tied to the rail in the corral is a single horse,
a small, brown-and-white pinto about twelve
hands in height. He wears a bridle but no saddle. Pauline comes through into the corral. As
she approaches the horse, Mr. Hefferman, a
man of about sixty and the owner of the farm,
comes out of the stable. He carries a currycomb and a brush.)*

Hefferman: Good morning, Pauline.

Pauline: Good morning, Mr. Hefferman.

*(Pauline pats the little horse and presses her
face lovingly against his. Hefferman places the
brush and comb on the fence.)*

Hefferman: I thought you might want to work
on him a little before he goes.

Pauline: Thank you.

Hefferman: They brought the new one.
(*gently*) Would you like to have a look at him? (*Pauline shakes her head.*) He's a fine-looking horse. (*She shakes her head again.*) Well, he's in the old stall whenever you get around to it.

(*Pauline unties the little horse, puts the lines over his neck, and swings up onto his back. Her long legs dangle almost to the ground. She turns the horse toward the lower gate. Hefferman smiles.*)

Hefferman: Going up to the hill?

(*Pauline just nods. Hefferman goes ahead of her as she walks the horse to the gate. Hefferman unlatches the gate. When she passes through, he closes it behind her. He watches as she starts down the field toward the river, the little horse stepping neatly in a medium walk. Hefferman turns, crosses the corral, and goes on up to the house.*)

SCENE THREE

(*Exterior. A stream. Day.*
As they come through the stream, Pauline stops to let the horse drink. It is a clear, bright morning. The birds are singing and on the banks of the river there are wild flowers, but Pauline seems unaffected by the beauty around her. When the horse has had enough, she pulls his head up and they climb the other bank, which leads shortly to the base of a long, high hill.*)

SCENE FOUR

(*Exterior. The bottom of the hill. Day.*
From another camera angle, along the base of the hill, with Pauline and the horse in the distance, we get the full perspective of the hill. At the top is a giant oak tree. We then see a closer shot of Pauline and the horse climbing the hill.*)

SCENE FIVE

(*Exterior. The hill. Day.*
The camera angle is from atop the hill, beside the oak tree, looking down across the countryside. The camera pans slowly to show the gentle curve across the base of the hill, a great stretch of a ride, a place to let a horse out and run. The pan carries us over to Pauline and the horse coming up the hill. The camera angle shifts to Pauline's POV of the tree as they come up onto the level at the top of the hill. The grass is eaten down as though she had come here many times to let the horse graze. She slips off his back and lets the reins drop to the ground. She sits with her back against the tree and watches her little horse grazing serenely. Slowly the pinto comes to Pauline. She looks at him and finally speaks to him.*)

Pauline: I'm sorry I grew so big. I really didn't mean to . . . grow so big. Why can't people mind their own business? You'd think they had nothing better to do than worry about how we look riding down the road together. (*She gets up on her knees, putting her arms around his neck, leaning her head against him.*) Stanley, I love you. I don't care how ridiculous we are. I don't want another horse. I want you. (*After a moment she finds a burr in his mane. She gets up fully, pulls it out, and speaks to him as though she were trying to cheer him up.*) I wonder how many burrs I've pulled out of your mane? Hundreds. Thousands, I guess! Six years of pulling burrs. It must be thousands. And that's not counting the ones you get in your tail. If you count those it might be millions. (*She teases him.*) Even trillions! (*Pauline swings onto the horse's back.*) Oh, come on.

SCENE SIX

(*Exterior. The hill and fields. Day.*
She starts down the hill, and we follow their ride back to the corral in a series of beautiful pastoral shots dissolving one into the other.*)

Pauline: I wonder what it's going to be like without you? I wonder what I'll do? I'll take long walks, all by myself, far out across the fields. I'll go down to the stream where I used to let you drink and watch the water running over the little brown stones. And one day I'll look up and I'll see you standing very still against the blue sky and just as I raise my hand to wave to you, he'll pull your head around. You'll be gone, and I'll walk back through the fields feeling very sad and very lonely.

SCENE SEVEN

(Exterior. The fields and corral. Day.
Pauline and the horse approach the lower gate of the corral. A figure sitting on a fence in the corral leaps down and comes to the lower gate to open it for them. His name is Martin. He is a likable, gregarious, just-turned fifteen-year-old, stocky in build and short for his age, about one hundred sixty-two centimetres tall. As Pauline and the horse come through the gate, Martin greets them cheerfully.)

Martin: Hi!

Pauline: *(coldly)* Hi.

(Pauline rides the horse into the corral, slips off his back, and ties him to the rail. Martin closes the gate and follows them.)

Martin: Well...here I am.

(Pauline picks up the currycomb and brush and begins working on the horse.)

Pauline: He's not ready yet.

Martin: He looks fine to me, just as he is.

Pauline: He's not leaving here until he's groomed. If you don't feel like waiting around, I'll bring him over to your place when I'm finished.

Martin: You don't have to do that. I'll wait. *(He watches for a moment.)* Maybe I can help you.

Pauline: I'd rather do it myself, thank you.

(Martin nods, climbs onto the fence, and sits watching her. After a while of stony silence he speaks.)

Martin: Look, I just want you to know, I didn't have anything to do with this. All I know is, your father phoned up my father and before I knew it I had a horse. To tell you the truth, I couldn't care one way or the other. *(Pauline looks up.)* You know, my father's on a great-outdoors kick. He wants to put the whole family on horseback. I wish he'd buy me a motor-bike instead. It's not that I'm afraid of them. Horses, I mean. Is...is this one tame?

Pauline: You mean gentle?

Martin: Yeah. Is he gentle?

Pauline: No.

Martin: *(worried)* Oh. *(Finally he smiles, figuring that she's putting him on.)* He looks gentle to me.

Pauline: That's because I'm the only one who can come near him.

Martin: You're kidding!

(Pauline steps back.)

Pauline: Try him.

Martin: No thanks. *(Pauline goes back to grooming the horse.)* What...what does he do?

Pauline: He bites.

Martin: You're kidding. A horse?

Pauline: That's right. He kicks, too.

(Martin comes down off the fence.)

Martin: Oh, for crying out loud!

Pauline: *(laying it on)* And when you try to ride him in the morning, he bucks.

(Martin is ready to leave.)

Martin: What the heck did my father buy me a horse like that for?

Pauline: And one thing I must warn you. Sometimes he rears. He rears right up on his hind legs. He paws the air and rolls his eyes and snorts through wide-spread nostrils. And once, he tried to fall back on top of me and crush me with his mighty horse's weight!

(Martin has caught on. He looks relieved.)

Martin: You're putting me on. Aren't you? *(As Pauline resumes her work, Martin climbs back on the fence.)* I don't blame you. I did the same thing once myself. I used to have an electric train. Automatic switches, cars that uncoupled themselves. You know. The whole bit. I was supposed to give it away to my little cousin because I wasn't using it any more. Only, when he came to get it I told him it was very dangerous to play with because he might get electrocuted and die, and I held a little piece of metal across the tracks and it made a few sparks and he started crying and yelling and everybody came running, and... anyway, he got the train, and I really didn't miss it that much. *(Pauline is not impressed. Martin shrugs.)* I hear you got a new horse. How do you like him?

Pauline: I don't know.

Martin: Maybe you just have to get used to him. It's the same with me. I'll have to get used to my horse, too. *(Pauline looks up at the strange words "my horse." Pause.)* I hear he's very big. Your new one, I mean. Seventeen hands? Is that right? It's not seventeen feet, is it?

Pauline: Hardly.

Martin: To tell you the truth, I haven't the faintest idea what seventeen hands means. All I know is that it's supposed to be big. How big is this one?

Pauline: Twelve hands.

Martin: Then seventeen hands is...is almost half again as big. Isn't it? Hey, that's not a horse, that's an elephant! *(Pauline looks up coldly.)* What colour is he?

Pauline: I don't know.

Martin: Haven't you seen him yet?

Pauline: No.

Martin: When's he coming?

Pauline: He's already here.

Martin: And you haven't seen him?

Pauline: No.

Martin: Where is he?

(Pauline turns and looks at the stable.)

Pauline: In there.

Martin: Could I have a look at him?

Pauline: *(strongly)* No!

Martin: O.K. He's your horse.

Pauline: I don't want anybody looking at him. I don't want anybody stroking him or saying kind things to him. He's going back. I don't want another horse.

Martin: Look. Why don't you keep your horse? This one, I mean. Why don't we just forget the whole thing. My father'll phone up your father, and your father can phone the guy who sold him the horse that's seventeen hands—or—feet—or—whatever—it is tall... and you'll have your horse back. *(Martin comes down off the fence.)* What do you say?

Pauline: *(softening)* I can't.

Martin: Sure you can. You want him back, don't you?

Pauline: Of course.

Martin: Then take him. *(Pauline, fighting back the tears, shakes her head.)* Oh, for crying out loud! Look, I don't want the horse. I don't even know how to ride one. So would you please do me a favour and take your horse back before I get killed.

Pauline: *(desperately)* I can't.

Martin: Why?

(Pauline is beginning to choke, trying to laugh to keep from crying.)

Pauline: Because...because my father won't board him any more. He says I'm making a fool of myself...because I've grown too big for him...and we look so funny together that people...the people...

(Martin is embarrassed. He is almost moved but afraid to show it. Through the choking and tears, Pauline senses his embarrassment. She tries her best to stop.)

Pauline: I'm sorry if you have to take a horse that you don't want.

Martin: That's all right. I'll just have to learn to ride. That's all.

Pauline: I could teach you if you like.

Martin: Sure, why not. Maybe we could go for rides together. That is, if you keep your new horse. *(Pauline turns away and begins to work on the pinto once again.)* Is he really hard to manage? This one, I mean.

(Pauline hugs the horse affectionately.)

Pauline: He's very gentle and very kind. And he understands everything.

Martin: I just hope he understands me.

Pauline: He will if you give him a chance.

Martin: How long have you had him?

Pauline: Since I was eight.

Martin: *(really impressed)* You're kidding!

Pauline: He knows all about me. All my secrets.

Martin: *(This fact is too much.)* Oh, great! What am I doing taking him away from you?

Pauline: It's not your fault.

Martin: Yeah, but why me? I don't even know anything about horses. I don't appreciate that horse.

Pauline: You will when you get to know him.

Martin: I wish my father wouldn't do these things. I feel lousy. I really do.

Pauline: Please don't. I understand.

Martin: I just want you to know that you can come and see him whenever you want.

Pauline: Thank you.

Martin: In fact, I hope you do.

Pauline: Why?

Martin: I don't know...because... *(He shrugs.)* I like you.

Pauline: Thank you. I like you too.

Martin: Who, me? Martin the horse thief?

Pauline: *(laughing)* You're not a horse thief.

Martin: I'm one of the roughest, toughest horse thieves in the country, pardner.

Pauline: You are not.

Martin: Am so.

Pauline: *(laughing)* You can't even *ride* a horse.

Martin: Don't have to. I'm so tough I just pick 'em up and *carry* 'em away.

(They both laugh, then fall silent, and stand for a moment looking at one another. Finally, a little embarrassed, Pauline resumes working on the horse.)

Martin: Do you have a boyfriend?

Pauline: No.

Martin: Great!

(Martin grins. Pauline smiles. Martin begins to take a little walk about the corral, hands in pockets, strutting ever so slightly. He picks up a stone and pitches it out across the corral. He takes another one and uses a more exaggerated pitching style. He looks at Pauline for approval. Pauline smiles.)

Martin: I was a pitcher back home. *(He picks up another stone, takes his stance, checks the imaginary bases, begins a very slow and dramatic wind-up, and lets fly across the corral. Pauline laughs.)* That's what you call style.

Pauline: I'll bet you're good.

Martin: Pretty good.

(He comes back and leans against the fence.)

Pauline: Would you like to help me?

Martin: Sure.

(Pauline hands him the brush and they begin to work together, silently, enjoying each other's company, looking up now and then to meet one another's eyes and to smile. It is a moment in which nothing really needs to be said. Nevertheless, after a while, Martin is compelled to express himself in words. He steps back from his work.)

Martin: You know, I think I'm going to like it out here in the country. I mean it. You know what I like about it? The space! *(He begins to gesture like someone inspired.)* There's so much space. Fields, and hills, and sky! My gosh, you can actually see the sky. You can smell the air! *(Pauline is enjoying this immensely.)* You've got so much freedom to be yourself. You don't have to feel that there's a crowd of people looking over your shoulder. It's as if you have all this space, and you're alone in the middle of it, and you can do whatever you like. Look at us. Look at the way we hit it off together. *(Pauline smiles.)* I think it's terrific! I'll bet if we were in the city we'd never get a chance to know one another. We'd probably be so worried about what people were going to say, or how we'd look walking down the street together, that we'd be afraid to stop long enough to talk to each other. Do you know what I mean?

Pauline: I...I'm not sure.

Martin: What I mean is... *(Suddenly he realizes where this is leading. He and Pauline face one another, and for a moment neither can speak.)*

Pauline: Do you mean that we'd look funny walking down the street together? *(Martin is unable to answer.)* Is that what you mean? Is it because I'm...I'm taller than you are? Is it because I'm so big for my age? Would you be ashamed to be seen with me back home where you come from? Would your friends all laugh at you? Do you think that you don't have to worry about it out here because there's nobody to see us? Is that it?

Martin: I didn't mean it that way...I...

Pauline: Yes you did. Only you're wrong. There are people here, too. I know. Maybe there aren't as many, but the ones who are here can hurt you just as much. *(She unhitches the horse.)* Your horse is ready now. You'd better lead him until he gets used to you.

(For a moment Martin hesitates. He is truly ashamed.)

Martin: Look, I...
(Pauline smiles a gentle, forgiving smile and hands him the lead. Martin begins to take the horse away. He stops and turns.)

Martin: I'm an idiot. I really am. I'm such an idiot. What the heck's the matter with me? Why don't I learn to shut up once in a while? I do it all the time!

Pauline: It's all right. It doesn't matter. *(Martin begins to lead the horse off again.)* Good-bye, Stanley.

Martin: What?

Pauline: That's his name. Stanley.

Martin: Gee, what a funny name for a horse. *(He smacks his head.)* You see what I mean!

(Exasperated, he leads the horse out through the corral gate and on up the road. Pauline watches them go and, as she does, her face begins to lose its composure.)

Pauline: *(almost to herself)* Stanley! *(She runs to the gate. Again to herself.)* Good-bye.

(Martin and the horse are well up the road. After a moment, Pauline turns back to the rail. The camera angle shows us her view of the empty rail. She comes forward sadly, picks up the grooming tools, and starts to walk to the barn.)

SCENE EIGHT

(Exterior. The stable. Day.
We see the door to the stable. The upper half of the door is open, leaving the inside black and ominous. Pauline stops. Her sadness leaves her. She turns to go but realizes she must put the brush and comb back where they belong. Yet there is more. There is, stirring within her, something that urges her to the stable doorway. Slowly, hesitatingly, she approaches it.)

SCENE NINE

(Interior. The stable. Day.
Pauline is inside, standing in the half-light, loking down the length of stalls. Hardly aware of it, she places the brush and comb on a shelf and begins to move forward, a hot, growing anger building steadily within her, burning her

eyes. *The camera angle shifts to her POV. In a stall at the end of the aisle a great, black horse stands out conspicuously. For a moment Pauline hesitates, and then quickly she moves into the stall and unties the horse. She backs him, forces him harshly, out into the aisle, and stands looking at him with contempt. She begins to shake her head from side to side in a rhythm that gradually encompasses her whole body, until at last she begins to cry, gasping out.)*

Pauline: You freak. You stupid freak. You ugly, stupid freak. You big, gangling, gawky, stupid, ugly freak!

(She throws her arms about the horse and breaks into huge, choking sobs. Suddenly getting a hold of herself, she reaches up for one of the bridles and saddles hanging near the stall and expertly slips it on the horse. He moves nervously, trying to break away from her, but she forces her weight against him and starts to saddle him up.)

SCENE TEN

(Exterior. The corral. Day.
 She brings him out into the harsh daylight. Across the open corral, we see Hefferman watching her.)

SCENE ELEVEN

(Exterior. The corral and fields. Day.
 She unlatches the gate that leads to the hills and fields beyond the stable. Quickly swinging up onto his back, she turns the horse out, whipping him brutally with the long reins. The horse lunges forward, stretching himself in a powerful, driving gallop that sends them hurtling on down across the fields in a reckless, frenzied ride.)

SCENE TWELVE

(Exterior. The creek. Day.
 They hit the small creek with a splash and spray of water, churning through it quickly and scrambling up the other bank.)

SCENE THIRTEEN

(Exterior. The hill. Day.
 From their POV we see the long, high hill with the single giant oak tree. Pauline veers the horse away from the hill, and instead of climbing it, they begin to charge along the entire length of its base. It is a wild, flat-out ride that becomes increasingly dangerous, more and more terrifying until suddenly, from Pauline's POV, the world seems to flip upside down. There is a great heaving thud and the neighing of a horse.)

SCENE FOURTEEN

(Exterior. The field. Day.
 The horse is scrambling to his feet. Pauline lies on the ground. For just an instant, Pauline is still; then slowly she sits up, winded and breathing heavily. The horse trots off across the field, makes a wide arc, and comes back at a walk. Pauline is on her feet watching him. The horse stops a short distance away, and for the first time we have a chance to see him as the proud and magnificent creature that he is. Pauline walks toward him as though she were ready to match that pride with her own. She catches the reins and, without hesitating, swings up onto his back. She starts him up, slowly at first, to get the feel of him under her. She moves him into a canter, then stops. She starts and stops again. She turns him in circles, this way and that, beginning to marvel at his response. She runs her hands along his neck and shoulders as though she were making contact for the first time. She looks down at her own feet and legs, fitting handsomely against the horse's sides.)

SCENE FIFTEEN

(Exterior. The hill. Day.
 From the top of the hill, beside the tree, we

look down on the horse and rider doing figure eights in the fields below.)

SCENE SIXTEEN

(Exterior. The fields. Day.

   She starts him again slowly, then into a careful canter, where she has a chance to move her own body with the horse and feel one with him. She begins to laugh and to cry at the same time with the sheer joy of knowing how well they look and ride together...how well they complement one another. The canter goes into a gallop. In the final shot, we see rider and horse as one riding away.)

(Fade out)

Caution:
Enquiries regarding the performance of this play, professional or amateur, should be directed to Mr. Ron Taylor, 142 Willow Avenue, Toronto, Ontario M4E 3K3.

COURTROOM JUSTICE

The witnesses give testimony, the two sides present their arguments, the jury leaves the room for the eagerly awaited decision—there is perhaps no more theatrical and dramatic situation than a courtroom scene. Often the choices in the courtroom are not of a clear-cut, black-and-white nature.

This unit examines two historical figures who were put on trial for their beliefs. Though hundreds of years apart in time, both Joan of Arc and Louis Riel sought to change the societies in which they lived. Both figures were caught up in a clash of cultures and were worshipped by their followers for what they were attempting to do. The trial setting concentrates the arguments of the central characters and those who opposed them. At the same time, the setting creates tension for the viewer as to the outcome of the struggle.

In the excerpt from George Bernard Shaw's *Saint Joan*, we watch the young Joan defend herself against the forces of both church and state as they try to crush her with charges of blasphemy and witchcraft. A selection from John Coulter's *Riel* uses the actual transcript of Riel's 1885 trial for treason to show the court battle that surrounded a figure from our own history.

Saint Joan

(Excerpt)

George Bernard Shaw

CHARACTERS

Joan—the Maid of Orleans, who believes God has sent her to save her French countrymen from the English

Peter Cauchon, the Bishop of Beauvais—a French clergyman determined to give Joan a fair trial and, if possible, have her accept Church doctrine

The Inquisitor—a scholarly examiner who is intent on defending the Church's point of view

Brother Martin Ladvenu—a priest who is compassionate toward Joan

John de Stogumber, the Chaplain—an English clergyman determined to get

Joan convicted and executed

Canon D'Estivet, the Promoter—Joan's prosecutor, always ready to stress all the legal details at the trial

Canon de Courcelles—another clergyman at the trial, as determined as de Stogumber to get Joan found guilty

The Executioner of Rouen

The Earl of Warwick—commander of the English forces, a man more concerned with political matters than with religious ones

The Assessors—the judges at Joan's trial

The Executioner's Assistants

"What God has made me do I will never go back on. . . . And in case the Church should bid me do anything contrary to the command I have from God, I will not consent to it, no matter what it may be."

(Rouen, the 30th of May, 1431. A great stone hall in the castle, arranged for a trial-at-law, but not a trial-by-jury, the court being the bishop's court with the Inquisition participating: hence there are two raised chairs side by side for the bishop and the Inquisitor as judges. Rows of chairs radiating from them at an obtuse angle are for the canons, the doctors of law and theology, and the Dominican monks, who act as assessors. In the angle is a table for the scribes, with stools. There is also a heavy rough wooden stool for the prisoner. All these are at the inner end of the hall. The further end is open to the courtyard through a row of arches. The court is shielded from the weather by screens and curtains.

Looking down the great hall from the middle of the inner end, the judicial chairs and scribes' table are to the right. The prisoner's stool is to the left. There are arched doors right and left. It is a fine sun-shiny May morning. All of the characters are present except Joan, the Executioner, and the Earl of Warwick.)

Cauchon: The court sits.

The Inquisitor: Let the accused be brought in.

Ladvenu: (*calling*) The accused. Let her be brought in.

(*Joan, chained by the ankles, is brought in through the arched door behind the prisoner's stool by a guard of English soldiers. With them is the Executioner and his assistants. They lead her to the prisoner's stool and place themselves behind it after taking off her chain. She wears a page's black suit. Her long imprisonment and the strain of the examinations which have preceded the trial have left their mark on her; but her vitality still holds; she confronts the court unabashed, without a trace of the awe which their formal solemnity seems to require for the complete success of its impressiveness.*)

The Inquisitor: (*kindly*) Sit down, Joan. (*She sits on the prisoner's stool.*) You look very pale today. Are you not well?

Joan: Thank you kindly: I am well enough. But the bishop sent me some carp; and it made me ill.

Cauchon: I am sorry. I told them to see that it was fresh.

Joan: You meant to be good to me, I know; but it is a fish that does not agree with me. The English thought you were trying to poison me...

Cauchon: (*together*)   What!

The Chaplain: No, my lord.

Joan: (*continuing*) They are determined that I shall be burnt as a witch; and they sent their doctor to cure me; but he was forbidden to bleed me because the silly people believe that a witch's witchery leaves her if she is bled; so he only called me filthy names. Why do you leave me in the hands of the English? I should be in the hands of the Church. And why must I be chained by the feet to a log of wood? Are you afraid I will fly away?

D'Estivet: (*harshly*) Woman: it is not for you to question the court: it is for us to question you.

Courcelles: When you were left unchained, did you not try to escape by jumping from a tower sixty feet high? If you cannot fly like a witch, how is it that you are still alive?

Joan: I suppose because the tower was not so high then. It has grown higher every day since you began asking me questions about it.

D'Estivet: Why did you jump from the tower?

Joan: How do you know that I jumped?

D'Estivet: You were found lying in the moat. Why did you leave the tower?

Joan: Why would anybody leave a prison if they could get out?

D'Estivet: You tried to escape?

Joan: Of course I did; and not for the first time, either. If you leave the door of the cage open the bird will fly out.

D'Estivet: (*rising*) That is a confession of heresy. I call the attention of the court to it.

Joan: Heresy, he calls it! Am I a heretic because I try to escape from prison?

D'Estivet: Assuredly, if you are in the hands of the Church and you willfully take yourself out of its hands, you are deserting the Church; and that is heresy.

Joan: It is great nonsense. Nobody could be such a fool as to think that.

D'Estivet: You hear, my lord, how I am reviled in the execution of my duty by this woman. (*He sits down indignantly.*)

Cauchon: I have warned you before, Joan, that you are doing yourself no good by these pert answers.

Joan: But you will not talk sense to me. I am reasonable if you will be reasonable.

The Inquisitor: (*interposing*) This is not yet in order. You forget, Master Promoter, that the proceedings have not been formally opened. The time for questions is after she has sworn on the Gospels to tell us the whole truth.

Joan: You say this to me every time. I have said again and again that I will tell you all that concerns this trial. But I cannot tell you the whole truth: God does not allow the whole truth to be told. You do not understand it when I tell it. It is an old saying that he who tells too much truth is sure to be hanged. I am weary of this argument: we have been over it nine times already. I have sworn as much as I will swear; and I will swear no more.

Courcelles: My lord: she should be put to the torture.

The Inquisitor: You hear, Joan? That is what happens to the obdurate. Think before you answer. *(to the Executioner)* Has she been shown the instruments?

The Executioner: They are ready, my lord. She has seen them.

Joan: If you tear me limb from limb until you separate my soul from my body, you will get nothing out of me beyond what I have told you. What more is there to tell that you could understand? Besides, I cannot bear to be hurt; and if you hurt me I will say anything you like to stop the pain. But I will take it all back afterwards; so what is the use of it?

Ladvenu: There is much in that. We should proceed mercifully.

Courcelles: But the torture is customary.

The Inquisitor: It must not be applied wantonly. If the accused will confess voluntarily, then its use cannot be justified.

Courcelles: But this is unusual and irregular. She refuses to take the oath.

Ladvenu: *(disgusted)* Do you want to torture the girl for the mere pleasure of it?

Courcelles: *(bewildered)* But it is not a pleasure. It is the law. It is customary. It is always done.

The Inquisitor: That is not so, master, except when the inquiries are carried on by people who do not know their legal business.

Courcelles: But the woman is a heretic. I assure you it is always done.

Cauchon: *(decisively)* It will not be done

today if it is not necessary. Let there be an end of this. I will not have it said that we proceeded on forced confessions. We have sent our best preachers and doctors to this woman to exhort and implore her to save her soul and body from the fire: we shall not now send the Executioner to thrust her into it.

Courcelles: Your lordship is merciful, of course. But it is a great responsibility to depart from the usual practice.

Joan: Thou art a rare noodle, master. Do what was done last time is thy rule, eh?

Courcelles: *(rising)* Thou wanton: dost thou dare call me noodle?

The Inquisitor: Patience, master, patience: I fear you will soon be only too terribly avenged.

Courcelles: *(mutters)* Noodle indeed! *(He sits down, much discontented.)*

The Inquisitor: Meanwhile, let us not be moved by the rough side of a shepherd lass's tongue.

Joan: Nay, I am no shepherd lass, though I have helped with the sheep like anyone else. I will do a lady's work in the house—spin or weave—against any woman in Rouen.

The Inquisitor: This is not a time for vanity, Joan. You stand in great peril.

Joan: I know it: have I not been punished for my vanity? If I had not worn my cloth-of-gold surcoat in battle like a fool, that Burgundian soldier would never have pulled me backward off my horse; and I should not have been here.

The Chaplain: If you are so clever at woman's work, why do you not stay at home and do it?

Joan: There are plenty of other women to do it; but there is nobody to do my work.

Cauchon: Come! We are wasting time on trifles. Joan: I am going to put a most solemn question to you. Take care how you answer; for your life and salvation are at stake on it. Will you for all you have said and done, be it good or bad, accept the judgment of God's Church on earth? More especially as to the acts and words that are imputed to you in this trial by the promoter here, will you submit your case to the inspired interpretation of the Church Militant?

Joan: I am a faithful child of the Church. I will obey the Church...

Cauchon: *(hopefully leaning forward)* You will?

Joan: ...provided it does not command anything impossible.

(Cauchon sinks back in his chair with a heavy sigh. The Inquisitor purses his lips and frowns. Ladvenu shakes his head pitifully.)

D'Estivet: She imputes to the Church the error and folly of commanding the impossible.

Joan: If you command me to declare that all that I have done and said, and all the visions and revelations I have had, were not from God, then that is impossible: I will not declare it for anything in the world. What God made me do I will never go back on; and what He has commanded or shall command I will not fail to do in spite of any man alive. That is what I mean by impossible. And in case the Church should bid me do anything contrary to the command I have from God, I will not consent to it, no matter what it may be.

The Assessors: *(shocked and indignant, speaking together)* Oh! The Church contrary to God! What do you say now? Flat heresy. This is beyond everything.

D'Estivet: *(throwing down his brief)* My lord: do you need anything more than this?

Cauchon: Woman: you have said enough to burn ten heretics. Will you not be warned? Will you not understand?

The Inquisitor: If the Church Militant tells you that your revelations and visions are sent by the devil to tempt you to your damnation, will you not believe that the Church is wiser than you?

Joan: I believe that God is wiser than I; and it

is His commands that I will do. All the things that you call my crimes have come to me by the command of God. I say that I have done them by the order of God: it is impossible for me to say anything else. If any churchman says the contrary I shall not mind him: I shall mind God alone, whose command I always follow.

Ladvenu: *(pleading with her urgently)* You do not know what you are saying, child. Do you want to kill yourself? Listen. Do you not believe that you are subject to the Church of God on earth?

Joan: Yes. When have I ever denied it?

Ladvenu: Good. That means, does it not, that you are subject to our Lord the Pope, to the cardinals, the archbishops, and the bishops for whom his lordship stands here today?

Joan: God must be served first.

D'Estivet: Then your voices command you not to submit yourself to the Church Militant?

Joan: My voices do not tell me to disobey the Church; but God must be served first.

Cauchon: And you, and not the Church, are to be the judge?

Joan: What other judgment can I judge by but my own?

The Assessors: *(scandalized)* Oh! *(They cannot find words.)*

Cauchon: Out of your own mouth you have condemned yourself. We have striven for your salvation to the verge of sinning ourselves: we have opened the door to you again and again; and you have shut it in our faces and in the face of God. Dare you pretend, after what you have said, that you are in a state of grace?

Joan: If I am not, may God bring me to it: if I am, may God keep me in it!

Ladvenu: That is a very good reply, my lord.

Courcelles: Were you in a state of grace when you stole the bishop's horse?

Cauchon: *(rising in a fury)* Oh, devil take the bishop's horse and you too! We are here to try

a case of heresy; and no sooner do we come to the root of the matter than we are thrown back by idiots, who understand nothing but horses. *(Trembling with rage, he forces himself to sit down.)*

The Inquisitor: Gentlemen, gentlemen: in clinging to these small issues you are the Maid's best advocates. I am not surprised that his lordship has lost patience with you. What does the promoter say? Does he press these trumpery matters?

D'Estivet: I am bound by my office to press everything; but when the woman confesses a heresy that must bring upon her the doom of excommunication, of what consequence is it that she has been guilty also of offences which expose her to minor penances? I share the impatience of his lordship as to these minor charges. Only, with great respect, I must emphasize the gravity of two very horrible and blasphemous crimes which she does not deny. First, she has intercourse with evil spirits, and is therefore a sorceress. Second, she wears men's clothes, which is indecent, unnatural, and abominable; and in spite of our most earnest remonstrances and entreaties, she will not change them even to receive the sacrament.

Joan: Is the blessed St. Catherine an evil spirit? Is St. Margaret? Is Michael the Archangel?

Courcelles: How do you know that the spirit which appears to you is an archangel? Does he not appear to you as a naked man?

Joan: Do you think God cannot afford clothes for him?

(The assessors cannot help smiling, especially as the joke is against Courcelles.)

Ladvenu: Well answered, Joan.

The Inquisitor: It is, in effect, well answered. But no evil spirit would be so simple as to appear to a young girl in a guise that would scandalize her when he meant her to take him for a messenger from the Most High. Joan: the Church instructs you that these apparitions are demons seeking your soul's perdition. Do you accept the instruction of the Church?

Joan: I accept the messenger of God. How could any faithful believer in the Church refuse him?

Cauchon: Wretched woman: again I ask you, do you know what you are saying?

The Inquisitor: You wrestle in vain with the devil for her soul, my lord: she will not be saved. Now as to this matter of the man's dress. For the last time, will you put off that impudent attire and dress as becomes your sex?

Joan: I will not.

D'Estivet: *(pouncing)* The sin of disobedience, my lord.

Joan: *(distressed)* But my voices tell me I must dress as a soldier.

Ladvenu: Joan, Joan: does not that prove to you that the voices are the voices of evil spirits? Can you suggest to us one good reason why an angel of God should give you such shameless advice?

Joan: Why, yes: what can be plainer common sense? I was a soldier living among soldiers. I am a prisoner guarded by soldiers. If I were to dress as a woman they would think of me as a woman; and then what would become of me? If I dress as a soldier they think of me as a soldier, and I can live with them as I do at home with my brothers. That is why St. Catherine tells me I must not dress as a woman until she gives me leave.

Courcelles: When will she give you leave?

Joan: When you take me out of the hands of the English soldiers. I have told you that I should be in the hands of the Church and not left night and day with four soldiers of the Earl of Warwick. Do you want me to live with them in petticoats?

Ladvenu: My lord: what she says is, God knows, very wrong and shocking; but there is a grain of worldly sense in it such as might impose on a simple village maiden.

Joan: If we were as simple in the village as you are in your courts and palaces, there would soon be no wheat to make bread for you.

Cauchon: That is the thanks you get for trying to save her, Brother Martin.

Ladvenu: Joan: we are all trying to save you. His lordship is trying to save you. The Inquisitor could not be more just to you if you were his own daughter. But you are blinded by a terrible pride and self-sufficiency.

Joan: Why do you say that? I have said nothing wrong. I cannot understand.

The Inquisitor: The blessed St. Athanasius has laid it down in his creed that those who cannot understand are damned. It is not enough to be simple. It is not enough even to be what simple people call good. The simplicity of a darkened mind is no better than the simplicity of a beast.

Joan: There is great wisdom in the simplicity of a beast, let me tell you; and sometimes great foolishness in the wisdom of scholars.

Ladvenu: We know that, Joan: we are not so foolish as you think us. Try to resist the temptation to make pert replies to us. Do you see that man who stands behind you? *(He indicates the Executioner.)*

Joan: *(turning and looking at the man)* Your torturer? But the bishop said I was not to be tortured.

Ladvenu: You are not to be tortured because you have confessed everything that is necessary to your condemnation. That man is not only the torturer: he is also the Executioner. Executioner: let the Maid hear your answers to my questions. Are you prepared for the burning of a heretic this day?

The Executioner: Yes, master.

Ladvenu: Is the stake ready?

The Executioner: It is. In the market place. The English have built it too high for me to get near her and make the death easier. It will be a cruel death.

Joan: *(horrified)* But you are not going to burn me now?

The Inquisitor: You realize it at last.

Ladvenu: There are eight hundred English soldiers waiting to take you to the market place the moment the sentence of excommunication has passed the lips of your judges. You are within a few short moments of that doom.

Joan: *(looking round desperately for rescue)* Oh, God!

Ladvenu: Do not despair, Joan. The Church is merciful. You can save yourself.

Joan: *(hopefully)* Yes: my voices promised me I should not be burnt. St. Catherine bade me be bold.

Cauchon: Woman: are you quite mad? Do you not yet see that your voices have deceived you?

Joan: Oh, no: that is impossible.

Cauchon: Impossible! They have led you straight to your excommunication and to the stake which is there waiting for you.

Ladvenu: *(pressing the point hard)* Have they kept a single promise to you since you were taken at Compiègne? The devil has betrayed you. The Church holds out its arms to you.

Joan: *(despairing)* Oh, it is true: it is true: my voices have deceived me. I have been mocked by devils: my faith is broken. I have dared and dared; but only a fool will walk into a fire: God, who gave me my common sense, cannot will me to do that.

Ladvenu: Now God be praised that He has saved you at the eleventh hour! *(He hurries to the vacant seat at the scribes' table and snatches a sheet of paper, on which he sets to work writing eagerly.)*

Cauchon: Amen!

Joan: What must I do?

Cauchon: You must sign a solemn recantation of your heresy.

Joan: Sign? That means to write my name. I cannot write.

Cauchon: You have signed many letters before.

Joan: Yes; but someone held my hand and guided the pen. I can make my mark.

The Chaplain: *(who has been listening with growing alarm and indignation)* My lord: do you mean that you are going to allow this woman to escape us?

The Inquisitor: The law must take its course, Master de Stogumber. And you know the law.

The Chaplain: *(rising, purple with fury)* I know that there is no faith in a Frenchman. *(There is a tumult, which he shouts down.)* I know what my lord the Cardinal of Winchester will say when he hears of this. I know what the Earl of Warwick will do when he learns that you intend to betray him. There are eight hundred men at the gate who will see that this abominable witch is burnt in spite of your teeth.

The Assessors: *(talking in the background)* What is this? What did he say? He accuses us of treachery! This is past bearing. No faith in a Frenchman! Did you hear that? This is an intolerable fellow. Who is he? Is this what English churchmen are like? He must be mad or drunk.

The Inquisitor: *(rising)* Silence, pray! Gentlemen: pray silence! Master Chaplain: bethink you a moment of your holy office: of what you are and where you are. I direct you to sit down.

The Chaplain: *(folding his arms doggedly, his face working convulsively)* I will NOT sit down.

Cauchon: Master Inquisitor: this man has called me a traitor to my face before now.

The Chaplain: So you are a traitor. You are all traitors. You have been doing nothing but begging this damnable witch on your knees to recant all through this trial.

The Inquisitor: *(placidly resuming his seat)* If you will not sit, you must stand: that is all.

The Chaplain: I will NOT stand. *(He flings himself back into his chair.)*

Ladvenu: *(rising with the paper in his hand)* My lord: here is the form of recantation for the Maid to sign.

Cauchon: Read it to her.

Joan: Do not trouble. I will sign it.

The Inquisitor: Woman: you must know what you are putting your hand to. Read it to her, Brother Martin. And let all be silent.

Ladvenu: *(reading quietly)* "I, Joan, commonly called the Maid, a miserable sinner, do confess that I have most grievously sinned in the following articles. I have pretended to have revelations from God and the angels and the blessed saints, and perversely rejected the Church's warnings that these were temptations by demons. I have blasphemed abominably by wearing an immodest dress, contrary to the Holy Scripture and the canons of the Church. Also I have clipped my hair in the style of a man and, against all the duties which have made my sex specially acceptable in heaven, have taken up the sword, even to the shedding of human blood, inciting men to slay each other, invoking evil spirits to delude them, and stubbornly and most blasphemously imputing these sins to Almighty God. I confess to the sin of sedition, to the sin of idolatry, to the sin of disobedience, to the sin of pride, and to the sin of heresy. All of which sins I now renounce and abjure and depart from, humbly thanking you doctors and masters who have brought me back to the truth and into the grace of our Lord. And I will never return to my errors but will remain in communion with our Holy Church and in obedience to our Holy Father the Pope of Rome. All this I swear by God Almighty and the Holy Gospels, in witness whereto I sign my name to this recantation."

The Inquisitor: You understand this, Joan?

Joan: *(listless)* It is plain enough, sir.

The Inquisitor: And it is true?

Joan: It may be true. If it were not true, the fire would not be ready for me in the market place.

Ladvenu: *(taking up his pen and a book and going to her quickly lest she should compromise herself again)* Come, child: let me guide your hand. Take the pen. *(She does so; and they begin to write, using the book as a desk)* J-e-h-a-n-e. So. Now make your mark by yourself.

Joan: *(makes her mark and gives him back the pen, tormented by the rebellion of her soul against her mind and body)* There!

Ladvenu: *(replacing the pen on the table and handing the recantation to Cauchon with a reverence)* Praise be to God, my brothers, the lamb has returned to the flock; and the shepherd rejoices in her more than in ninety and nine just persons. *(He returns to his seat.)*

The Inquisitor: *(taking the paper from Cauchon)* We declare thee by this act set free from the danger of excommunication in which thou stoodest. *(He throws the paper down to the table.)*

Joan: I thank you.

The Inquisitor: But because thou has sinned most presumptuously against God and the Holy Church, and that thou mayst repent thy errors in solitary contemplation and be shielded from all temptation to return to them, we, for the good of thy soul and for a penance that may wipe out thy sins and bring thee finally unspotted to the throne of grace, do condemn thee to eat the bread of sorrow and drink the water of affliction to the end of thy earthly days in perpetual imprisonment.

Joan: *(rising in consternation and terrible anger)* Perpetual imprisonment! Am I not then to be set free?

Ladvenu: *(mildly shocked)* Set free, child, after such wickedness as yours! What are you dreaming of?

Joan: Give me that writing. *(She rushes to the table; snatches up the paper; and tears it into fragments.)* Light your fire: do you think I

dread it as much as the life of a rat in a hole? My voices were right.

Ladvenu: Joan! Joan!

Joan: Yes: they told me you were fools (*the word gives great offence*) and that I was not to listen to your fine words nor trust to your charity. You promised me my life; but you lied. (*There are indignant exclamations.*) You think that life is nothing but not being stone dead. It is not the bread and water I fear: I can live on bread: when have I asked for more? It is no hardship to drink water if the water be clean. Bread has no sorrow for me, and water no affliction. But to shut me from the light of the sky and the sight of the fields and flowers; to chain my feet so that I can never again ride with the soldiers nor climb the hills; to make me breathe foul damp darkness and keep from me everything that brings me back to the love of God when your wickedness and foolishness tempt me to hate Him: all this is worse than the furnace in the Bible that was heated seven times. I could do without my warhorse; I could drag about in a skirt; I could let the banners and the trumpets and the knights and soldiers pass me and leave me behind as they leave the other women, if only I could still hear the wind in the trees, the larks in the sunshine, the young lambs crying through the healthy frost, and the blessed, blessed church bells that send my angel voices floating to me on the wind. But without these things I cannot live; and by your wanting to take them away from me, or from any human creature, I know that your counsel is of the devil, and that mine is of God.

The Assessors: (*in great commotion, speaking together*) Blasphemy! blasphemy! She is possessed. She said our counsel was of the devil. And hers of God. Monstrous! The devil is in our midst.

D'Estivet: (*shouting above the din*) She is a relapsed heretic, obstinate, incorrigible, and altogether unworthy of the mercy we have shown her. I call for her excommunication.

The Chaplain: (*to the Executioner*) Light your fire, man. To the stake with her.

(*The Executioner and his assistants hurry out through the courtyard.*)

Ladvenu: You wicked girl: if your counsel were of God, would He not deliver you?

Joan: His ways are not your ways. He wills that I go through the fire to His bosom; for I am His child, and you are not fit that I should live among you. That is my last word to you.

(*The soldiers seize her.*)

Cauchon: (*rising*) Not yet.

(*They wait. There is a dead silence. Cauchon turns to the Inquisitor with an inquiring look. The Inquisitor nods affirmatively. They rise solemnly and intone the sentence antiphonally.*)

Cauchon: We decree that thou art a relapsed heretic.

The Inquisitor: Cast out from the unity of the Church.

Cauchon: Sundered from her body.

The Inquisitor: Infected with the leprosy of heresy.

Cauchon: A member of Satan.

The Inquisitor: We declare that thou must be excommunicated.

Cauchon: And now we do cast thee out, segregate thee, and abandon thee to the secular power.

The Inquisitor: Admonishing the same secular power that it moderate its judgment of thee in respect of death and division of the limbs. (*He resumes his seat.*)

Cauchon: And if any true sign of penitence appear in thee, to permit our Brother Martin to administer to thee the sacrament of penance.

The Chaplain: Into the fire with the witch. (*He rushes at her and helps the soldiers to push her out.*)

(*Joan is taken away through the courtyard. The assessors rise in disorder and follow the soldiers, except Ladvenu, who has hidden his face in his hands.)*

Cauchon: *(rising again in the act of sitting down)* No, no: this is irregular. The representative of the secular arm should be here to receive her from us.

The Inquisitor: *(also on his feet again)* That man is an incorrigible fool.

Cauchon: Brother Martin: see that everything is done in order.

Ladvenu: My place is at her side, my lord. You must exercise your own authority. *(He hurries out.)*

Cauchon: These English are impossible: they will thrust her straight into the fire. Look!

(He points to the courtyard, in which the glow and flicker of fire can now be seen reddening the May daylight. Only the bishop and the Inquisitor are left in the court.)

Cauchon: *(turning to go)* We must stop that.

The Inquisitor: *(calmly)* Yes; but not too fast, my lord.

Cauchon: *(halting)* But there is not a moment to lose.

The Inquisitor: We have proceeded in perfect order. If the English choose to put themselves in the wrong, it is not our business to put them in the right. A flaw in the procedure may be useful later on: one never knows. And the sooner it is over, the better for that poor girl.

Cauchon: *(relaxing)* That is true. But I suppose we must see this dreadful thing through.

The Inquisitor: One gets used to it. Habit is everything. I am accustomed to the fire: it is soon over. But it is a terrible thing to see a young and innocent creature crushed between these mighty forces, the Church and the Law.

Cauchon: You call her innocent!

The Inquisitor: Oh, quite innocent. What does she know of the Church and the Law? She did not understand a word we were saying. It is

the ignorant who suffer. Come, or we shall be late for the end.

Cauchon: *(going with him)* I shall not be sorry if we are: I am not so accustomed as you.

(They are going out when the Earl of Warwick, the English commander, comes in, meeting them.)

Warwick: Oh, I am intruding. I thought it was all over. *(He makes a feint of retiring.)*

Cauchon: Do not go, my lord. It is all over.

The Inquisitor: The execution is not in our hands, my lord; but it is desirable that we should witness the end. So by your leave... *(He bows and goes out through the courtyard.)*

Cauchon: There is some doubt whether your people have observed the forms of law, my lord.

Warwick: I am told that there is some doubt whether your authority runs in this city, my lord. It is not in your diocese. However, if you will answer for that I will answer for the rest.

Cauchon: It is to God that we both must answer. Good morning, my lord.

Warwick: My lord, good morning.

(They look at one another for a moment with unconcealed hostility. Then Cauchon follows the Inquisitor out. Warwick looks round. Finding himself alone, he calls for attendance.)

Warwick: Hallo: some attendance here! *(silence)* Hallo, there! *(silence)* Hallo! Brian, you young blackguard, where are you? *(silence)* Guard! *(silence)* They have all gone to see the burning: even that child.

(The silence is broken by someone frantically howling and sobbing.)

Warwick: What in the devil's name...?

(The chaplain staggers in from the courtyard like a demented creature, his face streaming with tears, making the piteous sounds that Warwick has heard. He stumbles to the prisoner's stool and throws himself upon it with heart-rending sobs.)

Warwick: *(going to him and patting him on the shoulder)* What is it, Master John? What is the matter?

The Chaplain: *(clutching at his hands)* My lord, my lord: for Christ's sake pray for my wretched guilty soul.

Warwick: *(soothing him)* Yes, yes: of course I will. Calmly, gently...

The Chaplain: *(blubbering miserably)* I am not a bad man, my lord.

Warwick: No, no: not at all.

The Chaplain: I meant no harm. I did not know what it would be like.

Warwick: *(hardening)* Oh! You saw it then?

The Chaplain: I did not know what I was doing. I am a hot-headed fool; and I shall be damned to all eternity for it.

Warwick: Nonsense! Very distressing, no doubt; but it was not your doing.

The Chaplain: *(lamentably)* I let them do it. If I had known, I would have torn her from their hands. You don't know: you haven't seen: it is so easy to talk when you don't know. You madden yourself with words: you damn yourself because it feels grand to throw oil on the flaming hell of your own temper. But when it is brought home to you; when you see the thing you have done; when it is blinding your eyes, stifling your nostrils, tearing your heart, then—then... *(falling on his knees)* O God, take away this sight from me! O Christ, deliver me from this fire that is consuming me! She cried to Thee in the midst of it: Jesus! Jesus! Jesus! She is in Thy bosom; and I am in hell for evermore.

Warwick: *(summarily hauling him to his feet)* Come, come, man! You must pull yourself together. We shall have the whole town talking of this. *(He throws him not too gently into a chair at the table.)* If you have not the nerve to see these things, why do you not do as I do and stay away?

The Chaplain: *(bewildered and submissive)* She asked for a cross. A soldier gave her two sticks tied together. Thank God he was an Englishman! I might have done it; but I did not: I am a coward, a mad dog, a fool. But he was an Englishman too.

Warwick: The fool! They will burn him too if the priests get hold of him.

The Chaplain: *(shaken with a convulsion)* Some of the people laughed at her. They would have laughed at Christ. They were French people, my lord: I know they were French.

Warwick: Hush! Someone is coming. Control yourself.

(Ladvenu comes back through the courtyard to Warwick's right hand, carrying a bishop's cross which he has taken from a church. He is very grave and composed.)

Warwick: I am informed that it is all over, Brother Martin.

Ladvenu: *(enigmatically)* We do not know, my lord. It may have only just begun.

Warwick: What does that mean, exactly?

Ladvenu: I took this cross from the church for her that she might see it to the last: she had only two sticks that she put into her bosom. When the fire crept round us, and she saw that if I held the cross before her I should be burnt myself, she warned me to get down and save myself. My lord: a girl who could think of another's danger in such a moment was not inspired by the devil. When I had to snatch the cross from her sight, she looked up to heaven. And I do not believe that the heavens were empty. I firmly believe that her Saviour appeared to her then in His tenderest glory. She called to Him and died. This is not the end for her, but the beginning.

Warwick: I am afraid it will have a bad effect on the people.

Ladvenu: It had, my lord, on some of them. I heard laughter. Forgive me for saying that I hope and believe it was English laughter.

The Chaplain: *(rising frantically)* No: it was not. There was only one Englishman there that disgraced his country; and that was the mad dog, de Stogumber. *(He rushes wildly* *out, shrieking.)* Let them torture him. Let them burn him. I will go pray among her ashes. I am no better than Judas: I will hang myself.

Warwick: Quick, Brother Martin: follow him: he will do himself some mischief. After him quick.

(Ladvenu hurries out, Warwick urging him. The Executioner comes in by the door behind the judges' chairs; and Warwick, returning, finds himself face to face with him.)

Warwick: Well, fellow: who are you?

The Executioner: *(with dignity)* I am not addressed as fellow, my lord. I am the Master Executioner of Rouen: it is a highly skilled mystery. I am come to tell your lordship that your orders have been obeyed.

Warwick: I crave your pardon, Master Executioner; and I will see that you lose nothing by having no relics to sell. I have your word, have I, that nothing remains, not a bone, not a nail, not a hair?

The Executioner: Her heart would not burn, my lord; but everything that was left is at the bottom of the river. You have heard the last of her.

Warwick: *(with a wry smile, thinking of what Ladvenu said)* The last of her? Hm! I wonder!

(Curtain)

Caution:
Enquiries regarding performance of this excerpt, amateur or professional, should be directed to the Society of Authors, 84 Drayton Gardens, London, England SW10 9SD.

Riel
(Excerpt)
John Coulter

CHARACTERS

Louis Riel—leader of the Métis

The Judge

The Court Clerk

The Crown Attorney (usually called the **Crown**)

The Defence Attorney (usually called the **Defence**)

Major General Frederick Middleton—leader of the military forces against the Métis

Charles Nolin—Riel's cousin

Father Alexis André—a priest who knows Riel

François Roy—a doctor at the lunatic asylum of Beaufort

Dr. Jukes—senior surgeon of the Mounted Police

Police Officer Bromley-Witheroe—the officer in charge of Riel

A Woman—a Métis who knows Riel

The Sheriff

The Foreman of the Jury

"The Northwest...is my mother country. And I am sure my mother country will not kill me...any more than my mother did..."

SCENE ONE

(The Courtroom, Regina.
The voice of the clerk of the Court is heard from offstage.)

Voice of the Clerk: Oyez, oyez, oyez!

(Clerk enters, down right, gowned and holding papers in his hand. As he enters he is speaking.)

Clerk: That the said Louis Riel...not regarding the duty of his allegiance to our sovereign Lady the Queen, nor having the fear of God in his heart, but being moved and seduced by the instigation of the devil as a false traitor against our said Lady the Queen, here stands charged before my lord the Queen's Justice...

(While the clerk has been speaking, four separate areas have been spotlighted. In Spot One, down left, Judge Richardson is standing before the raised seat which is the bench. In Spot Two, up left centre, Riel stands behind a rail which is the dock. Spot Three, down right of centre, and Spot Four, down right, are for the time being unoccupied. In the unlit area, up right, stand, in separate groups, the six jurymen, Crown and Defence counsel, witnesses, and

the public. The clerk now moves to vicinity of the bench. An usher's "knock-knock" is heard.)

Clerk: Order! Order!

(Judge Richardson bows deeply to the Court and sits down. All others remain standing.)

Clerk: *(gabbling it off rapidly)* Oyez oyez oyez all persons having business with my lord the Queen's Justice draw near and give attention and you shall be heard God save the Queen.

(All present, except Riel, sit down.)

Judge: *(as to himself, consulting his papers)* Queen versus Riel. High treason. *(calls)* Louis Riel. *(Riel bows deeply and remains standing.)* Counsel for the Crown. *(The counsel for the Crown steps forward into Spot Three, bows to the judge, and retires.)* Counsel for the Defence. *(The counsel for the Defence steps forward into Spot Three, bows to the judge, and retires.)* Arraign the prisoner.

Clerk: *(rising from his position below the bench)* On this the sixth day of July in the year of our Lord, 1885, at the town of Regina, Louis Riel, you stand charged on oath that with divers other false traitors armed and arrayed in a warlike manner, you did levy and make war against our Lady the Queen, and did maliciously and traitorously attempt by force of arms to destroy the Constitution and Government of the Realm. . . and to depose our said Lady the Queen from the style, honour, and kingly name of the Imperial Crown of the Realm to the evil example of others in like case offending. Louis Riel, are you guilty or not guilty?

Riel: I have the honour to answer the Court I am not guilty.

Clerk: You may sit down.

(Riel bows and sits down. The judge nods to the Crown Attorney, who enters Spot Three.)

Judge: Proceed.

Crown: The jury assembled here must pass judgment in the most serious trial that has ever taken place in Canada. In the presence of witnesses the prisoner stated that in one week the government police would be wiped out of existence. A few days later he told another witness that the rebellion had commenced; that he had been waiting fifteen years to get this opportunity. He wrote and signed an ultimatum to Major Crozier of the North West Mounted Police in which he stated: "We intend to commence a war of extermination upon all who have shown themselves hostile to our rights." I think you will be satisfied before this case is over that this matter is brought about by the personal vanity of the man on trial. I would like to call as witness Major General Frederick Middleton.

(Middleton enters Spot Four. The oath in brief form may be taken by successive witnesses.)

Crown: General Middleton, you commanded the Canadian militia in its campaign against the rebels at Batoche and Duck Lake?

Middleton: Yes, that is correct.

Crown: Did you at any time see the prisoner in the field of battle?

Middleton: I did. At Duck Lake. Although he did not appear to be armed, he led a charge on horseback and shouted encouragement to his troops.

Crown: Tell us what happened at Batoche.

Middleton: There was some severe fighting. Our troops encountered unexpectedly stiff opposition. The enemy were so skilfully concealed in rifle pits behind thick cover that we could neither see them nor get at them. Their commander, one Gabriel Dumont—who, I understand, was responsible for the actual military operations—showed uncommon skill, as well as a thorough grasp of Indian methods of warfare.

Crown: Can you say what part in all this, if any, was played by the prisoner?

Middleton: He seems to have been the ringleader. He managed to inspire his men with almost fanatical bravery and tenacity. We were unable to dislodge them until we could bring into play the superior firepower of our Gatling gun. That made short work of 'em.

Got 'em on the run. Soon they dispersed altogether, and I sent out scouts to search the woods as far as Batoche. Scouts Howrie and Armstrong came upon the prisoner wandering in the woods. He asked them for safe conduct. To be brought to me with the purpose, he said, of discussing terms. When he reached my tent he said he had come to ask for an armistice, to have the just demands and grievances of his people seriously weighed by Ottawa. I told him the people's demands and grievances weren't my affair. And that he would be taken in custody to Regina, where he'd have a chance to put his case before a court of law. And—well—here we are.

Crown: In what capacity did he present himself to you, with this absurd request for an armistice?

Middleton: He said he was leader of the Métis.

Crown: Did he speak to you on religious subjects?

Middleton: Oh, yes. From the first moment. Later, he spoke often of religion. He said the saints had talked to him. That visions had been vouchsafed to him. He told me St. Peter had appeared to him, in the Church of St. James at Washington, District of Columbia. He said St. Peter had ordered him to undertake his mission.

Crown: His mission?

Middleton: To lead the people of the Northwest. He said a bishop, or archbishop, called Bourget, I think, had already told him he had a mission. He seemed to have mission on the brain. It bored me. I remember thinking, oh, confound him, he's always bothering about the saints and his mission and religion. He's anxious I should know about his religion. I noticed that when any conversation reached a point where he wanted to evade or gain time to answer—he immediately turned to religious matters.

Crown: Ah! He used his ideas on religion in that way?

Middleton: I so regarded it.

Crown: Tell us any of the views he expressed on religion.

Middleton: He spoke about Rome and the Pope. He wanted the government of the Church to be located not in Rome but here, in the new world, in Canada.

Crown: The Vatican in Canada?

Middleton: Yes. He told me he thought Rome was all wrong and corrupt, and that the priests were narrow-minded and had interfered too much with the people. And others of his ideas were excessively good.

Crown: What were they?

Middleton: He thought that religion should be based on humanity and morality and charity. His view of hell was that God's mercy was too great to be sinned away by anyone in the short time he had to live. Also he wanted to purge the Christian Church of its relics of paganism—such as the names of the days of the week.

Crown: He wanted to give new names to the days of the week?

Middleton: Yes, instead of the present pagan names.

Crown: During all your interviews with him did you see anything to indicate unsoundness of mind?

Middleton: On the contrary, I should say he was a man of rather acute intellect; in fact, deucedly clever.

Crown: And the idea of mental aberration never occurred to you?

Middleton: I believe it was put on—for a purpose.

Crown: Thank you.

(The Crown gives place in Spot Three to the Defence.)

Defence: What experience have you had in dealing with people of unsound mind?

Middleton: None at all.

Defence: But you think yourself qualified to give an opinion as to sanity?

Middleton: Not a medical opinion. But I think that in living with him several days I would know if I was living with a lunatic.

Defence: Are you aware that medical experts say it takes four months to detect insanity in many cases?

Middleton: Living with him it would be different.

Defence: Have you seen any document signed by the prisoner?

Middleton: Yes.

Defence: Was there anything peculiar in the manner of the signature?

Middleton: The signature was sometimes Louis Riel and sometimes Louis David Riel. I understand he included David to identify himself with the Biblical hero—the boy who slew the giant with a slingshot.

Judge: Was this told you by Riel himself?

Middleton: No, your Honour.

Defence: Any other peculiarity you observed about his signature?

Middleton: The word *exovede*.

Defence: Exovede?

Middleton: It frequently appeared after his name. He told me he invented it—from the Latin words, *ex*, from, and *ovile*, flock. From the flock. He said he used it to show he was assuming no authority except as one of the flock, an ordinary member of society. He said that his council, being composed of exovedes, was to be called exovedate.

Defence: *(with careful point)* And in all this— you see no indication whatever of mental aberration?

Middleton: As I said, I think he put it all on— for a purpose.

Defence: Thank you.

(Middleton retires. The Defence steps out of Spot Three.)

Clerk: Charles Nolin.

(Nolin enters Spot Four. The Crown enters Spot Three.)

Crown: You know the prisoner?

Nolin: He is my cousin.

Crown: You have frequently seen him since he returned from Montana?

Nolin: When he returned he was a guest in my house for several weeks.

Crown: Did he talk to you about his ideas and plans?

Nolin: He never stopped talking about them.

Crown: Tell us something of what he said.

Nolin: He said he was sending out messengers all over the country with secret messages to rouse the Indians and Métis. Calling them to come and help. He said that together we could defeat the police and militia and bring Canada to her knees. He said he had plans to bring foreign armies here, to drive out Canada and take possession of Manitoba and the Northwest for the Métis and Indians. He said if we didn't drive out or destroy the white men we would be overrun and driven out or destroyed ourselves. He said the white men from the east would keep on swarming in to grab our lands. And that we would soon be no better than so many hungry, mangy coyotes to be hunted and shot at. We were to go on living our own kind of life, respecting and keeping up our own old customs and laws, and fighting for that to the death; or be despised and pushed aside and go down, down, down till we were lost.

Crown: He seriously thought that a scattering of Métis and Indians had a right, and duty, to fence off these vast empty lands against the spread of population from all the rest of the overcrowded world?

Nolin: He said what was ours was ours and we should fight and fight to hold it. Any man who wouldn't take up arms and fight to hold it was a traitor. He said we were to rise in arms. He had asked God and God had told him. He had waited fifteen years for God to tell him. And God had told him. It was God's time. We were to rise in arms.

Crown: Did you believe this?

Nolin: No.

Crown: But many did?

Nolin: They thought he was a prophet. He played on this. He could do what he liked with them. They were ready to die for him.

Crown: And many of them did?

Nolin: Yes. There was much bloodshed and great misery.

Crown: Would it be true to say that prisoner was the chief instigator of this rising in arms?

Nolin: He was the one that roused the people to get together and fight; but Gabriel Dumont was the one that planned and led the fighting here, like Ambroise Lépine did fifteen years ago at Fort Garry.

Crown: But prisoner was the one who roused them to fight?

Nolin: Without him it would not have happened. It might have flared up but it would have fizzled out.

Crown: One last question. When the fighting started, did prisoner himself take any active part in it?

Nolin: He was the one that went about the rifle pits giving the order to fire.

(The Crown gives place to the Defence.)

Defence: Prisoner, you say, is your cousin?

Nolin: Yes.

Defence: You have—or had—great affection and admiration for him?

Nolin: We were on friendly terms.

Defence: But you did admire him?

Nolin: I thought he was—clever—a cut above the rest of us.

Defence: Were you ever envious or jealous of his cleverness?

Nolin: No.

Defence: You have mentioned the trouble at Fort Garry. Is it true that there, as here again, you were with your cousin and his cause at first and later decided to desert them?

Nolin: I had to be with him at first. It was the only way to save my life. I did not think he would fight. I did not want to fight.

(During the examination of this witness, Riel shows signs of exasperation and resentment.)

Defence: When you thought he would not fight, you were with him to save your life. When you thought he would fight and might be defeated, you again decided to save your life?

Nolin: I did not want to fight, there or here. Here, when I'd had enough, he had me arrested and court-martialled. I was condemned to death but reprieved. Then I escaped.

Defence: And now you are here to give evidence against him! You have said that at the rifle pits he gave orders to fire. Did he himself fire?

Nolin: He had no rifle. He was always afraid of firearms. When the shooting started he went about carrying a crucifix.

Defence: What for? What did he do with the crucifix?

Nolin: When a volley was fired by the police and militia he lifted up the crucifix and gave the order to fire in return. He said: "In the name of God the Father who created us, reply to that!" Next time it would be: "In the name of Jesus Christ who redeemed us, reply to that!" Next it would be: "In the name of the Holy Ghost who sanctifies us, reply to that!" And so on, calling on the saints one after another.

Defence: Did this strike you as in any way unusual or peculiar?

Nolin: He was always trying to make out there was something out of the ordinary about him. That he was a prophet. Speaking for God. He even dressed up sometimes like a sort of priest—in a black suit with a purple waistcoat and a big cross hanging on his front.

Defence: Did *that* strike you as indicating anything not quite normal in his mentality?

Nolin: I think he knew what he was doing.

(Riel, unable to restrain himself any longer, suddenly rises.)

Riel: Your Honour, would you permit me a little while to...

Judge: *(surprised and a little flustered)* Eh? What?

Riel: I have some questions...

Judge: At the proper time. You will be given every opportunity.

Riel: Is there any legal way that I could be allowed to speak? To ask some questions?

Judge: You should suggest any questions to your own counsel.

Riel: *(to Defence)* Do you allow me to speak? I have some observations, some questions to ask this witness...

Defence: *(interrupting)* I don't think this is the proper time, your Honour.

Riel: Before this man leaves the witness box...

Judge: I agree it is not the proper time.

(Riel reluctantly sits down.)

Defence: I think it is necessary that the prisoner should thoroughly understand that anything that is done in his behalf in this case must be done through me.

Judge: The statute of high treason states that the prisoner can defend himself personally or by counsel.

Defence: But after counsel has been accepted...

Riel: *(rising again)* Your Honour, this case comes to be extraordinary. The Crown are trying to show that I am guilty. It is their duty. My counsel, my good friends and lawyers, whom I respect, are trying to show that I am insane. It is their line of defence. I reject it. I indignantly deny that I am insane. I am not insane! I declare...

Judge: Now you must stop.

Riel: The chance to ask important questions of the witness is slipping by. My good counsel does not know what questions to ask because he does not know this man and because he is from Quebec and does not understand our ways out here...

Judge: I have said you must stop. Now stop at once.

Riel: I will stop and obey your Court.

Crown: *(rising, smiling, and soothing)* Your Honour, the prosecution does not object to the prisoner putting questions to witnesses.

Defence: *(becoming angry)* Your Honour, the prisoner is actually obstructing the proper management of his case and he must not be allowed to interfere in it.

Judge: Isn't that a matter between yourself and your client?

Defence: I don't pretend to argue with the Court, but if I am to continue the case the prisoner must be made to abandon his attitude.

Riel: *(again rising)* I cannot abandon my dignity. Here I have to defend myself against the accusation of high treason. Or I have to allow the plea that I am insane and consent to the animal life of an asylum. I don't care much about animal life if I am not allowed to carry with it the moral existence of an intellectual being.

Judge: *(peremptorily)* Now stop.

Riel: *(beaten and sitting)* Yes, your Honour.

Judge: *(to the Defence)* Proceed.

Defence: *(to Nolin)* You may go. *(to the clerk)* Call Father André.

Clerk: Father Alexis André.

(Father André enters Spot Four. He is a noticeably unkempt bearded man in a greasy cassock.)

Defence: What is your name in religion?

André: Alexis André, Oblat.

Defence: Since how long have you been in this country?

André: Since 1865 in the Saskatchewan.

Defence: You know of the political activities of the population?

André: I do.

Defence: Do you know of petitions and resolutions being sent to the federal government?

André: Yes.

Defence: Did these petitions and resolutions—adopted at public meetings and sent to the government—have any result?

André: The continual silence or evasions of the government produced great dissatisfaction and drove the people to think their only hope lay in resort to force. And I...

(The counsel for the Crown intervenes, coming into the spot with the Defence.)

Crown: *(to the Judge)* I must object to this class of question. My learned friend has opened a case of treason justified only by the insanity of the prisoner, and he is now seeking to justify armed rebellion for the redress of their grievances.

Judge: Which is like trying the government.

Crown: And that isn't open to any one on trial for high treason. *(withdraws)*

Defence: *(to the Judge)* I don't want to justify the rebellion. I want to show the state of things in the country and that the prisoner was justified in coming back across the border from Montana.

Judge: That, I think, is not questioned.

Defence: *(bows to the Judge and turns again to the witness)* You have had occasion to meet the prisoner between July 1884 and the time of the rebellion?

André: Yes.

Defence: Have you spoken to him on politics and religion?

André: Frequently.

Defence: Did he speak in a sensible manner?

André: Not on politics and religion. On these subjects he did not have his intelligence of mind. I want to state a fact to the Court regarding the prisoner. You know the life of that man affected us during a certain time.

Defence: In what way?

André: He was a fervent Catholic, attending to his religious duties. But he stated things that frightened the priests. And he was subject to violent outbursts in which he would flout the authority and holy office of the priests. It is true that when the rebellious and hot-tempered mood had passed he would appear sad and contrite. He would then outdo himself in being extravagantly apologetic and polite, even abasing himself. Once, all the priests met together to decide if the man could be allowed to continue in his religious duties. They unanimously decided that, on questions of religion and politics, there was no way of explaining his conduct except that he was insane.

Defence: Insane?

André: Insane.

(The Crown replaces the Defence in Spot Three.)

Crown: You say the prisoner made statements that frightened the priests. What statements?

André: He wanted to change the Mass and the liturgy, the ceremonies and the symbols. He thought only the first person in the Trinity was God, and he did not admit the doctrine of the Divine Presence. God was not present in the Host according to him, but only an ordinary man six feet high.

Crown: Do you deny that a man may be a great reformer of religious questions without being a fool?

André: I do not deny history.

Crown: Is it not a fact that the Métis are extremely religious and that religion has a great influence on them?

André: Yes. It was just because he was so religious and appeared so devout that he exercised such a great influence on them.

Crown: He was at pains to appear devout to the Métis?

André: I did not say "he was at pains."

Crown: But you do say he appeared devout to the Métis?

André: Yes.

Crown: You heard the evidence of the previous witnesses?

André: Yes.

Crown: You heard them give their opinion that prisoner sometimes used religion for a purpose?

André: I have said that where religion is concerned I believe the prisoner is of unsound mind.

Crown: Thank you.

(André and the Crown withdraw.)

Clerk: François Roy, doctor of medicine.

(Dr. Roy enters Spot Four. The Defence enters Spot Three.)

Defence: You are a doctor of medicine?

Roy: Yes.

Defence: In the city of Quebec?

Roy: Yes. For a great many years I have been medical superintendent and one of the proprietors of the lunatic asylum of Beaufort.

Defence: You have made a special study of the diseases of the brain?

Roy: Yes.

Defence: Were you superintendent of the asylum at Beaufort in 1875 and 1876?

Roy: Yes.

Defence: In those years did you see the prisoner?

Roy: Many times.

Defence: Where?

Roy: In the asylum.

Defence: As a patient?

Roy: Yes.

Defence: Was he admitted with all the formalities required by law?

Roy: Yes.

Defence: Did you study the mental disease by which the prisoner was afflicted?

Roy: Yes—megalomania.

Defence: In a case of this kind, could a casual observer, without medical experience, form an estimate as to the state of the man's mind?

Roy: Not usually.

Defence: You were present at the examination of witnesses here today?

Roy: Yes.

Defence: You heard their evidence as to the prisoner's views on religion?

Roy: I did.

Defence: From what you heard can you say whether he was then of sound mind?

Roy: I believe he was of unsound mind.

Defence: Do you believe he was capable or incapable of knowing the nature and quality of the acts which he did?

Roy: I believe he was not master of his acts.

Defence: Will you swear that the man did not know what he was doing, or whether he was contrary to law in reference to his particular delusion?

Roy: That is my belief.

(The Defence gives place to the Crown in Spot Three.)

Crown: Under what name was the prisoner in your asylum?

Roy: Under the name of Larochelle.

Crown: Did you know that the man was Riel?

Roy: He himself told me so.

Crown: From what facts in evidence did you say the prisoner was incapable of distinguishing between right and wrong?

Roy: They never could persuade him that his special mission didn't exist.

Crown: How would you describe his belief in his special mission?

Roy: As an insane delusion.

Crown: Do you say that any man claiming to be inspired is suffering from an insane delusion, so as not to be able to distinguish between right and wrong?

Roy: It is possible.

Crown: Does not the whole evidence sustain the theory that prisoner's claim to a special mission was a skilful fraud?

Roy: There is no evidence of fraud.

Crown: Do you say the evidence is inconsistent with fraud?

Roy: When the prisoner was under my care...

Crown: *(sharply)* Will you answer my question.

Roy: Put the question another way.

Crown: *(He pauses. Then, with a glance at the Judge, he continues.)* If you cannot answer my question, I may as well let you go. You may go.

(Roy and the Crown withdraw.)

Clerk: Dr. Jukes.

(Dr. Jukes enters Spot Four. The Crown re-enters Spot Three.)

Crown: You are at present the medical officer attached to the Mounted Police force?

Jukes: I am the senior surgeon of the Mounted Police.

Crown: In your medical capacity, insane persons come under your observation?

Jukes: Yes.

Crown: You know the prisoner?

Jukes: Yes.

Crown: Have you formed an opinion as to his sanity or insanity?

Jukes: I have seen nothing to induce me to believe he is insane.

Crown: Is he capable of knowing the nature and quality of any act which he would commit, so as to distinguish between right and wrong?

Jukes: Very acutely.

(Crown gives place to the Defence.)

Defence: You have heard of the mental disease

known as megalomania?

Jukes: Yes.

Defence: What are the symptoms?

Jukes: The patient has delusions, grandiose delusions.

Defence: That he is powerful?

Jukes: Yes.

Defence: A great soldier?

Jukes: Yes.

Defence: A great leader and statesman?

Jukes: Yes.

Defence: That he is identified with some heroic Biblical or other character?

Jukes: Yes.

Defence: That he is a great prophet with a mission divinely inspired?

Jukes: He may be a great anything and everything.

Defence: Do such insane persons believe they are in constant intercourse with God and are directed by Him?

Jukes: I have known patients of that kind.

Defence: From the evidence and your own observation you have no doubt that prisoner's conduct is compatible with a perfectly sound mind?

Jukes: I've heard nothing that might not be accounted for by other causes, for instance fraud or deception.

Defence: If it can be proved that a man is labouring under an insane delusion that he was in communication with the Holy Ghost and acting under direct inspiration of God and was bound to do a certain act, and did it, would he be responsible for that act?

Jukes: Views on that subject are so different, even among the sane.... There are men who have held very remarkable views on religion and who have always been declared to be insane—until they gathered great numbers of followers in a new sect—then they became

great prophets and great men; Mahomet, for instance.

Defence: You think the conduct of Mr. Riel compatible with the conduct of a man like Mahomet?

Jukes: *(carefully)* My opinion is, rather, that Mr. Riel is a man of great shrewdness and very great depth, and that he *might* have assumed, for the purpose of maintaining his influence with his followers, more than he really believed.

Defence: That is your impression, doctor?

Jukes: I have thought it *might* be so.

Defence: Are you in a position to say, doctor, on your oath, that this man is not insane?

Jukes: I have never spoken to him on a single subject on which he has spoken irrationally.

Defence: Thank you.

(Jukes leaves Spot Four. The Defence steps outside Spot Three.)

Clerk: Police Officer Bromley-Witheroe.

(The policeman enters Spot Four. The Defence re-enters Spot Three.)

Defence: You are an Englishman?

Policeman: I am.

Defence: And you have had a good education?

Policeman: *(with a deprecating smile)* Well, it may not be an answer but I *am* a university graduate.

Defence: The prisoner has been in your charge?

Policeman: Yes.

Defence: So you have had ample opportunity to observe him?

Policeman: I have.

Defence: Tell us what you have observed.

Policeman: He occupies the cell next to the guard room in the barracks. His little statue of St. Joseph stands on the table, and when he's telling his beads I've noticed that he holds it in his hand and hugs it. His countenance usually displays a calm composure, and his eyes are nearly always bent on the ground as if he were wrapped in contemplation and study.

Defence: Can you tell us more? Anything in his conduct that seemed to you different from that of the other prisoners?

Policeman: He wrote a great deal in a book which he describes as written with buffalo blood.

Defence: With buffalo blood?

Policeman: Yes. I understand it's about himself and what he calls his people, his mission in the Northwest. A sort of *apologia pro vita sua.*

Defence: Have you noticed any other peculiarity of conduct?

Policeman: Sometimes in his cell he talks all night.

Defence: To whom?

Policeman: There's no one visible in the cell with him. But he talks as though God were in the cell with him. He speaks intimately, addressing God by name. And sometimes it's one of the saints. Particularly St. Joseph. He addresses himself frequently as if to the actual presence of St. Joseph.

Defence: And at such times he speaks aloud?

Policeman: Not always. Frequently there's a prolonged, deeply earnest talking in a low voice. A sort of—urgent whispering. But often he talks aloud.

Defence: And continues in this all night?

Policeman: Well, we have to stop him, for the sake of prisoners trying to sleep in neighbouring cells.

Defence: On such occasions did Riel resent being stopped?

Policeman: No. When we spoke to him through the grid he seemed at first not to understand, as if he were still—apart—in some sort of trance or dream. When he did come to, and understood where he was and what we wanted, he would be apologetic and most polite, and would comply.

(Defence gives place to the Crown.)

Crown: In your observation of the prisoner did you at any time form the opinion you were dealing with a lunatic?

Policeman: If by lunatic you mean...

Crown: A person of unsound mind.

Policeman: I'm not sure what constitutes soundness of mind.

Crown: So you will not say that you thought the prisoner insane?

Policeman: No. He seems to me one of those...singular persons.... *(suddenly)* After all, people have called Hamlet insane.

Crown: *(pouncing)* Ah, but was not Hamlet "putting an antic disposition on"?

Policeman: Yes.

Crown: Do you think prisoner was "putting an antic disposition on"?

(The policeman pauses, uncertain.)

Crown: *(sharply)* Well, do you?

Policeman: *(slowly, considering it thoughtfully)* I have never quite been able to make up my mind.

Crown: Thank you.

(The Crown and the policeman withdraw. Spots Three and Four are out. Only Riel and the Judge are highlighted, in Spot Two and Spot One.)

Clerk: The prisoner Louis Riel.

Riel: *(rising and bowing gravely)* Your Honour. Honourable Court. You will have seen by the papers in the hands of the Crown, I am naturally inclined to think of God at the beginning of my actions. I wish, if I do, you will not take it as a mark of insanity or as a play of insanity. *(He clasps his hands and closes his eyes and prays, with deep humility and simplicity.)* Oh my God help me through Thy grace and the divine influence of Jesus Christ. Bless me. Bless the honourable Court. Bless all who are around me now through the grace of Jesus Christ our Saviour. Change the curiosity of those who are paying

attention to me now. Change that curiosity into sympathy for me. Amen. *(He opens his eyes and looks around. Then, not rhetorical, but intimate, tender.)* The day of my birth I was helpless, and my mother took care of me, and I lived. Today, although I am a man, I am as helpless before this Court in the Dominion of Canada and in this world as I was helpless on the knees of my mother, the day of my birth.

The Northwest also is my mother. It is my mother country. And I am sure my mother country will not kill me... any more than my mother did, forty years ago when I came into this world. Because, even if I have my faults, she is my mother and will see that I am true, and be full of love for me.

I believe I have a mission. *(The lights begin to dim out, slowly.)* I say humbly that through the grace of God—who is in this box with me—I am the Prophet of the New World.

First I worked to get free institutions for Manitoba. Now—though I was exiled from Manitoba for my pains—they have those institutions, and I am here, hounded, outlawed.... *(The stage is now dark.)*

SCENE TWO

(Vicinity of the Courtroom, Regina.
  Down right, a woman meets the sheriff.)

Woman: Please, sheriff, please...

Sheriff: What is it?

Woman: I know Louis Riel. I know him since he was a little boy. I want to tell the judge about Louis.

Sheriff: No, no, no, no, I'm sorry...

Woman: They don't understand Louis in there. It is wrong about him in there. It is not Louis. I know Louis. I know his mother. I knew his father, too, Jean Louis. He was for us too, the Métis people...

Sheriff: Yes, yes, I'm sorry, but it's quite impossible for me to... *(She clutches at him*

imploringly, and he impatiently casts her off.) Keep your hands off! Let go of me!

Woman: Don't put me away, please, sir, please.

Sheriff: You can't possibly speak to the judge.

Woman: Then the jury...

Sheriff: Nor any of the jury. Certainly not!

Woman: But they are kind men; they will want to know about Louis; they will see I come only to tell the truth for Louis.

Sheriff: You don't seem to understand. If you try to speak to them...

Woman: *(frantic)* I must, I must...

Sheriff: *(sternly)* Do you want to be sent to jail?!

(The policeman, walking from the left, has noticed and overheard; the sheriff by a nod and glance has him take over. The sheriff goes briskly on his way off, left; the policeman takes the woman's arm kindly and leads her off, right.)

Policeman: It'll be all right with him. He'll be all right. Come now, come. The law is very fair. It's better not to interfere. Better for him.

Woman: Not to interfere! His friends that knew him, not to interfere!

SCENE THREE

(The Courtroom, Regina.
  The lights gradually come up on Riel nearing the conclusion of his speech.)

Riel: ...Petition after petition was sent from the Northwest to the federal government, and so irresponsible is that government that in the course of several years, besides doing nothing to satisfy the just claims of the people, they hardly troubled even to reply. All they have done is to send police and more police. That fact indicates absolute lack of responsibility. Insanity of government! Insanity complicated with paralysis. I was called by the people to lead them in their struggle against this insanity. I came. I came back from exile—to help them. And when I was pounced upon by armed police, I answered with arms. That is what is called my crime of high treason, for which they hold me today and for which they would tear me in pieces. If you take the plea of the Defence that I am not responsible for my acts, acquit me completely. If you pronounce in favour of the Crown, which contends I am responsible, acquit me all the same. You are perfectly justified in declaring that, having my reason, I acted with sound mind in quarrelling with an insane and irresponsible government. If there is high treason, it is not mine but theirs—their high treason against the people of the Northwest.

Judge: *(wearied)* Now are you done?

Riel: If you have the kindness to permit me...

Judge: Well, if you must, you must.

Riel: I am glad the Crown has proved I am the leader of the Métis of the Northwest. That is important to remember. It means I stand in this dock not as myself only, but as the chosen representative and leader of a whole people—the Métis people. Can a whole people be guilty of treason? I beg you to think of that. I am their leader—and one day perhaps I will be acknowledged as more than a leader of the Métis—as a leader of good in this great country.

All my life I have worked for practical results. If I have succeeded, after my death my children will shake hands with the Protestants. I do not want those evils which exist in Europe to be repeated here. There will be at last a New World. But not in some days or years. It will take hundreds of years.

Yet, now, we make a beginning. We invite to our new world Italians, Poles, Bavarians, Belgians, the Swedes, the Irish, the Jews—all, all are welcome here, provided only they will help us with their work and with their money and by acknowledging Jesus Christ as the only hope of mankind and the Saviour of the world.

Now by the soil of this great land they have their start to make a nation. Who starts the nations? God. God is the maker of the universe. Our planet is in His hands. All the nations, the tribes, are members of His family. To each as a good Father He gives their inheritance. God cannot create a tribe, a nation, without locating it. We are not birds. We have to walk on the ground. And this is our ground, our country. And we will enrich it. We will cultivate it. This is the genius of civilization. Honourable Court, that is what, as a public man, Riel has said. Of this I am guilty. Of the charge against me I am not guilty. I am confident that for this I will not be destroyed.

Judge: Is *that* all?

Riel: Yes, that is all. Except to put my speech under the protection of my God my Saviour. He is the only one who can make it effective. And He will not fail me. If I have been astray, I have been acting not as an impostor but according to my conscience. Your Honour, that is what I have to say. *(He bows gravely to the Court and then kneels down in the dock in silent prayer.)*

Clerk: The jury will retire to consider their verdict.

Judge: Adjourned.

Clerk: Court adjourned.

SCENE FOUR

(Vicinity of Courtroom, Regina.
The Crown and Defence come walking slowly from the right, discussing the case.)

Crown: Must congratulate you. A most skilful defence.

Defence: Thank you. But the jury was with you to the last, I'm afraid.

Crown: Wish I could think so, but I'm not so sure. They showed lots of sympathy for him at times.

Defence: True, true—if only he hadn't squandered it by tiresome verbosity. French Canadians will still demand to know why he was tried by an exclusively Anglo-Saxon jury. Not even one Frenchman. And a jury of only six.

Crown: Our frontier ways are rough sometimes. A bit irregular. But—they get the job done.

(Dr. Jukes and Dr. Roy have come strolling from the left, similarly discussing the case.)

Jukes: They'll hang him, doctor.

Roy: Is it so sure? You and I do not agree about him. So—the jury may not either.

Jukes: We shall soon know. Meanwhile, I've found him a most interesting patient. Forces me to re-examine my settled beliefs on many points.

Roy: It is like this, with the deranged. To work with them, it is to see how—what is your word—how—*precarious* is our hold on what we call sanity. What *is* sanity? To think of this—it can be frightening.

Jukes: Speaking of fright, I hate to imagine what *he's* going through now, poor devil. Sitting in there...

Roy: Pardon. Kneeling. He prays. The jury considers, and he prays. He does not stop. He prays in French. In Latin. Mostly French. But sometimes in English! To make quite sure they will understand *(looking upward)* up there! But I think it is all right, up there. I think *they* know some French!

Jukes: Unless, up there, they've quite lost touch with the French! Quite given them up.

Roy: Ah, oui! And heaven now—full only of the English! This would be heaven!

Jukes: This levity, doctor...

Roy: M'm! Not—English.

Jukes: Well, a trifle heartless, perhaps. With prisoner in there, bracing himself for the verdict. Guilty? Not guilty? Must be absolutely agonizing.

(They are now joined by the Crown and the Defence.)

Roy: I think he genuinely believes his saints will save him.

Jukes: Certainly if faith—utter faith could sway a verdict...

Crown: A court of law's a most unfavourable climate for miracles of faith.

Defence: Even the faith of a prophet.

Jukes: Which reminds me—if it won't strike you as blasphemous, gentlemen—I've been thinking we know a little more now of the considerations Pilate had to weigh—in a case with, shall we say, certain parallels.

Crown: *(but lightly, smiling)* Doctor, I consider that remark one of the truest examples of profanity I've heard in a long time.

Jukes: But some truth in it, don't you think? And in that particular connection, gentlemen, isn't it striking how anxious the prisoner is to identify his own predicament with the—Easter tragedy?

Defence: That cross with himself hanging on it.

Crown: Passion for martyrdom.

Defence: Part of my case for him.

Jukes: Well, he may soon have what his heart desires. Jury may be ready. Shall we go in?

(They all go off right.)

SCENE FIVE

*(The Courtroom, Regina.
  The Court is assembled as before.)*

Clerk: Foreman of the jury.

(The foreman rises, bows, and remains standing.)

Clerk: Are the jury agreed upon their verdict?

Foreman: They are.

Clerk: How say you: Is the prisoner guilty or not guilty?

Foreman: Guilty.

Clerk: Look to your verdict as the Court records it. You find the prisoner, Louis Riel, guilty—so say you all?

Foreman: We do. *(He turns to the Judge.)* Your Honour, there's something more.

Judge: What is it?

Foreman: I've been asked by my brother jurors to recommend the prisoner to the mercy of the Crown.

Judge: Your recommendation will be conveyed to the proper authorities. Thank you.

(The foreman bows and sits down.)

Judge: Louis Riel, you have been found guilty of a crime the most pernicious that man can commit. You have been found guilty of high treason. For what you did your remarks form no excuse whatsoever, and the law requires you to answer for it. It's true, the jury have asked that Her Majesty give your case merciful consideration, but I can't hold out any hope that Her Majesty will open her hand in clemency to you. As for me, I have only one more duty to perform: that is, to tell you what the sentence of the law is upon you. All I can suggest or advise you is to prepare to meet your end.

(Riel clasps his hands before his breast and bows his head for the blow. The Judge puts on the black cap.)

Judge: It is now my painful duty to pass sentence upon you, and that is, that you be taken now to the police guardroom at Regina, and that you be kept there till the eighteenth September next, and that you then be taken to the place appointed for your execution, and there be hanged by the neck till you are dead. And may God have mercy on your soul.

(Spot One out on the Judge, leaving only Riel spotlighted. For an intense, silent moment Riel stands motionless.)

Riel: *(then, incredulous)* St. Joseph! *(then a cry of anguish)* St. Joseph!

(Blackout)

THE UNEXPECTED

A good dramatist can make us believe that even the most unrealistic situation is a fact. This is especially true in the case of fantasy and science fiction. We might end up in the most unexpected of worlds, with the most unusual of characters, but the writer must first have established a "normal" setting or framework for the events that follow.

Fantasy and science fiction are also means for commenting on human nature. Although a situation may have something of the supernatural about it, the people within that situation are human beings with the same feelings, fears, and aspirations that we have. Bringing in a character from another world—either literally or figuratively—allows the dramatist to bring into sharp focus the other characters.

In Maurice Valency's *Feathertop*, a witch brings a scarecrow to life and sends it out into the world to encounter real-life straw men. Gore Vidal's *Visit to a Small Planet* shows what happens when a stranger from another planet arrives on earth with the goal of ruling the world and starting a global war.

Feathertop

Maurice Valency

CHARACTERS

Mother Rigby—a witch

Diccon—her assistant

Feathertop—the scarecrow that Mother Rigby turns into a human being

Judge Gookin—the richest and the biggest fool in the Colonies

Polly Gookin—his daughter

Bob Endicott—Polly's suitor

Adam—Gookin's servant

Major Whitby—an officer in King George III's army

Graham Bell—King George III's tax collector

A Lady—at Gookin's dance

Several couples at the dance

"Walk, pumpkin head! Walk, Feathertop! I say, walk!"

(We fade in on a shot of Mother Rigby's fireplace: dancing flames, an iron pot on a crane seething over, weird shadows. We hear Mother Rigby singing an old ballad as she bends over her work.

The camera pulls back to show Mother Rigby's kitchen. The kitchen is a low-beamed room, the largest room in a small New England house of colonial design. It is the year 1770. There are cobwebs in the corners. Bunches of herbs and other witch's gear hang from the ceiling. On the wall hangs an old brass astrolabe alongside an old cutlass, a magic square on old parchment, etc. Mother Rigby puts the finishing touches to the scarecrow she has made. This has a ramshackle grandeur about it. It is plainly enough stuffed with straw. The head is a pumpkin. The tattered silk stockings fall lankly over the sticks that serve it for legs. But the embroidered coat and the doeskin breeches were once the last word in fine tailoring and the head has an oddly appealing look to it. An old tiewig gives the figure a cockiness as it sits sprawled out in the chimney corner.)

Mother Rigby: *(singing as she puts the last touches to it)*
Late, late yestreen I saw the new moon
With the old moon in her arm,
And I fear, I fear, my master dear,
That we will come to harm....
(When she has finished, she takes her pipe from the mantel shelf and fills it from an old tobacco pouch. She gazes at her work with satisfaction. A battered three-cornered hat hangs on a nail nearby. She fetches it down, chuckling, and sets it on the scarecrow's head. Then she stands her creation up in the corner. She stops humming her ballad and speaks in a sharp, professional tone.) Dic-

con! *(Diccon, her helper, appears at once.)* Diccon, a coal for my pipe! *(A glowing coal appears in Diccon's hand. He touches it to her pipe. Mother Rigby puffs abstractedly.)* Thank you. Sit down, Diccon. What think you of my scarecrow? He's worth looking at, eh? *(She turns to the scarecrow.)* And you are the fine gentleman, my boy. Fine enough to scare any crow in New England. Ah, there. Ah, there. *(She fishes an old feather out of the trash and mischievously sticks it in his hat.)* There, Feathertop, that's you. Now you're perfect. *(She stares at the firelight playing over Feathertop's honest features.)* Diccon, that puppet yonder is too good a piece of work to stand all summer long in a cornfield. Just because I'm a witch, I've half a mind to send him forth into the world to take his chance among other straw men of my acquaintance. *(She sets down her glass, chuckling.)* Judge Gookin, for instance—the richest as well as the biggest fool in the Colonies. Wouldn't that be a fine joke? *(She laughs.)* For two coppers, I'd do it. *(Two coins fall mysteriously, one after the other, on the table before her. She picks them up, laughing.)* So. So. The joke begins. Master Gookin wants very much to rise in the world—that I know. Well, I shall give him a leg up—I shall send him the finest gentleman ever seen in these parts—by far. *(laughs again)* What for, you wonder? I'll tell you, boy—but first I'll turn you into a man—and then—ah, then you'll hear the joke I've planned for Master Gookin! *(She sticks her pipe into the scarecrow's mouth.)* Come now, puff, darling! Puff! Puff just once. Breathe in a little smoke. Puff, I say! Puff! *(A little smoke trickles out of the pumpkin's mouth. She laughs exultantly.)* Ah, there! That's it, boy. Once more—puff! It's breath I'm giving you. Puff for your life, boy, puff! *(He begins puffing in earnest. The face changes. Upon the innocent and cheerful features of the scarecrow is superimposed a human face of the same contours. This shimmers into focus with each puff and then withdraws. Mother Rigby claps her hands.)* Ah, now it takes! Again, boy! Once more!

Once more! *(Feathertop emits a cloud of smoke that envelops the head completely. When it clears, the head is human.)* And now fetch us a puff to the very bottom of your bellows. There— *(The figure straightens up miraculously, the utmost in an elegant gentleman.)* See what a fine boy you've become? *(Feathertop smiles, pleased that he's done so well.)* But why are you skulking like a mouse in the corner? You've nothing to be ashamed of. *(She beckons.)* Step forth. The world awaits you. *(He looks frightened and eager by turns but ends by shaking his head. She beckons imperiously.)* Walk, pumpkin head! Walk, Feathertop! I say, walk! *(He hitches forward uncertainly and stands tottering. The rising sun streams in through the window, setting off his figure. He lifts his hand, trying to touch the sunlight.)* Steady! Steady, boy! *(He steadies himself. He steps out.)* That's it. That's splendid! *(He is now enjoying himself. He steps out with an impish grin, pretends to totter, then regains balance, and struts about comically. She is delighted by these unsolicited antics.)* Yes. Yes. Yes. Ha-ha-ha-ha. You're a proper marvel. And now that you're properly puffed up— *(She raises a hand. Her eye flashes. He shrinks back in terror.)* Speak! *(He takes the pipe from his lips and opens his mouth, trembling. He shakes his head. She insists.)* Speak! *(He gasps desperately.)* Speak or I'll—

Feathertop: *(in terror)* Ah—

Mother Rigby: I beg your pardon?

Feathertop: *(piteously)* Par-don.

Mother Rigby: *(laughs)* Pardon? What for? You haven't done anything yet. Well? Speak!

Feathertop: What—must—I—say?

Mother Rigby: Whatever comes into your head.

Feathertop: *(makes an effort to think. Then he puts the pipe to his lips and sucks in some smoke. A thought comes with it.)* Who— am—I?

Mother Rigby: You? You're my little Feathertop, that's who you are. You're the best witch's puppet ever seen in this world. I'm going to make a man of you.

Feathertop: *(pleased)* A man?

Mother Rigby: And no ordinary man. A man among men. Lift up your head, boy. Chin high.

Feathertop: Chin high. *(He laughs with delight.)*

Mother Rigby: Ah, what sparkle! What grace! *(Suddenly she fetches him a slap on the ear. Tears come into his eyes.)*

Feathertop: That hurt.

Mother Rigby: It was your birth pang. No person is complete without one. Congratulations, boy. You're born. Well? How do you like it?

Feathertop: I like it.

Mother Rigby: Do you so? Well, I'm delighted to hear it. Come then, say "Thank you, Mother."

Feathertop: Thank you, Mother.

Mother Rigby: With a proper bow. *(He tries.)* No, no—not like a pump handle. Like a fine gentleman. Like this. *(She bows.)*

Feathertop: *(imitates her with impish humour)* Thank you, Mother.

Mother Rigby: That's better. Bit homespun still. Back still creaks a bit. But many a fine gentleman's back creaks worse than yours and no one's the worse for it.

Feathertop: *(bows with the utmost grace)* Thank you, ma'am.

Mother Rigby: *(curtsies)* Ah, that's something like. You're a real wonder, I declare. So life interests you, does it? Well, there's quite a bit to it in one way or the other.

Feathertop: Where, ma'am?

Mother Rigby: Why, all about you, boy. Just open your eyes and you're certain to see it. *(He steps to the fire.)* That's fire. It burns. Don't touch.

Feathertop: No, ma'am. *(His coat catches a highlight of the fire. He passes a timid hand over its surface.)*

Mother Rigby: That's velvet.

Feathertop: It's smooth, ma'am.

Mother Rigby: *(smiles)* Not half as smooth as you, pet.

(He smells a bunch of dried herbs.)

Feathertop: Thank you, ma'am.

Mother Rigby: Them's herbs. Sweet?

Feathertop: *(gallantly)* Not half as sweet as you, ma'am.

Mother Rigby: *(laughing)* Well, now that's something I didn't expect to hear! Diccon, do you mark the boy? What a piece of work he's turned out, to be sure. *(admiringly)* Lad, I count myself a better witch because of you.

Feathertop: You're a wonderful witch, ma'am.

Mother Rigby: Listen to him, now. A feather and a puff of smoke, and he's all compliments and manners. Well, my handsome boy, you've come a long way since sunrise, there's no denying it. You should be quite a man by nightfall at this rate, if you have scope.

Feathertop: Scope, ma'am?

Mother Rigby: And scope you shall have. I'm going to send you forth into the world—what do you say to that—the great, wide, the wonderful world, boy.

Feathertop: Will I like it, Mother?

Mother Rigby: I think so, aye. For I've given you great natural advantages, boy, including a coat that once belonged to a French duke—'tis no ordinary garment. Besides, you're tall and slender and you have modesty. You're bound to cut a fine figure among the other stuffed shirts that go strutting and posing about the world.

Feathertop: I shall endeavour to live up to it, ma'am.

Mother Rigby: Oh, you will, you will, never fear. You've a well-turned leg. Your chest is full. And your head's empty. There's a perfect natural endowment for any sort of career.

Without any more, you could be a general and command an army. And as for your heart—there's more heart in that waistcoat, depend on it, than you'll find in many a banker or statesman. Yes, yes, boy—barring accidents, you will go far in this world. *(He puffs fruitlessly.)* Only mind—your pipe's out.

Feathertop: *(distressed)* Oh.

Mother Rigby: Knock out the ashes. *(He does so. She hands him her pouch.)* Fill it, boy. Quickly. *(He begins filling it.)* Mark me now, you do stand in some need of education, for you're young, though remarkably grown for your age. I can't send you to Harvard College, there's no time, and besides they'd only stuff your head with rubbish. Well, there are but three things a man needs to know, and I'll teach you those directly. Diccon! *(Diccon appears.)* For the rest, what passes for learning in this world is mostly smoke, and you'll find plenty of that in your pipe. Diccon, a coal! *(Diccon lights the pipe and goes. Feathertop puffs away contentedly.)* Now, boy, mark me well—

Feathertop: With all my heart, ma'am.

Mother Rigby: If you wish to get on in this world, look wise, ask no questions, tell no lies.

Feathertop: Look wise. Ask no questions. Tell no lies.

Mother Rigby: Can you remember that? *(He nods.)* With that much learning, you can hold your own with the wisest heads in the New World—nay, in the Old World, too.

Feathertop: But, Mother, how if I'm asked—

Mother Rigby: What, boy?

Feathertop: Where I hail from, who I am?

Mother Rigby: Gentlemen never answer such questions and 'tis rude to ask. Keep your mouth shut and others will tell your lies for you. Only see you don't get caught up in them yourself.

Feathertop: Never fear, Mother. I'm no scatterbrain.

Mother Rigby: Oh, you're not? That's good to know. And now we must look to your fortune, my innocent, for in this world a man without money might as well be dead. Here's two coppers for you.

Feathertop: What am I to do with them, ma'am?

Mother Rigby: You may jingle them together in your pocket, but on no account spend them.

Feathertop: But what if I should have need?

Mother Rigby: You won't. You're a rich man, by the looks of you, and that's all that matters. The rich have no need of money—they have credit. 'Tis a type of witchcraft I don't deal in, but you'll find out soon enough how it goes.

Feathertop: *(pockets the money)* Trust me for that, ma'am.

Mother Rigby: I do, boy, I do. You have a good head on your shoulders, a clear, fine, empty head, that's the point. The rest will come. In the meantime, bow and smile. And, above all, listen. So long as you listen, people will consider that you're a marvellously witty fellow.

Feathertop: One never tires of listening to *you*, ma'am.

Mother Rigby: *(smiles)* I know. I know. *(admiringly)* 'Twouldn't surprise me a bit if you rose to be governor and ruled us all.

Feathertop: I'm not so ambitious, ma'am. 'Twill be enough if I learn to rule myself. But I've a strange longing to see the world.

Mother Rigby: So? And where do you wish to begin, my fine gentleman?

Feathertop: 'Tis all one to me, Mother. I have seen none of it yet.

Mother Rigby: Boston? No, 'tis too big; you'd be lost in Boston. Philadelphia? 'Tis too grand. *(She thinks.)* Feathertop, my boy—

Feathertop: Mother?

Mother Rigby: Straight down that path, a half hour's walk will bring you to Judge Gookin's house. 'Tis a fine, big house.

Feathertop: Finer than this, ma'am?

Mother Rigby: *(chuckles)* A little. Master Gookin's the richest, as well as the biggest, fool in the Colonies. And he wants to rise in the world. Well, you shall give him a leg up.

Feathertop: I, ma'am?

Mother Rigby: You, lad. No one in these parts is good enough for his daughter, so he says. She must have a fine gentleman from abroad. Well, we shall send him one—the finest gentleman from abroad that ever was seen. Wait a bit, now— *(She picks an old garter out of a drawer and pins it to his coat. It turns into a jewelled cross.)* There! You're a Knight of the Garter. Lord Feathertop!

Feathertop: *(strutting about)* How I glitter! *(suddenly weak)* Mother—

Mother Rigby: Why, what ails you? Oh— *(His pipe has gone out.)* Diccon! *(Diccon appears.)* Quick! A coal for his pipe. *(Diccon obliges.)* Puff, lad, puff! *(He brightens up at once.)* Better now?

Feathertop: Much better, thank you. *(in the grand manner)* A trifling indisposition. Nothing at all, really.

Mother Rigby: *(hands him her tobacco pouch and chuckles)* I understand. All the same, remember, boy, stick to your pipe—your life is in it. A puff from time to time and you'll be as fit as a fiddle. There's nothing else but smoke holds you together. Here—there's tobacco in this pouch will keep you glittering a lifetime, and for a light all you need to do is to call for Diccon to bring you a coal.

Feathertop: *(gaily)* Diccon! A coal for my pipe! *(Diccon appears, glances at the burning pipe, then goes. Feathertop laughs.)* Why, it works like a charm, Mother.

Mother Rigby: Yes, it does. And now, hark ye, lad, while I think of it. When you see Polly Gookin—she's a pretty lass and she's certain to turn your head. Mind you don't lose it completely.

Feathertop: Trust me for that, Mother. I'm no fool.

Mother Rigby: Come, then, off you go. *(The door swings open by itself.)* 'Tis a beautiful morning, and the world's before you.

Feathertop: *(peers out dubiously)* Is that it there, Mother?

Mother Rigby: That's it there, boy.

Feathertop: *(jauntily)* Why then, I'm off.

Mother Rigby: Here, take my staff with you. *(She hands him her old stick. It turns into a gold-topped cane.)* This will lead you straight to Judge Gookin's door.

Feathertop: Good-bye, Mother. *(He wipes away a tear.)*

Mother Rigby: Why, the lad's sentimental.

Feathertop: I've my feelings, ma'am, like other people, I hope.

Mother Rigby: Have you so? Well—mind you don't show them too often. *(blows him a kiss)* Good luck, boy. Good luck, my darling.

Feathertop: *(waves his hat gallantly as he goes)* Good-bye, Mother, good-bye. *(He goes.)*

(The scene dissolves to a silhouette of Feathertop striding down a road against the morning sun, with Diccon behind him.
We next see a close-up of Feathertop's hat and stick on Judge Gookin's hall table. Polly Gookin and Bob Endicott are standing near them, speaking in low tones.)

Bob: Polly— *(Polly takes up the hat and perches it on her head.)* Take that off, Polly. 'Tis the stranger's hat.

Polly: I'll not take it off.

Bob: Polly, listen to me.

Polly: I'll not listen to you, Bob Endicott. I've listened to you enough.

Bob: But Polly, I mean to ask your father this very night—

Polly: You do? Oh, Bob! *(She throws her arms about his neck gaily and kisses him.)* And why not now, pray?

Bob: Oh, Polly, can I ask him for his daughter's hand in front of this Lord—Lord—what's-his-name?

Judge Gookin: *(off-stage)* Polly!

Polly: *(puts down hat)* It's Father.

Gookin: *(off-stage)* Polly!

Polly: I must go.

Bob: I'll come back tonight, Polly, and I'll ask him, never fear.

Polly: Mind you do, Bob Endicott, or I'll—

Gookin: *(off-stage)* Polly!

Polly: Good-bye.

(The scene changes to Judge Gookin's living room. Windsor chairs are drawn up to the fire. Feathertop sits in one at his ease, pipe in hand. Gookin is standing. The décor is colonial, elegant, and comfortable.)

Gookin: No, no, I won't hear of it! My Lord stay at the inn? What would they say of me in Boston? *(calls)* Polly! Polly, I say! I'm naught but a poor widower, sir, as you may know, but my daughter will see to it that whatever poor comforts this house can afford— *(calls)* Polly! Where the devil is the girl? *(A servant comes in with a tray, decanter, and glasses.)* Where's your mistress?

Adam: Miss Polly begs you will be patient. She will be down directly she's dressed.

Gookin: Primping, primping. Tell her she's wanted here. *(He pours a glass for Feathertop.)* And now, My Lord— *(He pours himself one.)* Pray tell me *(clinking glasses with Feathertop, who is not too sure of the procedure)* what brings a man of your position to our town?

Feathertop: *(takes a sip of the wine thoughtfully; the taste astonishes him)* What d'ye call this liquid?

Gookin: What? 'Tis wine, my lad. Port wine.

Feathertop: It makes the head spin.

Gookin: Surely you don't disapprove of spirits, My Lord.

Feathertop: Not in the least, sir. In this world you need to drink things to make the head spin. *(holds out his glass)* Another drop, Master Gookin.

Gookin: My Lord is here on no ordinary business, I'm sure.

Feathertop: I come only to see the world, Master Gookin.

Gookin: *(laughs knowingly)* Ah, indeed. To be sure. *(winks)* Secret business. Private business?

Feathertop: By no means. Public.

Gookin: Ah! On public business. Trust me, My Lord, I'll say nothing of it. Not a word. And the nature of— *(Feathertop gets up, his eye caught by a portrait of George III on the wall.)* I confess, I have been expecting this visit for some time.

Feathertop: *(pointing to the picture in wonder)* Why is that man so angry?

Gookin: Eh? Oh, I take your meaning, My Lord, yes. Ah, My Lord, you're right. His Majesty has good cause to be angry. Thank heaven you've come, My Lord. We look to you for deliverance.

Feathertop: *(in astonishment)* To me?

Gookin: Come now, 'tis as plain as a pikestaff. My Lord, be open with me. You were sent here, were you not?

Feathertop: Yes, I was indeed. But—

Gookin: Enough, My Lord, say no more. I understand. And look you, sir. *(He unlocks a casket.)* I have not been idle. Here, My Lord. The evidence.

Feathertop: The evidence—

Gookin: Enough to hang the lot of them, My Lord. A letter from Major Whitby offering to sell his fortress to the French whenever they desire it. Here he threatens to send his Hessians to sack a farm unless he is paid fifty pounds. Letters. Affidavits. Depositions. All as clear as day. You may open the hearings at once. Tomorrow. The sheriff takes bribes. The selectmen are perjurers. His Majesty's collector is a knave. Major Whitby is a traitor. The preacher has traffic with witches—

Feathertop: But are there no honest men in the land?

Gookin: All rogues. All blackguards. You must make a clean sweep, My Lord. I can see you are shocked.

Feathertop: I am astonished.

Gookin: My Lord, can you leave treachery unpunished? Can you permit honest folk to be abused? Can you look on idly while these wolves batten on the blood of the people?

Feathertop: No, certainly I can't do that.

Gookin: (*pours him out another glass*) My Lord, I say no more. The evidence is in your hands. You may sift it at your leisure.

Feathertop: You wish me to?

Gookin: I beg you to.

Feathertop: Very well, I shall.

Gookin: And when you see who the guilty are, My Lord, heads will roll, will they not?

Feathertop: Upon my word, they may. They may. (*inflating visibly*) I did not ask to be sent forth into your world, Master Gookin. But now that I'm here (*blowing out a cloud of smoke*) perhaps I shall be of some use in it. (*At this moment, Polly Gookin comes in. He sees her. He gasps with amazement.*)

Gookin: Be guided by me, My Lord. Hang a dozen of them first. After that—

Feathertop: (*rises*) Oh, lovely creature!

Gookin: What? (*He turns.*) Why, 'tis only my daughter, Polly.

Feathertop: How beautiful she is, your daughter!

Polly: (*curtsies*) My Lord.

Feathertop: (*bows*) My lady.

Gookin: The lass is to your taste, eh?

Feathertop: Aye, very much. Very much.

Gookin: She's a good girl, My Lord, and has a sweet singing voice. And she'll bring five

hundred a year to the man she marries. (*Adam comes in.*) What is it, Adam?

Adam: Major Whitby and the King's collector to present their compliments.

Gookin: I'll come out to them. By your leave, My Lord. (*He goes out with Adam.*)

Feathertop: Your name is Polly, lovely creature?

Polly: Polly Gookin, My Lord.

Feathertop: Polly Gookin. 'Tis a beautiful name, is it not?

Polly: It's mine.

Feathertop: 'Tis music in the ear. All of you is lovely, Mistress Polly. Your name, your eyes, your hair— (*He reaches out timidly and touches her hair.*) 'Tis softer than velvet. But your cheek is softer still— (*He strokes her cheek. She draws back.*)

Polly: My Lord, by your leave—!

Feathertop: Mistress Polly— (*He bends forward very naturally and kisses her on the lips.*)

Polly: Oh!

Feathertop: You are angry with me?

Polly: But what do you take me for, My Lord?

Feathertop: I have done something wrong?

Polly: Pray let me pass.

Feathertop: On my word, I meant no harm. And you're really none the worse for it. Don't be angry, Mistress Polly.

Polly: I'm not accustomed to your courtly ways, My Lord. We are simple country folk. All the same—

Feathertop: Among country folk, it is not permitted to kiss a lovely face?

Polly: Only if one intends to marry it, My Lord.

Feathertop: But I intend to marry it, Miss Polly. I very much intend to marry it.

Polly: You're but mocking me, My Lord. 'Tis not very gallant.

Feathertop: On my word, I'm not.

Polly: Let me go! Please! *(She breaks away.)*

Feathertop: Wait, Miss Polly, wait— *(She crosses to the door. Gookin comes in.)*

Gookin: My Lord, these scoundrels insist— What's amiss here? Where are you going?

Polly: *(brushing past)* I beg your pardon.

Feathertop: I have made your daughter angry, Master Gookin.

Gookin: What? Oh, bother the child—she's high-spirited. I'll bring her round. Major Whitby and the collector desire to be received. You'll not see them, I hope?

(Major Whitby and the collector come in.)

Whitby: I'm sure My Lord will see us, Master Gookin, if only out of curiosity. *(He bows.)* My Lord, your most humble and obedient servant, Major Whitby. In command of His Majesty's garrison. *(Feathertop bows curtly.)* And this is Mr. Graham Bell, His Majesty's collector.

Mr. Bell: My Lord.

Feathertop: I am much concerned for Miss Polly, Master Gookin.

Gookin: I'll see to it directly. *(calls)* Polly! *(to Feathertop)* I'll fetch her back. Polly! One moment, My Lord. *(He goes.)*

Whitby: Hark ye, My Lord—this Gookin . . .

Feathertop: Eh?

Whitby: A most pernicious liar, sir.

Mr. Bell: A thief, sir. A notorious knave. Not to be trusted for a moment. *(He whispers to Feathertop.)*

Whitby: Whatever he may have told you, My Lord—

Mr. Bell: Whatever he may have said—

Whitby: Believe no word of it—

Mr. Bell: Be guided by us, My Lord. We've been waiting for you night and day.

Whitby: Sh! Mum's the word!

(Gookin comes in.)

Mr. Bell: Your girl has spirit, Master Gookin.

Gookin: Aye. But what could My Lord have said to her to make her fly off like a jack-rabbit?

Feathertop: *(putting his pipe to his lips)* Only that I intend to marry her.

Gookin: To marry her! But, My Lord—!

Feathertop: Diccon! A coal for my pipe!

(Diccon appears, adding to the general astonishment. Feathertop puffs calmly.

The scene changes to a room in Gookin's house adjoining the ballroom, where a dance is in progress. Polly is standing before a long mirror, admiring her ball gown. Gookin stands behind her. There is a sound of string music.)

Gookin: *(exasperated)* "But, Father! But, Father! But, Father!" Can you sing no other tune? You want to travel in your own coach, I suppose, with your servants in livery and your house in town?

Polly: Oh, Father, I don't want anything like that.

Gookin: Well, I do. And here's the man can give them to you. Aye, and sent from heaven! A baron!

Polly: But, Father—

Gookin: "But, Father!" Now listen to me, girl, your father knows best, and we'll have no more of this nonsense. I shall send My Lord Feathertop in to you, and mind you cross him in nothing. Wait here.

(He goes off. The girl walks back to the mirror and makes a face at his retreating back. Bob comes in silently.)

Bob: Polly— *(The camera shows his reflection in the mirror. She turns.)*

Polly: *(in his arms)* Oh, Bob, Bob! I'm frightened!

Bob: Frightened? Of what?

Polly: This man. This baron.

Bob: Feathertop?

(Feathertop has just walked into the doorway. He stops on hearing his name.)

Polly: He's not like other people. He's strange.

Bob: But what's it to you, Polly?

Polly: Father—Father wants me to marry him.

Bob: Marry him? But you don't even know him. He's scarcely been here a day.

Polly: I know. I know. But Father—Oh, Bob, Bob, what are we going to do?

Bob: Do? Why, I'll—

(Feathertop blows out a cloud of smoke. They see him and turn. He comes in and bows.)

Feathertop: *(ignores Bob)* Miss Polly, your father bids me come and fetch you. It seems the dancing is about to begin. *(to Bob)* By your leave. *(He offers his arm to Polly, who takes it with a helpless look at Bob.)*

Bob: Sir.

Feathertop: *(stops)* Yes?

Bob: Nothing. Nothing.

(Feathertop smiles. He takes Polly out. Bob stares after them in desperation. The music strikes up.

The scene shifts to the dance floor. Several couples take places to dance a figure dance of the minuet variety. Feathertop and Polly join them.)

Feathertop: *(as the dance begins)* I may be a little awkward at this just at first, Miss Polly—

Polly: *(dancing)* Our New World dances must seem strange.

Feathertop: Your New World seems strange. *(He steps on her foot.)* Ah. Forgive me.

Polly: 'Tis no matter.

Feathertop: The young man yonder—Mr. Endicott—

Polly: Yes, My Lord?

Feathertop: He takes your fancy, Miss Polly?

Polly: We grew up together.

Feathertop: *(his dancing greatly improved)* He's not for you, Miss Polly. *(He draws her away from the other dancers.)*

Polly: How do you mean, My Lord?

(Camera moves to a lady dancing with Whitby.)

The Lady: Mark My Lord, how he dances, Major.

Whitby: 'Tis doubtless the latest fashion from Paris.

(Feathertop dances out of the room with Polly and into the adjoining room. The camera follows them.)

Feathertop: *(still dancing)* Miss Polly, I am but lately come into this world. I understand little enough of it.

Polly: It must seem trivial, My Lord, compared to the world you know.

Feathertop: It seems beautiful and wonderful beyond belief. Yet it bewilders me.

Polly: How bewilders you, My Lord?

Feathertop: Until I look at you, Miss Polly. Then all is clear.

Polly: What is clear, My Lord?

Feathertop: *(stops dancing; takes her hand)* What it is, and what I am, and what I have to do.

Polly: I don't understand, My Lord.

Feathertop: 'Tis a beautiful world, this world of yours, with its hills and its plains, its sunlight poured like a blessing from the sky, and its water bubbling like laughter from the depths. There should be joy in such a world, Miss Polly. It should be peopled with happy and lovely beings. Like you, Miss Polly. Not with miserable creatures like Judge Gookin.

Polly: My Lord!

Feathertop: *(nods)* Or Major Whitby. Or Mr. Bell, His Majesty's collector. Why should this beautiful world be filled with liars and hypocrites?

Polly: Is that not human nature, My Lord?

Feathertop: I had begun to think so. But then I saw you, Miss Polly. And then I understood. People are beautiful. They are good. But they are unhappy. They are afraid. And that makes them hateful and ugly. No matter. They shall be so no longer.

Polly: But My Lord—

Feathertop: *(more and more exalted)* I came among them in my innocence, and at once they turned to me for help. Very well. *(He takes her other hand.)* I shall not fail them.

Polly: Let me go, if you please, sir!

Feathertop: For your sake I shall help them. I shall heal them. I shall make all men equal and all men good. I shall exalt the humble. I shall abase the proud. I shall feed the hungry. Aye, the world will be the better for me.

Polly: *(frightened)* Please let me go.

Feathertop: But I shall need help, Miss Polly. I shall need inspiration, more than this poor pipe of mine can give. I shall need a vision of beauty to guide me. I shall need a hand to lead me. I shall need you—

Polly: You're hurting me.

Feathertop: I love you. *(He moves to take her in his arms. At this moment, half acceding, she sees his image in the glass. It is the scarecrow, pumpkin head and all. She screams.)* I love you. *(But now he sees it also and recoils in horror. He speaks to the image.)* Go away! *(He makes a threatening gesture. The image steps toward him with the same gesture. His words echo back from it as he shouts.)* Go away!

(Polly faints. The music stops. People rush in.)

Gookin: My Lord—

Whitby: My Lord—

Bob: What have you done to her? *(He kneels beside her.)* Polly!

Mr. Bell: She's fainted.

(Polly opens her eyes.)

Feathertop: Miss Polly—

Polly: *(sees him and starts up)* The scarecrow!

Whitby: Scarecrow?

Gookin: Pull yourself together, girl. Have you lost your wits?

Bob: *(to Gookin)* If she has, the fault is yours!

Gookin: Be so good as to leave my house, Mr. Endicott. My Lord, forgive the girl. She's yours.

Feathertop: *(totters; he speaks in a choked voice)* Fools! Fools!

Gookin: My Lord?

Feathertop: Give the girl to the man she loves. *(He takes up a massive candlestick and draws Gookin to the mirror.)* Or—do you prefer—

Gookin: What, My Lord?

Feathertop: Your Lord? There's your lord for you! There! *(They stare in horror at the reflection. He hurls the candlestick at the glass. It shatters.)* There. *(He makes a supreme effort and draws himself up. He surveys them each in turn. Then he puts his pipe in his mouth defiantly.)* Diccon. A coal for my pipe. *(Diccon appears.)*

Gookin: But, My Lord—My Lord—where are you going?

(Feathertop pauses at the door, looks at them, and blows a puff of smoke at them.
The scene changes to Mother Rigby's kitchen. She sits placidly rocking by her fire. The door flies open. Feathertop comes in, dejected.)

Mother Rigby: Well, well, boy! And I thought you'd make the whole world over!

Feathertop: So did I, Mother. But then I looked in a glass.

Mother Rigby: I know. I know.

Feathertop: And I saw myself as I am.

Mother Rigby: Alas, boy, I should have warned you.

Feathertop: I don't want to live!

Mother Rigby: Nonsense, boy—you're no different from the rest of them.

Feathertop: I don't want to live! I don't want to live!

(He hurls his pipe against the wall. He falls in a heap.)

Mother Rigby: What a pity! *(She picks up her pipe and fills it slowly.)* Poor little Feathertop! Of all the straw men who go bustling about this world, why should you alone have to know yourself and die for it? *(She sighs.)* Poor lad! Who knows what mighty thoughts passed through that pumpkin head in its little hour. And how you must have suffered! *(He looks up at her.)* Well, 'twas not in vain—at least you've put one thing right in the world. *(A flicker of interest appears in his eyes.)* Old Gookin has learned his lesson and the girl will have her boy. 'Tis not much—one good deed and that done unwillingly, but more than most people can boast of in a lifetime of iniquity. Well— *(She stares at her pipe a moment, then puts it to her lips.)* You shall be a scarecrow after all. 'Tis a useful and innocent vocation and will bring you no grief. *(She stares reflectively at the scarecrow lying in a heap on the floor and prods it with her toe.)* Diccon! *(She sits back in her rocker.)* A coal for my pipe! *(Diccon lights it. She puffs out a cloud which obscures the picture.)*

(Fade out)

Visit to a Small Planet

Gore Vidal

CHARACTERS

Kreton—a visitor to earth from another planet

Roger Spelding—an American television commentator

Mrs. Spelding—his wife

Ellen Spelding—their daughter

John Randolph—Ellen's boyfriend

General Powers—a forceful military commander

Aide—his assistant

Paul Laurent—the Secretary-General of the World Council

Second Visitor—another person from Kreton's planet

President of Paraguay

Two Technicians

"A war! I want one of your really splendid wars."

ACT I

(It is the day after tomorrow. We see the night sky, stars. Then slowly a luminous object arcs into view. As it is almost upon us, dissolve to the living room of the Spelding house in Maryland.

The room is comfortably balanced between the expensively decorated and the homely. Roger Spelding is concluding his TV broadcast. He is middle-aged, unctuous, resonant. His wife, bored and vague, knits while he talks at his desk. Two technicians are on hand, operating the equipment. His daughter, Ellen, a lively woman of twenty, fidgets as she listens.)

Spelding: *(into microphone)* ...and so, according to General Powers...who should know if anyone does...the flying object which has given rise to so much irresponsible conjecture is nothing more than a meteor passing through the earth's orbit. It is not, as many believe, a secret weapon of this country. Nor is it a space ship as certain lunatic elements have suggested. General Powers has assured me that it is highly doubtful there is any form of life on other planets capable of building a space ship. "If any travelling is to be done in space, we will do it first." And those are his exact words....Which winds up another week of news. *(crossing to pose with wife and daughter)* This is Roger Spelding, saying good night to Mother and Father America, from my old homestead in Silver Glen, Maryland, close to the warm pulse-beat of the nation.

Technician: Good show tonight, Mr. Spelding.

Spelding: Thank you.

Technician: Yes sir, you were right on time.

(Spelding nods wearily, his mechanical smile and heartiness suddenly gone.)

Mrs. Spelding: Very nice, dear. Very nice.

Technician: See you next week, Mr. Spelding.

Spelding: Thank you, boys.

(*Technicians go.*)

Spelding: Did you like the broadcast, Ellen?

Ellen: Of course I did, Daddy.

Spelding: Then what did I say?

Ellen: Oh, that's not fair.

Spelding: It's not very flattering when one's own daughter won't listen to what one says while millions of people...

Ellen: I always listen, Daddy, you know that.

Mrs. Spelding: We love your broadcasts, dear. I don't know what we'd do without them.

Spelding: Starve.

Ellen: I wonder what's keeping John?

Spelding: Certainly not work.

Ellen: Oh, Daddy, stop it! John works very hard and you know it.

Mrs. Spelding: Yes, he's a perfectly nice boy, Roger. I like him.

Spelding: I know, I know. He has every virtue except the most important one: he has no get-up-and-go.

Ellen: (*precisely*) He doesn't want to get up and he doesn't want to go because he's already where he wants to be on his own farm which is exactly where *I'm* going to be when we're married.

Spelding: More thankless than a serpent's tooth is an ungrateful child.

Ellen: I don't think that's right. Isn't it "more deadly—"

Spelding: Whatever the exact quotation is, I stand by the sentiment.

Mrs. Spelding: Please don't quarrel. It always gives me a headache.

Spelding: I never quarrel. I merely reason, in my simple way, with Miss Know-it-all here.

Ellen: Oh, Daddy! Next you'll tell me I should marry for money.

Spelding: There is nothing wrong with marry-ing a wealthy man. The horror of it has always eluded me. However, my only wish is that you marry someone hard-working, ambitious, a man who'll make his mark in the world. Not a boy who plans to sit on a farm all his life, growing peanuts.

Ellen: English walnuts.

Spelding: Will you stop correcting me?

Ellen: But Daddy, John grows walnuts...

(*John enters, breathlessly.*)

John: Come out! Quickly. It's coming this way. It's going to land right here!

Spelding: *What's* going to land?

John: The space ship. Look!

Spelding: Apparently you didn't hear my broadcast. The flying object in question is a meteor, not a space ship.

(*John has gone out to the terrace with Ellen. Spelding and Mrs. Spelding follow.*)

Mrs. Spelding: Oh, my! Look! Something *is* falling! Roger, you don't think it's going to hit the house, do you?

Spelding: The odds against being hit by a fall-ing object that size are, I should say, roughly, ten million to one.

John: Ten million to one or not, it's going to land right here and it's *not* falling.

Spelding: I'm sure it's a meteor.

Mrs. Spelding: Shouldn't we go down to the cellar?

Spelding: If it's not a meteor, it's an optical illu-sion...mass hysteria.

Ellen: Daddy, it's a real space ship. I'm sure it is.

Spelding: Or maybe a weather balloon. Yes, that's what it is. General Powers said only yesterday...

John: It's landing!

Spelding: I'm going to call the police...the army!

(*He bolts inside.*)

Ellen: Oh, look how it shines!

John: Here it comes!

Mrs. Spelding: Right in my rose garden!

Ellen: Maybe it's a balloon.

John: No, it's a space ship and right in your own backyard.

Ellen: What makes it shine so?

John: I don't know, but I'm going to find out.

(He runs off toward the light.)

Ellen: Oh, darling, don't! John, please! John, John, come back!

(Spelding, wide-eyed, returns.)

Mrs. Spelding: Roger, it's landed right in my rose garden.

Spelding: I got General Powers. He's coming over. He said they've been watching this thing. They...they don't know what it is.

Ellen: You mean it's nothing of ours?

Spelding: They believe it... *(swallows hard)* ...it's from outer space.

Ellen: And John's down there! Daddy, get a gun or something.

Spelding: Perhaps we'd better leave the house until the army gets here.

Ellen: We can't leave John.

Spelding: I can. *(peers nearsightedly)* Why, it's not much larger than a car. I'm sure it's some kind of meteor.

Ellen: Meteors are blazing hot.

Spelding: This is a cold one...

Ellen: It's opening...the whole side's opening! *(shouts)* John! Come back! Quick...

Mrs. Spelding: Why, there's a man getting out of it! *(sighs)* I feel much better already. I'm sure if we ask him, he'll move that thing for us. Roger, you ask him.

Spelding: *(ominously)* If it's really a man.

Ellen: John's shaking hands with him. *(calls)* John darling, come on up here...

Mrs. Spelding: And bring your friend...

Spelding: There's something wrong with the way that creature looks...if it is a man and not a...not a monster.

Mrs. Spelding: He looks perfectly nice to me.

(John and the visitor (Kreton) appear. He is in his forties, a mild, pleasant-looking man with side-whiskers and dressed in the fashion of 1860. He pauses when he sees the three people, in silence for a moment. They stare back at him, equally interested.)

Kreton: I seem to've made a mistake. I *am* sorry. I'd better go back and start over again.

Spelding: My dear sir, you've only just arrived. Come in, come in. I don't need to tell you what a pleasure this is...Mister...Mister...

Kreton: Kreton....This *is* the wrong costume, isn't it?

Spelding: Wrong for what?

Kreton: For the country and the time.

Spelding: Well, it's a trifle old-fashioned.

Mrs. Spelding: But really awfully handsome.

Kreton: Thank you.

Mrs. Spelding: *(to her husband)* Ask him about moving that thing off my rose bed.

(Spelding leads them all into the living room.)

Spelding: Come on in and sit down. You must be tired after your trip.

Kreton: Yes, I am a little. *(looks around delightedly)* Oh, it's better than I'd hoped!

Spelding: Better? What's better?

Kreton: The house...that's what you call it? Or is this an apartment?

Spelding: This is a house in the State of Maryland, U.S.A.

Kreton: In the late twentieth century! To think this is really the twentieth century. I must sit down a moment and collect myself. The *real* thing! *(He sits down.)*

Ellen: You...you're not an American, are you?

Kreton: What a nice thought! No, I'm not.

John: You sound more English.

Kreton: Do I? Is my accent very bad?

John: No, it's quite good.

Spelding: Where *are* you from, Mr. Kreton?

Kreton: *(evasively)* Another place.

Spelding: On this earth, of course.

Kreton: No, not on this planet.

Ellen: Are you from Mars?

Kreton: Oh, dear, no, not Mars. There's nobody on Mars...at least no one I know.

Ellen: I'm sure you're testing us and this is all some kind of publicity stunt.

Kreton: No, I really am from another place.

Spelding: I don't suppose you'd consent to my interviewing you on television?

Kreton: I don't think your authorities will like that. They are terribly upset as it is.

Spelding: How do you know?

Kreton: Well, I...pick up things. For instance, I know that in a few minutes a number of people from your army will be here to question me and they...like you...are torn by doubt.

Spelding: How extraordinary!

Ellen: Why did you come here?

Kreton: Simply a visit to your small planet. I've been studying it for years. In fact, one might say, you people are my hobby. Especially this period of your development.

John: Are you the first person from your... your planet to travel in space like this?

Kreton: Oh, my, no! Everyone travels who wants to. It's just that no one wants to visit you. I can't think why. *I* always have. You'd be surprised what a thorough study I've made. *(recites)* The planet earth is divided into five continents with a number of large islands. It is mostly water. There is one moon. Civilization is only just beginning...

Spelding: Just beginning! My dear sir, we have had...

Kreton: *(blandly)* You are only in the initial stages, the most fascinating stage as far as I'm concerned....I do hope I don't sound patronizing.

Ellen: Well, we are very proud.

Kreton: I know, and that's one of your most endearing, primitive traits. Oh, I can't believe I'm here at last!

(General Powers, a vigorous product of the National Guard, and his Aide enter.)

Powers: All right, folks. The place is surrounded by troops. Where is the monster?

Kreton: I, my dear general, am the monster.

Powers: What are you dressed up for, a fancy-dress party?

Kreton: I'd hoped to be in the costume of the period. As you see, I am about a hundred years too late.

Powers: Roger, who is this joker?

Spelding: This is Mr. Kreton...General Powers. Mr. Kreton arrived in that thing outside. He is from another planet.

Powers: I don't believe it.

Ellen: It's true. We saw him get out of the flying saucer.

Powers: *(to his Aide)* Captain, go down and look at that ship. But be careful. Don't touch anything. And don't let anybody else near it. *(The Aide goes.)* So you're from another planet.

Kreton: Yes. My, that's a very smart uniform, but I prefer the ones made of metal, the ones you used to wear. You know—with the feathers on top.

Powers: That was five hundred years ago.... Are you *sure* you're not from the earth?

Kreton: Yes.

Powers: Well, I'm not. You've got some pretty tall explaining to do.

Kreton: Anything to oblige.

Powers: All right, which planet?

Kreton: None that you have ever heard of.

Powers: Where is it?

Kreton: You wouldn't know.

Powers: This solar system?

Kreton: No.

Powers: Another system?

Kreton: Yes.

Powers: Look, buster, I don't want to play games; I just want to know where you're from. The law requires it.

Kreton: It's possible that I could explain it to a mathematician but I'm afraid I couldn't explain it to you. Not for another five hundred years, and by then of course *you'd* be dead, because you people do die, don't you?

Powers: What?

Kreton: Poor, fragile butterflies, such brief little moments in the sun. . . . You see, *we* don't die.

Powers: You'll die, all right, if it turns out you're a spy or a hostile alien.

Kreton: I'm sure you wouldn't be so cruel.

(The Aide returns; he looks disturbed.)

Powers: What did you find?

Aide: I'm not sure, general.

Powers: *(heavily)* Then do your best to describe what the object is like.

Aide: Well, it's elliptical, with a four-metre diameter. And it's made of an unknown metal which shines and inside there isn't anything.

Powers: Isn't anything?

Aide: There's nothing inside the ship. No instruments, no food, nothing.

Powers: *(to Kreton)* What did you do with your instrument board?

Kreton: With my what? Oh, I don't have one.

Powers: How does the thing travel?

Kreton: I don't know.

Powers: You don't know. Now look, mister, you're in pretty serious trouble. I suggest you do a bit of co-operating. You claim you travelled here from outer space in a machine with no instruments. . .

Kreton: Well, these cars are rather common in my world and I suppose, once upon a time, I must've known the theory on which they operate, but I've long since forgotten. After all, general, we're not mechanics, you and I.

Powers: Roger, do you mind if we use your study?

Spelding: Not at all. Not at all, general.

Powers: Mr. Kreton and I are going to have a chat. *(to his Aide)* Put in a call to the chief of staff.

Aide: Yes, general.

(Spelding rises, leads Kreton and Powers into the next room, a handsomely furnished study with many books and a globe of the world.)

Spelding: This way, gentlemen. *(Kreton sits down comfortably beside the globe, which he twirls thoughtfully. At the door, Spelding speaks in a low voice to Powers.)* I hope I'll be the one to get the story first, Tom.

Powers: There isn't any story. Complete censorship. I'm sorry, but this house is under martial law. I've a hunch we're in trouble.

(He shuts the door. Spelding turns and rejoins his family.)

Ellen: I think he's wonderful, whoever he is.

Mrs. Spelding: I wonder how much damage he did to my rose garden. . .

John: It's sure hard to believe he's really from outer space. No instruments, no nothing. . . boy, they must be advanced scientifically.

Mrs. Spelding: Is he spending the night, dear?

Spelding: What?

Mrs. Spelding: Is he spending the night?

Spelding: Oh, yes, yes, I suppose he will be.

Mrs. Spelding: Then I'd better go make up the bedroom. He seems perfectly nice to me. I like his whiskers. They're so very. . .comforting. Like Grandfather Spelding's.

(She goes.)

Spelding: *(bitterly)* I *know* this story will leak out before I can interview him. I just know it.

Ellen: What does it mean, we're under martial law?

Spelding: It means we have to do what General Powers tells us to do. *(He goes to the window as a soldier passes by.)* See?

John: I wish I'd taken a closer look at that ship when I had the chance.

Ellen: Perhaps he'll give us a ride in it.

John: Travelling in space! Just like those stories. You know—intergalactic drive stuff.

Spelding: *If* he's not an impostor.

Ellen: I have a feeling he isn't.

John: Well, I better call the family and tell them I'm all right.

(He crosses to the telephone near the door which leads into hall.)

Aide: I'm sorry, sir, but you can't use the phone.

Spelding: He certainly can. This is my house...

Aide: *(mechanically)* This house is a military reservation until the crisis is over: order of General Powers. I'm sorry.

John: How am I to call home to say where I am?

Aide: Only General Powers can help you. You're also forbidden to leave this house without permission.

Spelding: You can't do this!

Aide: I'm afraid, sir, we've done it.

Ellen: Isn't it exciting!

(Cut to the study.)

Powers: Are you deliberately trying to confuse me?

Kreton: Not deliberately, no.

Powers: We have gone over and over this for two hours now, and all that you've told me is

that you're from another planet in another solar system...

Kreton: In another dimension. I think that's the word you use.

Powers: In another dimension and you have come here as a tourist.

Kreton: Up to a point, yes. What did you expect?

Powers: It is my job to guard the security of this country.

Kreton: I'm sure that must be very interesting work.

Powers: For all I know, you are a spy, sent here by an alien race to study us, preparatory to invasion.

Kreton: Oh, none of my people would *dream* of invading you.

Powers: How do I know that's true?

Kreton: You don't, so I suggest you believe me. I should also warn you—I can tell what's inside.

Powers: What's inside?

Kreton: What's inside your mind.

Powers: You're a mind reader?

Kreton: I don't really read it. I hear it.

Powers: What am I thinking?

Kreton: That I am either a lunatic from the earth or a spy from another world.

Powers: Correct. But then you could've guessed that. *(frowns)* What am I thinking now?

Kreton: You're making a picture. Three silver stars. You're pinning them on your shoulder, instead of the two stars you now wear.

Powers: *(startled)* That's right. I was thinking of my promotion.

Kreton: If there's anything I can do to hurry it along, just let me know.

Powers: You can. Tell me why you're here.

Kreton: Well, we don't travel much, my people. We used to, but since we see everything through special monitors and recreators, there is no particular need to travel. However, *I* am a hobbyist. I love to gad about.

Powers: *(taking notes)* Are you the first to visit us?

Kreton: Oh, no! We started visiting you long before there were people on the planet. However, we are seldom noticed on our trips. I'm sorry to say I slipped up, coming in the way I did...but then this visit was all rather impromptu. *(laughs)* I am a creature of impulse, I fear.

(The Aide looks in.)

Aide: Chief of staff on the telephone, general.

Powers: *(picks up phone)* Hello, yes, sir. Powers speaking. I'm talking to him now. No, sir. No, sir. No, we can't determine what method of power was used. He won't talk. Yes, sir. I'll hold him there. I've put the house under martial law...belongs to a friend of mine, Roger Spelding, the TV commentator. Roger Spelding, the TV...what? Oh, no, I'm sure he won't say anything. Who...oh, yes, sir. Yes, I realize the importance of it. Yes, I will. Good-bye. *(hangs up)* The President of the United States wants to know all about you.

Kreton: How nice of him! And I want to know all about him. But I do wish you'd let me rest a bit first. Your language is still not familiar to me. I had to learn them all, quite exhausting.

Powers: You speak *all* our languages?

Kreton: Yes, all of them. But then it's easier than you might think, since I can see what's inside.

Powers: Speaking of what's inside, we're going to take your ship apart.

Kreton: Oh, I wish you wouldn't.

Powers: Security demands it.

Kreton: In that case, *my* security demands you leave it alone.

Powers: You plan to stop us?

Kreton: I already have...listen.

(We hear far-off shouting. The Aide rushes into the study.)

Aide: Something's happened to the ship, general. The door's shut and there's some kind of wall around it, an invisible wall. We can't get near it.

Kreton: I hope there was no one inside.

Powers: *(to Kreton)* How did you do that?

Kreton: I couldn't begin to explain. Now if you don't mind, I think we should go in and see our hosts.

(He rises, goes into living room. Powers and his Aide look at each other.)

Powers: Don't let him out of your sight.

(Cut to the living room as Powers picks up phone. Kreton is with John and Ellen.)

Kreton: I don't mind curiosity, but I really can't permit them to wreck my poor ship.

Ellen: What do you plan to do, now you're here?

Kreton: Oh, keep busy. I have a project or two... *(sighs)* I can't believe you're real!

John: Then we're all in the same boat.

Kreton: Boat? Oh, yes! Well, I should have come ages ago but I...I couldn't get away until yesterday.

John: Yesterday? It took you a *day* to get here?

Kreton: One of *my* days, not yours. But then you don't know about time yet.

John: Oh, you mean relativity.

Kreton: No, it's much more involved than that. You won't know about time until...now let me see if I remember...no, I don't, but it's about two thousand years.

John: What do we do between now and then?

Kreton: You simply go on the way you are, living your exciting primitive lives...you have no idea how much fun you're having now.

Ellen: I hope you'll stay with us while you're here.

Kreton: That's very nice of you. Perhaps I will. Though I'm sure you'll get tired of having a visitor underfoot all the time.

Ellen: Certainly not. And Daddy will be deliriously happy. He can interview you by the hour.

John: What's it like in outer space?

Kreton: Dull.

Ellen: I should think it would be divine!

(Powers enters.)

Kreton: No, general, it won't work.

Powers: What won't work?

Kreton: Trying to blow up my little force field. You'll just plough up Mrs. Spelding's garden.

(Powers snarls and goes into the study.)

Ellen: Can you tell what we're *all* thinking?

Kreton: Yes. As a matter of fact, it makes me a bit giddy. Your minds are not at all like ours. You see, we control our thoughts while you...well, it's extraordinary the things you think about!

Ellen: Oh, how awful! You can tell *everything* we think?

Kreton: Everything! It's one of the reasons I'm here, to intoxicate myself with your primitive minds...with the wonderful rawness of your emotions! You have no idea how it excites me! You simply seethe with unlikely emotions.

Ellen: I've never felt so sordid.

John: From now on I'm going to think about agriculture.

Spelding: *(entering)* You would.

Ellen: Daddy!

Kreton: No, no. You must go right on thinking about Ellen. Such wonderfully *purple* thoughts!

Spelding: Now see here, Powers, you're carrying this martial-law thing too far...

Powers: Unfortunately, until I have received word from Washington as to the final disposition of this problem, you must obey my orders—no telephone calls, no communica-

tion with the outside.

Spelding: This is unsupportable.

Kreton: Poor Mr. Spelding! If you like, I shall go. That would solve everything, wouldn't it?

Powers: You're not going anywhere, Mr. Kreton, until I've had my instructions.

Kreton: I sincerely doubt if you could stop me. However, I put it up to Mr. Spelding. Shall I go?

Spelding: Yes! *(Powers gestures a warning.)* Do stay, I mean, we want you to get a good impression of us...

Kreton: And of course you still want to be the first journalist to interview me. Fair enough. All right, I'll stay on for a while.

Powers: Thank you.

Kreton: Don't mention it.

Spelding: General, may I ask our guest a few questions?

Powers: Go right ahead, Roger. I hope you'll do better than I did.

Spelding: Since you read our minds, you probably already know what our fears are.

Kreton: I do, yes.

Spelding: We are afraid that you represent a hostile race.

Kreton: And I have assured General Powers that my people are not remotely hostile. Except for me, no one is interested in this planet's present stage.

Spelding: Does this mean you might be interested in a *later* stage?

Kreton: I'm not permitted to discuss your future. Of course my friends think me perverse to be interested in a primitive society, but there's no accounting for tastes, is there? You are my hobby. I love you. And that's all there is to it.

Powers: So you're just here to look around... sort of going native.

Kreton: What a nice expression! That's it exactly. I am going native.

Powers: *(grimly)* Well, it is my view that you have been sent here by another civilization for the express purpose of reconnoitring prior to invasion.

Kreton: That *would* be your view! The wonderfully primitive assumption that all strangers are hostile. You're almost too good to be true, general.

Powers: You deny your people intend to make trouble for us?

Kreton: I deny it.

Powers: Then are they interested in establishing communication with us? Trade? That kind of thing?

Kreton: We have always had communication with you. As for trade, well, we do not trade...that is something peculiar only to your social level. *(quickly)* Which I'm not criticizing! As you know, I approve of everything you do.

Powers: I give up.

Spelding: You have no interest then in...well, trying to dominate the earth.

Kreton: Oh, yes!

Powers: I thought you just said your people weren't interested in us.

Kreton: *They're* not, but *I* am.

Powers: You!

Kreton: Me...I mean I. You see, I've come here to take charge.

Powers: Of the United States?

Kreton: No, of the whole world. I'm sure you'll be much happier and it will be great fun for me. You'll get used to it in no time.

Powers: This is ridiculous. How can one man take over the world?

Kreton: *(gaily)* Wait and see!

Powers: *(to Aide)* Grab him!

(Powers and Aide rush Kreton but within half a metre of him, they stop, stunned.)

Kreton: You can't touch me. That's part of the game. *(He yawns.)* Now, if you don't mind,

I shall go up to my room for a little lie-down.

Spelding: I'll show you the way.

Kreton: That's all right, I know the way. *(touches his brow)* Such savage thoughts! My head is vibrating like a drum. I feel quite giddy, all of you thinking away. *(He starts to the door and pauses beside Mrs. Spelding.)* No, it's not a dream, dear lady. I shall be here in the morning when you wake up. And now, good night, dear, wicked children...

(He goes as we fade out.)

ACT II

(Fade in on Kreton's bedroom next morning. He lies fully clothed on bed with cat on his lap.)

Kreton: Poor cat! Of course I sympathize with you. Dogs *are* distasteful. What? Oh, I can well believe they do; yes, yes, how disgusting. They don't ever groom their fur! But you do *constantly*, such a fine coat. No, no, I'm not just saying that. I really mean it—exquisite texture. Of course, I wouldn't say it was *nicer* than skin but even so....What? Oh, no! They *chase* you! Dogs chase you for no reason at all except pure malice? You poor creature. Ah, but you *do* fight back! That's right! Give it to them—slash, bite, scratch! Don't let them get away with a trick....No! Do dogs really do that? Well, I'm sure *you* don't. What...oh, well, yes, I completely agree about mice. They *are* delicious! *(aside)* Ugh! *(to the cat)* Pounce, snap, and there is a heavenly dinner. No, I don't know any mice yet...they're not very amusing? But after all, think how you must terrify them because you are so bold, so cunning, so beautifully predatory! *(There is a knock at the door.)* Come in.

Ellen: *(enters with a tray of food)* Good morning. I brought you your breakfast.

Kreton: How thoughtful! *(examines bacon)* Delicious, but I'm afraid my stomach is not like yours, if you'll pardon me. I don't eat. *(removes a pill from his pocket and swallows it)* This is all I need for the day. *(indi-*

cates the cat) Unlike this creature, who would eat her own weight every hour, given a chance.

Ellen: How do you know?

Kreton: We've had a talk.

Ellen: You can *speak* to the cat?

Kreton: Not speak exactly, but we communicate. I look inside and the cat co-operates. Bright red thoughts, very exciting, though rather on one level.

Ellen: Does kitty like us?

Kreton: No, I wouldn't say she did. But then she has very few thoughts not connected with food. Have you, my quadruped criminal? *(He strokes the cat, which jumps to the floor.)*

Ellen: You know you've really upset everyone.

Kreton: I supposed that I would.

Ellen: Can you really take over the world, just like that?

Kreton: Oh, yes.

Ellen: What do you plan to do when you *have* taken over?

Kreton: Ah, that is my secret.

Ellen: Well, I think you'll be a very nice president—*if* they let you, of course.

Kreton: What a sweet girl you are! Marry him right away.

Ellen: Marry John?

Kreton: Yes. I see it in your head *and* in his. He wants you very much.

Ellen: Well, we plan to get married this summer, if Father doesn't fuss too much.

Kreton: Do it before then. I shall arrange it all, if you like.

Ellen: How?

Kreton: I can convince your father.

Ellen: That sounds awfully ominous. I think you'd better leave poor Daddy alone.

Kreton: Whatever you say. *(sighs)* Oh, I love it

so! When I woke up this morning I had to pinch myself to prove I was really here.

Ellen: We were all doing a bit of pinching too. Ever since dawn we've had nothing but visitors and phone calls and troops outside in the garden. No one has the faintest idea what to do about you.

Kreton: Well, I don't think they'll be confused much longer.

Ellen: How do you plan to conquer the world?

Kreton: I confess I'm not sure. I suppose I must make some demonstration of strength, some coloured trick that will frighten everyone . . . though I much prefer taking charge quietly. That's why I've sent for the President.

Ellen: The President? *Our* President?

Kreton: Yes, he'll be along any minute now.

Ellen: But the President just doesn't go around visiting people.

Kreton: He'll visit me. *(chuckles)* It may come as a surprise to him, but he'll be in this house in a very few minutes. I think we'd better go downstairs now. *(to the cat)* No, I will not give you a mouse. You must get your own. Be self-reliant. Beast!

(Dissolve to the study. Powers is reading book entitled The Atom and You. *Muffled explosions off-stage.)*

Aide: *(entering)* Sir, nothing seems to be working. Do we have the general's permission to try a fission bomb on the force field?

Powers: No . . . no. We'd better give it up.

Aide: The men are beginning to talk.

Powers: *(thundering)* Well, keep them quiet! *(contritely)* I'm sorry, captain. I'm on edge. Fortunately, the whole business will soon be in the hands of the World Council.

Aide: What will the World Council do?

Powers: It will be interesting to observe them.

Aide: You don't think this Kreton can really take over the world, do you?

Powers: Of course not. Nobody can.

(Dissolve to living room. Mrs. Spelding and Spelding are alone.)

Mrs. Spelding: You still haven't asked Mr. Kreton about moving that thing, have you?

Spelding: There are too many important things to ask him.

Mrs. Spelding: I hate to be a nag, but you know the trouble I have had getting anything to grow in that part of the garden...

John: *(enters)* Good morning.

Mrs. Spelding: Good morning, John.

John: Any sign of your guest?

Mrs. Spelding: Ellen took his breakfast up to him a few minutes ago.

John: They don't seem to be having much luck, do they? *(To Spelding)* I sure hope you don't mind my staying here like this.

(Spelding glowers.)

Mrs. Spelding: Why, we love having you! I just hope your family aren't too anxious.

John: One of the G.I.'s finally called them, said I was staying here for the weekend.

Spelding: The rest of our lives, if something isn't done soon.

John: Just how long do you think that'll be, Dad?

Spelding: Who knows?

(Kreton and Ellen enter.)

Kreton: Ah, how wonderful to see you again! Let me catch my breath....Oh, your minds! It's not easy for me, you know—so many crude thoughts blazing away! Yes, Mrs. Spelding, I will move the ship off your roses.

Mrs. Spelding: That's awfully sweet of you.

Kreton: Mr. Spelding, if any interviews are to be granted, you will be the first, I promise you.

Spelding: That's very considerate, I'm sure.

Kreton: So you can stop thinking *those* particular thoughts. And now where is the President?

Spelding: The President?

Kreton: Yes, I sent for him. He should be here. *(goes to terrace window)* Ah, that must be he.

(A swarthy man in uniform with a sash across his chest is standing, bewildered, on the terrace. Kreton opens the glass doors.)

Kreton: Come in, sir! Come in, Your Excellency. Good of you to come on such short notice.

(The man enters.)

President: *(speaking with a Spanish accent)* Where am I?

Kreton: You *are* the President, aren't you?

President: Of course I am the President. What am I doing here? I was dedicating a bridge and I find myself...

Kreton: *(aware of his mistake)* Oh, dear! Where was the bridge?

President: Where do you think, you idiot—in Paraguay!

Kreton: *(to others)* I seem to've made a mistake. Wrong President. *(He gestures and the man disappears.)* Seemed rather upset, didn't he?

John: You can make people come and go just like that?

Kreton: Just like that.

(Powers looks into the room from the study.)

Powers: Good morning, Mr. Kreton. Could I see you for a moment?

Kreton: By all means.

(He goes to the study.)

Spelding: I believe I am going mad.

(Cut to the study. The Aide stands at attention while Powers addresses Kreton.)

Powers: ...and so we feel—the government of the United States feels—that this problem is too big for any one country. Therefore, we have turned the whole affair over to Paul Laurent, the Secretary-General of the World Council.

Kreton: Very sensible. I should've thought of that myself.

Powers: Mr. Laurent is on his way here now. And may I add, Mr. Kreton, you've made me look singularly ridiculous.

Kreton: I'm awfully sorry. *(pause)* No, you can't kill me.

Powers: You were reading my mind again.

Kreton: I can't really help it, you know. And such *black* thoughts today, but intense, very intense.

Powers: I regard you as a menace.

Kreton: I know you do, and I think it's awfully unkind. I do mean well.

Powers: Then go back where you came from and leave us alone.

Kreton: No, I'm afraid I can't do that just yet...

(The telephone rings; the Aide answers it.)

Aide: He's outside? Sure, let him through. *(To Powers)* The Secretary-General of the World Council is here, sir.

Powers: *(to Kreton)* I hope you'll listen to *him*.

Kreton: Oh, I shall, of course. I love listening.

(The door opens and Paul Laurent, middle-aged and serene, enters. Powers and his Aide stand to attention. Kreton goes forward to shake hands.)

Laurent: Mr. Kreton?

Kreton: At your service, Mr. Laurent.

Laurent: I welcome you to this planet in the name of the World Council.

Kreton: Thank you, sir, thank you.

Laurent: Could you leave us alone for a moment, general?

Powers: Yes, sir.

(Powers and his Aide go. Laurent smiles at Kreton.)

Laurent: Shall we sit down?

Kreton: Yes, yes, I love sitting down. I'm afraid my manners are not quite suitable, yet.

(They sit down.)

Laurent: Now, Mr. Kreton, in violation of all the rules of diplomacy, may I come to the point?

Kreton: You may.

Laurent: Why are you here?

Kreton: Curiosity. Pleasure.

Laurent: You are a tourist, then, in this time and place?

Kreton: *(nods)* Yes. Very well put.

Laurent: We have been informed that you have extraordinary powers.

Kreton: By your standards, yes, they must seem extraordinary.

Laurent: We have also been informed that it is your intention to...to take charge of this world.

Kreton: That is correct.... What a remarkable mind you have! I have difficulty looking inside it.

Laurent: *(laughs)* Practice. I've attended so many conferences.... May I say that your conquest of our world puts your status of tourist in a rather curious light?

Kreton: Oh, I said nothing about *conquest*.

Laurent: Then how else do you intend to govern? The people won't allow you to direct their lives without a struggle.

Kreton: But I'm sure they will if I ask them to.

Laurent: You believe you can do all this without—well, without violence?

Kreton: Of course I can. One or two demonstrations and I'm sure they'll do as I ask. *(smiles)* Watch this.

(Pause. Then we hear shouting. Powers bursts into the room.)

Powers: Now what've you done?

Kreton: Look out the window, Your Excellency. *(Laurent goes to the window. A rifle floats by, followed by an alarmed soldier.)* Nice, isn't it? I confess I worked out a number of rather melodramatic tricks last night. Incidentally, all the rifles of all the soldiers in all the world are now floating in the air. *(gestures)* Now they have them back.

Powers: *(to Laurent)* You see, sir, I didn't exaggerate in my report.

Laurent: *(awed)* No, no, you certainly didn't.

Kreton: You were sceptical, weren't you?

Laurent: Naturally. But now I . . . now I think it's possible.

Powers: That this . . . this gentleman is going to run everything?

Laurent: Yes, yes I do. And it might be wonderful.

Kreton: You *are* more clever than the others. You begin to see that I mean only good.

Laurent: Yes, only good. General, do you realize what this means? We can have one government . . .

Kreton: With innumerable bureaus and intrigue . . .

Laurent: *(excited)* And the world could be incredibly prosperous, especially if he'd help us with his superior knowledge.

Kreton: *(delighted)* I will, I will. I'll teach you to look into one another's minds. You'll find it devastating but enlightening—all that self-interest, those *lurid* emotions . . .

Laurent: No more countries. No more wars . . .

Kreton: *(startled)* What? Oh, but I like a lot of countries. Besides, at this stage of your development you're supposed to have lots of countries and lots of wars . . . innumerable wars . . .

Laurent: But you can help us change all that.

Kreton: *Change* all that? My dear sir, I am your friend.

Laurent: What do you mean?

Kreton: Why, your deepest pleasure is violence. How can you deny that? It is the whole point to you, the whole point to my hobby . . . and you are my hobby, all mine.

Laurent: But our lives are devoted to *control-* *ling* violence, not creating it.

Kreton: Now, don't take me for an utter fool. After all, I can see into your minds. My dear fellow, don't you *know* what you are?

Laurent: What are we?

Kreton: You are savages. I have returned to the dark ages of an insignificant planet simply because I want the glorious excitement of being among you and revelling in your savagery! There is murder in all your hearts and I love it! It intoxicates me!

Laurent: *(slowly)* You hardly flatter us.

Kreton: I didn't mean to be rude, but you did ask me why I am here and I've told you.

Laurent: You have no wish then to . . . to help us poor savages.

Kreton: I couldn't even if I wanted to. You won't be civilized for at least two thousand years, and you won't reach the level of my people for about a million years.

Laurent: *(sadly)* Then you have come here only to . . . to observe?

Kreton: No, more than that. I mean to regulate your pastimes. But don't worry—I won't upset things too much. I've decided I don't want to be known to the people. You will go right on with your countries, your squabbles, the way you always have, while I will *secretly* regulate things through you.

Laurent: The World Council does not govern. We only advise.

Kreton: Well, I shall advise you and you will advise the governments and we shall have a lovely time.

Laurent: I don't know what to say. You obviously have the power to do as you please.

Kreton: I'm glad you realize that. Poor General Powers is now wondering if a hydrogen bomb might destroy me. It won't, general.

Powers: Too bad.

Kreton: Now, Your Excellency, I shall stay in this house until you have laid the groundwork for my first project.

Laurent: And what is that to be?

Kreton: A war! I want one of your really splendid wars, with all the trimmings, all the noise and the fire...

Laurent: A war! You're joking. Why, at this moment we are working as hard as we know how *not* to have a war.

Kreton: But secretly you want one. After all, it's the one thing your little race does well. You'd hardly want me to deprive you of your simple pleasures, now would you?

Laurent: I think you must be mad.

Kreton: Not mad, simply a philanthropist. Of course, I myself shall get a great deal of pleasure out of a war (the vibrations must be incredible), but I'm doing it mostly for you. So, if you don't mind, I want you to arrange a few incidents, so we can get one started spontaneously.

Laurent: I refuse.

Kreton: In that event, I shall select someone else to head the World Council. Someone who *will* start a war. I suppose there exist a few people here who might like the idea.

Laurent: How can you do such a horrible thing to us? Can't you see that we don't want to be savages?

Kreton: But you have no choice. Anyway, you're just pulling my leg! I'm sure you want a war as much as the rest of them do, and that's what you're going to get—the biggest war you've ever had!

Laurent: *(stunned)* Heaven help us!

Kreton: *(exuberant)* Heaven won't! Oh, what fun it will be! I can hardly wait! *(He strikes the globe of the world a happy blow as we fade out.)*

ACT III

(Fade in on the study, two weeks later. Kreton is sitting at a desk on which a map is spread out. He has a pair of dividers, some models of jet aircraft. Occasionally he pretends to dive-

bomb, imitating the sound of a bomb going off. Powers enters.)

Powers: You wanted me, sir?

Kreton: Yes, I wanted those figures on radioactive fallout.

Powers: They're being made up now, sir. Anything else?

Kreton: Oh, my dear fellow, why do you dislike me so?

Powers: I am your military aide, sir; I don't have to answer that question. It is outside the sphere of my duties.

Kreton: Aren't you at least happy about your promotion?

Powers: Under the circumstances, no, sir.

Kreton: I find your attitude baffling.

Powers: Is that all, sir?

Kreton: You have never once said what you thought of my war plans. Not once have I got a single word of encouragement from you, a single compliment...only black thoughts.

Powers: Since you read my mind, sir, you know what I think.

Kreton: True, but I can't help but feel that deep down inside of you there is just a twinge of professional jealousy. You don't like the idea of an outsider playing your game better than you do. Now confess!

Powers: I am acting as your aide only under duress.

Kreton: *(sadly)* Bitter, bitter...and to think I chose you especially as my aide. Think of all the other generals who would give anything to have your job.

Powers: Fortunately, they know nothing about my job.

Kreton: Yes, I do think it wise not to advertise my presence, don't you?

Powers: I can't see that it makes much difference, since you seem bent on destroying our world.

Kreton: I'm not going to destroy it. A few

dozen cities, that's all, and not very nice cities either. Think of the fun you'll have building new ones when it's over.

Powers: How many millions of people do you plan to kill?

Kreton: Well, quite a few, but they love this sort of thing. You can't convince me they don't. Oh, I know what Laurent says. But he's a misfit, out of step with this time. Fortunately, my new World Council is more reasonable.

Powers: Paralysed is the word, sir.

Kreton: You don't think they like me either?

Powers: You *know* they hate you, sir.

Kreton: But love and hate are so confused in your savage minds, and the vibrations of the one are so very like those of the other that I can't always distinguish. You see, we neither love nor hate in my world. We simply have hobbies. *(He strokes the globe of the world tenderly.)* But now to work. Tonight's the big night; first, the sneak attack, then—boom! *(He claps his hands gleefully.)*

(Dissolve to the living room, to John and Ellen.)

Ellen: I've never felt so helpless in my life.

John: Here we all stand around doing nothing while he plans to blow up the world.

Ellen: Suppose we went to the newspapers.

John: He controls the press. When Laurent resigned they didn't even print his speech.

(A gloomy pause.)

Ellen: What are you thinking about, John?

John: Walnuts.

(They embrace.)

Ellen: Can't we do anything?

John: No, I guess there's nothing.

Ellen: *(vehemently)* Oh! I could kill him!

(Kreton and Powers enter.)

Kreton: Very good, Ellen, *very* good! I've never felt you so violent.

Ellen: You heard what I said to John?

Kreton: Not in words, but you were absolutely bathed in malevolence.

Powers: I'll get the papers you wanted, sir.

(Powers exits.)

Kreton: I don't think he likes me very much, but your father does. Only this morning he offered to handle my public relations, and I said I'd let him. Wasn't that nice of him?

John: I think I'll go get some fresh air.

(He goes out through the terrace door.)

Kreton: Oh, dear! *(sighs)* Only your father is really entering the spirit of the game. He's a much better sport than you, my dear.

Ellen: *(exploding)* Sport! That's it! You think we're sport. You think we're animals to be played with; well, we're not. We're people and we don't want to be destroyed.

Kreton: *(patiently)* But I am not destroying you. You will be destroying one another of your own free will, as you have always done. I am simply a...a kibitzer.

Ellen: No, you are a vampire!

Kreton: A vampire? You mean I drink blood? Ugh!

Ellen: No, you drink emotions, our emotions. You'll sacrifice us all for the sake of your... your vibrations!

Kreton: Touché. Yet what harm am I really doing? It's true I'll enjoy the war more than anybody; but it will be *your* destructiveness after all, not mine.

Ellen: You could stop it.

Kreton: So could you.

Ellen: I?

Kreton: Your race. They could stop altogether but they won't. And I can hardly intervene in their natural development. The most I can do is help out in small, practical ways.

Ellen: We are not what you think. We're not so...so primitive.

Kreton: My dear girl, just take this one household. Your mother dislikes your father but she is too tired to do anything about it, so she knits and she gardens and she tries not to think about him. Your father, on the other hand, is bored with all of you. Don't look shocked—he doesn't like you any more than you like him...

Ellen: Don't say that!

Kreton: I am only telling you the truth. Your father wants you to marry someone important; therefore he objects to John. While you, my girl...

Ellen: *(with a fierce cry, grabs vase to throw)* You devil! *(The vase breaks in her hand.)*

Kreton: You see? That proves my point perfectly. *(gently)* Poor savage, I cannot help what you are. *(briskly)* Anyway, you will soon be distracted from your personal problems. Tonight is the night. If you're a good girl, I'll let you watch the bombing.

(Dissolve to study. A clock on the wall shows that the time is eleven forty-five. Powers and the Aide gloomily await the war.)

Aide: General, isn't there anything we can do?

Powers: It's out of our hands.

(Kreton, dressed as a Hussar with shako, enters.)

Kreton: Everything on schedule?

Powers: Yes, sir. Planes left for their targets at twenty-two hundred.

Kreton: Good...good. I myself shall take off shortly after midnight to observe the attack first-hand.

Powers: Yes, sir.

(Kreton goes into the living room, where the family is gloomily assembled.)

Kreton: *(enters from study)* And now the magic hour approaches! I hope you're all as thrilled as I am.

Spelding: You still won't tell us who's attacking whom?

Kreton: You'll know in exactly...fourteen minutes.

Ellen: *(bitterly)* Are we going to be killed too?

Kreton: Certainly not! You're quite safe, at least in the early stages of the war.

Ellen: Thank you.

Mrs. Spelding: I suppose this will mean rationing again.

Spelding: Will...will we see anything from here?

Kreton: No, but there should be a good picture on the monitor in the study. Powers is tuning in right now.

John: *(at the window)* Hey look, up there! Coming this way!

(Ellen joins him.)

Ellen: What is it?

John: Why...it's *another* one! And it's going to land.

Kreton: *(surprised)* I'm sure you're mistaken. No one would dream of coming here.

(He has gone to the window, too.)

Ellen: It's landing!

Spelding: Is it a friend of yours, Mr. Kreton?

Kreton: *(slowly)* No, no, not a friend...

(Kreton retreats to the study; he inadvertently drops a lace handkerchief beside the sofa.)

John: Here he comes.

Ellen: *(suddenly bitter)* Now we have two of them.

Mrs. Spelding: My poor roses.

(The new Visitor enters in a gleam of light from his ship. He is wearing a most futuristic costume. Without a word, he walks past the awed family into the study. Kreton is cowering behind the globe. Powers and the Aide stare, bewildered, as the Visitor gestures sternly and Kreton reluctantly removes shako and sword. They communicate by odd sounds.)

Visitor: *(to Powers)* Please leave us alone.

(Cut to the living room as Powers and the Aide enter from the study.)

Powers: *(to Ellen)* Who on earth was that?

Ellen: It's another one, another visitor.

Powers: Now we're done for.

Ellen: I'm going in there.

Mrs. Spelding: Ellen, don't you dare!

Ellen: I'm going to talk to them.

(She starts to the door.)

John: I'm coming, too.

Ellen: *(grimly)* No, alone. I know what I want to say.

(Cut to interior of the study, to Kreton and the other Visitor as Ellen enters.)

Ellen: I want you both to listen to me...

Visitor: You don't need to speak. I know what you will say.

Ellen: That you have no right here? That you mustn't...

Visitor: I agree. Kreton has no right here. He is well aware that it is forbidden to interfere with the past.

Ellen: The past?

Visitor: *(nods)* You are the past, the dark ages; we are from the future. In fact, we are *your* descendants on another planet. We visit you from time to time, but we never interfere because it would change *us* if we did. Fortunately, I have arrived in time.

Ellen: There won't be a war?

Visitor: There will be no war. And there will be no memory of any of this. When we leave here you will forget Kreton and me. Time will turn back to the moment before his arrival.

Ellen: *(to Kreton)* Why did you want to hurt us?

Kreton: *(heartbroken)* Oh, but I didn't! I only wanted to have...well, to have a little fun, to indulge my hobby...against the rules, of course.

Visitor: *(to Ellen)* Kreton is a rarity among us. Mentally and morally he is retarded. He is a child, and he regards your period as his toy.

Kreton: A child, now really!

Visitor: He escaped from his nursery and came back in time to you...

Kreton: And *everything* went wrong, everything! I wanted to visit 1860...that's my *real* period. But then something happened to the car and I ended up here. Not that I don't find you nearly as interesting but...

Visitor: We must go, Kreton.

Kreton: *(to Ellen)* You did like me just a bit, didn't you?

Ellen: Yes, yes I did, until you let your hobby get out of hand. *(to Visitor)* What is the future like?

Visitor: Very serene, very different...

Kreton: Don't believe him; it is dull, dull, dull beyond belief! One simply floats through eternity; no wars, no excitement...

Visitor: It is forbidden to discuss these matters.

Kreton: I can't see what difference it makes, since she's going to forget all about us anyway.

Ellen: Oh, how I'd love to see the future...

Visitor: It is against...

Kreton: Against the rules—how tiresome you are. *(to Ellen)* But, alas, you can never pay us a call because you aren't born yet! I mean where we are, you are not. Oh, Ellen, dear, think kindly of me, until you forget.

Ellen: I will.

Visitor: Come. Time has begun to turn back. Time is bending.

(He starts to door. Kreton turns conspiratorially to Ellen.)

Kreton: Don't be sad, my girl. I shall be back one bright day, but a bright day in 1860. I dote on the Civil War, so exciting...

Visitor: Kreton!

Kreton: Only next time I think it'll be more fun if the *South* wins! *(He hurries after the Visitor.)*

(Cut to the clock as the hands spin backward.

Dissolve to the living room, exactly the same as the first scene: Spelding, Mrs. Spelding, Ellen.)

Spelding: There is nothing wrong with marrying a wealthy man. The horror of it has always eluded me. However, my only wish is that you marry someone hard-working, ambitious, a man who'll make his mark in the world. Not a boy who is content to sit on a farm all his life, growing peanuts.

Ellen: English walnuts! And he won't just sit there.

Spelding: Will you stop contradicting me?

Ellen: But Daddy, John grows walnuts...

(John enters.)

John: Hello, everybody.

Mrs. Spelding: Good evening, John.

Ellen: What kept you, darling? You missed Daddy's broadcast.

John: I saw it before I left home. Wonderful broadcast, sir.

Spelding: Thank you, John.

(John crosses to the window.)

John: That meteor you were talking about— well, for a while it looked almost like a space ship or something. You can just barely see it now.

(Ellen joins him at window. They watch, arms about one another.)

Spelding: Space ship! Nonsense! Remarkable what some people will believe, *want* to believe. Besides, as I said in the broadcast—if there's any travelling to be done in space, we'll do it first.

(He notices Kreton's handkerchief on the sofa and picks it up. They all look at it, puzzled, as we cut to a shot of the starry night against which two space ships vanish in the distance, one serene in its course, the other erratic, as we fade out.)

Caution:
Enquiries regarding the performance of this play, professional or amateur, should be directed to Little, Brown and Company, 34 Beacon Street, Boston, Massachusetts 02106.

Glossary of Dramatic and Film Terms

Act—a division in a play which may include several related scenes.

Antagonist—a character in a drama who is in opposition to the hero.

Aside—a remark or speech made by an actor that other actors are not supposed to hear.

Atmosphere—the mood established by the impression made upon the audience.

Background—the part of a scene that is at a distance from the viewer.

Caricature—a dramatic impression which makes the subject look ridiculous through the exaggeration of certain aspects of the person's character.

Characterization—the clues and details provided by an author which will make the characters more believable.

Chorus—the commentators and reactors to the events of a play. Like the narrator, they often bridge the gap betwen play and audience.

Closet Drama—a play meant to be read rather than performed.

Close-Up—a camera shot taken at close range, such as of an actor's face. Sometimes it is abbreviated "CU."

Comedy—a work of literature that is not of a serious nature.

Complication—situations in drama which present the characters with a problem.

Conflict—the struggle in which characters engage to solve the problem.

Crisis—that point in the drama beyond which the conflict cannot continue and must be resolved.

Cue—the lines immediately preceding an actor's own lines.

Cut—to go quickly from one camera shot to another.

Dialect—a characteristic speech pattern common to a particular group from a specific geographic region.

Dialogue—conversation between two or more characters.

Dissolve—to fade a shot gradually from the camera's point of view and have another take its place.

Dramatic Irony—a situation in which the audience knows the facts but the characters do not.

Exposition—introductory background material.

Extras—minor characters, often with few, if any, lines.

Fade In or Fade Out—to become gradually more or less distinct visually or audibly.

Farce—a play in which the characters are realistic but the situation is exaggerated.

Foreground—the part of a scene that is close to the viewer.

Foreshadowing—hints of what is to come.

Frame—the section of a scene that the camera sees.

Genre—a type of literary composition, such as the short story, novel, drama, or essay.

Hero/Heroine—the main figure of a play.

History Play—a play which is based largely upon fact. *Riel* is an example of a history play.

Incident—a detail of plot.

Irony—an event or outcome of events opposite to what is expected. Also, a form of expression in which the intended meaning is the opposite of what is said.

Line—the words that an actor speaks in a play or film.

Melodrama—a drama of improbable, romantic, violent action which usually ends happily.

Montage—the combination of a series of separate pictures or camera shots to make a composite picture.

Motivation—the purpose behind a character's actions.

Narrator—the linking character between play and audience. The narrator often speaks with the voice of the author.

Offstage or Offscreen—away from the part of the stage or screen that the viewer can see. Sometimes it is simply called "off."

Onstage or Onscreen—in the part of the stage or screen that the viewer can see. Sometimes it is simply called "on."

Pan—to move the camera to the left or right to follow the action.

Parable—a narrative that teaches a lesson.

Plot—the events which make up the story upon which a drama is based.

Point of View—the position from which a scene is viewed. Sometimes it is abbreviated "POV."

Protagonist—the character with whom the audience is in greatest sympathy.

Satire—a technique that holds conventions and attitudes up to ridicule to expose falsity and hypocrisy.

Scene—a section of a play or film in which a single point is made.

Set—the physical location of the acting area.

Setting—the physical, social, chronological locale of the play.

Shot—a picture or scene photographed with a camera.

Stereotype—a character or situation seen as conforming to a fixed and conventional view.

Subplot—the secondary plot in a drama which occurs along with the main action.

Surprise Ending—the unexpected development at the end of a play.

Suspense—the uncertainty, created by the conflict, as to the outcome of the drama.

Symbol—something that stands for something else. A sword may stand for war, or an olive branch for peace.

Synopsis—a summary of a story.

Teaser—the opening scene of a television production, used to capture the viewer's attention.

Theme—the underlying idea of or reason for writing a play.

Tragedy—a drama in which the main character suffers great misfortune, often as a result of his or her own decisions and actions.

Voice-Over—lines spoken by an offscreen character while a scene is presented visually. Sometimes it is abbreviated "VO."